CONTROL AND
DYNAMIC SYSTEMS

Advances in Theory and Applications

Volume 24

CONTROL AND DYNAMIC SYSTEMS

ADVANCES IN THEORY AND APPLICATIONS

Edited by
C. T. LEONDES

School of Engineering and Applied Science
University of California, Los Angeles
Los Angeles, California

VOLUME 24: DECENTRALIZED/DISTRIBUTED CONTROL AND DYNAMIC SYSTEMS
Part 3 of 3

1986

ACADEMIC PRESS, INC.
Harcourt Brace Jovanovich, Publishers
Orlando San Diego New York Austin
Boston London Sydney Tokyo Toronto

ACADEMIC PRESS RAPID MANUSCRIPT REPRODUCTION

ACADEMIC PRESS, INC.
Orlando, Florida 32887

United Kingdom Edition published by
ACADEMIC PRESS INC. (LONDON) LTD.
24–28 Oval Road, London NW1 7DX

LIBRARY OF CONGRESS CATALOG CARD NUMBER: 64-8027

ISBN 0–12–012724–5

PRINTED IN THE UNITED STATES OF AMERICA

86 87 88 89 9 8 7 6 5 4 3 2 1

CONTENTS

System Zeros in the Decentralized Control of Large-Scale Systems

Thomas A. Kennedy

Direct Model Reference Adaptive Control for a Class of MIMO Systems

Kenneth M. Sobel and Howard Kaufman

Passive Adaptation in Control System Design

D. D. Sworder and D. S. Chou

PREFACE

In the series *Control and Dynamic Systems* this is the third volume of a trilogy whose theme is advances in techniques for the analysis and synthesis of decentralized or distributed control and dynamic systems. The subject of decentralized but coordinated systems is emerging as a major issue in industrial and aerospace systems, and so this is an appropriately significant theme for this series at this time. The three volumes of this trilogy will thus comprise the most comprehensive treatment of the theory of this broad and complex subject and its many potential applications to date. It is in the various complex "real world" applications that many practitioners may find these three volumes particularly useful. This includes the articles on the many computational issues and techniques appearing in the textbook literature for the first time.

The first article in this volume, "A Two-Level Parameter Estimation Algorithm for Large-Scale Systems," by M. P. Spathopoulos, deals with the vital issue of parameter estimation or determination in large-scale systems, which are rather characteristic of decentralized systems. Some rather powerful new results are presented and verified by computer simulations which demonstrate that these new techniques have the potential in diverse applications of producing considerable savings in memory, computational effort, and in alleviating numerical inaccuracies. There are a number of other significant advantages of the techniques in this article, not the least of which is its suitability for multiprocessing systems. As in earlier *Control and Dynamic Systems,* an essential design concept is that of suboptimal control techniques and related suboptimal bounds. The next article by Sinai presents a rather comprehensive treatment of this issue of central importance to a well-developed theory of decentralized control. Substantial savings in computational requirements result, greater insight into uncertainties associated with modeling large-scale systems is gained, and numerous other advantages also result. The article "Decentralized Control Using Observers," by Shahian, presents a rather comprehensive treatment, with many new results of observers suitable for large-scale decentralized systems. The next article, "System Zeros in the Decentralized Control of Large-Scale Systems," by Kennedy, presents many new and rather powerful results on the use of system zeros in the decentralized control of large-scale systems, that decentralized transmission zeros are crucial to the stability of composite closed-loop systems under a high-gain decentralized feedback. Fundamental relations to system controllability and observability are also developed. Model reference adaptive control techniques have constituted an area of great interest in the past. What is essential if such techniques are to be developed and applied to decentralized control systems is an extension of model reference adaptive control to multiple-input multiple-output (MIMO) systems. The article "Direct Model Reference Adaptive Control for a Class of MIMO Systems" by Sobel and Kaufman provides the necessary and essential results. Finally, the last article of this volume, "Passive Adaptation in Control System Design," by Sworder and Chou, presents some simplified but highly effective and powerful control techniques. Such a simplified but effective techniques approach is essential to a well-rounded theory of the very broad and rather complex subject of decentralized but coordinated control systems.

When the theme for this trilogy of volumes, of which this is the third and last, was decided upon there seemed little doubt that it was most timely. However, because of the substantially important contributions of the authors all volumes promise to be not only timely but of substantial lasting value.

A Two-Level Parameter Estimation Algorithm for Large-Scale Systems

M. P. SPATHOPOULOS

Department of Electrical Engineering
Imperial College of Science and Technology
London SW7 2BT, England

I. INTRODUCTION

System identification may be defined as the set of techniques employed in building up mathematical models for real processes. This is done by determining difference or differential equations, such that they describe the process in accordance with some predetermined criterion. The mathematical models must be capable of representing the actual process (system) behavior. The accuracy of identification can be measured by the difference between the output of the real system and that of the model. Usually system identification can be split into two distinct phases: structure determination and parameter estimation.

The structure of the model is usually determined from the a priori physical knowledge that we have on the process. Parameter estimation is defined as the experimental determination of values of parameters that govern the dynamic and/or nonlinear behavior, assuming that the structure of the process model is known. Parameter estimation usually requires experimental data on the inputs and outputs of the system. It then enables us to put precise values on the parameters so that the model describes the real process and not a class of such processes. The observed data or actual system behavior can be used for the determination of unknown system parameters within the structure of the model, which minimizes a given error criterion.

In large-scale systems the application of parameter estimation techniques is a very difficult task, due to the high dimensionality inherent in the system. Several methods have been proposed to deal with this difficulty, such as reducing the order of the system, using perturbation techniques, and sensitivity analysis [3]. Efforts have been devoted to decompose large-scale problems into several smaller coupled subproblems. Hierarchical system theory [7,11], which deals with system decomposition and coordination, can be applied effectively to decouple these subproblems while at the same time allowing for the coordination of their solutions to yield the original problem's solution.

Physical and conceptual hierarchical structures of large systems may occur in different ways. The system may be composed of interconnected subsystems with well-defined physical boundaries. In other cases the system structure may be categorized according to a natural property such as time behavior or may be characterized by its order of priority of different parts of the system. Hierarchical system theory can then be applied to these structures, where the physical and conceptual structures are viewed basically the same.

Although the problem of optimization and control of large-scale systems composed of interconnected dynamic subsystems has previously been tackled from a deterministic point of view, there is no general, well-established procedure developed for stochastic problems such as the parameter estimation problem. Arafeh and Sage [1] have considered this problem and have developed an interesting algorithm based on decomposition – coordination techniques. However, their algorithm is suboptimal and it converges to the optimal solution only at the end of the observation period. An attempt using the maximum a posteriori approach has been done in [8]. Hassan [4] applied a partitioning approach for the optimal Kalman filter for large-scale systems in which, after a finite number of iterations between the subsystems and the coordinator, the optimum Kalman estimator was achieved. This method was limited to two subsystems only. Hassan *et al.* [5] generalized the previous approach and developed a decentralized computational algorithm for the global Kalman filter using the multiple projection idea. The new filter used a hierarchical structure to perform successive orthogonalizations on the measured subspaces of each subsystem within a two-level structure in order to provide the optimal estimate.

This ensured substantial savings in computation time, stability, and reduction of numerical inaccuracies. Thus, this idea has proven to be an efficient technique for dealing with large-scale interconnected dynamic systems. More recently Hassan *et al.* [6] developed a new decentralized algorithm for the parameter estimation problem by using the multiple projection approach developed in [5]. This chapter gives a description of the algorithm and proves that the algorithm gives the minimum variance estimate after N iterations between the coordinator level and the subsystems level, where N is the number of subsystems. It develops the basic parameter estimation algorithm and then generalizes it to the recursive case. Simulation results of two examples have indicated that this two-level algorithm provides accurate estimates while requiring a modest computation effort.

II. LEAST SQUARE ESTIMATION--THE MULTIPLE PROJECTION APPROACH

A. *INTRODUCTION*

Before the algorithm is derived, the basic principles of least squares estimation are introduced and the multiple projection idea is analyzed.

In systems analysis, a fundamental problem is to provide values for the unknown states or parameters of a system given noisy measurements that are some functions of these states or parameters. If we consider a certain number of measurements $\{z_1, z_2, \ldots, z_N\}$ which depend on a parameter θ, we can define a function $K_N(z_1, z_2, \ldots, z_N)$ which will be called the estimate of θ. Since the measurements z_i are, in general, random, the estimate $K_N(\cdot)$ will also be a random variable. Since all functions of z_i could be estimates, the problem is to find an estimate (which is a function of z_i) that is optimal with respect to some criterion. Also this estimate should possess certain convergence properties with respect to the real value of the parameters.

There are three principal estimators: (a) The maximum likelihood estimator (MLE, (b) the Bayes' estimator, and (c) the least square estimator.

The MLE uses as its criterion the a priori conditional probability density function $p(z_N|\theta)$. The Bayes' estimator uses as its criterion the a posteriori probability density function $p(\theta|z_N)$. The criterion for the least mean-square estimator is to minimize the mean-square estimation error. For the scalar case, it is expressed as

$$\min E\{(\theta - \hat{\theta})^2\}, \tag{1}$$

where $\hat{\theta}$ is the estimate of θ.

In the case where θ is a vector, we minimize

$$E\{(\underline{\theta} - \underline{\hat{\theta}})^T Q(\underline{\theta} - \underline{\hat{\theta}})\} \tag{2}$$

where Q is a nonnegative definite symmetrical weighting matrix.

The least mean-square estimate is reviewed in the following section.

B. *LEAST SQUARE ESTIMATION OF ONE RANDOM VECTOR IN TERMS OF ANOTHER*

Problem 1. Consider two jointly distributed random vectors X and Y with respective dimensions n and m and with joint probability density function $f_{X,Y}(\cdot, \cdot)$. Find the estimator $\hat{X}$ of X in terms of Y that is best in the sense that $\hat{X}$ minimizes $E\{||X - g(Y)||^2\}$ over all functions g mapping R^m into R^n.

Proposition 1. The least square estimator $\hat{X}$ of X in terms of Y in the sense of the above problem is the conditional expectation

$$\hat{X} = E\{X|Y\} \tag{3}$$

of X given Y, and the corresponding minimum mean-square error is the conditional variance $E\{||X - E\{X|Y\}||^2\}$.

Proof. It is known that

$$E\{||X - g(Y)||^2\} = E_Y\left\{E_{X|Y}||X - g(Y)||^2|Y\right\}.$$

We would like to minimize

$$E_{X|Y}\{X^TX - 2g(Y)^TX + g(Y)^Tg(Y)|Y\}.$$

This is written as

$$E\{X^TX|Y\} - 2g(Y)^TE\{X|Y\} + g(Y)^Tg(Y)$$
$$= E\{||g(Y) - E\{X|Y\}||^2\} + E\{||X||^2|Y\} - ||E\{X|Y\}||^2. \tag{4}$$

The only term on the right-hand side of Eq. (4) involving g(Y) is the first and this is uniquely minimized by setting

$$\hat{X} = g(y) = E\{X|Y\}. \tag{5}$$

It is easy to show that for any nonnegative matrix Q, $\hat{X} = E\{X|Y\}$ minimizes $E\{[X - g(Y)]^TQ[X - g(Y)]\}$ over all functions $g: R^m \to R^n$. In fact, if Q is positive definite the proof is unchanged if $||q||^2$ is interpreted to mean q^TQq and w^Tq is replaced by w^TQq. If Q is nonnegative definite the same identification may be made but $||q|| = |q^TQq|^{1/2}$ is in this case only a seminorm, and while $\hat{X} = E\{X|Y\}$ minimizes the first term on the right-hand side of Eq. (4), it does not do so uniquely.

Properties. The least square estimator is

(a) *linear*, that is,

$$E\{AX + b|Y\} = AE\{X|Y\} + b = A\hat{X} + b, \tag{6}$$

where A is a deterministic matrix and b is a deterministic vector;

(b) *unbiased*, that is,

$$E\{X - \hat{X}\} = E\{X\} - E\{E\{X|Y\}\} = E\{X\} - E\{X\} = 0; \tag{7}$$

and (c) the estimation error $\tilde{X} \triangleq X - \hat{X}$ is *uncorrelated* with any function g of the random vector Y, that is,

$$E\{g(Y)\tilde{X}^T\} = 0. \tag{8}$$

Proof. For every value y of Y we have

$$\begin{aligned} E\{g(Y)\tilde{X}^T|Y = y\} &= E\{g(y)[X - X(y)]^T|Y = y\} \\ &= g(y)E\{X^T - \hat{X}^T(y)|Y = y\} \\ &= g(y)[\hat{X}^T(y) - \hat{X}^T(y)] = 0. \end{aligned}$$

The proof that $E\{g(Y)\tilde{X}^T\} = 0$ comes immediately from the fact that

$$E\{E\{g(Y)\tilde{X}^T|Y\}\} = E\{g(Y)\tilde{X}^T\}.$$

C. *LEAST SQUARE ESTIMATION OF GAUSSIAN RANDOM VECTORS*

Gaussian random vectors play a major role in probability and system theory. Their importance stems largely from two facts: first, they possess many distinctive mathematical properties; and second, the Gaussian distribution bears close resemblance to the probability laws of many physical random phenomena. The importance of Gaussian random vectors in estimation and control theory is due largely to the following facts.

(a) The probability density function of a Gaussian random vector is completely specified by a knowledge of its mean and covariance.

(b) Uncorrelated jointly Gaussian random vectors are independent.

(c) Linear functions of Gaussian random vectors are themselves Gaussian random vectors.

(d) The conditional expectation of one jointly Gaussian random vector given another is a Gaussian random vector that is a linear function of the conditioning vector.

Let X, Y be jointly distributed Gaussian random vectors with respective dimensions n and m whose composite vector $Z = [X^T, Y^T]^T$ is $N(\mu, P)$. Thus we have a mean

$$E\{Z\} = \mu = \begin{bmatrix} \mu_x \\ \mu_y \end{bmatrix} = \begin{bmatrix} E\{X\} \\ E\{Y\} \end{bmatrix}$$

and a covariance

$$\text{cov}[Z, Z] = P = \begin{bmatrix} P_{xx} & P_{xy} \\ P_{yx} & P_{yy} \end{bmatrix} = \begin{bmatrix} \text{cov}[X, X] & \text{cov}[X, Y] \\ \text{cov}[Y, X] & \text{cov}[Y, Y] \end{bmatrix}.$$

Then the following properties hold (for proofs see [9]).

Property 1. If $W = AZ$, where A is any nonrandom $q \times r$ matrix, then W is $N(A\mu, APA^T)$.

Property 2. The conditional probability density of the vector X given the vector Y is Gaussian with mean $E\{X|Y\}$ and covariance

$$P_{xx} - P_{xy}P_{yy}^{-1}P_{yx}.$$

Property 3. The least square estimator of X in terms of Y is the random vector

$$\hat{X} = E\{X|Y\} = E\{X\} + P_{xy}P_{yy}^{-1}[Y - E\{Y\}], \tag{9}$$

and since this random vector is a linear function of the random vector Y, it follows immediately from Property (1) that $E\{X|Y\}$ is a Gaussian vector with mean value $E\{X\}$ and covariance

$$\text{cov}[\hat{X}, \hat{X}] = P_{xy}P_{yy}^{-1}P_{yx}. \tag{10}$$

Thus, $\hat{X}$ is $N\left(E\{X\}, P_{xy}P_{yy}^{-1}P_{yx}\right)$.

Property 4. The least square estimation error $\tilde{X} = X - E\{X|Y\}$ is the difference between two jointly Gaussian vectors and is therefore a Gaussian random vector with zero mean and covariance equal to the conditional covariance

$$\text{cov}[\tilde{X}, \tilde{X}] = P_{xx} - P_{xy}P_{yy}^{-1}P_{yx} \tag{11}$$

of X given Y. Thus $\tilde{X} = N\left(0, P_{xx} - P_{xy}P_{yy}^{-1}P_{yx}\right)$.

Property 5. Any function of the least square estimation error $\tilde{X} = X - E\{X|Y\}$ is independent of any function of the random vector Y since it is Gaussian and uncorrelated with any function of the random vector Y.

It is important to remark that when X and Y are jointly Gaussian the least square estimator $\hat{X}$ of X in terms of Y is a *linear* function of Y. If X and Y are not Gaussian random vectors the $E\{X|Y\}$ will be a *nonlinear* function of the random vector Y.

Problem 2. With the assumptions of Problem (1) find the linear estimator $X = A^0Y + b^0$ of X in terms of Y that is best in the sense that $\hat{X}$ minimizes

$$E\{\|X - AY - b\|^2\} \triangleq E\{[X - AY - b]^T[X - AY - b]\}$$

over all linear estimators AY + b of X in terms of Y.

This problem is called the linear least square estimator of X in terms of Y. When X and Y are jointly Gaussian, the least square estimator is already linear in Y and it must therefore coincide with the linear least square estimator.

The linear least square estimator has all the properties of the least square estimator. Below is given one important property which introduces the multiple projection idea.

Property 6. If Y and Y are uncorrelated, then the best linear estimator of X in terms of both Y and Z (i.e., in terms of the composite vector $[Y^T Z^T]^T$) may be written

$$E\{X|Y, Z\} = E\{X|Y\} + E\{X|Z\} - E\{X\}. \tag{12}$$

Proof. Defining $W = [Y^T, Z^T]^T$, we have

$$P_{ww} = \mathrm{cov}[W, W] = \begin{bmatrix} \mathrm{cov}[Y, Y] & \mathrm{cov}[Y, Z] \\ \mathrm{cov}[Z, Y] & \mathrm{cov}[Z, Z] \end{bmatrix},$$

and since Z, Y are uncorrelated,

$$P_{ww} = \begin{bmatrix} P_{yy} & 0 \\ 0 & P_{zz} \end{bmatrix}. \tag{13}$$

Also,

$$\begin{aligned} P_{xw} &= \mathrm{cov}[X, W] = [\mathrm{cov}[X, Y] \ \mathrm{cov}[X, Z]] \\ &= [P_{xy} \ P_{xz}]. \end{aligned} \tag{14}$$

Then, using Eq. (9), we have

$$E\{X|Y, Z\} = E\{X\} + [P_{xy} \ P_{xz}] \begin{bmatrix} P_{yy} & 0 \\ 0 & P_{zz} \end{bmatrix}^{-1} \times \begin{bmatrix} Y - E\{Y\} \\ Z - E\{Z\} \end{bmatrix}. \tag{15}$$

Then, on expanding the right-hand side of Eq. (15), we have

$$E\{X|Y, Z\} = E\{X\} + \underbrace{P_{xy}P_{yy}^{-1}[Y - E\{Y\}]}_{E\{X|Y\} - E\{X\}} + \underbrace{P_{xz}P_{zz}^{-1}[Z - E\{Z\}]}_{E\{X|Z\} - E\{X\}} \quad \text{Q.E.D.}$$

The corresponding estimation error has covariance

$$P_{xx} - P_{xy}P_{yy}^{-1}P_{yx} - P_{xz}P_{zz}^{-1}P_{zx} = P_{\tilde{x}^Y\tilde{x}^Y} - P_{xz}P_{zz}^{-1}P_{zx}, \tag{16}$$

where $P_{\tilde{x}^Y\tilde{x}^Y}$ is the covariance of $\tilde{X}^Y \triangleq X - E\{X|Y\} = X - \hat{X}^Y$. This expression follows by substituting Eqs. (13) and (14) into Eq. (11), with W replacing Y.

Alternatively, with convenience for later applications in mind, we can write

$$E\{X|Y, Z\} = E\{X|Y\} + E\{\tilde{X}^Y\}Z . \tag{17}$$

This is a direct consequence of the observation that, writing $\hat{X}^Y$ for $E\{X|Y\}$ and $\tilde{X}^Y$ for $X - \hat{X}^Y$,

$$\hat{X}^Z = E\{X|Z\} = E\{\hat{X}^Y + \tilde{X}^Y|Z\} = E\{\tilde{X}^Y|Z\} + E\{X\}$$

since $\hat{X}^Y$ is a linear function of Y and Y is by assumption uncorrelated with Z, so that $E\{\hat{X}^Y|Z\} = E\{X\}$.

An alternative expression for the covariance of the estimation error is

$$P_{\tilde{X}\tilde{X}} = P_{\tilde{X}^Y\tilde{X}^Y} - P_{\tilde{X}^Y Z} P_{ZZ}^{-1} P_{Z\tilde{X}^Y}, \tag{18}$$

where $P_{\tilde{X}^Y\tilde{X}^Y} = \text{cov}[\tilde{X}^Y, \tilde{X}^Y]$ and $P_{\tilde{X}^Y Z} = \text{cov}[\tilde{X}^Y, Z]$. Equation (18) comes from Eq. (16) and the fact that

$$P_{XZ} = P_{\tilde{X}^Y Z} . \tag{19}$$

Indeed,

$$P_{XZ} = \text{cov}[\hat{X}^Y + \tilde{X}^Y, Z] = \text{cov}[\hat{X}^Y, Z] + \text{cov}[\tilde{X}^Y, Z]$$

$$= \text{cov}[\tilde{X}^Y, Z] = P_{\tilde{X}^Y Z},$$

since $\text{cov}[\hat{X}^Y, Z] = 0$. Now we are ready to introduce the multiple projection idea.

D. *THE MULTIPLE PROJECTION APPROACH*

The multiple projection technique is based on the following theorem (cf. Luenberger [13, p. 92]).

Theorem. Let X be a member of space H of random variables which is a closed subspace of L_2 and let $\hat{X}^1$ denote its orthogonal projection on a closed subspace X of H (thus, $\hat{X}^1$ is the best estimate of X in $\mathcal{X}$). Let Y be an m vector of random variables generating a subspace $\mathcal{Y}$ of H and let $\hat{Y}$ denote the m-dimensional vector of the projections of the components of Y onto $\mathcal{X}$ (thus, $\hat{Y}$ is the vector of best estimates of Y in $\mathcal{X}$). Let $\tilde{Y} = Y - \hat{Y}$. Then the projection of X on the subspace $\mathcal{X} \oplus \mathcal{Y}$, denoted by $\hat{X}$, is

$$\hat{X} = \hat{X}^1 + E\{X\tilde{Y}^T\}[E\{\tilde{Y}\tilde{Y}^T\}]^{-1}\tilde{Y},$$

where $E\{\cdot\}$ is the expected value. For proof cf. Luenberger [13].

The above equation can be interpreted as follows: $\hat{X}$ is $\hat{X}^1$ plus the best estimate of X in the subspace $\tilde{\mathcal{Y}}$ generated by $\tilde{Y}$.

The linear square estimation $\hat{X}$ of the random vector X in terms of Y can be interpreted geometrically as the orthogonal projection of the vector X on the space generated by the vector Y. It has already proved that if Y, Z are Gaussian, uncorrelated random vectors, the best estimation of X in terms of Y and Z is $\hat{X}^1$ (i.e., $E\{X|Y\}$) plus the best estimation of X on the subspace generated by Z (i.e., $E\{X|Z\}$), which in fact is the orthogonal projection of X on the subspace generated by the vector $\tilde{Z}^Y = Z - \hat{Z}^Y = Z - E\{Z|Y\}$ since $\hat{Z}^Y = E\{Z\}$. Thus Property 6 can be considered as a special case of the above theorem.

Speaking in terms of the linear square estimator, we shall try to explain how this theorem is expressed algebraically in more general cases.

Property 7. If Y and Z are correlated, then the best estimator of X in terms of both Y and Z may be written as

$$E\{X|Y, Z\} = E\{X|Y, \tilde{Z}^Y\} = E\{X|Y\} + E\{X|\tilde{Z}^Y\} - E\{X\} \tag{20}$$

$$= E\{X|Y\} + E\{\tilde{X}^Y|\tilde{Z}^Y\}, \tag{21}$$

where $\tilde{Z}^Y = Z - E\{Z|Y\}$ and $\tilde{X}^Y = X - E\{X|Y\}$.

The covariance of the estimation error is given by

$$P_{\tilde{x}^y\tilde{x}^y} - P_{\tilde{x}^y\tilde{z}^y}P^{-1}_{\tilde{z}^y\tilde{z}^y}P_{\tilde{z}^y\tilde{x}^y}. \tag{22}$$

Indeed, this follows from Property 6, the observation that the random vector $\tilde{Z}^Y = Z - \hat{Z}^Y$ is uncorrelated with Y, and the observation that $E\{X|Y, Z\} = E\{X|Y, \tilde{Z}^Y\}$ since the knowledge of Y and Z is clearly *equivalent* to a knowledge of Y and $\tilde{Z}^Y$.

Property 8. More generally, the best linear estimator

$$\hat{X}^{k+1} \triangleq E\{X|Y_1, Y_2, \ldots, Y_k, Y_{k+1}\}$$

of X in terms of the random vector $Y_1, Y_2, \ldots, Y_k, Y_{k+1}$ may be written recursively as

$$\begin{aligned}\hat{X}^{k+1} &= \hat{X}^k + E\left\{\tilde{X}^k|\tilde{Y}^k_{k+1}\right\}\\ &= \hat{X}^k + E\left\{X|\tilde{Y}^k_{k+1}\right\} - E\{X\},\end{aligned} \tag{23}$$

where

$$\tilde{X}^k \triangleq X - \hat{X}^k \triangleq X - E\{X|Y_1, Y_2, \ldots, Y_k\},$$

$$\tilde{Y}^k_{k+1} \triangleq Y_{k+1} - E\{Y_{k+1}|Y_1, Y_2, \ldots, Y_k\}.$$

The covariance of the corresponding estimation error may also be written recursively as

$$P_{\tilde{x}^{k+1}\tilde{x}^{k+1}} = P_{\tilde{x}^k\tilde{x}^k} - P_{\tilde{x}^k\tilde{y}^k_{k+1}}P^{-1}_{\tilde{y}^k_{k+1}\tilde{y}^k_{k+1}}P_{\tilde{y}^k_{k+1}\tilde{x}^k}. \tag{24}$$

Remark. This is simply a restatement of Property 7 with Y replaced by $\left[Y_1^T, Y_2^T, \ldots, Y_k^T\right]^T$ and Z replaced by Y_{k+1}.

The random vector $\tilde{Y}^k_{k+1}$ defined previously is sometimes called the innovation in Y_{k+1} with respect to $Y_1, Y_2, \ldots, Y_k$. As shown in Property 5, $\tilde{Y}^k_{k+1}$ is uncorrelated with the composite vector $\left[Y_1^T, Y_2^T, \ldots, Y_k^T\right]^T$ and therefore with $Y_1, Y_2, \ldots, Y_{k-1}$ and Y_k separately. It might therefore be viewed as "the component" of Y_{k+1} that conveys new information not already present in Y_1 through Y_k. This viewpoint can be made quite precise by viewing the least square linear estimation problem as a minimum-norm problem in an appropriately defined inner product space R of random variables and solving it using the multiple projection theorem [13]. In this formulation, the least square linear estimator becomes the orthogonal projection of (the components of) X on the subspace of R generated by (the components of) the random vectors $Y_1, Y_2, \ldots, Y_k, Y_{k+1}$. The characterization of the best linear estimator becomes the one whose estimation error is uncorrelated with Y_1 through Y_{k+1} and is merely a statement of the orthogonality of the projection, that $X - \hat{X}^{k+1}$ must be orthogonal to the vectors that generate the subspace. The iterative calculation of the innovations $Y_1, \tilde{Y}_2^1, \tilde{Y}_3^2, \ldots, \tilde{Y}_k^{k+1}, \tilde{Y}_{k+1}^k$ is nothing more than the application of the well-known Gram–Schmidt orthogonalization procedure to generate an orthogonal basis for the subspace, and because the innovations sequence $\left\{\tilde{Y}_i^{i-1}\right\}$ and the sequence of original vectors $\{Y_i\}$ generate the same subspace, they convey *equivalent information* insofar as the linear estimation is concerned. The updating formula (23) is an easily proven observation that the projection of a vector on a subspace is the sum of its projections on each of the orthogonal basis vectors of that subspace.

E. EXAMPLE: STATE ESTIMATION

Consider the system composed of N interconnected linear dynamical subsystems defined by

$$\underline{x}_i(k+1) = \phi_{ii}\underline{x}_i(k) + \sum_{\substack{j=1 \\ i \neq j}}^{N} \phi_{ij}\underline{x}_j(k) + \underline{w}_i(k),$$

$$i = 1, 2, \ldots, N, \tag{25}$$

with the outputs given by

$$\underline{y}_i(k+1) = H_i \underline{x}_i(k+1) + \underline{v}_i(k+1),$$
$$i = 1, 2, \ldots, N, \tag{26}$$

where $\underline{w}_i$, $\underline{v}_i$ are uncorrelated zero-mean Gaussian white noise sequences. Consider the Hilbert space $\mathcal{Y}$ formed by the measurements of the overall systems. At the instant k this space is denoted by $\mathcal{Y}_k$. The optimal minimum variance estimate $\hat{\underline{x}}_i(k+1/k+1)$ is given by

$$\begin{aligned}\hat{\underline{x}}_i(k+1/k+1) &= E\{\underline{x}_i(k+1)/\mathcal{Y}_{k+1}\}\\ &= E\{\underline{x}_i(k+1)/\mathcal{Y}_k, \underline{y}_1(k+1), \underline{y}_2(k+1),\\ &\qquad \ldots, \underline{y}_N(k+1)\}\\ &= E\{\underline{x}_i(k+1)/\mathcal{Y}_k, \underline{y}_1(k+1),\\ &\qquad \ldots, \underline{y}_{N-1}(k+1)\}\\ &\quad + E\{\underline{x}_i(k+1)/\tilde{\underline{y}}_N^{N-1}(k+1/k+1)\},\end{aligned} \tag{27}$$

where

$$\tilde{\underline{y}}_N^{N-1}(k+1/k+1) = \underline{y}_N(k+1) - E\{\underline{y}_N(k+1)/\mathcal{Y}_k, \underline{y}_1(k+1), \ldots, \underline{y}_{N-1}(k+1)\}. \tag{28}$$

Equation (27) states algebraically the geometrical result of the multiple projection theorem. Further decomposing the first term on the right-hand side of Eq. (27), we finally obtain

$$\begin{aligned}\hat{\underline{x}}_i(k+1/k+1) &= E\{\underline{x}_i(k+1)/\mathcal{Y}_k\}\\ &\quad + E\{\underline{x}_i(k+1)/\tilde{\underline{y}}_1(k+1/k)\}\\ &\quad + \sum_{r=2}^{N} E\left\{\underline{x}_i(k+1)/\tilde{\underline{y}}_r^{r-1}(k+1/k+1)\right\},\end{aligned} \tag{29}$$

i.e., the optimal estimate $\hat{\underline{x}}_i(k + 1/k + 1)$ of the ith subsystem is given by the projection of $\underline{x}_i(k + 1)$ on the space generated by all measurements up to k (Y_k) and the projection of $\underline{x}_i(k + 1)$ on the subspace generated by $\tilde{Y}_1(k + 1/k) \oplus Y_2^1(k + 1/k + 1) \oplus \cdots + \tilde{Y}_N^{N-1}(k + 1/k + 1)$, where $\tilde{Y}_i^{i-1}(k + 1)$ is the subspace generated by the subspace of measurements $Y_i(k + 1)$ and the projection of it on the subspaces generated by $Y(k) \oplus Y_1(k + 1) \oplus Y_2(k + 1) \oplus \cdots \oplus Y_{i-1}(k + 1)$. Equation (29) has been used in [5] to derive the algebraic structure of a new decentralized Kalman filter.

III. THE MULTIPLE PROJECTION ALGORITHM

A. *PROBLEM FORMULATION*

A detailed description of the nonrecursive multiple projection algorithm is presented in this section. It is shown that the algorithm gives the minimum variance estimator error, after N iterations, between the coordinator level and the subsystems level, where N is the number of subsystems. Extension to the case of recursive estimation is also included.

It is assumed that the following linear static model is given:

$$\underline{z} = H\,\underline{\theta} + \underline{v}, \tag{30}$$

where $\underline{z} \in R^n$ is the measurement vector, $\underline{\theta} \in R^m$ the random constant parameter vector to be estimated, $\underline{v} \in R^n$ the vector of measurement errors, and $H \in R^{n\times m}$ the modulation (transformation) matrix with known elements. It is assumed that $\underline{\theta}$ and $\underline{v}$ are independent Gaussian random vectors with the statistical parameters

$$E\{\underline{\theta}\} = \underline{\mu}_\theta, \qquad \mathrm{var}\{\underline{\theta}\} = P,$$

$$E\{\underline{v}\} = \underline{0}, \qquad \mathrm{var}\{\underline{v}\} = Q.$$

The matrix Q is a full matrix. We would like to find the minimum variance estimate which minimizes the mean square error:

$$E\{(\underline{\theta} - \hat{\underline{\theta}})^T(\underline{\theta} - \hat{\underline{\theta}})\}, \tag{31}$$

where $\hat{\underline{\theta}}$ is the estimate of $\underline{\theta}$. As shown in the previous section, the best estimate of $\hat{\underline{\theta}}$ which minimizes Eq. (31) is

$$\hat{\underline{\theta}} = E\{\underline{\theta}|\underline{z}\}. \tag{32}$$

B. DEVELOPMENT OF THE NONRECURSIVE ALGORITHM

The algorithm procedure starts by decomposing the measurement vector $\underline{z}$ and the parameter vector $\underline{\theta}$ into N subvectors such that

$$\underline{z} = \left\{\underline{z}_1^T, \underline{z}_2^T, \ldots, \underline{z}_N^T\right\}^T,$$

$$\underline{z}_i \in R^{n_i} \quad \text{with} \quad \sum_{i=1}^{N} n_i = n; \tag{33}$$

and

$$\underline{\theta} = \left\{\underline{\theta}_1^T, \underline{\theta}_2^T, \ldots, \underline{\theta}_N^T\right\}^T,$$

$$\underline{\theta}_i \in R^{m_i} \quad \text{with} \quad \sum_{i=1}^{N} m_i = m. \tag{34}$$

The expression which describes the ith measurement submodel is given by

$$\underline{z}_i = H_{ii}\underline{\theta}_i + \sum_{\substack{j=1 \\ i\neq j}}^{N} H_{ij}\underline{\theta}_j + \underline{v}_i. \tag{35}$$

The main results are summarized by the following lemmas.

Lemma 1. The optimal (minimum variance) estimator $\hat{\underline{\theta}}_i^N$ is given by

$$\hat{\underline{\theta}}_i^N = \underline{\mu}_{\theta_i} + P_{\theta_i z_1} P_{z_1 z_1}^{-1} \left(\underline{z}_1 - \sum_{j=1}^{N} H_{1j} \underline{\mu}_{\theta_j} \right)$$

$$+ \sum_{j=2}^{N} P_{\tilde{\theta}_i^{j-1} \tilde{z}_j^{j-1}} P_{\tilde{z}_j^{j-1} \tilde{z}_j^{j-1}}^{-1} \underline{\tilde{z}}_j^{j-1}$$

$$= \hat{\underline{\theta}}_i^r + \sum_{j=r+1}^{N} P_{\tilde{\theta}_i^{j-1} \tilde{z}_j^{j-1}} P_{\tilde{z}_j^{j-1} \tilde{z}_j^{j-1}}^{-1} \underline{\tilde{z}}_j^{j-1}, \tag{36}$$

where

$$\hat{\underline{\theta}}_i^r = \underline{\mu}_{\theta_i} + P_{\theta_i z_1} P_{z_1 z_1}^{-1} \left(\underline{z}_1 - \sum_{j=1}^{N} H_{1j} \underline{\mu}_{\theta_j} \right)$$

$$+ \sum_{l=2}^{r} P_{\tilde{\theta}_i^{l-1} \tilde{z}_l^{l-1}} P_{\tilde{z}_l^{l-1} \tilde{z}_l^{\ell-1}}^{-1} \underline{\tilde{z}}_l^{l-1} \tag{37}$$

is the estimator after r iterations between the two levels.

Proof. The linear least square estimation of $\underline{\theta}_i$ in terms of $\underline{z}$ is given by

$$\hat{\underline{\theta}}_i^N = E\{\underline{\theta}_i | \underline{z}\} = E\{\underline{\theta}_i | \underline{z}_1, \underline{z}_2, \ldots, \underline{z}_N\}.$$

Using Eq. (23),

$$\hat{\underline{\theta}}_i^N = \hat{\underline{\theta}}_i^{N-1} + E\left\{\tilde{\underline{\theta}}_i^{N-1} | \underline{\tilde{z}}_N^{N-1}\right\}$$

$$= \hat{\underline{\theta}}_i^{N-1} + E\left\{\underline{\theta}_i | \underline{\tilde{z}}_N^{N-1}\right\} - E\{\underline{\theta}_i\}$$

$$= \hat{\underline{\theta}}_i^1 + \sum_{j=2}^{N} E\left\{\underline{\theta}_i | \underline{\tilde{z}}_j^{j-1}\right\} - (N-1)\underline{\mu}_{\theta_i} \tag{38}$$

where

$$\hat{\underline{\theta}}_i^1 = E\{\underline{\theta}_i | \underline{z}_1\}$$

and

$$\underline{\tilde{z}}_j^{j-1} = \underline{z}_j - E\{\underline{z}_j | \underline{z}_1, \underline{z}_2, \ldots, \underline{z}_{j-1}\} = \underline{z}_j - \underline{\hat{z}}_j^{j-1}.$$

The first term of Eq. (38) is calculated using Eq. (9) to yield

$$E\{\underline{\theta}_i | \underline{z}_1\} = \underline{\mu}_{\theta_i} + P_{\theta_i z_1} P_{z_1 z_1}^{-1} (\underline{z}_1 - E\{\underline{z}_1\}), \tag{39}$$

and since $E\{\underline{v}_j\} = 0$,

$$\begin{aligned} E\{\underline{z}_1\} &= E\left\{\sum_{j=1}^{N} H_{1j}\underline{\theta}_j + \underline{v}_j\right\} \\ &= \sum_{j=1}^{N} H_{1j}\underline{\mu}_{\theta_j}. \end{aligned} \tag{40}$$

Therefore, Eq. (39) becomes

$$E\{\underline{\theta}_i | \underline{z}_1\} = \underline{\mu}_{\theta_i} + P_{\theta_i z_1} P_{z_1 z_1}^{-1} \left(\underline{z}_1 - \sum_{j=1}^{N} H_{1j}\underline{\mu}_{\theta_j}\right). \tag{41}$$

Turning to the second terms of Eq. (38), it follows immediately from Eq. (9) that

$$\begin{aligned} E\left\{\underline{\theta}_i | \underline{\tilde{z}}_j^{j-1}\right\} &= \underline{\mu}_{\theta_i} + P_{\theta_i \tilde{z}_j^{j-1}} P_{\tilde{z}_j^{j-1} \tilde{z}_j^{j-1}}^{-1} \\ &\quad \times \left(\underline{\tilde{z}}_j^{j-1} - E\left\{\underline{\tilde{z}}_j^{j-1}\right\}\right) \quad \left(E\left\{\underline{\tilde{z}}_j^{j-1}\right\} = 0\right) \\ &= \underline{\mu}_{\theta_i} + P_{\theta_i \tilde{z}_j^{j-1}} P_{\tilde{z}_j^{j-1} \tilde{z}_j^{j-1}}^{-1} \underline{\tilde{z}}_j^{j-1}. \end{aligned} \tag{42}$$

Substituting Eqs. (41) and (42) into Eq. (38), we obtain

$$\begin{aligned} \underline{\hat{\theta}}_i^N &= \underline{\mu}_{\theta_i} + P_{\theta_i z_1} P_{z_1 z_1}^{-1} \left(\underline{z}_1 - \sum_{j=1}^{N} H_{1j}\underline{\mu}_{\theta_j}\right) \\ &\quad + \sum_{j=2}^{N} P_{\theta_i \tilde{z}_j^{j-1}} P_{\tilde{z}_j^{j-1} \tilde{z}_j^{j-1}}^{-1} \underline{\tilde{z}}_j^{j-1}. \end{aligned}$$

By replacing the vector Z by $\tilde{\underline{z}}_j^{j-1}$, the vector Y by the composite vector $\left[\underline{z}_1^T, \underline{z}_2^T, \ldots, \underline{z}_{j-1}^T\right]^T$, and the vector X by the vector $\underline{\theta}$ in Eq. (19), we have

$$P_{\theta_i \tilde{z}_j^{j-1}} = P_{\tilde{\theta}_i^{j-1} \tilde{z}_j^{j-1}};$$

and, finally, we obtain

$$\hat{\underline{\theta}}_i^N = \underline{\mu}_{\theta_i} + P_{\theta_i z_1} P_{z_1 z_1}^{-1} \left(\underline{z}_1 - \sum_{j=1}^{N} H_{1j} \underline{\mu}_{\theta_j} \right)$$

$$+ \sum_{j=2}^{N} P_{\tilde{\theta}_i^{j-1} \tilde{z}_j^{j-1}} P_{\tilde{z}_j^{j-1} \tilde{z}_j^{j-1}}^{-1} \tilde{\underline{z}}_j^{j-1}$$

$$= \hat{\underline{\theta}}_i^r + \sum_{j=r+1}^{N} P_{\tilde{\theta}_i^{j-1} \tilde{z}_j^{j-1}} P_{\tilde{z}_j^{j-1} \tilde{z}_j^{j-1}}^{-1} \tilde{\underline{z}}_j^{j-1}, \tag{43}$$

where

$$\hat{\underline{\theta}}_i^r = \underline{\mu}_{\theta_i} + P_{\theta_i z_1} P_{z_1 z_1}^{-1} \left(\underline{z}_1 - \sum_{j=1}^{N} H_{1j} \underline{\mu}_{\theta} \right)$$

$$+ \sum_{l=2}^{r} P_{\tilde{\theta}_i^{l-1} \tilde{z}_l^{l-1}} P_{\tilde{z}_l^{l-1} \tilde{z}_l^{l-1}}^{-1} \underline{z}_l^{l-1}, \tag{44}$$

which is the desired result and completes the proof. Evaluation of the associated error quantities is given in terms of the subsequent lemmas.

Lemma 2. The covariance matrices $P_{\theta_i z_j}$, $P_{z_i z_i}$, and $P_{z_i z_j}$ are given by

$$P_{\theta_i z_j} = \sum_{r=1}^{N} P_{\theta_i \theta_r} H_{jr}^T, \tag{45}$$

$$P_{z_i z_i} = H_{ii}\left(P_{\theta_i\theta_i}H_{ii}^T + \sum_{\substack{j=1\\i\neq j}}^{N} P_{\theta_i\theta_j}H_{ij}^T\right) + \left(\sum_{\substack{j=1\\i\neq j}}^{N} H_{ij}P_{\theta_j\theta_i}\right)H_{ii}^T$$

$$+ \sum_{\substack{r=1\\r\neq i}}^{N} H_{ir} \sum_{\substack{j=1\\i\neq j}}^{N} P_{\theta_r\theta_j}H_{ij}^T + Q_{ii}, \tag{46}$$

$$P_{z_i z_j} = H_{ii}\left(P_{\theta_i\theta_j}H_{jj}^T + \sum_{\substack{l=1\\l\neq j}}^{N} P_{\theta_i\theta_l}H_{jl}^T\right) + \left(\sum_{\substack{r=1\\r\neq i}}^{N} H_{ir}P_{\theta_r\theta_j}\right)H_{jj}^T$$

$$+ \sum_{\substack{r=1\\i\neq r}}^{N} H_{ir} \sum_{\substack{l=1\\l\neq j}}^{N} P_{\theta_r\theta_l}H_{jl}^T + Q_{ij}. \tag{47}$$

Proof. The starting point is the definition of $P_{\theta_i z_j} = \mathrm{cov}[\underline{\theta}_i, \underline{z}_j]$ as

$$P_{\theta_i z_j} = E\left\{[\underline{\theta}_i - \underline{\mu}_{\theta_i}][\underline{z}_j - E\{\underline{z}_j\}]^T\right\}$$

$$= E\left\{[\underline{\theta}_i - \underline{\mu}_{\theta_i}]\left[\sum_{r=1}^{N} (\underline{\theta}_r - \underline{\mu}_{\theta_r})^T H_{jr}^T + \underline{v}_j^T\right]\right\}$$

$$= \sum_{r=1}^{N} P_{\theta_i\theta_r}H_{jr}^T. \tag{48}$$

Similarly, $P_{z_i z_i}$ is given by

$$P_{z_i z_i} = E\left\{[\underline{z}_i - E\{\underline{z}_i\}][\underline{z}_i - E\{\underline{z}_i\}]^T\right\}$$

$$= E\left\{\left[H_{ii}(\underline{\theta}_i - \underline{\mu}_{\theta_i}) + \sum_{\substack{j=1\\i\neq j}}^{N} H_{ij}(\underline{\theta}_j - \underline{\mu}_{\theta_j}) + \underline{v}_i\right]\right.$$

$$\left.\times\left[(\underline{\theta}_i - \underline{\mu}_{\theta_j})^T H_{ii}^T + \sum_{\substack{j=1\\i\neq j}}^{N} (\underline{\theta}_j - \underline{\mu}_{\theta_j})^T H_{ij}^T + \underline{v}_i^T\right]\right\}.$$

After some algebraic manipulations, the above expression reduces to

$$P_{z_i z_i} = H_{ii} P_{\theta_i \theta_i} H_{ii}^T + H_{ii} \sum_{\substack{j=1 \\ i \neq j}}^{N} P_{\theta_i \theta_j} H_{ij}^T + \left(\sum_{\substack{j=1 \\ i \neq j}}^{N} H_{ij} P_{\theta_j \theta_i} \right) H_{ii}^T + \sum_{\substack{r=1 \\ r \neq i}}^{N} H_{ir} \sum_{\substack{j=1 \\ i \neq j}}^{N} P_{\theta_r \theta_j} H_{ij}^T + Q_{ii}. \tag{49}$$

In a similar fashion, $P_{z_i z_j}$ takes the form

$$P_{z_i z_j} = E\left\{ \left[H_{ii}(\underline{\theta}_i - \underline{\mu}_{\theta_i}) + \sum_{\substack{r=1 \\ r \neq i}}^{N} H_{ir}(\underline{\theta}_r - \underline{\mu}_{\theta_r}) + \underline{v}_i \right] \times \left[(\underline{\theta}_j - \underline{\mu}_{\theta_j})^T H_{jj}^T + \sum_{\substack{l=1 \\ l \neq j}}^{N} (\underline{\theta}_l - \underline{\mu}_{\theta_l})^T H_{jl}^T + \underline{v}_j^T \right] \right\}.$$

Expanding the right-hand side and rearranging, we arrive at

$$P_{z_i z_j} = H_{ii} P_{\theta_i \theta_j} H_{jj}^T + H_{ii} \sum_{\substack{l=1 \\ l \neq j}}^{N} P_{\theta_i \theta_l} H_{jl}^T + \left(\sum_{\substack{r=1 \\ r \neq i}}^{N} H_{ir} P_{\theta_r \theta_j} \right) H_{jj}^T + \sum_{\substack{r=1 \\ i \neq r}}^{N} H_{ir} \sum_{\substack{l=1 \\ l \neq j}}^{N} P_{\theta_r \theta_l} H_{jl}^T + Q_{ij}, \tag{50}$$

which completes the proof. Note that by symmetry $P_{z_i z_j} = P_{z_j z_i}^T$.

Lemma 3. The measurement estimation error $\underline{\tilde{z}}_j^r$ and the corresponding covariance matrices

$$P_{\tilde{z}_r^{r-1}\tilde{z}_r^{r-1}}, \quad P_{\tilde{z}_j^{r-1}\tilde{z}_j^{r-1}}, \quad \text{and} \quad P_{\tilde{z}_j^{r-2}\tilde{z}_{j-1}^{r-2}}$$

are given by

$$\underline{\tilde{z}}_j^r = \underline{\tilde{z}}_j^{r-1} - P_{\tilde{z}_j^{r-1}\tilde{z}_r^{r-1}} P^{-1}_{\tilde{z}_r^{r-1}\tilde{z}_r^{r-1}} \underline{\tilde{z}}_r^{r-1}, \tag{51}$$

$$P_{\tilde{z}_r^{r-1}\tilde{z}_r^{r-1}} = P_{\tilde{z}_r^{r-2}\tilde{z}_r^{r-2}} - P_{\tilde{z}_r^{r-2}\tilde{z}_{r-1}^{r-2}} P^{-1}_{\tilde{z}_{r-1}^{r-2}\tilde{z}_{r-1}^{r-2}} P_{\tilde{z}_{r-1}^{r-2}\tilde{z}_r^{r-2}}; \tag{52}$$

and, in general,

$$P_{\tilde{z}_j^{r-1}\tilde{z}_j^{r-1}} = P_{\tilde{z}_j^{r-2}\tilde{z}_j^{r-2}} - P_{\tilde{z}_j^{r-2}\tilde{z}_{r-1}^{r-2}} P^{-1}_{\tilde{z}_{r-1}^{r-2}\tilde{z}_{r-1}^{r-2}} P_{\tilde{z}_{r-1}^{r-2}\tilde{z}_j^{r-2}}, \tag{53}$$

$$P_{\tilde{z}_j^{r-2}\tilde{z}_{j-1}^{r-2}} = P_{\tilde{z}_j^{r-3}\tilde{z}_{j-1}^{r-3}} - P_{\tilde{z}_j^{r-3}\tilde{z}_{r-2}^{r-3}} P^{-1}_{\tilde{z}_{r-2}^{r-3}\tilde{z}_{r-2}^{r-3}} P_{\tilde{z}_{r-2}^{r-3}\tilde{z}_{j-1}^{r-3}}. \tag{54}$$

Proof. The one-step measurement error $\underline{\tilde{z}}_i^1$ is derived as

$$\begin{aligned}
\underline{\tilde{z}}_i^1 &= \underline{z}_i - E(\underline{z}_i | \underline{z}_1) \\
&= \underline{z}_i - E\{\underline{z}_i\} - P_{z_i z_1} P^{-1}_{z_1 z_1} (\underline{z}_1 - E\{\underline{z}_1\}); \qquad i = 2, \ldots, N \\
&= \underline{z}_i - \sum_{j=1}^{N} (H_{ij}\underline{\mu}_{\theta_j}) - P_{z_i z_1} P^{-1}_{z_1 z_1} \left(\underline{z}_1 - \sum_{j=1}^{N} (H_{1j}\underline{\mu}_{\theta_j}) \right).
\end{aligned} \tag{55}$$

The associated measurement error variance matrix is

$$\begin{aligned}
P_{\tilde{z}_i^1 \tilde{z}_i^1} &= E\left[\underline{\tilde{z}}_i^1 \underline{\tilde{z}}_i^{1T} \right] \quad \text{since} \quad E\left\{ \underline{\tilde{z}}_i^1 \right\} = 0 \\
&= E\left\{ \left[(\underline{z}_i - E\{\underline{z}_i\}) - P_{z_i z_1} P^{-1}_{z_1 z_1} (\underline{z}_1 - E\{\underline{z}_1\}) \right] \right. \\
&\qquad \left. \times \left[(z_i - E\{\underline{z}_i\}) - P_{z_i z_1} P^{-1}_{z_1 z_1} (\underline{z}_1 - E\{\underline{z}_1\}) \right]^T \right\}
\end{aligned}$$

$$= P_{z_i z_i} - P_{z_i z_1} P^{-1}_{z_1 z_1} P_{z_1 z_i} - P_{z_i z_1} P^{-1}_{z_1 z_1} P_{z_1 z_i}$$

$$+ P_{z_i z_1} P^{-1}_{z_1 z_1} P_{z_1 z_i}$$

$$= P_{z_i z_i} - P_{z_i z_1} P^{-1}_{z_1 z_1} P_{z_1 z_i}. \tag{56}$$

To obtain the measurement estimation error $\underline{\tilde{z}}_j^r$, we have

$$\underline{\tilde{z}}_j^r = \underline{z}_j - E\{\underline{z}_j | \underline{z}_1, \ldots, \underline{z}_r\} \quad \text{[and using Eqs. (23) and (9)]}$$

$$= \underline{z}_j - E\{\underline{z}_j | \underline{z}_1, \ldots, \underline{z}_{r-1}\} - E\left\{\underline{z}_j | \underline{\tilde{z}}_r^{r-1}\right\} + E\{\underline{z}_j\}$$

$$= \underline{\tilde{z}}_j^{r-1} - \left[E\{\underline{z}_j\} + P_{z_j \tilde{z}_r^{r-1}} P^{-1}_{\tilde{z}_r^{r-1} \tilde{z}_r^{r-1}} \left(\underline{\tilde{z}}_r^{r-1} - \underbrace{E\left\{\underline{\tilde{z}}_r^{r-1}\right\}}_{=0}\right)\right]$$

$$+ E\{\underline{z}_j\}$$

$$= \underline{\tilde{z}}_j^{r-1} - P_{z_j \tilde{z}_r^{r-1}} P^{-1}_{\tilde{z}_r^{r-1} \tilde{z}_r^{r-1}} \underline{\tilde{z}}_r^{r-1}.$$

Since

$$P_{z_j \tilde{z}_r^{r-1}} = P_{\tilde{z}_j^{r-1} \tilde{z}_r^{r-1}},$$

thus

$$\underline{\tilde{z}}_j^r = \underline{\tilde{z}}_j^{r-1} - P_{\tilde{z}_j^{r-1} \tilde{z}_r^{r-1}} P^{-1}_{\tilde{z}_r^{r-1} \tilde{z}_r^{r-1}} \underline{\tilde{z}}_r^{r-1}. \tag{57}$$

Proceeding further, we obtain

$$\underline{\tilde{z}}_j^{r-1} = \underline{\tilde{z}}_j^{r-2} - P_{\tilde{z}_j^{r-2} \tilde{z}_{r-1}^{r-2}} P^{-1}_{\tilde{z}_{r-1}^{r-2} \tilde{z}_{r-1}^{r-2}} \underline{\tilde{z}}_{r-1}^{r-2}.$$

By definition

$$P_{\tilde{z}_j^{r-1} \tilde{z}_j^{r-1}} = E\left\{\underline{\tilde{z}}_j^{r-1} \underline{\tilde{z}}_j^{r-1^T}\right\}$$

since $E\left\{\underline{\tilde{z}}_j^{r-1}\right\} = 0$, and thus, using Eq. (57),

$$P_{\tilde{z}_j^{r-1}\tilde{z}_j^{r-1}} = E\left\{\left[\underline{\tilde{z}}_j^{r-2} - P_{\tilde{z}_j^{r-2}\tilde{z}_{r-1}^{r-2}}P^{-1}_{\tilde{z}_{r-1}^{r-2}\tilde{z}_{r-1}^{r-2}}\underline{\tilde{z}}_{r-1}^{r-2}\right] \times \left[\underline{\tilde{z}}_j^{r-2} - P_{\tilde{z}_j^{r-2}\tilde{z}_{r-1}^{r-2}}P^{-1}_{\tilde{z}_{r-1}^{r-2}\tilde{z}_{r-1}^{r-2}}\underline{\tilde{z}}_{r-1}^{r-2}\right]^T\right\}$$

$$= P_{\tilde{z}_j^{r-2}\tilde{z}_j^{r-2}} - P_{\tilde{z}_j^{r-2}\tilde{z}_{r-1}^{r-2}}P^{-1}_{\tilde{z}_{r-1}^{r-2}\tilde{z}_{r-1}^{r-2}}P_{\tilde{z}_{r-1}^{r-2}\tilde{z}_j^{r-2}}. \tag{58}$$

Putting j = r, we obtain expression (52) for

$P_{\tilde{z}_r^{r-1}\tilde{z}_r^{r-1}}$.

Finally, to obtain the covariance matrix

$P_{\tilde{z}_j^{r-2}\tilde{z}_{j-1}^{r-2}}$,

we have

$$P_{\tilde{z}_j^{r-2}\tilde{z}_{j-1}^{r-2}} = E\left\{\underline{\tilde{z}}_j^{r-2}\underline{\tilde{z}}_{j-1}^{r-2^T}\right\} \tag{59}$$

since

$$E\left\{\underline{\tilde{z}}_j^{r-2}\right\} = 0 \quad \text{and} \quad E\left\{\underline{\tilde{z}}_{j-1}^{r-2}\right\} = 0.$$

Also, from Eq. (57) it follows that

$$\underline{\tilde{z}}_j^{r-2} = \underline{\tilde{z}}_j^{r-3} - P_{\tilde{z}_j^{r-3}\tilde{z}_{r-2}^{r-3}}P^{-1}_{\tilde{z}_{r-2}^{r-3}\tilde{z}_{r-2}^{r-3}}\underline{\tilde{z}}_{r-2}^{r-3} \tag{60}$$

and

$$\tilde{z}_{j-1}^{r-2} = \underline{\tilde{z}}_{j-1}^{r-3} - P_{\tilde{z}_{j-1}^{r-3}\tilde{z}_{r-2}^{r-3}}P^{-1}_{\tilde{z}_{r-2}^{r-3}\tilde{z}_{r-2}^{r-3}}\underline{\tilde{z}}_{r-2}^{r-3}. \tag{61}$$

Substituting Eqs. (60) and (61) into Eq. (59), we obtain

$$P_{\tilde{z}_j^{r-2}\tilde{z}_{j-1}^{r-2}} = E\left\{\left[\underline{\tilde{z}}_j^{r-3} - P_{\tilde{z}_j^{r-3}\tilde{z}_{r-2}^{r-3}}P^{-1}_{\tilde{z}_{r-2}^{r-3}\tilde{z}_{r-2}^{r-3}}\underline{\tilde{z}}_{r-2}^{r-3}\right] \times \left[\underline{\tilde{z}}_{j-1}^{r-3} - P_{\tilde{z}_{j-1}^{r-3}\tilde{z}_{r-2}^{r-3}}P^{-1}_{\tilde{z}_{r-2}^{r-3}\tilde{z}_{r-2}^{r-3}}\underline{\tilde{z}}_{r-2}^{r-3}\right]^T\right\}.$$

With some manipulations, the above expression reduces to

$$P_{\tilde{z}_j^{r-2}\tilde{z}_{j-1}^{r-2}} = P_{\tilde{z}_j^{r-3}\tilde{z}_{j-1}^{r-3}} - P_{\tilde{z}_j^{r-3}\tilde{z}_{r-2}^{r-3}} P^{-1}_{\tilde{z}_{r-2}^{r-3}\tilde{z}_{r-2}^{r-3}} P_{\tilde{z}_{r-2}^{r-3}\tilde{z}_{j-1}^{r-3}}, \tag{62}$$

which concludes the proof.

We are now in a position to derive a formula for the propagation of the parameter estimation error and its associated variance – covariance matrices.

Lemma 4. The variance and covariance matrices of the parameter estimation error propagate according to

$$P_{\tilde{\theta}_i^r\tilde{\theta}_i^r} = P_{\tilde{\theta}_i^{r-1}\tilde{\theta}_i^{r-1}} - P_{\tilde{\theta}_i^{r-1}\tilde{z}_r^{r-1}} P^{-1}_{\tilde{z}_r^{r-1}\tilde{z}_r^{r-1}} P_{\tilde{z}_r^{r-1}\tilde{\theta}_i^{r-1}}; \tag{63}$$

$$P_{\tilde{\theta}_i^r\tilde{\theta}_j^r} = P_{\tilde{\theta}_i^{r-1}\tilde{\theta}_j^{r-1}} - P_{\tilde{\theta}_i^{r-1}\tilde{z}_r^{r-1}} P^{-1}_{\tilde{z}_r^{r-1}\tilde{z}_r^{r-1}} P_{\tilde{z}_r^{r-1}\tilde{\theta}_j^{r-1}}, \tag{64}$$

$$i = 1, \ldots, N, \quad j = 1, \ldots, N, \quad i \neq j;$$

$$P_{\tilde{\theta}_i^{r-1}\tilde{z}_r^{r-1}} = P_{\tilde{\theta}_i^{r-2}\tilde{z}_r^{r-2}} - P_{\tilde{\theta}_i^{r-2}\tilde{z}_{r-1}^{r-2}} P^{-1}_{\tilde{z}_{r-1}^{r-2}\tilde{z}_{r-1}^{r-2}} P_{\tilde{z}_{r-1}^{r-2}\tilde{z}_r^{r-2}}. \tag{65}$$

Proof. The parameter estimation error $\underline{\tilde{\theta}}_i^r$ is given by

$$\begin{aligned}
\underline{\tilde{\theta}}_i^r &= \underline{\theta}_i - E\{\underline{\theta}_i \mid \underline{z}_1, \ldots, \underline{z}_r\} \\
&= \underline{\theta}_i - E\{\underline{\theta}_i \mid \underline{z}_1, \ldots, \underline{z}_{r-1}\} - E\left\{\underline{\theta}_i \mid \underline{\tilde{z}}_r^{r-1}\right\} + \underline{\mu}_{\theta_i} \\
&= \underline{\tilde{\theta}}_i^{r-1} - P_{\theta_i\tilde{z}_r^{r-1}} P^{-1}_{\tilde{z}_r^{r-1}\tilde{z}_r^{r-1}} \underline{\tilde{z}}_r^{r-1} \\
&= \underline{\tilde{\theta}}_i^{r-1} - P_{\tilde{\theta}_i^{r-1}\tilde{z}_r^{r-1}} P^{-1}_{\tilde{z}_r^{r-1}\tilde{z}_r^{r-1}} \underline{\tilde{z}}_r^{r-1},
\end{aligned} \tag{66}$$

where the covariance matrix $P_{\tilde{\theta}_i^r\tilde{\theta}_i^r}$ is obtained as follows:

$$P_{\tilde{\theta}_i^r\tilde{\theta}_i^r} = E\left\{\underline{\tilde{\theta}}_i^r \underline{\tilde{\theta}}_i^{r^T}\right\} \quad \text{since} \quad E\left\{\underline{\tilde{\theta}}_i^r\right\} = 0.$$

Therefore,

$$P_{\tilde{\theta}_i^r \tilde{\theta}_i^r} = E\left\{\left[\underline{\tilde{\theta}}_i^{r-1} - P_{\tilde{\theta}_i^{r-1}\tilde{z}_r^{r-1}} P^{-1}_{\tilde{z}_r^{r-1}\tilde{z}_r^{r-1}} \underline{\tilde{z}}_r^{r-1}\right] \times \left[\underline{\tilde{\theta}}_i^{r-1} - P_{\tilde{\theta}_i^{r-1}\tilde{z}_r^{r-1}} P^{-1}_{\tilde{z}_r^{r-1}\tilde{z}_r^{r-1}} \underline{\tilde{z}}_r^{r-1}\right]^T\right\},$$

from which we obtain

$$P_{\tilde{\theta}_i^r \tilde{\theta}_i^r} = P_{\tilde{\theta}_i^{r-1}\tilde{\theta}_i^{r-1}} - P_{\tilde{\theta}_i^{r-1}\tilde{z}_r^{r-1}} P^{-1}_{\tilde{z}_r^{r-1}\tilde{z}_r^{r-1}} P_{\tilde{z}_r^{r-1}\tilde{\theta}_i^{r-1}}. \tag{67}$$

In a parallel development we can prove that

$$P_{\tilde{\theta}_i^r \tilde{\theta}_j^r} = P_{\tilde{\theta}_i^{r-1}\tilde{\theta}_j^{r-1}} - P_{\tilde{\theta}_i^{r-1}\tilde{z}_r^{r-1}} P^{-1}_{\tilde{z}_r^{r-1}\tilde{z}_r^{r-1}} P_{\tilde{z}_r^{r-1}\tilde{\theta}_j^{r-1}}, \qquad i = 1, \ldots, N, \quad j = 1, \ldots, N, \quad i \neq j. \tag{68}$$

Finally, to determine

$$P_{\tilde{\theta}_i^{r-1}\tilde{z}_r^{r-1}},$$

using the fact that $E\{\underline{\tilde{\theta}}_i^{r-1}\} = 0$ and $E\{\underline{\tilde{z}}_r^{r-1}\} = 0$, we proceed as follows

$$P_{\tilde{\theta}_i^{r-1}\tilde{z}_r^{r-1}} = E\left\{\underline{\tilde{\theta}}_i^{r-1} \underline{\tilde{z}}_r^{r-1^T}\right\}, \tag{69}$$

but

$$\underline{\tilde{\theta}}_i^{r-1} = \underline{\tilde{\theta}}_i^{r-2} - P_{\tilde{\theta}_i^{r-2}\tilde{z}_{r-1}^{r-2}} P^{-1}_{\tilde{z}_{r-1}^{r-2}\tilde{z}_{r-1}^{r-2}} \underline{\tilde{z}}_{r-1}^{r-2} \tag{70}$$

and

$$\underline{\tilde{z}}_r^{r-1} = \underline{\tilde{z}}_r^{r-2} - P_{\tilde{z}_r^{r-2}\tilde{z}_{r-1}^{r-2}} P^{-1}_{\tilde{z}_{r-1}^{r-2}\tilde{z}_{r-1}^{r-2}} \underline{\tilde{z}}_{r-1}^{r-2}. \tag{71}$$

From substituting Eqs. (70) and (71) in Eq. (69), we obtain

$$P_{\tilde{\theta}_i^{r-1}\tilde{z}_r^{r-1}} = E\left\{\left[\underline{\tilde{\theta}}_i^{r-2} - P_{\tilde{\theta}_i^{r-2}\tilde{z}_{r-1}^{r-2}} P^{-1}_{\tilde{z}_{r-1}^{r-2}\tilde{z}_{r-1}^{r-2}} \underline{\tilde{z}}_{r-1}^{r-2}\right] \times \left[\underline{\tilde{z}}_r^{r-2} - P_{\tilde{z}_r^{r-2}\tilde{z}_{r-1}^{r-2}} P^{-1}_{\tilde{z}_{r-1}^{r-2}\tilde{z}_{r-1}^{r-2}} \underline{\tilde{z}}_{r-1}^{r-2}\right]^T\right\}$$

$$= P_{\tilde{\theta}_i^{r-2}\tilde{z}_r^{r-2}} - P_{\tilde{\theta}_i^{r-2}\tilde{z}_{r-1}^{r-2}} P^{-1}_{\tilde{z}_{r-1}^{r-2}\tilde{z}_{r-1}^{r-2}} P_{\tilde{z}_{r-1}^{r-2}\tilde{z}_r^{r-2}}. \tag{72}$$

Note that by symmetry

$$P_{\tilde{\theta}_i^{r-1}\tilde{\theta}_j^{r-1}} = P^T_{\tilde{\theta}_j^{r-1}\tilde{\theta}_i^{r-1}} \quad \text{and} \quad P_{\tilde{\theta}_i^{r-1}\tilde{z}_r^{r-1}} = P^T_{\tilde{z}_r^{r-1}\tilde{\theta}_i^{r-1}}.$$

Remark. Setting $r = N$ in all the above equations, we obtain the optimal solution.

Special case. Consider the case where the sequence $\{\underline{v}_k\}$ consists of independent, zero-mean, uncorrelated Gaussian variables. This means that the covariance matrix is block diagonal, that is

$$E\{\underline{v}\underline{v}^T\} = \begin{bmatrix} Q_1 & & & & 0 \\ & Q_2 & & & \\ & & \ddots & & \\ & & & Q_k & \\ 0 & & & & \ddots \; Q_N \end{bmatrix}.$$

Now we show that the optimal minimum variance estimate $\hat{\underline{\theta}}_i$ is also obtained after N iterations between the two levels. The kth iteration is given by the following procedure:

$$\hat{\underline{z}}_k^{k-1} = E\{\underline{z}_k | \underline{z}_1, \underline{z}_2, \ldots, \underline{z}_{k-1}\}$$

$$= \sum_{i=1}^{N} H_{ki}\hat{\underline{\theta}}_i^{k-1} + \underbrace{E\{\underline{v}_k | \underline{z}_1, \underline{z}_2, \ldots, \underline{z}_{k-1}\}}_{=0}$$

$$= \sum_{i=1}^{N} H_{ki}\hat{\underline{\theta}}_i^{k-1}. \tag{73}$$

The second term ($=E\{\underline{v}_k\}$) is zero by virtue of the uncorrelated nature of $\{\underline{v}_k\}$, and consequently

$$E\{\underline{v}_k\underline{z}_{k-i}^T\} = 0 \quad \forall i = 1, \ldots, k - 1.$$

Also,

$$\underline{\tilde{z}}_k^{k-1} = \underline{z}_k - \underline{\hat{z}}_k^{k-1}$$

$$= \sum_{r=1}^{N} H_{kr}\underline{\theta}_r + \underline{v}_k - \sum_{i=1}^{N} H_{ki}\underline{\hat{\theta}}_i^{k-1}$$

$$= \sum_{r=1}^{N} H_{kr}\underline{\tilde{\theta}}_r^{k-1} + \underline{v}_k, \tag{74}$$

$$P_{\tilde{z}_k^{k-1}\tilde{z}_k^{k-1}} = E\left\{\underline{\tilde{z}}_k^{k-1}\underline{\tilde{z}}_k^{k-1^T}\right\}; \tag{75}$$

and finally, substituting Eq. (74) into Eq. (75), we obtain

$$P_{\tilde{z}_k^{k-1}\tilde{z}_k^{k-1}} = \sum_{i=1}^{N} H_{ki} \sum_{r=1}^{N}\left[P_{\tilde{\theta}_i^{k-1}\tilde{\theta}_r^{k-1}}H_{kr}^T\right] + Q_k, \tag{76}$$

$$P_{\tilde{\theta}_i^{k-1}\tilde{z}_k^{k-1}} = E\left\{\underline{\tilde{\theta}}_i^{k-1}\underline{\tilde{z}}_k^{k-1^T}\right\}; \tag{77}$$

and, substituting Eq. (74) into Eq. (77), we obtain

$$P_{\tilde{\theta}_i^{k-1}\tilde{z}_k^{k-1}} = \sum_{r=1}^{N} P_{\tilde{\theta}_i^{k-1}\tilde{\theta}_r^{k-1}}H_{kr}^T. \tag{78}$$

The other equations we need have already been derived:

$$\underline{\hat{\theta}}_i^k = \underline{\hat{\theta}}_i^{k-1} + P_{\tilde{\theta}_i^{k-1}\tilde{z}_k^{k-1}}P^{-1}_{\tilde{z}_k^{k-1}\tilde{z}_k^{k-1}}\underline{\tilde{z}}_k^{k-1}, \tag{79}$$

$$P_{\tilde{\theta}_i^k\tilde{\theta}_i^k} = P_{\tilde{\theta}_i^{k-1}\tilde{\theta}_i^{k-1}} - P_{\tilde{\theta}_i^{k-1}\tilde{z}_k^{k-1}}P^{-1}_{\tilde{z}_k^{k-1}\tilde{z}_k^{k-1}}P_{\tilde{z}_k^{k-1}\tilde{\theta}_i^{k-1}}, \tag{80}$$

$$P_{\tilde{\theta}_i^k\tilde{\theta}_j^k} = P_{\tilde{\theta}_i^{k-1}\tilde{\theta}_j^{k-1}} - P_{\tilde{\theta}_i^{k-1}\tilde{z}_k^{k-1}}P^{-1}_{\tilde{z}_k^{k-1}\tilde{z}_k^{k-1}}P_{\tilde{z}_k^{k-1}\tilde{\theta}_j^{k-1}}. \tag{81}$$

Corollary. Expressions (52) and (76) are equivalent.

Proof.

$$P_{\tilde{z}_k^{k-1}\tilde{z}_k^{k-1}} = \sum_{i=1}^{N} H_{ki} \sum_{r=1}^{N}\left[P_{\tilde{\theta}_i^{k-1}\tilde{\theta}_r^{k-1}}H_{kr}^T\right] + Q_k.$$

Using Eqs. (81) and (78), we take

$$P_{\tilde{z}_k^{k-1}\tilde{z}_k^{k-1}} = \sum_{i=1}^{N} H_{ki} \sum_{r=1}^{N}$$

$$\times \left[\left(P_{\tilde{\theta}_i^{k-2}\tilde{\theta}_r^{k-2}} - P_{\tilde{\theta}_i^{k-2}\tilde{z}_{k-1}^{k-2}} P^{-1}_{\tilde{z}_{k-1}^{k-2}\tilde{z}_{k-1}^{k-2}} P_{\tilde{z}_{k-1}^{k-2}\tilde{\theta}_r^{k-2}}\right) H_{kr}^T\right]$$

$$+ Q_k$$

$$= P_{\tilde{z}_k^{k-2}\tilde{z}_k^{k-2}} - \sum_{i=1}^{N} H_{ki} \sum_{r=1}^{N}$$

$$\times P_{\tilde{\theta}_i^{k-2}\tilde{z}_{k-1}^{k-2}} P^{-1}_{\tilde{z}_{k-1}^{k-2}\tilde{z}_{k-1}^{k-2}} P_{\tilde{z}_{k-1}^{k-2}\tilde{\theta}_r^{k-2}} H_{kr}^T$$

$$= P_{\tilde{z}_k^{k-2}\tilde{z}_k^{k-2}} - \sum_{i=1}^{N} H_{ki} \sum_{r=1}^{N}$$

$$\times \left(\sum_{l=1}^{N} P_{\tilde{\theta}_i^{k-2}\tilde{\theta}_l^{k-2}} H_{k-1\ l}^T\right) P^{-1}_{\tilde{z}_{k-1}^{k-2}\tilde{z}_{k-1}^{k-2}}$$

$$\times \left(\sum_{l=1}^{N} H_{k-1\ l} P_{\tilde{\theta}_r^{k-2}\tilde{\theta}_l^{k-2}}^T\right) H_{kr}^T$$

$$= P_{\tilde{z}_k^{k-2}\tilde{z}_k^{k-2}} - \sum_{i=1}^{N} H_{ki} \sum_{l=1}^{N}\left[P_{\tilde{\theta}_i^{k-2}\tilde{\theta}_l^{k-2}} H_{k-1\ l}^T\right]$$

$$\times P^{-1}_{\tilde{z}_{k-1}^{k-2}\tilde{z}_{k-1}^{k-2}} \sum_{r=1}^{N} \sum_{l=1}^{N}\left[H_{k-1\ l} P_{\tilde{\theta}_r^{k-2}\tilde{\theta}_l^{k-2}}^T\right] H_{kr}^T$$

$$= P_{\tilde{z}_k^{k-2}\tilde{z}_k^{k-2}} - P_{\tilde{z}_k^{k-2}\tilde{z}_{k-1}^{k-2}} P^{-1}_{\tilde{z}_{k-1}^{k-2}\tilde{z}_{k-1}^{k-2}} P_{\tilde{z}_{k-1}^{k-2}\tilde{z}_k^{k-2}} \qquad \text{Q.E.D.}$$

Similarly, it can be proven that expression (78) is equivalent to expression (65).

Finally, we consider a recursive version of this algorithm.

C. DEVELOPMENT OF THE RECURSIVE ALGORITHM

Let us assume that Eq. (30) is obtained after k measurements. Rewriting Eq. (30), we obtain

$$\underline{z}_k = H_k\underline{\theta} + \underline{v}_k.$$

Now if we received a new measurement k + 1 given by

$$\underline{\zeta}_{k+1} = h_{k+1}\underline{\theta} + v'_{k+1}, \tag{82}$$

by adjoining this new observation to the previous observation we obtain

$$\underline{z}_{k+1} = H_{k+1}\underline{\theta} + \underline{v}_{k+1}, \tag{83}$$

where

$$\underline{z}_{k+1} = \begin{bmatrix} \underline{z}_k \\ \hline \underline{\zeta}_{k+1} \end{bmatrix}, \quad H_{k+1} = \begin{bmatrix} H_k \\ \hline h_{k+1} \end{bmatrix}, \quad \underline{v}_{k+1} = \begin{bmatrix} \underline{v}_k \\ \hline \underline{v}'_{k+1} \end{bmatrix}.$$

The minimum variance estimator based on k + 1 measurement $\hat{\underline{\theta}}_{k+1}$ is given by

$$\begin{aligned}\hat{\underline{\theta}}_{k+1} &= E\{\underline{\theta}|\underline{z}_{k+1}\} = E\{\underline{\theta}|\underline{z}_k, \zeta_{k+1}\} \\ &= E\{\underline{\theta}|\underline{z}_k\} + E\left\{\underline{\theta}|\tilde{\underline{\zeta}}^k_{k+1}\right\} - \underline{\mu}_\theta \qquad \text{[from Eq. (23)]} \\ &= \hat{\underline{\theta}}_k + \underline{\mu}_\theta + P_{\theta\tilde{\zeta}^k_{k+1}} P^{-1}_{\tilde{\zeta}^k_{k+1}\tilde{\zeta}^k_{k+1}} \tilde{\underline{\zeta}}^k_{k+1} - \underline{\mu}_\theta.\end{aligned}$$

Therefore

$$\hat{\underline{\theta}}_{k+1} = \hat{\underline{\theta}}_k + P_{\theta\tilde{\zeta}^k_{k+1}} P^{-1}_{\tilde{\zeta}^k_{k+1}} \tilde{\underline{\zeta}}^k_{k+1}, \tag{84}$$

where the innovation vector $\tilde{\underline{\zeta}}^k_{k+1}$ is given by

$$\begin{aligned}\tilde{\underline{\zeta}}^k_{k+1} &= \underline{\zeta}_{k+1} - E\{\underline{\zeta}_{k+1}|\underline{z}_k\} \\ &= \underline{\zeta}_{k+1} - h_{k+1}E\{\underline{\theta}|\underline{z}_k\} - E\left\{\underline{v}'_{k+1}|\underline{z}_k\right\}.\end{aligned}$$

Assuming that $E\left\{\underline{v}'_{k+1}\underline{v}_k^T\right\} = 0$, then $E\left\{\underline{v}'_{k+1}\underline{z}_k^T\right\} = 0$. Moreover,

$$\underline{\tilde{\zeta}}^k_{k+1} = \underline{\zeta}_{k+1} - h_{k+1}\underline{\hat{\theta}}_k = h_{k+1}\underline{\tilde{\theta}}_k + \underline{v}'_{k+1}, \tag{85}$$

for which the covariance matrix $P_{\tilde{\zeta}^k_{k+1}\tilde{\zeta}^k_{k+1}}$ is given by

$$P_{\tilde{\zeta}^k_{k+1}\tilde{\zeta}^k_{k+1}} = E\left\{\left[h_{k+1}\underline{\tilde{\theta}}_k + \underline{v}'_{k+1}\right]\left[\underline{\tilde{\theta}}_k^T h_{k+1}^T + \underline{v}'^T_{k+1}\right]\right\}.$$

Hence

$$P_{\tilde{\zeta}^k_{k+1}\tilde{\zeta}^k_{k+1}} = h_{k+1}P_{\tilde{\theta}_k\tilde{\theta}_k}h_{k+1}^T + Q'_{k+1}. \tag{86}$$

Also, the covariance matrix $P_{\theta\tilde{\zeta}^k_{k+1}}$ can be derived as follows:

$$P_{\theta\tilde{\zeta}^k_{k+1}} = E\left\{[\underline{\theta} - \underline{\mu}_\theta]\left[\underline{\tilde{\zeta}}^k_{k+1} - \underbrace{E\left\{\tilde{\zeta}^k_{k+1}\right\}}_{=0}\right]^T\right\}$$

$$= E\left\{\left[\underline{\hat{\theta}}_k + \underline{\tilde{\theta}}_k - \underline{\mu}_\theta\right]\underline{\tilde{\zeta}}^{k^T}_{k+1}\right\}$$

$$= \underbrace{E\left\{\underline{\hat{\theta}}_k\tilde{\zeta}^{k^T}_{k+1}\right\}}_{=0} + E\left\{\underline{\tilde{\theta}}_k\underline{\tilde{\theta}}_k^T h_{k+1}^T\right\} - \underline{\mu}_\theta \underbrace{E\left\{\underline{\tilde{\zeta}}^{k^T}_{k+1}\right\}}_{=0} + \underbrace{E\left\{\underline{\tilde{\theta}}_k\underline{v}'^T_{k+1}\right\}}_{=0}.$$

Thus

$$P_{\theta\tilde{\zeta}^k_{k+1}} = P_{\tilde{\theta}_k\tilde{\theta}_k}h_{k+1}^T = P^T_{\tilde{\zeta}^k_{k+1}\theta}. \tag{87}$$

Finally, the resulting recursive equation of the covariance matrix of the estimation error after k + 1 measurements can be obtained using the following procedure:

$$P_{\tilde{\theta}_{k+1}\tilde{\theta}_{k+1}} = E\left\{\left[\underline{\theta} - \underline{\hat{\theta}}_{k+1}\right]\left[\underline{\theta} - \underline{\hat{\theta}}_{k+1}\right]^T\right\}$$

$$= E\left\{\left[\underline{\theta} - \underline{\hat{\theta}}_k - P_{\theta\tilde{\zeta}^k_{k+1}}P^{-1}_{\tilde{\zeta}^k_{k+1}\tilde{\zeta}^k_{k+1}}\underline{\tilde{\zeta}}^k_{k+1}\right]\right.$$

$$\left.\times\left[\underline{\theta} - \underline{\hat{\theta}}_k - P_{\theta\tilde{\zeta}^k_{k+1}}P^{-1}_{\tilde{\zeta}^k_{k+1}\tilde{\zeta}^k_{k+1}}\underline{\tilde{\zeta}}^k_{k+1}\right]^T\right\}$$

$$= E\left\{\left[\underline{\tilde{\theta}}_k - P_{\theta\tilde{\zeta}^k_{k+1}} P^{-1}_{\tilde{\zeta}^k_{k+1}\tilde{\zeta}^k_{k+1}} \underline{\tilde{\zeta}}^k_{k+1}\right]\right.$$

$$\left.\times \left[\underline{\tilde{\theta}}_k - P_{\theta\zeta^k_{k+1}} P^{-1}_{\tilde{\zeta}^k_{k+1}\tilde{\zeta}^k_{k+1}} \underline{\tilde{\zeta}}^k_{k+1}\right]^T\right\}.$$

Hence

$$P_{\tilde{\theta}_{k+1}\tilde{\theta}_{k+1}} = P_{\tilde{\theta}_k\tilde{\theta}_k} - P_{\theta\tilde{\zeta}^k_{k+1}} P^{-1}_{\tilde{\zeta}^k_{k+1}\tilde{\zeta}^k_{k+1}} P_{\tilde{\zeta}^k_{k+1}\theta}. \tag{88}$$

Note that using Eq. (19),

$$P_{\theta\tilde{\zeta}^k_{k+1}} = P_{\tilde{\theta}_k\tilde{\zeta}^k_{k+1}}.$$

The vectors $\underline{\zeta}_{k+1}$ and $\underline{\theta}$ have not been decomposed. If $\underline{\zeta}_{k+1}$ is of high dimension, we can decompose $\underline{\zeta}_{k+1}$ and $\underline{\theta}$ and again use the multiple projection idea.

Next we extend the above recursive algorithm by decomposing the vectors $\underline{\zeta}_{k+1}$ and $\underline{\theta}$. This extended recursive algorithm now combines the best of both versions, keeping recursive characteristics together with a decentralized nature.

Let us assume that Eq. (35) is obtained after k measurements. Rewriting Eq. (35), we obtain

$$\underline{z}^k_i = H^k_{ii}\underline{\theta}_i + \sum_{\substack{j=1 \\ i\neq j}}^{N} H^k_{ij}\underline{\theta}_j + \underline{v}^k_i. \tag{89}$$

The new measurement k + 1 is given by

$$\underline{\zeta}^{k+1}_i = h^{k+1}_{ii}\underline{\theta}_i + \sum_{\substack{j=1 \\ i\neq j}}^{N} h^{k+1}_{ij}\underline{\theta}_j + \underline{v}'^{k+1}_i. \tag{90}$$

By adjoining this new observation to the previous observation, we obtain

$$\underline{z}^{k+1}_i = H^{k+1}_{ii}\underline{\theta}_i + \sum_{\substack{j=1 \\ i\neq j}}^{N} H^{k+1}_{ij}\underline{\theta}_j + \underline{v}^{k+1}_i, \tag{91}$$

where

$$\underline{z}_i^{k+1} = \begin{bmatrix} \underline{z}_i^k \\ \underline{\zeta}_i^{k+1} \end{bmatrix}, \quad H_{ij}^{k+1} = \begin{bmatrix} H_{ij}^k \\ h_{ij}^{k+1} \end{bmatrix}, \quad \underline{v}_i^{k+1} = \begin{bmatrix} \underline{v}_i^k \\ \underline{v}_i'^{k+1} \end{bmatrix}.$$

The minimum variance estimator $\hat{\underline{\theta}}_i^{k+1}$ is given by

$$\begin{aligned}
\hat{\underline{\theta}}_i^{k+1} &= E\left\{\underline{\theta}_i \mid \underline{z}^{k+1}\right\} \\
&= E\left\{\underline{\theta}_i \mid \underline{z}^k, \underline{\zeta}_1^{k+1}, \underline{\zeta}_2^{k+1}, \ldots, \underline{\zeta}_N^{k+1}\right\} \qquad \text{[and using Eq. (23)]} \\
&= E\left\{\underline{\theta}_i \mid \underline{z}^k\right\} + E\left\{\underline{\theta}_i \mid \tilde{\underline{\zeta}}_1^k\right\} + \sum_{j=1}^{N-1} E\left\{\underline{\theta}_i \mid \tilde{\underline{\zeta}}_{j+1}^j\right\} - N\mu_{\theta_i} \\
&= \hat{\underline{\theta}}_i^k + P_{\theta_i \tilde{\zeta}_1^k} P_{\tilde{\zeta}_1^k \tilde{\zeta}_1^k}^{-1} \tilde{\underline{\zeta}}_1^k + \sum_{j=2}^{N} P_{\theta_i \tilde{\zeta}_j^{j-1}} P^{-1}_{\tilde{\zeta}_j^{j-1} \tilde{\zeta}_j^{j-1}} \tilde{\underline{\zeta}}_j^{j-1} \\
&= \hat{\underline{\theta}}_i^k + P_{\tilde{\theta}_i^k \tilde{\zeta}_1^k} P^{-1}_{\tilde{\zeta}_1^k \tilde{\zeta}_1^k} \tilde{\underline{\zeta}}_1^k + \sum_{j=2}^{N} P_{\tilde{\theta}_i^{j-1} \tilde{\zeta}_j^{j-1}} P^{-1}_{\tilde{\zeta}_j^{j-1} \tilde{\zeta}_j^{j-1}} \tilde{\underline{\zeta}}_j^{j-1},
\end{aligned} \tag{92}$$

where the innovation vector $\tilde{\underline{\zeta}}_1^k$ is given by

$$\begin{aligned}
\tilde{\underline{\zeta}}_1^k &= \underline{\zeta}_1^{k+1} - E\left\{\underline{\zeta}_1^{k+1} \mid \underline{z}^k\right\} \\
&= \underline{\zeta}_1^{k+1} - h_{11}^{k+1} E\left\{\underline{\theta}_1 \mid \underline{z}^k\right\} - \sum_{j=1}^{N} h_{1j}^{k+1} E\left\{\underline{\theta}_j \mid \underline{z}^k\right\} - E\left\{\underline{v}_1'^{k+1} \mid \underline{z}^k\right\}.
\end{aligned}$$

Assuming $E\left\{\underline{v}_1'^{k+1} \underline{v}_i^{k^T}\right\} = 0$, $i = 1, \ldots, N$, thus

$$\begin{aligned}
\tilde{\underline{\zeta}}_1^k &= \underline{\zeta}_1^{k+1} - h_{11}^{k+1} \hat{\underline{\theta}}_1^k - \sum_{j=1}^{N} h_{1j}^{k+1} \hat{\underline{\theta}}_j^k \\
&= h_{11}^{k+1} \tilde{\underline{\theta}}_1^k + \sum_{j=1}^{N} h_{1j}^{k+1} \tilde{\underline{\theta}}_j^k + \underline{v}_1'^{k+1}.
\end{aligned} \tag{93}$$

Working as previously, we easily conclude that the covariance matrix $P_{\tilde{\zeta}_1^k \tilde{\zeta}_1^k}$ is given by

$$P_{\tilde{\zeta}_1^k \tilde{\zeta}_1^k} = \sum_{r=1}^{N} h_{1r}^{k+1} \sum_{j=1}^{N} P_{\tilde{\theta}_r^k \tilde{\theta}_j^k} h_{1j}^{k+1^T} + Q_{11}^{\prime k+1}. \tag{94}$$

Also, the covariance $P_{\tilde{\theta}_i^k \tilde{\zeta}_1^k}$ is given by

$$P_{\tilde{\theta}_i^k \tilde{\zeta}_1^k} = \sum_{r=1}^{N} P_{\tilde{\theta}_i^k \tilde{\theta}_r^k} h_{1r}^{k+1^T}, \tag{95}$$

and the covariance matrix of the estimation error after k + 1 measurements is given by

$$\begin{aligned} P_{\tilde{\theta}_i^{k+1} \tilde{\theta}_j^{k+1}} &= P_{\theta_i \theta_j}^{(k+1)} = P_{\tilde{\theta}_i^N \tilde{\theta}_j^N}^{(k)} \\ &= P_{\tilde{\theta}_i^k \tilde{\theta}_j^k} - P_{\tilde{\theta}_i^k \tilde{\zeta}_1^k} P_{\tilde{\zeta}_1^k \tilde{\zeta}_1^k}^{-1} P_{\tilde{\zeta}_1^k \tilde{\theta}_j^k} \\ &\quad - \sum_{l=2}^{N} P_{\tilde{\theta}_i^{l-1} \tilde{\zeta}_l^{l-1}} P_{\tilde{\zeta}_l^{l-1} \tilde{\zeta}_l^{l-1}}^{-1} P_{\tilde{\zeta}_l^{l-1} \tilde{\theta}_j^{l-1}}. \end{aligned} \tag{96}$$

The third terms of Eqs. (92) and (96) are obtained from the equations used in the nonrecursive algorithm, substituting H_{ij} by h_{ij}^{k+1}, $\underline{z}_i$ by $\underline{\zeta}_i^{k+1}$, Q_{ij} by $Q_{ij}^{\prime k+1}$, and $P_{\theta_i \theta_j}$ by

$$P_{\tilde{\theta}_i^k \tilde{\theta}_j^k} = P_{\theta_i \theta_j}^{(k)}.$$

Note that with the above notation,

$$P_{\tilde{\theta}_i^r \tilde{\theta}_j^r}$$

of the nonrecursive algorithm becomes

$$P_{\tilde{\theta}_i^r \tilde{\theta}_j^r}^{(k)}$$

and denotes the covariance matrix of the parameter estimation error after k recursions and after r iterations between the two levels of the hierarchy.

Special case. Assume that $E\left\{\underline{v}_i'^k \underline{v}_{i-1}'^{k^T}\right\} = 0$, $i = 2, \ldots, N$, that is $E\left\{\underline{v}'^k \underline{v}'^{k^T}\right\}$ is in block diagonal form.

In order to calculate the third term of Eq. (92), we can use the equations of the special case of the nonrecursive algorithm and the same substitution as above.

Remarks.

(a) It is obvious that

$$\tilde{\underline{z}}_i^0 = \underline{z}_i \quad \left(\hat{\underline{z}}_i^0 = 0\right) \quad \text{and} \quad \tilde{\underline{\theta}}_i^0 = \underline{\theta}_i,$$

and consequently,

$$P_{\tilde{z}_i^0 \tilde{z}_j^0} = P_{z_i z_j}, \quad P_{\tilde{\theta}_i^0 \tilde{\theta}_j^0} = P_{\theta_i \theta_j}$$

(b) The philosophy of multiple projection is based on decomposition of the measurement vector $\underline{z}$ to facilitate building up partitioned estimation algorithms. Although in the nonrecursive algorithm we have considered decomposing the parameter vector $\underline{\theta}$ in agreement with $\underline{z}$, the developed algorithm can still be implemented without the decomposition of $\underline{\theta}$ by replacing $\underline{\theta}_i$ or $\underline{\theta}_j$ by $\underline{\theta}$. This is suitable for situations where a small number of parameters is encountered.

(c) The matrix $\left(H_{ii} P_{\theta_i \theta_i} H_{ii}^T + Q_{ii}\right)$ used in the algorithmic procedure is always invertable, even if rank $(H_{ii}) < n_i$. This is so because Q_{ii} has nonzero diagonal terms since there is always measurement noise in the system.

(d) The number of the subvectors of the measurement vector $\underline{z}$ need not be equal to the number of subvectors of the parameter vector $\underline{\theta}$. The algorithm can be easily generalized when N measurement subvectors and M parameter subvectors are considered.

(e) Without loss of generality, consider that the measurement and parameter vectors per subsystem have dimensions n/N and m/N, respectively. Then, under the assumption that the measurement matrix H is block diagonal, the number of elementary multiplications required for the global (single-level) estimator is given by [5]

$$1.5m^2 + 1.5m^3 + mn\left\{\frac{1}{N} + \frac{2n + m}{2N} + n + 1 + \frac{m + 1}{2}\right\}$$
$$+ n^2 \frac{(3n + 1)}{2}.$$

The required number of multiplications for the two-level estimator using a monoprocessor system is

$$1.4m^2 + 1.5m^3 + N\left\{\frac{mn}{N^2} + \frac{mn(2n + m)}{2N^3} + \frac{n^2(3n/N + 1)}{2N^2}\right.$$
$$\left. + N\left[\frac{m^2n + mn^2}{N^3} + \frac{mn}{N^2} + \frac{mn(m + N)}{2N^3}\right] + \frac{N(N - 1)m^2n}{2N^3}\right\}.$$

It is easy to see that when m becomes large, the new two-level structure gives substantial saving in the computational effort required.

(f) For the nonrecursive version there is no restriction on the type of noise signals. However, the recursive version deals only with uncorrelated noise and thus gives unbiased estimates.

IV. IMPLEMENTATION OF THE ALGORITHM

To illustrate the implementation of the new two-level algorithm, we consider system (30) being decomposed into two subsystems. In this case three processors are used to carry out the two-level estimation structure. One processor represents the coordinator and each of the remaining two is linked to a subsystem. The minimum variance estimate, after two iterations, can be obtained by the following procedure.

Step 1. Subsystems 1 and 2 give to the coordinator the matrices $P_{\theta_1\theta_1}$, H_{11}, H_{12} and $P_{\theta_2\theta_2}$, H_{21}, H_{22}, respectively. Also, the coordinator provides communication from subsystem 2 to subsystem 1 for the mean value $\underline{\mu}_{\theta_2}$.

The subsystems calculate the matrices

$$P_{\theta_1 z_1},\ P_{\theta_2 z_1},\ P_{z_1 z_1} \qquad \text{(subsystem 1)}$$

and

$$P_{\theta_1 z_2},\ P_{\theta_2 z_2},\ P_{z_2 z_2} \qquad \text{(subsystem 2)}.$$

The coordinator calculates the matrix $P_{z_1 z_2}$.

Subsystem 1 calculates the estimate after one iteration:

$$\underline{\hat{\theta}}_1 = \underline{\mu}_{\theta_1} + P_{\theta_1 z_1} P_{z_1 z_1}^{-1} (\underline{z}_1 - H_{11} \cdot \underline{\mu}_{\theta_1} - H_{12} \cdot \underline{\mu}_{\theta_2}),$$

$$\underline{\hat{\theta}}_2 = \underline{\mu}_{\theta_2} + P_{\theta_2 z_1} P_{z_1 z_1}^{-1} (\underline{z}_1 - H_{11} \cdot \underline{\mu}_{\theta_1} - H_{12} \cdot \underline{\mu}_{\theta_2}).$$

At the end of this step subsystem 1 calculates the covariance matrices of the estimation error after one iteration,

$$P_{\tilde{\theta}_1^1 \tilde{\theta}_1^1},\ P_{\tilde{\theta}_1^1 \tilde{\theta}_2^1},\ P_{\tilde{\theta}_2^1 \tilde{\theta}_2^1}.$$

Step 2. The coordinator gives to subsystem 1 the term $P_{z_1 z_2}$, and then subsystem 1 calculates the terms

$$\underline{P}_1 = P_{z_2 z_1} P_{z_1 z_1}^{-1} (\underline{z}_1 - H_{11}\underline{\mu}_{\theta_1} - H_{12}\underline{\mu}_{\theta_2}),$$

$$P_2 = P_{z_2 z_1} (P_{z_1 z_1} P_{z_1 z_2}),$$

$$P_3 = P_{\theta_1 z_1} \left(P_{z_1 z_1}^{-1} P_{z_1 z_2}\right),$$

$$P_4 = P_{\theta_2 z_1} \left(P_{z_1 z_1}^{-1} P_{z_1 z_2}\right).$$

The coordinator communicates $\underline{P}_1$, P_2, P_3, P_4 and the mean value $\underline{\mu}_{\theta_1}$, from subsystem 1 to subsystem 2.

Then subsystem 2 calculates the terms after one iteration:

$$\underline{\tilde{z}}_2^1 = \underline{z}_2 - H_{21}\underline{\mu}_{\theta_1} - H_{22}\underline{\mu}_{\theta_2} - \underline{P}_1,$$

$$P_{\tilde{z}_2^1\tilde{z}_2^1} = P_{z_2z_2} - P_2,$$

$$P_{\tilde{\theta}_1^1\tilde{z}_2^1} = P_{\theta_1z_2} - P_3,$$

$$P_{\tilde{\theta}_2^1\tilde{z}_2^1} = P_{\theta_2z_2} - P_4.$$

Now subsystem 2 calculates the terms

$$\underline{\hat{\theta}}_3 = P_{\tilde{\theta}_1^1\tilde{z}_2^1}\left(P^{-1}_{\tilde{z}_2^1\tilde{z}_2^1}\underline{\tilde{z}}_2^1\right),$$

$$\underline{\theta}_4 = P_{\tilde{\theta}_2^1\tilde{z}_2^1}\left(P^{-1}_{\tilde{z}_2^1\tilde{z}_2^1}\underline{\tilde{z}}_2^1\right).$$

These terms communicate through the coordinator with terms $\underline{\hat{\theta}}_1$ and $\underline{\hat{\theta}}_2$ of subsystem 1 and give to the coordinator the estimation after two iterations as

$$\underline{\hat{\theta}}_1 = \underline{\hat{\theta}}_1 + \underline{\hat{\theta}}_3, \quad \underline{\hat{\theta}}_2 = \underline{\hat{\theta}}_2 + \underline{\hat{\theta}}_4.$$

At the end of this step the coordinator transmits from subsystem 1 to subsystem 2 the matrices

$$P_{\tilde{\theta}_1^1\tilde{\theta}_1^1}, \quad P_{\tilde{\theta}_1^1\tilde{\theta}_2^1}, \quad \text{and} \quad P_{\tilde{\theta}_2^1\tilde{\theta}_2^1},$$

and then subsystem 2 calculates the covariance matrices of the estimation error after two iterations,

$$P_{\tilde{\theta}_1^2\tilde{\theta}_1^2}, \quad P_{\tilde{\theta}_1^2\tilde{\theta}_2^2}, \quad P_{\tilde{\theta}_2^2\tilde{\theta}_2^2}.$$

The flow of information within the two-level structure is shown in Fig. 1.

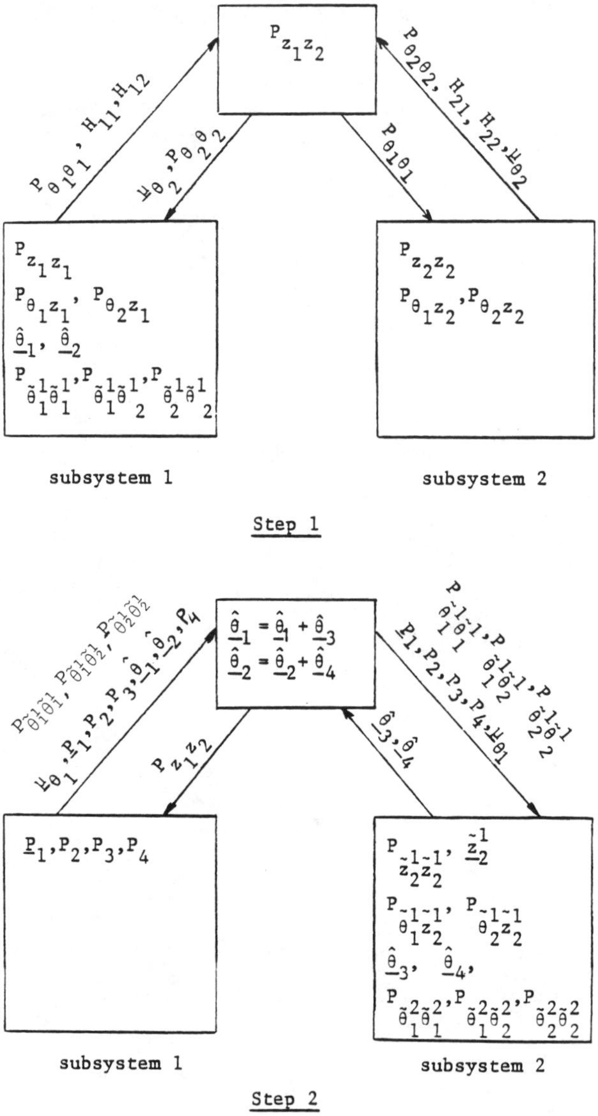

Fig. 1. Implementation of the algorithm.

V. SIMULATION RESULTS

A single input – single output discrete transfer function with unknown coefficients

$$\frac{y(z)}{u(z)} = \frac{b_0 + b_1 z^{-1} + \cdots + b_n z^{-n}}{1 + a_1 z^{-1} + \cdots + a_n z^{-n}}$$

can be rewritten as

$$y(k) = -\sum_{i=1}^{n} a_i y(k - 1) + b_0 u(k) + \sum_{i=1}^{n} b_i u(k - 1) + v(k),$$

where the random variable $v(k)$ takes into account the uncertainty or noise in the model. If we study the evaluation of the system for L samples (where $L \gg n$), we can put the problem in a form which is analogous to the static model of our problem:

$$\begin{bmatrix} y_{k+1} \\ y_{k+2} \\ \vdots \\ y_{k+L} \end{bmatrix} = \begin{bmatrix} -y_k & \cdots & -y_{k-n+1} & u_{k+1} & \cdots & u_{k-n+1} \\ \vdots & & \vdots & \vdots & & \vdots \\ -y_{k+L-1} & & & u_{k+L} & & \end{bmatrix} \begin{bmatrix} a_1 \\ a_2 \\ \vdots \\ a_n \\ b_0 \\ b_1 \\ \vdots \\ b_n \end{bmatrix} + \begin{bmatrix} v_{k+1} \\ \\ \\ v_{k+L} \end{bmatrix},$$

or $\underline{z} = H\underline{\theta} + \underline{v}$. Two specific models were used in order to test both versions of the new algorithm.

Model 1 had the parameter values $b_0 = 0$, $b_1 = 1$, $b_2 = 0.5$, $a_1 = -1.5$, $a_2 = 0.7$.

Model 2 had the parameter values $b_0 = 1$, $b_1 = 0.1$, $b_2 = -0.8$, $b_3 = 0$, $b_4 = -0.45$, $a_1 = -2.3$, $a_2 = 1.93$, $a_3 = -0.713$, $a_4 = 0.1102$, $a_5 = -0.0056$.

A Gaussian, zero-mean, unit-variance random signal was used in exciting both models during simulation studies. The measurement vector $\underline{z}$ was decomposed into subvectors $\underline{z}_1 \in R^{n_1}$, $\underline{z}_2 \in R^{n_2}$, and $\underline{z}_3 \in R^{n_3}$, with $n_1 + n_2 + n_3 = L$. The parameter vector $\underline{\theta} = [-a_1 \cdots -a_n b_0 \cdots b_m]^T$, where $m \leq n$, was decomposed into $\underline{\theta}_1 \in R^{m_1}$, $\underline{\theta}_2 \in R^{m_3}$, where $m_1 < n$, $m_2 = n - m_1$, and $m_3 = m + 1$.

The simulation results for the nonrecursive algorithm are given in Tables I and II for models 1 and 2, respectively.

The recursive (nondecomposed) algorithm was then tested since the decomposed (extended) algorithm can be simply considered as a combination of the recursive (nondecomposed) and the nonrecursive algorithm. For simplicity, we present the simulation results of model 1 for different operating conditions.

Case 1. $Q = 0.1$, $P_{\theta\theta} = I$, $\underline{\mu}_\theta = \underline{0}$, and 100 recursions. The behavior of the parameter estimation and the error variance is shown in Figs. 2–6.

Case 2. $Q = 0.1$, $P_{\theta\theta} = I$, $\underline{\mu}_\theta = \underline{0}$, and 1000 recursions. In Figs. 7–11, the behavior of the parameter estimation is plotted.

Case 3. $Q = 1$, $P_{\theta\theta} = I$, $\underline{\mu}_\theta = \underline{0}$, and 100 recursions. We present, in Figs. 12 and 13, the behavior of the estimation of the parameters b_1 and b_2 and its error variances.

Case 4. $Q = 1$, $P_{\theta\theta} = 10I$, $\underline{\mu}_\theta = \underline{1}$, and 100 recursions. In Figs. 14 and 15 the effect of changing the initial values on the performance of the algorithm is given for the parameters b_1 and b_2.

TABLE I. Simulation Results of Model 1[a]

Dimensions of subsystems	Initial data	Estimation results: After one iteration	After two iterations	After three iterations
$n_1=20$, $m_1=1$ $n_2=10$, $m_2=1$ $n_3=10$, $m_3=3$	$\underline{\mu}_\theta=\underline{0}$ $P_{\theta\theta}=I$ $Q=0.1$	$\theta_1=1.5086$, $\theta_2=-0.7421$, $\theta_3=0.0856$, $\theta_4=0.9904$, $\theta_5=0.4990$, $P_{\theta\theta}=diag\{0.1822, 0.2743, 0.8204, 0.8250, 1.0749\}\times 10^{-2}$	$\theta_1=1.5085$, $\theta_2=-0.7264$, $\theta_3=0.0853$, $\theta_4=0.9828$, $\theta_5=0.4974$, $P_{\theta\theta}=diag\{0.1334, 0.1417, 0.3866, 0.3947, 0.4972\}\times 10^{-2}$	$\theta_1=1.5121$, $\theta_2=-0.7435$, $\theta_3=0.0339$, $\theta_4=0.9358$, $\theta_5=0.4388$, $P_{\theta\theta}=diag\{0.1103, 0.1103, 0.2596, 0.2668, 0.3190\}\times 10^{-2}$
$n_1=30$, $m_1=1$ $n_2=40$, $m_2=1$ $n_3=30$, $m_3=3$	$\underline{\mu}_\theta=\underline{0}$ $P_{\theta\theta}=I$ $Q=0.1$	$\theta_1=1.5057$, $\theta_2=-0.7320$, $\theta_3=0.0576$, $\theta_4=0.9540$ $\theta_5=0.4737$, $P_{\theta\theta}=diag\{0.1452, 0.1481, 0.3656, 0.3665, 0.4849\}\times 10^{-2}$	$\theta_1=1.4967$, $\theta_2=-0.7214$, $\theta_3=0.0078$, $\theta_4=0.9348$, $\theta_5=0.4565$, $P_{\theta\theta}=diag\{0.8448, 0.8423, 1.7422, 1.8365, 2.3793\}\times 10^{-3}$	$\theta_1=1.4934$, $\theta_2=-0.7198$, $\theta_3=-0.0268$, $\theta_4=0.9281$, $\theta_5=0.4253$, $P_{\theta\theta}=diag\{0.6767, 0.6601, 1.1310, 1.1585, 1.4644\}\times 10^{-3}$
$n_1=30$, $m_1=1$ $n_2=40$, $m_2=1$ $n_3=30$, $m_3=3$	$\underline{\mu}_\theta=\underline{1}$ $P_{\theta\theta}=10I$ $Q=0.1$	$\theta_1=1.5079$, $\theta_2=-0.7340$, $\theta_3=0.0589$, $\theta_4=0.9578$, $\theta_5=0.4740$, $P_{\theta\theta}=diag\{0.1458, 0.1484, 0.3670, 0.3680, 0.4876\}\times 10^{-2}$	$\theta_1=1.4983$, $\theta_2=-0.7228$, $\theta_3=-0.7159$, $\theta_4=0.9369$, $\theta_5=0.4564$, $P_{\theta\theta}=diag\{0.8474, 0.8428, 1.7454, 1.8404, 2.3854\}\times 10^{-3}$	$\theta_1=1.4946$, $\theta_2=-0.7210$, $\theta_3=-0.0265$, $\theta_4=0.9294$, $\theta_5=0.4250$, $P_{\theta\theta}=diag\{0.6784, 0.6609, 1.1330, 1.1600, 1.4670\}\times 10^{-3}$

[a] All figures are rounded to four decimals.

TABLE II. Simulation Results of Model 2[a]

Dimensions of subsystems	Initial data	Estimation results: After one iteration	After two iterations	After three iterations
$n_1=20,\ m_1=2$ $n_2=40,\ m_2=3$ $n_3=40,\ m_3=5$	$\underline{\mu}_\theta=\underline{0}$ $P_{\theta\theta}=I$ $Q=0.1$	$\theta_1=2.1780,\ \theta_2=1.6558,$ $\theta_3=0.4870,\ \theta_4=-0.0659,$ $\theta_5=0.0134,\ \theta_6=1.0387,$ $\theta_7=0.2029,\ \theta_8=-0.7861,$ $\theta_9=-0.0542,\ \theta_{10}=-0.5073,$ $P_{\theta\theta}=diag\{0.1510,\ 0.8274,$ $1.0414,\ 0.6862,$ $0.1136,\ 0.0687,$ $0.1758,\ 0.1743,$ $0.3015,\ 0.1811\}$ $\times 10^{-1}$	$\theta_1=2.1533,\ \theta_2=-1.6383,$ $\theta_3=0.5714,\ \theta_4=-0.1768,$ $\theta_5=0.0534,\ \theta_6=1.0087,$ $\theta_7=0.1967,\ \theta_8=-0.7817$ $\theta_9=-0.1899,\ \theta_{10}=-0.5656,$ $P_{\theta\theta}=diag\{0.6493,\ 3.6310,$ $4.9130,\ 3.0405,$ $0.4154,\ 0.2122,$ $0.8379,\ 0.8442,$ $1.1726,\ 0.8735\}$ $\times 10^{-2}$	$\theta_1=2.2282,\ \theta_2=-1.7853,$ $\theta_3=0.6781,\ \theta_4=-0.2064,$ $\theta_5=0.0626,\ \theta_6=0.9648,$ $\theta_7=0.1009,\ \theta_8=-0.8501,$ $\theta_9=-0.1402,\ \theta_{10}=-0.5589,$ $P_{\theta\theta}=diag\{0.4222,\ 2.3881,$ $3.0568,\ 1.8290,$ $0.2533,\ 0.1155,$ $0.5113,\ 0.4680,$ $0.7562,\ 0.5391\}$ $\times 10^{-2}$
$n_1=20,\ m_1=2$ $n_2=40,\ m_2=3$ $n_3=40,\ m_3=5$	$\underline{\mu}_\theta=\underline{0}$ $P_{\theta\theta}=I$ $Q=0.01$	$\theta_1=2.2655,\ \theta_2=-1.8489,$ $\theta_3=0.6465,\ \theta_4=-0.1014,$ $\theta_5=0.0111,\ \theta_6=1.0115,$ $\theta_7=0.1281,\ \theta_8=-0.7966,$ $\theta_9=-0.0177,\ \theta_{10}=-0.4678$ $P_{\theta\theta}=diag\{0.2443,\ 1.3832,$ $1.6871,\ 1.1154,$ $0.1852,\ 0.0803,$ $0.2234,\ 0.2276,$ $0.5001,\ 0.2629\}$ $\times 10^{-2}$	$\theta_1=2.2427,\ \theta_2=-1.8152,$ $\theta_3=0.6589\ \ \theta_4=-0.1367,$ $\theta_5=0.0241,\ \theta_6=1.0041,$ $\theta_7=0.1420,\ \theta_8=-0.7866,$ $\theta_9=-0.0679,\ \theta_{10}=-0.4919.$ $P_{\theta\theta}=diag\{1.0762,\ 6.0539,$ $8.0247,\ 4.7447,$ $0.6323,\ 0.1871,$ $1.2016,\ 1.1868,$ $1.6162,\ 1.2096\}$ $\times 10^{-3}$	$\theta_1=2.2738,\ \theta_2=-1.8852,$ $\theta_3=0.7187,\ \theta_4=-0.1564,$ $\theta_5=0.0268,\ \theta_6=0.9928,$ $\theta_7=0.1057,\ \theta_8=-0.8025,$ $\theta_9=-0.0401,\ \theta_{10}=-0.4918.$ $P_{\theta\theta}=diag\{0.7428,\ 4.0369,$ $4.9504,\ 2.9496,$ $0.4079,\ 0.0967,$ $0.8290,\ 0.7416,$ $1.0988,\ 0.7702\}$ $\times 10^{-3}$

[a]All figures are rounded to four decimals.

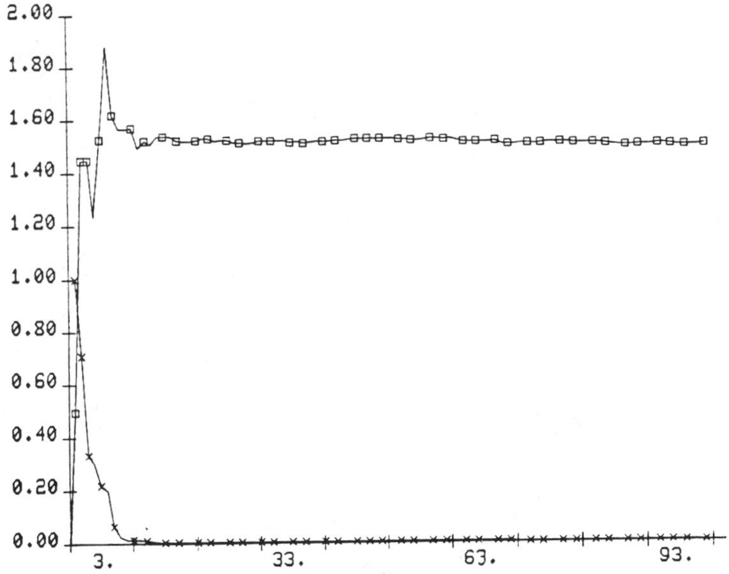

Fig. 2. One hundred recursions for model 1 ($Q = 0.1$, $P_{\theta\theta} = I$, $\underline{\mu}_\theta = \underline{0}$). x -- $P_{\theta_1\theta_1}$, □ -- θ_1.

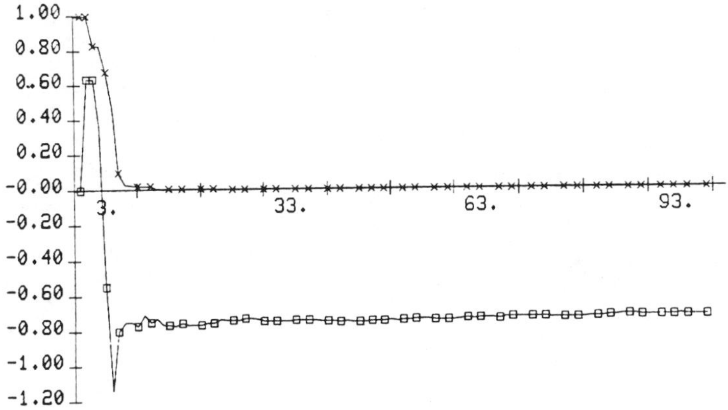

Fig. 3. One hundred recursions for model 1 ($Q = 0.1$, $P_{\theta\theta} = I$, $\underline{\mu}_\theta = \underline{0}$). x -- $P_{\theta_2\theta_2}$, □ -- θ_2.

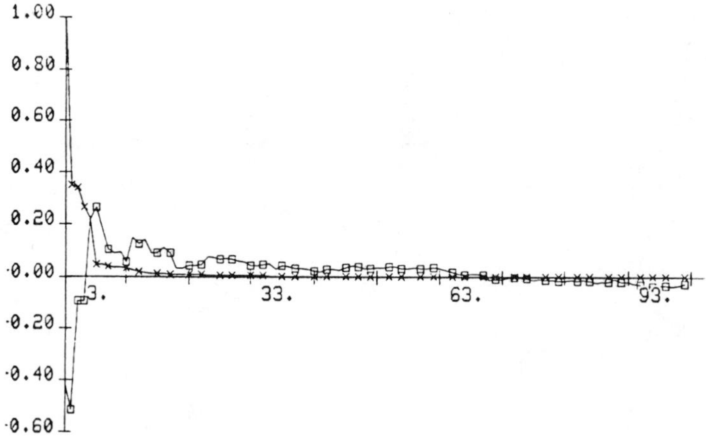

Fig. 4. One hundred recursions for model 1 ($Q = 0.1$, $P_{\theta\theta} = I$, $\underline{\mu}_\theta = \underline{0}$). X -- $P_{\theta_3\theta_3}$, □ -- θ_3.

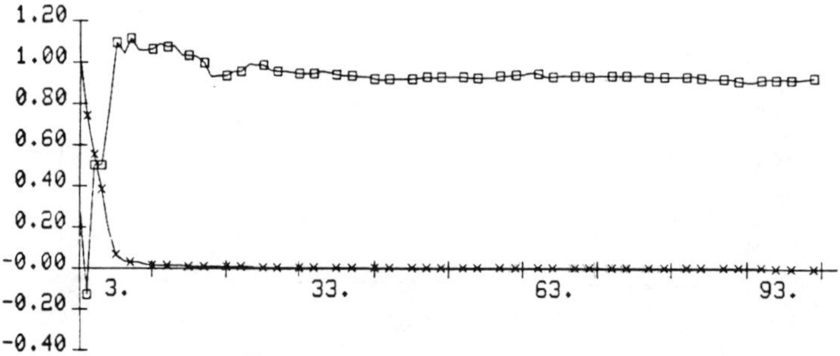

Fig. 5. One hundred recursions for model 1 ($Q = 0.1$, $P_{\theta\theta} = I$, $\underline{\mu}_\theta = \underline{0}$). X -- $P_{\theta_4\theta_4}$, □ -- θ_4.

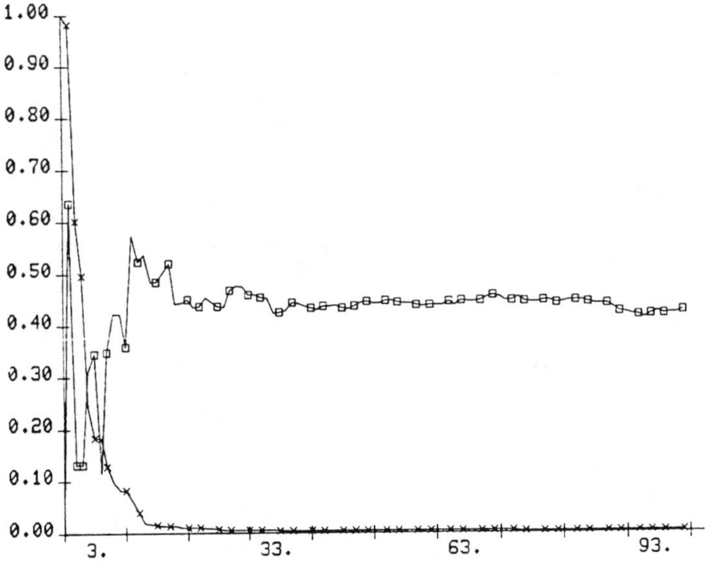

Fig. 6. One hundred recursions for model 1 ($Q = 0.1$, $P_{\theta\theta} = I$, $\underline{\mu}_\theta = 0$). X -- $P_{\theta_5\theta_5}$, □ -- θ_5.

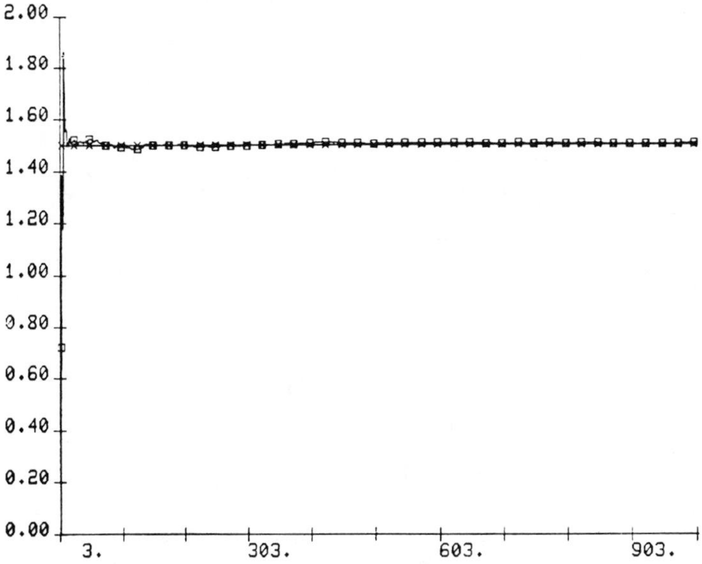

Fig. 7. One thousand recursions for model 1 ($Q = 0.1$, $P_{\theta\theta} = I$, $\underline{\mu}_\theta = \underline{0}$). X -- a_1, □ -- θ_1.

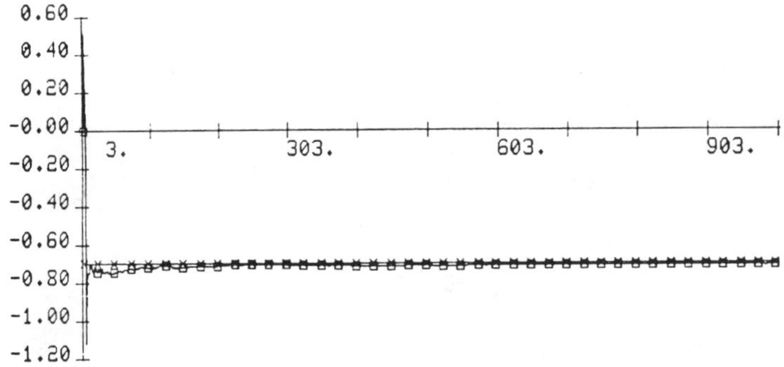

Fig. 8. One thousand recursions for model 1 ($Q = 0.1$, $P_{\theta\theta} = I$, $\underline{\mu}_\theta = \underline{0}$). X -- a_2, □ -- θ_2.

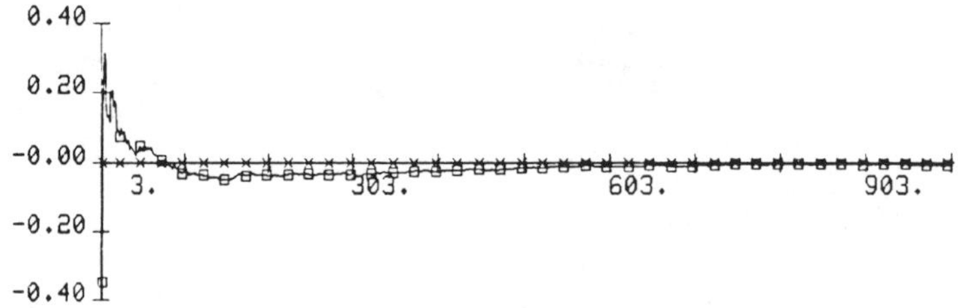

Fig. 9. One thousand recursions for model 1 ($Q = 0.1$, $P_{\theta\theta} = I$, $\underline{\mu}_\theta = \underline{0}$). X -- b_0, □ -- θ_3.

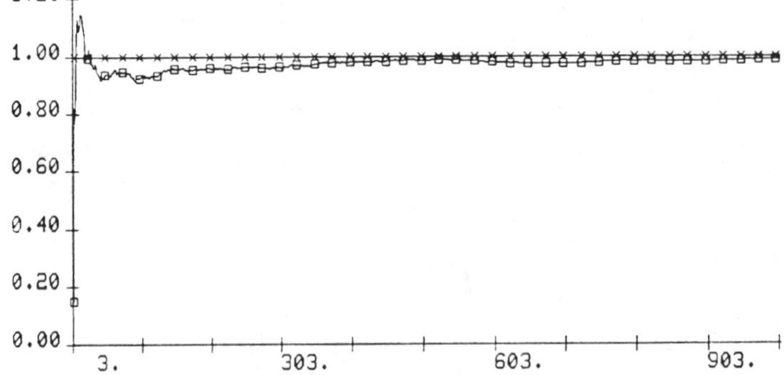

Fig. 10. One thousand recursions for model 1 ($Q = 0.1$, $P_{\theta\theta} = I$, $\underline{\mu}_\theta = \underline{0}$). X -- b_1, □ -- θ_4.

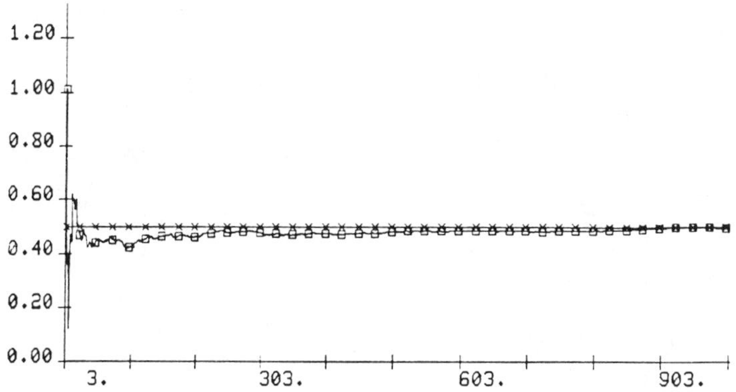

Fig. 11. *One thousand recursions for model 1* ($Q = 0.1$, $P_{\theta\theta} = I$, $\underline{\mu}_\theta = \underline{0}$). X -- b_2, □ -- θ_5.

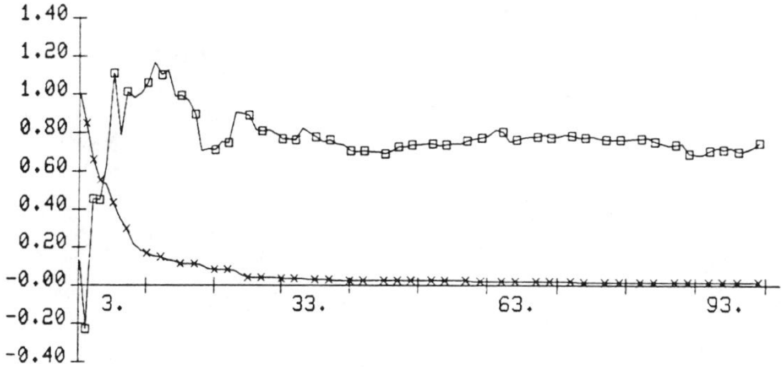

Fig. 12. *One hundred recursions for model 1* ($Q = 1$, $P_{\theta\theta} = I$, $\underline{\mu}_\theta = \underline{0}$). X -- $P_{\theta_4\theta_4}$, □ -- θ_4.

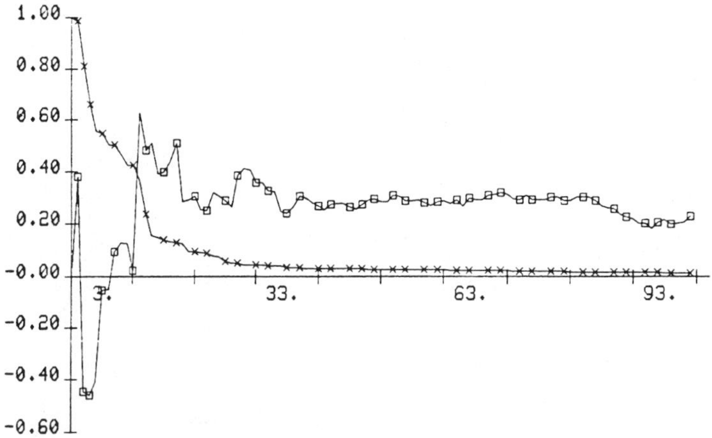

Fig. 13. *One hundred recursions for model 1* ($Q = 1$, $P_{\theta\theta} = I$, $\underline{\mu}_\theta = \underline{0}$). X -- $P_{\theta_5\theta_5}$, □ -- θ_5.

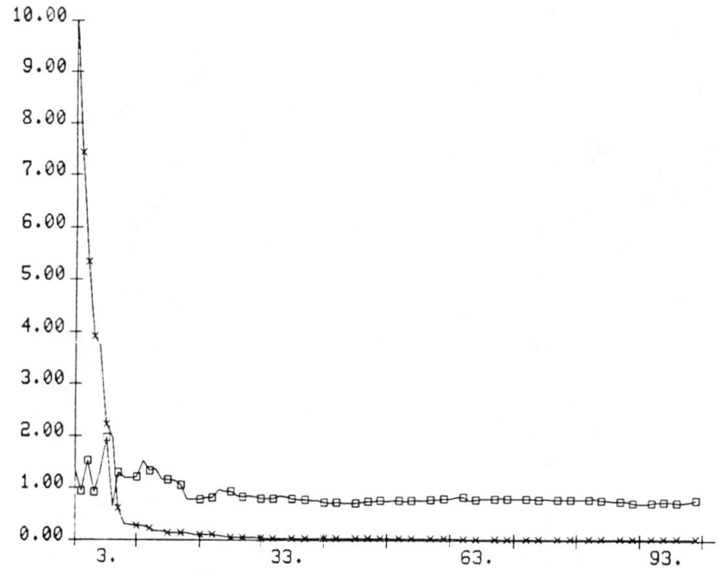

Fig. 14. One hundred recursions for model 1 (Q = 1, $P_{\theta\theta}$ = 10I, $\underline{\mu}_\theta$ = $\underline{1}$). x -- $P_{\theta_4\theta_4}$, □ -- θ_4.

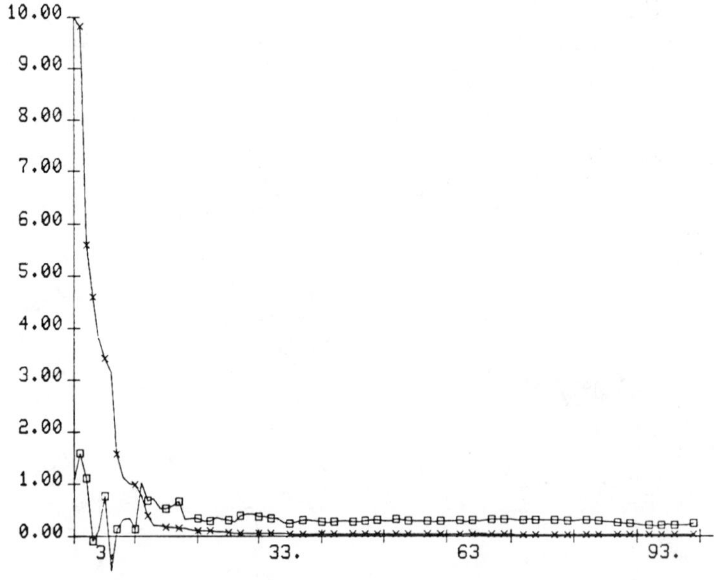

Fig. 15. One hundred recursions for model 1 (Q = 1, $P_{\theta\theta}$ = 10I, $\underline{\mu}_\theta$ = $\underline{1}$). x -- $P_{\theta_5\theta_5}$, □ -- θ_5.

Case 5. $Q = 2$, $P_{\theta\theta} = I$, $\underline{\mu}_\theta = \underline{0}$, and 1000 recursions. Figures 16 – 20 show the behavior of the algorithm.

From the above results we note the following.

(1) The new two-level algorithm has a good performance in estimating the unknown parameters. This is evident by noting the rapid decrease of the estimation error after a few recursions.

(2) Increasing the number of recursions, the estimates converge absolutely to the real values, which implies that the estimation procedure is unbiased.

(3) The increase in noise variance has the effect of decreasing the estimation error at a slower rate. Comparing the results of Figs. 5 and 16 with those of Figs. 12 and 13, we see that the effect of increasing the noise variance means that more information (measurements) is required to achieve the same estimation error variance. More measurements are also required when the number of parameters is increased, as in model 2.

(4) The effect of changing the initial values is only noticeable during the first few recursions (Figs. 14 and 15); otherwise, the convergence is unaffected.

(5) We have tested the algorithm when a variance of arbitrary magnitude is used. It was found that the parameter estimation procedure converged to the real values which, in turn, confirmed the unbiasedness of our two-level algorithm. This effect is shown in Figs. 21 and 22.

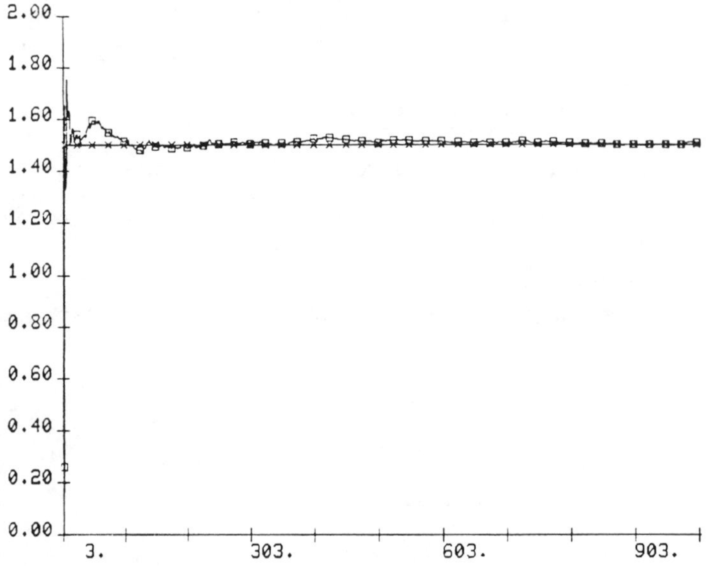

Fig. 16. One thousand recursions for model 1 ($Q = 2$, $P_{\theta\theta} = I$, $\underline{\mu}_\theta = \underline{0}$). X -- a_1, □ -- θ_1.

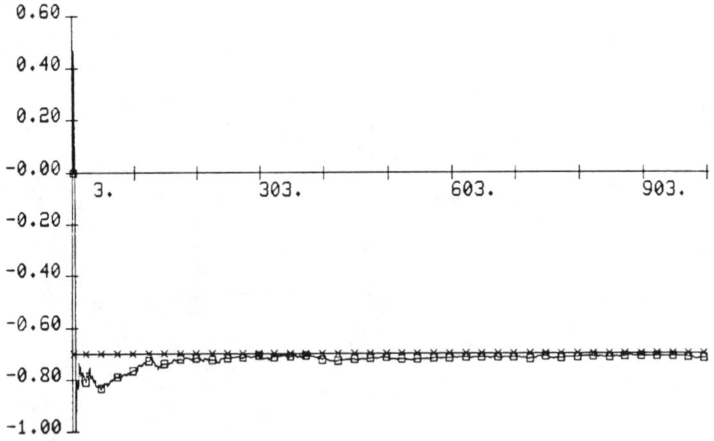

Fig. 17. One thoudand recursions for model 1 ($Q = 2$, $P_{\theta\theta} = I$, $\underline{\mu}_\theta = \underline{0}$). X -- a_2, □ -- θ_2.

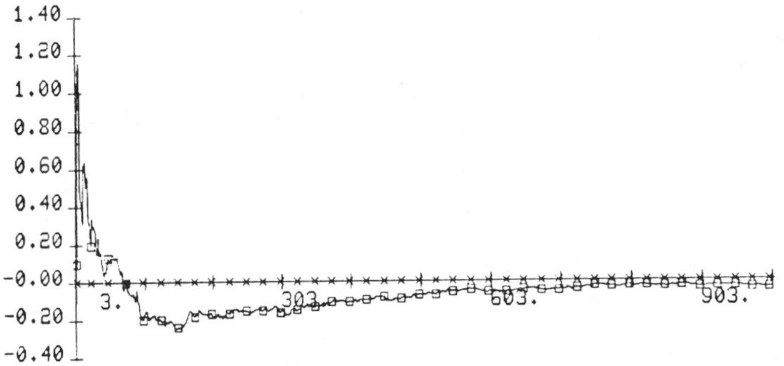

Fig. 18. *One thousand recursions for model 1* ($Q = 2$, $P_{\theta\theta} = I$, $\underline{\mu}_\theta = \underline{0}$). X -- b_0, □ -- θ_3.

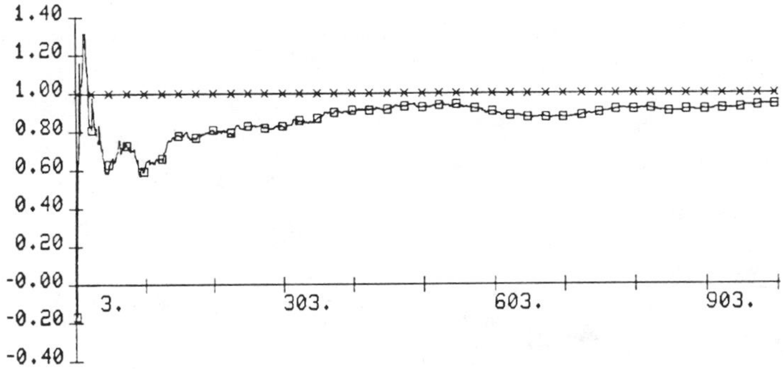

Fig. 19. *One thousand recursions for model 1* ($Q = 2$, $P_{\theta\theta} = I$, $\underline{\mu}_\theta = \underline{0}$). X -- b_1, □ -- θ_4.

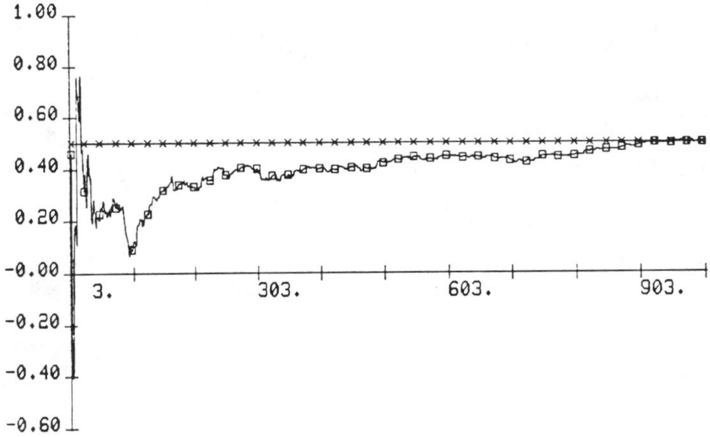

Fig. 20. *One thousand recursions for model 1* ($Q = 2$, $P_{\theta\theta} = I$, $\underline{\mu}_\theta = \underline{0}$). X -- b_2, □ -- θ_5.

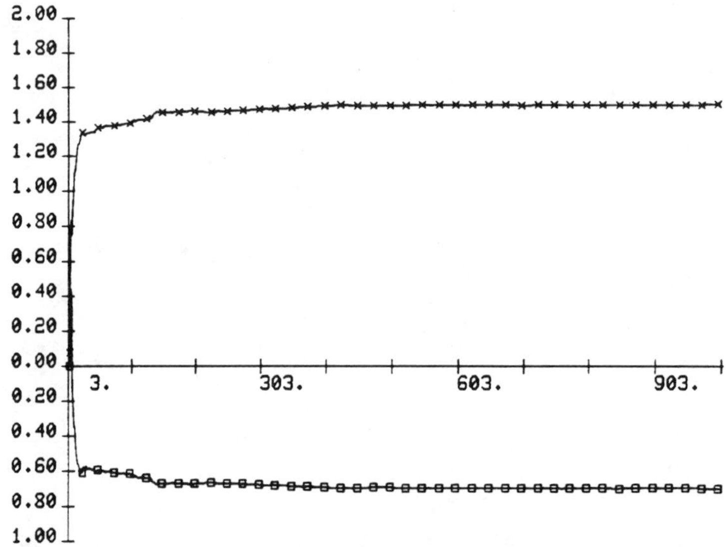

Fig. 21. One thousand recursions for model 1 (variance of arbitrary magnitude). X -- θ_1, □ -- θ_2.

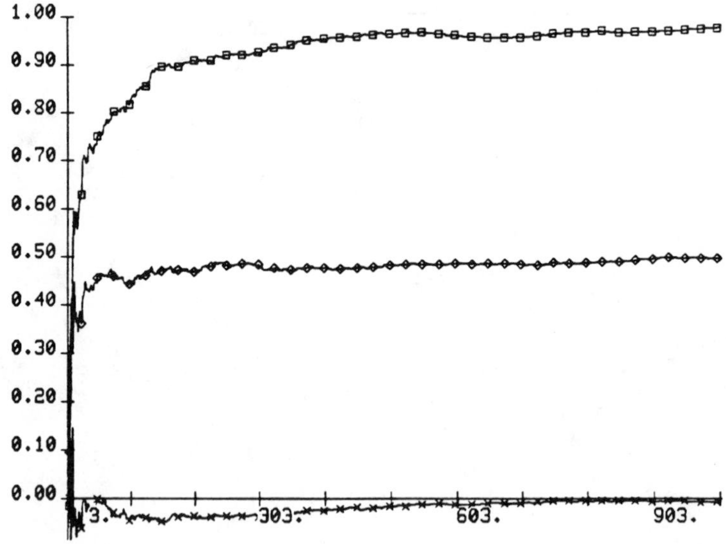

Fig. 22. One thousand recursions for model 1 (variance of arbitrary magnitude). X -- θ_3, ◇ -- θ_5, □ -- θ_4.

VI. CONCLUSIONS

Using the multiple projection approach, an efficient two-level parameter estimation algorithm is developed. It is shown that the new algorithm procides considerable savings in memory space and computational effort. It also reduces the effect of numerical inaccuracies. Both the recursive and nonrecursive versions of the algorithm are considered. By virtue of its nature, our algorithm is very suitable for multiprocessing systems. Simulation of the two-level estimation algorithm on two system examples under different operating conditions clearly shows the power of our algorithm in estimating the unknown parameters of control models.

REFERENCES

1. S. ARAFEH and A. P. SAGE, "Multi-Level Discrete Time Identification in Large Scale Systems," *Int. J. Syst. Sci. 5*, No. 8, 753-791 (1974).

2. P. EYKHOFF, "Systems Identification," Wiley, New York, 1974.

3. N. J. GUINZY and A. P. SAGE, "Modeling and Identification of Large Scale Systems Using Sensitivity Analysis," *Int. J. Control 17*(5), 1073-1087 (1973).

4. M. F. HASSAN, "Optimum Kalman Filter for Large-Scale Systems Using the Partitioning Approach," *IEEE Trans. Syst. Man Cybern. SMC-6*, October 1976.

5. M. F. HASSAN, G. SALUT, M. G. SINGH, and A. TITLI, "A Decentralized Computational Algorithm for the Global Kalman Filter," *IEEE Trans. Autom. Control AC-23*, No. 2, 262-268 (1978).

6. M. F. HASSAN, M. S. MAHMOUD, M. G. SINGH, and M. P. SPATHOPOULOS, "A Two Level Parameter Estimation Algorithm Using the Multiple Projection Approach," *Automatica 18*, No. 5, 621-630 (1982).

7. M. S. MAHMOUD, "Multilevel Systems Control and Applications: A Survey," *IEEE Trans. Syst. Man Cybern. SMC-7*, No. 3, 125-143 (1977).

8. P. CHEMOUIL, M. R. KATEBI, D. SASTRAY, and M. G. SINGH, "Parameter Estimation in Large Scale Systems Using the Maximum a Posteriori Approach," *CSC Report*, No. 484, UMIST, Manchester, England (1980).

9. I. B. RHODES, "A Tutorial Introduction to Estimation and Filtering," *IEEE Trans. Autom. Control AC-16*, No. 6, 688-706, December 1971.

10. A. P. SAGE and J. L. MELSA, "Estimation Theory with Applications to Communication and Control," McGraw-Hill, New York, 1971.

11. M. G. SINGH, "Dynamical Hierarchical Control," North-Holland Publ., Amsterdam, 1977.

12. M. G. SINGH and A. TITLI, "Systems: Decomposition, Control and Optimisation," Pergamon Press, New York, 1978.

13. D. G. LUENBERGER, "Optimisation by Vector Space Methods," Wiley, New York, 1969.

14. M. F. HASSAN, M. S. MAHMOUD, M. G. SINGH, and M. P. SPATHOPOULOS, "A Two Level Parameter Estimation Algorithm Using the Multiple Projection Approach," *CSC Report*, No. 518, UMIST, Manchester, England (1981).

15. M. P. SPATHOPOULOS, "The Multiple Projection Algorithm for Parameter Estimation in Large Scale Systems," M.Sc. Dissertation, UMIST, Manchester, England (1981).

Suboptimality Bounds on Decentralized Control and Estimation of Large-Scale Discrete-Time Linear Systems

MASSOUD SINAI

School of Engineering and Applied Science
University of California at Los Angeles
Los Angeles, California 90024

I. INTRODUCTION

Problems with classical information patterns have been the subject of research for many years. This research has revealed some interesting results in terms of their form of solution. The classical information pattern is based on two basic assumptions: first, the availability of all information about system dynamics, noise statistics, and the entire observed data to the controller; and second, perfect recall with respect to past data and actions taken by the controller or all controllers at all instants of time. Under such assumptions, the number of controllers is irrelevant to the theoretical formulation and the controls are all computed from a single problem, the centralized control problem.

However, the above two assumptions tend to be of an unrealistic nature, especially if we are dealing with large-scale systems. Physical separation of different parts of the system leads to a high cost of establishing communication links and the vulnerability of systems operations due to a complicated network of links. These are only a few of the many problems. Even if such links are made, because of different and large delays in receiving the same data in different parts of the system, the assumptions of classical information patterns are still under question. Also, the need for updating or eliminating parts of old data, due to limited computer memory, poses another challenge to the assumption regarding perfect recall of past data. Furthermore, the rise in the ratio of communication to local processing cost, due to recent advances in microprocessor technology, provides designers with an inexpensive local data processing alternative.

Under the strict assumption of centrality of information, linear quadratic systems possess interesting solutions. For linear systems with white Gaussian additive noise and a quadratic performance index, the optimal control problem consists of two separate problems [1,2], the state reconstruction problem and the control problem. The state reconstructor is a linear finite dimensional filter with its order equal to the order of the system. The control problem corresponds to the deterministic system which results from ignoring noise effects. Finally, the state in the solution to the deterministic problem is replaced by the reconstructed state, the output of the filter, to achieve the stochastic control (certainty equivalence) [3,4].

Research on control systems with several control stations (decentralized control) has been an area of significant interest in recent years. Survey papers by Sandell *et al.* [5] and Athans [6] are excellent introductions to the topic. They also indicate various disciplines of applications and the large number of authors interested in this research area. However, the present state of decentralized control is unsatisfactory, and a unified approach to nonclassical information patterns is yet to be accepted. Books by Measaroic *et al.* [7], Wismer [8], Ho and Mitter [9], Singh [10], Sacks [11], Jamshidi [12], and Siljak [13] present different approaches and various aspects of large-scale systems and decentralized control. The generally accepted underlying approach to decentralized control problems is the concept of a team. According to Marshak [14], a team is a group of persons (controllers) each of whom makes decisions based on different information but who receive a common reward from the results of those decisions. Decentralized control problems can be formulated alternatively using a game theoretic approach, a cooperative game whose players share a common objective. Upon such formulation great difficulty is revealed with the state reconstruction problem. The Kalman filter, a finite-order filter, is sufficient to estimate the state of the system under the classical information assumption. However, due to the "second guessing" problem, as suggested by Rhodes and Luenberger [15] and William [16], a finite-order filter is not sufficient for nonclassical information cases. Also, since the publication of Wistenhausen's counterexample [18], the possibility of a nonlinear solution to a linear – quadratic – Gaussian (LQG) problem with nonclassical information is a well-known fact. Therefore, the search for the optimal solution to decentralized control problems cannot be limited to the class of linear functions; nonlinear solutions should also be considered. Generally speaking, a nonclassical constraint on information or control results in the inapplicability of current standard optimization procedures.

Different techniques have been adopted successfully by researchers to alleviate hardship and convert some decentralized control problems into forms consistent with available optimization techniques. Information structures in general and a class of information structures that ensures the linearity (affineness) of the solution are investigated in [18 – 27]. When the linearity of solution is assured, the search for the optimal solution can be limited to linear functions and the optimal solution is found by standard techniques. While the search for the optimal solution can be limited to the class of linear (affine) functions for specific information structures, it is almost impossible to attain the optimal solution for other problems. The separation property does not hold; a finite-order filter is not optimal and the search for the solution cannot be limited to linear (affine) functions.

However, a feasible approach is to use an a priori restricted optimization problem with all conventional properties of standard LQG problems. The reconstructed state for the controller is limited to the outputs of a linear filter with the order of the filter equal to the order of the system. Controllers use linear instantaneous functions for the outputs of their state estimators as their controls. The matrix minimum principle (Athans [28]) or standard dynamic programming techniques can be used to find feedback and filter gains. This method has been applied to decentralized control problems and the necessary conditions for continuous-time (Chu [29], Looze and Sandell [30], Levine and Athans [32], Chong and Athans [32], Sandell and Athans [33]) and for discrete time systems (Yoshikawa [34] and Pisacane *et al.* [35] have been derived.

Large-scale systems may be assumed to consist of smaller interacting subsystems, each controlled by a different controller. Having access to all information and observations regarding its own subsystem, an optimal solution can be found in a local sense, ignoring the effects of interaction between subsystems. The decentralized control problem is therefore converted to a number of independent subsystem optimization problems. The performance index for the system is defined as the sum of individual subsystem performance indices. Interaction between subsystems is then considered as perturbations interfering with individual subsystem's autonomy, performing in an optimal manner as a result. The overall performance index would be different from that of the individual subsystems acting independently. Two different approaches have been considered with respect to perturbing effects of subsystem interactions. The first method is to use a multilevel technique to reduce or cancel the effect of subsystem interactions. Individual subsystems have to report to a coordinator about their observations and actions. The coordinator, with some prior knowledge of the overall system, would modify decisions to achieve a better overall performance index. The amount of information reported to the coordinator has a significant impact on the role of the coordinator. If the coordinator knows about all observations and decisions of the subsystems, he can act as a central agent, derive a globally optimal solution, and suppress decisions made by subsystems. The high cost of communication, plus the possibility of a centralized controller contrary to the autonomy of subsystems, are setbacks in multilevel techniques. Different aspects of multilevel techniques are considered by Sundareshan [36 – 38], Siljak and Sundareshan [39], Siljak and Vukcevic [40], and Darwish *et al.* [41].

The effect of interaction for a system consisting of subsystems which have been optimized by local feedbacks can be studied directly. This approach is based on performance deterioration (Rissanen [42] and Popov [43]). Deterministic problems are considered by Baily and Ramparyan [44], Laub and Baily [45], and Siljak and Sundareshan [39]. Performance bounds for the system have been established when decentralized control of system decomposition is applied to the interconnected system. Suboptimality is measured as the ratio of the upper bound on the performance index of the interconnected system to the sum of the optimal performance indices of the subsystems. Krtolica and Siljak [46] have considered the stochastic control problem and derived numerous results for both decentralized control and estimation problems.

With the increasing complexity and sophistication of control systems, the incorporation of a digital computer as the controller in the systems has become a necessity. Recent technological advances in utilizing the microprocessor as an inexpensive and reliable data processor have provided a major technological breakthrough for decentralized control. However, the use of a digital data processor, capable of working only on a time-sequence basis, requires analytical models to assume discrete-time characters at some point in their development. Most of the research in the area of decentalized control is, however, concerned with continuous systems not directly implementable on a digital computer. More research therefore should be focused on the study of discrete time systems. This study is limited to discrete time systems to serve this purpose.

II. SUBOPTIMALITY BOUNDS ON DECENTRALIZED CONTROL

A. *PROBLEM DEFINITION*

Let us consider a discrete time dynamic system described by a linear stochastic equation of the form

$$x(t + 1) = A(t)x(t) + B(t)u(t) + v(t), \tag{1}$$

where $x(t)$ is an n vector (state of the system), $u(t)$ is a p vector (input to the system), $A(t)$ is an $n \times n$ matrix, $B(t)$ is an $n \times p$ matrix, $x(t_0)$ is a Gaussian n vector with mean x_0 and covariance R_0, T is the time index defined on the time interval $[t_0, t_{f-1}]$, $T_a \triangleq \{t_0, t_0 + 1, \ldots, t_f\}$, $v(t)$ is a zero-mean white Gaussian noise whose covariance matrix is given by $R_V(t)$, and $R_V(t)$ is positive semidefinite for all $t \in T$.

It is assumed that the system can be decomposed into s interconnected subsystems described by s linear stochastic difference equations of the form

$$x_i(t + 1) = A_i(t) + B_i u_i(t) + \sum_j A_{ij}(t) x_j(t) + v_i(t),$$

$$i \in I \triangleq \{1, 2, \ldots, s\}, \quad t \in T_a, \tag{2}$$

$$J = \{1, 2, \ldots, s\},$$

where $x_i(t)$ is an n_i vector (state of the ith subsystem), $u_i(t)$ is a p_i vector (input to the ith subsystem), $A_i(t)$ is an $n_i \times n_i$ matrix, $B_i(t)$ is an $n_i \times p_i$ matrix, $A_{ij}(t)$ is an $n_i \times n_j$ matrix, and $v_i(t)$ is a zero-mean white Gaussian noise to the ith subsystem. Also,

$$\sum_I n_i = n \tag{3}$$

and

$$\sum_I p_i = p. \tag{4}$$

A fundamental assumption with respect to validation of such decomposition is that the matrix $B(t)$ of Eq. (1) is of block diagonal form, or

$$B = \text{block diag}[B_i]. \tag{5}$$

However, no such assumption is required for system noise $v(t)$, and subsystem noises may be correlated.

When all interconnection matrices A_{ij} are zero, the subsystems are decoupled. An important role is played by decoupled systems in the context of decentralized control. For convenience, a new matrix is defined as

$$A_D \triangleq \text{block diag}[A_i] \tag{6}$$

and

$$A_C \triangleq A - A_D. \tag{7}$$

The subscripts D and C, respectively, stand for decoupled and coupled systems. Using the above definitions, the system (1) and (2) may be rewritten as

$$x(t + 1) = A_D x(t) + Bu(t) + A_C x(t) + v(t). \tag{8}$$

Together with the dynamic system (1), a performance index of the following form is associated:

$$J \triangleq E \sum_{T} \left[x'(t)Q_x x(t) + u'(t)Q_u u(t)\right]. \tag{9}$$

The expected value of the quadratic term, J, is considered as a measure of system performance, where

$$Q_x(t) = \text{block diag}[Q_{x1}(t), Q_{x2}(t), \ldots, Q_{xs}(t)]; \tag{10}$$

$$Q_u(t) = \text{block diag}[Q_{u1}(t), Q_{u2}(t), \ldots, Q_{us}(t)]; \tag{11}$$

$Q_{xi}(t)$, $t \in T$, and $i \in I$ are symmetric positive semidefinite matrices of $n_i \times n_i$ dimension; and $Q_{ui}(t)$, $t \in T$, $i \in I$ are symmetric positive definite matrices of $p_i \times p_i$ dimension.

The expected value $E[\cdot]$ is taken over all random variables involved in the system.

By choosing matrices $Q_x(t)$ and $Q_u(t)$ in block diagonal forms, a decentralized control strategy can be found to be implemented for the system (8). This choice of matrices $Q_x(t)$ and $Q_u(t)$ implies that for each decoupled subsystem

$$x_i(t + 1) = A_i(t)x_i(t) + B_i(t) + v_i(t), \tag{12}$$

a cost is associated of the form

$$J_i \triangleq E \sum_T \left[x_i'(t)Q_{xi}(t)x_i(t) + u_i'(t)Q_{ui}(t)u_i(t)\right], \tag{13}$$

with

$$J = \sum_I J_i \tag{14}$$

and

$$\min_u [J] = \sum_I \min_{u_i} [J_i] \tag{15}$$

for the case $A_c \equiv 0$.

From the results of LQG theory, as presented in [47], the optimal control law for subsystems is given by a linear feedback form, that is,

$$u_i^0(t) = -L_i(t)x_i(t), \tag{16}$$

where the matrix $L_i(t)$ is given by

$$L_i(t) = \left[Q_{ui} + B_i'(t)S_i(t+1)B_i(t)\right]^{-1} \times B_i'(t)S_i(t+1)A_i(t) \tag{17}$$

and $S_i(t)$ is a positive semidefinite symmetric solution of the discrete time Ricatti equation

$$S_i(t) = [A_i(t) - B_i(t)L_i(t)]'S_i(t+1)[A_i(t) - B_i(t)L_i(t)] \times L_i'(t)Q_{ui}(t)L_i(t) + Q_{xi}(t) \tag{18}$$

for $t \in T$ and

$$S_i(t_f) = 0, \quad i \in I. \tag{19}$$

By virtue of relation (15), the optimal control law for the system of

$$x(t+1) = A_D x(t) + B(t)u(t) + v(t) \tag{20}$$

and cost of Eq. (9) is given by the decentralized control law

$$u^0 = -L(t)x(t), \tag{21}$$

where L(t) is of block diagonal form,

$$L(t) = \text{block diag}[L_i(t)], \tag{22}$$

and $L_i(t)$, $i \in I$, are given by Eqs. (17) and (18).

The control law (16) provides a decentralized scheme for calculation and implementation of the control laws. The necessary information as required by Eq. (16) to obtain feedback gain matrices $L_i(t)$ consists only of subsystem information, and each controller can proceed to find its own control law without access to any other subsystem information. Also, during the operation of the system, no on-line data need be exchanged between subsystems. This is clear from Eq. (16), where the control laws are limited to local information about the state of the system, $x_i(t)$, as measured by each subsystem, and thus all difficulties with respect to on-line data communication are avoided. It also should be pointed out that the independence of feedback gains from future measurements provides freedom for time and memory management of the computer system if it is to be used as the control unit. All feedback gains $L_i(t)$ can be precalculated and stored in the computer memory before the operation of the system starts if a minimal computation time is required during the on-line control of the system. However, a portion of computer memory is to be dedicated for storing this information during the operation of the system.

When the control law (16) is used together with the decoupled system of Eq. (20), it results in a value for the performance index:

$$J^0 = x_0' S(t_0) x(t_0) + \text{tr } S(t_0) R_0 + \sum_T \text{tr } S(t+1) R_v(t). \tag{23}$$

If the same control law is applied to the coupled system of Eq. (2), the value of performance would be different in general, from J^0 as given by Eq. (23). J^0, however, could be used as a reference point for relative comparisons of system performance. This is well justified by the fact that the optimal control, and therefore the minimal cost, in general, cannot be obtained. An upper bound for the value of the performance index is sought when the decentralized control law (16) is used with the coupled system. J^0, the minimum cost for the decoupled system divided by the upper bound, serves as a suboptimality index or indicates how the performance of the system is compared to the decoupled case. The bigger the suboptimality index is, the smaller the performance index is expected to be, and a better performance is achieved.

B. DERIVATION OF NECESSARY CONDITIONS

Let us define $\Delta(t)$ as

$$\Delta(t) \triangleq x'(t+1)S(t+1)x(t+1) - x'(t)S(t)x(t), \tag{24}$$

where $S(t)$ is the solution to the discrete time Ricatti equation (18) and initial condition (19). The following equality holds:

$$\sum_{T} \Delta(t) = -x'(t_0)S(t_0)x(t_0). \tag{25}$$

For x normal with mean $\bar{x}$ and covariance R and for any square matrix S of appropriate dimension, we have

$$E[x'Sx] = \bar{x}'S\bar{x} + \text{tr } SR. \tag{26}$$

For the coupled system where feedback control law (21) is used, the dynamic of the system is given by

$$x(t+1) = (A - BL)x(t) + v(t) \tag{27}$$

and

$$x'(t+1)S(t+1)x(t+1)$$

$$= [(A - BL)x(t) + v(t)]'S(t+1) \times [(A - BLx(t) + v(t)]. \quad (28)$$

Using the fact that $x(t)$ and $v(t)$ are independent random vectors with

$$E[v(t)] = 0, \quad (29)$$

therefore

$$E[\Delta(t)] = \operatorname{tr} R_V S(t+1) + \operatorname{tr}\Big[(A - BL)'S(t+1)(A - BL) - (A_D - BL)'S(t+1)(A_D - BL) - L'Q_u L - Q_x\Big] \times E[x(t)x'(t)]. \quad (30)$$

Taking the summation from t_0 to $t_f - 1$,

$$\sum_T E[\Delta(t)] = \sum_T \operatorname{tr} T_V S(t+1) + \sum_T \operatorname{tr}\Big[(A - BL)'S(t+1)(A - BL) - (A_D - BL)'S(t+1)(A_D - BL)\Big]E[(x(t)x'(t))] - \sum_T \operatorname{tr}\Big[L'(t)Q_u L(t) + Q_x\Big]E[x(t)x'(t)]. \quad (31)$$

By defining

$$\overline{X}(t) = E[x(t)x'(t)], \quad (32)$$

we will have

$$\sum_T \operatorname{tr}\Big[L'(t)Q_u L(t)Q_x\Big]\overline{X}(t)$$

$$= x_0'S(t_0)x_0 + \operatorname{tr} S(t_0)R_0 + \sum_T R_V S(t+1)$$

$$+ \sum_T \operatorname{tr}\Big[(A - BL)'S(t + 1)(A - BL) - (A_D - BL)'S(t + 1)(A_D BL)\Big]\overline{X}(t) \tag{33}$$

or

$$J^a = J^0 + \sum_T \operatorname{tr}\Big[(A - BL)'S(t + 1)(A - BL) - (A_D - BL)'S(t + 1)(A_D - BL)\Big]\overline{X}(t). \tag{34}$$

Subtracting from both sides of the above equality the term

$$J^0 + (1 - \mu)J^a \tag{35}$$

results in

$$\mu J^a - J^0 = \sum_T \operatorname{tr}\Big[(A - BL)'S(t + 1)(A - BL) - (A_D - BL)'S(t + 1)(A_D - BL) - L'(t)Q_u L(t) - Q_x + \mu\big(L'(t)Q_u L(t) + Q_x\big)\Big]\overline{X}(t), \tag{36}$$

or equivalently

$$\mu J^a - J^0 = \sum_T \operatorname{tr}\Big[(A - BL)'S(t + 1)(A - BL) - S(t) + \mu\big(L'(t)Q_u L(t)Q_u L(t) + Q_x\big)\Big]\overline{X}(t). \tag{37}$$

If the matrix $F(t)$ defined by

$$F(t) \triangleq (A - BL)'S(t + 1)(A - BL) - S(t) + \mu\big[L'(t)Q_u L(t) + Q_x\big] \tag{38}$$

is negative semidefinite for all $t \in [t_0, t_f]$, then

$$\sum_T \operatorname{tr}\Big[(A - BL)'S(t + 1)(A - BL) - S(t) + \mu\big(L'(t)Q_u L(t) + Q_x\big)\Big]\overline{X}(t) = \sum E[x'(t)F(t)x(t)] \leq 0, \tag{39}$$

and therefore

$$\mu J^a - J^0 \leq 0 \tag{40}$$

or

$$J^a \leq \mu^{-1} J^0. \tag{41}$$

If T_a, the set of time indexes, is finite, an upper bound on the value of the performance index is found from Eq. (41). However, the definition of suboptimality as given by Siljak [46] and Kwakernaak and Sivan [48] also considers the infinite time case. A time average of performance index is to be used to the infinite time problem also include:

$$J = (t_f - t_0 - 1)^{-1} E\left[\sum_T x'(t)Q_x x(t) + u'(t)Q_u u(t)\right]. \tag{42}$$

The modification in performance index is necessary even when time-invariant systems under strict assumptions of complete controllability are considered. This is due to the fact that even if the system is stable, due to the presence of noise, the performance index of Eq. (13) does not converge and is to be modified. Further assumptions to guarantee the existence of a steady state (infinite time) are required and will be addressed in the following derivations and in the statements of the theorems.

To complete the derivation, consider the infinite time case. It is evident that the results of previous parts of this proof also apply for the time-average cost function when $t_f < \infty$. Therefore, if F(t) is negative semidefinite and taking limits, then

$$\lim_{t_f \to \infty} \left\{ (t_f - t_0 - 1)^{-1} E\left[\sum x'Q_x x + u'Q_u u\right]\right\}$$
$$\leq \mu^{-1} \lim_{t_f \to \infty} \left\{ (t_f - t_0 - 1)^{-1} \left[x_0' S(t_0) x_0 + \operatorname{tr} S(t_0) R_0 + \sum_T \operatorname{tr} R_v S(t+1)\right]\right\}. \tag{43}$$

Expectations in the above expression are well defined for $t_f \to \infty$, and further assumptions on subsystems are required to guarantee that the limit for the right-hand side of the above inequality exists, which implies

$$J_\infty^a \leq \mu^{-1} J_\infty^0. \tag{44}$$

Stabilizability and detectability on the part of subsystems ensure the existence of steady state feedback gains and, furthermore, the closed-loop subsystems are asymptotically stable. When the subsystems are asymptotically stable, the steady state covariance sequence will converge and the limit to the right-hand side exists. As in the finite case, the negative semidefiniteness of matrix F establishes an upper bound on the value of the performance index. The following is the main theorem regarding the bounds on decentralized control.

Theorem 1. Suppose all subsystems defined by triples (A_i, B_i, D_i) are stabilizable and detectable, where D_i, $i = 1, 2, \ldots, s$, are defined by

$$D_i D_i' = Q_{xi}. \tag{45}$$

Furthermore, the matrix F(t) defined as

$$F(t) = A_{cl}' S(t+1) A_{cl} - S(t) + \mu\left[Q_x + L'(t) Q_u L(t)\right] \tag{46}$$

is negative semidefinite for all discrete time intervals $[t_0, t_f]$. Then the decentralized control law of

$$u_i = -L_i(t) x(t) \tag{47}$$

is suboptimal with degree μ for the coupled time-invariant system (8) and performance index (42).

C. *ALTERNATIVE CONDITIONS AND COROLLARIES*

In the derivation of Theorem 1 the time-invariance property of the system is used only when infinite time problems are considered. All results for LQG finite time problems are still valid even if the time-independence assumption is dropped. So long as the limits in the derivation of Theorem 1 exits, the proof of the time-variant case is similar to that of time-invariant case. A general relationship between the suboptimality index μ and the coupling matrix A_c is provided by Theorem 1. If A_c is specified, the suboptimality index μ can be derived using the following corollary.

Corollary 2. For the time-invariant system of Theorem 1, if A_c is specified, the suboptimality index μ is given by

$$\mu = \min_{t, x \neq 0} \frac{x'\left[S(t) - A_{cl}'S(t+1)A_{cl}\right]x}{x'\left[Q_x + L'(t)Q_u L(t)\right]x} . \tag{48}$$

It is evident that if μ [as defined by Eq. (48)] for a specified A_c is positive and finite, then the matrix F(t) [as defined in the statement of Theorem 1] is negative semidefinite for any time interval $[t_0, t_f]$.

The quadratic term $x'Sx$ for an S symmetric matrix is bounded from below and above by Eq. (49), where λ_m and λ_M are minimum and maximum eigenvalues of their arguments:

$$\lambda_m(S)x'x \leq x'Sx \leq \lambda_M(S)x'x. \tag{49}$$

Equation (49) can be applied to evaluate the maximum and minimum values of the quadratic terms in expression (48). Since the denominator of expression (48) is positive definite, its maximum eigenvalue is positive and finite. If a positive number can be found as the minimum value of the nominator, μ exists and can be found from the following definitions:

$$\eta^* = \min_t \eta(t) \triangleq \lambda_m[s(t)] - \lambda_M\left[A'_{cl}S(t+1)A_{cl}\right]. \tag{50}$$

The suboptimality index μ can be found from the following useful corollary.

Corollary 3. The time-invariant system of Theorem 1 is suboptimal if η^* as defined by Eq. (50) is positive. The suboptimality index is given by

$$\mu^* = \min_t[\eta(t)/\xi(t)], \tag{51}$$

where

$$\xi(t) = \lambda_M\left[Q_u + L'(t)Q_uL(t)\right]. \tag{52}$$

The quadratic term $x'(t)S(t)x(t)$, where $S(t)$ is the solution that the decoupled discrete time Ricatti equation associated with the decoupled system (12), can be used as the Lyapanov function for the coupled system. The state of the system $x(t+1)$ for the closed-loop coupled system is given by

$$x(t+1) = (A - BL)x(t). \tag{53}$$

Using the above expression for $x(t+1)$, $\Delta(x'sx)$ is defined as

$$\Delta(x'(t)S(t)x(t)) \triangleq x'(t+1)S(t+1)x(t+1) - x'(t)S(t)x(t), \tag{54}$$

and using the definition of matrix $F(t)$, we have

$$\Delta(x'(t)S(t)x(t)) = x'(t)\left[F(t) - \mu\left(Q_x + L'(t)Q_uL(t)\right)\right]x(t). \tag{55}$$

If the matrix $F(t)$ is negative semidefinite and μ is positive, the resulting matrix inside the brackets in Eq. (54) is negative definite. From the stability theory of discrete time systems (Astrom [47] and Sivan and Kwakernaak [48]), the negative definiteness of Eq. (54) implies asymptotic stability of the system. Therefore, existence of a suboptimality index guarantees stability of the system which is formalized in Corollary 4.

Corollary 4. If μ, as found in Theorem 1 or Corollaries 2 and 3, is positive, the closed-loop system of Theorem 1 with decentralized control law (16)–(19) is asymptotically stable.

It should be pointed out here that if the suboptimality index μ, as defined by Theorem 1 and its associated corollaries, is negative, the system does not have a finite degree of suboptimality. Also, if a positive μ can be found, it ensures the stability of the coupled system. The suboptimality index μ, if found for a class of interconnection matrices A_c, will form a partial ordering in that class and can serve as a measure of relative goodness between the class members.

Three classes of interconnection matrices can immediately be identified.

(1) A_c^P represents all interconnection matrices A_c for which the performance of the coupled system is better than that of the decoupled system, corresponding to the case where $\mu > 1$.

(2) A_c^N represents all interconnection matrices A_c for which the performance of the coupled system is worse than that of the decoupled system, corresponding to the case where $1 < \mu < 1$.

(3) A_c^0 represents all interconnection matrices A_c for which the performance of the coupled system is as good as that of the decoupled system, corresponding to the case where $\mu = 1$.

Theorem 1 provides a means to find the degree of suboptimality for a decentralized control policy. In general, the performance of the system would be different from that of the decoupled system which is used as a reference point. The method to obtain the suboptimality index, if it exists, is presented in Corollaries 2 and 3. If the suboptimality index exists, the stability of system is assured by Corollary 4.

III. NEUTRAL INTERCONNECTIONS

A. *PROBLEM DEFINITION*

Various conditions for suboptimality of decentralized control have been derived in previous parts of this chapter. The conditions are general and are derived for all time intervals, including the infinite time problem. If we are only concerned about the steady state performance of the system, and not the transient performance, simpler conditions may be obtained. Specific conditions under which the coupling matrix A_C has no effect on the steady state performance of the system can be derived.

B. *NECESSARY CONDITIONS*

1. *Deterministic Systems*

Let us again consider the discrete time-invariant coupled system

$$x(t + 1) = (A_C + A_D)x(t) + Bu(t) \tag{56}$$

over the infinite time interval. The performance index to be minimized is

$$J_\infty = \sum_{T\infty} \left[x'(t)Q_x x(t) + u'(t)Q_u u(t)\right]. \tag{57}$$

Matrices A_D, B, Q_x, and Q_u are block diagonal with A_i, B_i, Q_{xi}, and Q_{ui} corresponding to the ith subsystem.

When $A_C \equiv 0$, the optimal control is given by the feedback law:

$$u(t) = -\bar{L}x(t), \tag{58}$$

$$\bar{L} = \text{block diag}[\bar{L}_i], \tag{59}$$

where the time-invariant feedback gain $\bar{L}$ is given by

$$\bar{L} \triangleq \left[Q_u + B'\bar{S}B\right]^{-1} B\bar{S}A_D \tag{60}$$

and $\bar{S}$ is the positive semidefinite solution of the algebraic Ricatti equation

$$\bar{S} = (A_d - B\bar{L})'\bar{S}(A - B\bar{L}) + Q_x + \bar{L}'Q_u\bar{L}. \tag{61}$$

Furthermore, the minimum value of the performance index is given by

$$\bar{J} = \min J = x'(t_0)\bar{S}x(t_0). \tag{62}$$

The implementation of the decentralized control law (58) for the coupled system (56) will result in a value of the performance index which is generally different from J_∞^0.

If the closed-loop coupled system

$$x(t + 1) = \left(A_C + A_D - B\bar{L}\right)x(t) \tag{63}$$

is stable, then the infinite time cost converges. The cost is given by

$$J_\infty^0 = \sum_{T\infty} x'(t)Q_x x(t) + u'(t)Q_u u(t) \tag{64}$$

$$= \sum_{T\infty} x'(t_0)(A - B\bar{L})'^{(t_f - t_0)}$$

$$\times \left[Q_x + \bar{L}'Q_u L\right](A - B\bar{L})^{(t_f - t_0)} x(t_0), \tag{65}$$

which is a convergent sum if the closed-loop system is stable. The value of the summation is given by

$$J_\infty^0 = x'(t_0)\Omega x'(t_0), \tag{66}$$

where Ω is the positive semidefinite solution of

$$\Omega = (A - B\bar{L})'\Omega(A - B\bar{L}) + Q_x + \bar{L}'Q_u\bar{L}. \tag{67}$$

The above equation can be changed to

$$\Omega = \left(A_D - B\bar{L}\right)'\Omega\left(A_D - B\bar{L}\right) + Q_x + \bar{L}'Q_u\bar{L}$$
$$+ A_C'\Omega\left(A_C - B\bar{L}\right) + (A_D - BL)'\Omega A_C + A_C'\Omega A_C. \tag{68}$$

If the following condition holds for Ω,

$$A_C'\Omega(A_D - BL) + A_D - BL)'\Omega A_C + A_C'\Omega A_C = 0, \tag{69}$$

then the algebraic equation for Ω is

$$\Omega = A_D - B\bar{L}\ '\Omega\ A_D - B\bar{L}\ + Q_x + \bar{L}'Q_u\bar{L}, \tag{70}$$

which is exactly the algebraic equation for $\bar{S}$. By uniqueness of the solution of the above algebraic Ricatti equation, we conclude that

$$\Omega = \bar{S}, \tag{71}$$

and therefore

$$A_C'\bar{S}\left(A_D - B\bar{L}\right) + (A_D - BL)'\bar{S}A_C + A_C'\bar{S}A_C = 0; \tag{72}$$

but

$$A_C'\bar{S}A_C = A_C'\bar{S}(1/2A_C) + (1/2A_C)'\bar{S}A_C \tag{73}$$

and

$$A_C'\bar{S}\left(1/2A_C + A_D - B\bar{L}\right) + \left(1/2A_C + A_D - B\bar{L}\right)'\bar{S}A_C = 0. \tag{74}$$

If we define

$$\hat{S} = A_C'\bar{S}\left(1/2A_C + A_D - B\bar{L}\right), \tag{75}$$

then

$$\hat{S} + \hat{S}' = 0, \tag{76}$$

which implies that $\hat{S}$ as defined by Eq. (75) is skew symmetric.

Theorem 5. The interconnection matrix A_C has no effect on the performance index of the time-invariant system

$$x(t + 1) = (A_C + A_D)x(t) + Bu(t), \tag{77}$$

with u(t) given by the decentralized control law

$$u(t) = \bar{L}x(t) \tag{78}$$

if the matrix

$$\hat{S} \triangleq A_C'\bar{S}\left(1/2A_C + A_D - B\bar{L}\right) \tag{79}$$

is skew symmetric and the resulting closed-loop coupled system is stable.

2. *Stochastic Systems*

Motivated by the results of Theorem 5 for deterministic systems, let us now consider the corresponding stochastic system

$$x(t + 1) = Ax(t) + Bu(t) + v(t) \tag{80}$$

and the performance index

$$J = \lim_{t_f \to \infty}\left[\frac{1}{t_f - t_0 - 1}\right]\sum_{T}\left[x'(t)Q_x x(t) + u'(t)Q_u u(t)\right]. \tag{81}$$

If the closed-loop system is stable, there exists a steady state covariance matrix, and furthermore,

$$\lim_{t_f \to \infty} [\mathrm{tr}\, P(t + 1)\bar{S} - \mathrm{tr}\, P(t)\bar{S}] = 0, \tag{82}$$

but

$$\mathrm{tr}\, P(t + 1)\bar{S} - \mathrm{tr}\, P(t)\bar{S}$$

$$= E[x'(t + 1)\bar{S}x(t + 1) - x'(t)\bar{S}x(t)], \tag{83}$$

where

$$x(t + 1) = (A - B\bar{L})x(t) + v(t). \tag{84}$$

Therefore,

$$E[x'(t + 1)\bar{S}x(t + 1)]$$

$$= E[x'(t)(A - B\bar{L})'\bar{S}(A - B\bar{L})x(t)] + \mathrm{tr}\, \bar{S}R_v \tag{85}$$

since x(t) and v(t) are independent. Substituting for $\bar{S}$ results in

$$E[x'(t)\bar{S}x(t)] = E\Big\{x'(t)\Big[\big(A_D - B\bar{L}\big)'\bar{S}\big(A_D - B\bar{L}\big) + Q_x + \bar{L}'Q_u\bar{L}\Big]x(t)\Big\}; \tag{86}$$

therefore,

$$E\Big[x'(t)Q_x x(t) + u'(t)Q_u u(t)\Big] = \text{tr } R_v\bar{S} + \text{tr } P\Big[A_C'\bar{S}A_C + A_C'\bar{S}(A_d - BL) + (A_d - BL)\bar{S}A_C\Big]. \tag{87}$$

Also,

$$\lim_{t_f\to\infty} J = x'(t)Q_x x(t) + u'(t)Q_u u(t). \tag{88}$$

Hence, if the matrix $\hat{S}$ defined by

$$\hat{S} \triangleq A_C'\bar{S}\big(1/2A_C + A_D - B\bar{L}\big) \tag{89}$$

is skew symmetric, the performance of the coupled system is similar to that of the decoupled system.

Theorem 6. For the stochastic linear time-invariant system

$$x(t + 1) = Ax(t) + Bu(t) + v(t), \tag{90}$$

with performance index (81) and decentralized control law

$$u(t) = -\bar{L}x(t), \tag{91}$$

the coupling matrix A_C has no effect on the performance of the system if the matrix

$$\hat{S} \triangleq A_C'\bar{S}\big(1/2A_C + A_D - B\bar{L}\big) \tag{92}$$

is skew symmetric and the closed-loop system is stable.

IV. SUBOPTIMALITY BOUNDS ON DECENTRALIZED ESTIMATION

By the duality theorem of Ref. [46], the results obtained for suboptimality of decentralized control can be applied to the problem of decentralized estimation when the subsystem noises are not correlated.

A. PROBLEM DEFINITION

Consider the state estimation problem for the system described by

$$x(t + 1) = A_D x(t) + B(t)u(t) + A_C x(t) + v(t), \tag{93}$$

$$y(t) = C(t)x(t) + w(t), \tag{94}$$

where $x(t)$, A_D, B, $u(t)$, and A_C are the same as defined for the optimal control problem. C is a $q \times n$ block diagonal matrix:

$$C = \text{block diag}[C_1, \ldots, C_s]. \tag{95}$$

$w_i(t)$ is a zero-mean white Gaussian sequence independent of the initial state x_0 and system noise $v(t)$:

$$E[w(t)] = 0, \quad t \in T, \tag{96}$$

$$E[w(t)w'(t)] = R_w(t), \tag{97}$$

$$R_w(t) = \text{block diag}[R_{wi}(t)], \tag{98}$$

where R_{wi} is the subsystem observation noise covariance matrix and is a $q_i \times q_i$ symmetric positive definite matrix. Also, $v(t)$, the system's input noise, is a zero-mean white Gaussian sequence, and

$$E[v(t)v'(t)] = R_v(t), \tag{99}$$

$$R_v(t) = \text{block diag}[R_{vi}(t)]. \tag{100}$$

R_{vi} is the ith subsystem input noise covariance matrix and is a $p_i \times p_i$ symmetric positive definite matrix.

For the decoupled subsystem

$$x(t+1) = A_D x(t) + v(t), \tag{101}$$

$$y(t) = Cx(t), \tag{102}$$

the minimum of the mean-square estimation error will be achieved by the Kalman filter

$$\hat{x}(t+1) = A_D \hat{x}(t) + K(t)[y(t) - C\hat{x}(t)], \tag{103}$$

where K(t), the gain of Kalman filter, is given by

$$K(t) = A_D P(t) C' \left[CP(t)C' + R_w(t) \right]^{-1}. \tag{104}$$

P(t), the estimation error covariance matrix, is governed by

$$P(t+1) = [A_D - K(t)C]P(t)[A_D - K(t)C]' + R_v + K(t)R_w K'(t) \tag{105}$$

with boundary conditions

$$P(t_0) = 0. \tag{106}$$

Since all of the matrices in Eqs. (103)–(105) are of block diagonal form, the resulting Kalman gain is also of block diagonal form. The resulting state estimator is of decentralized form, and there is no need to exchange the observed data between the subsystems during the operation of the system. Only local observations regarding the subsystem state are required for the least square estimation. Therefore, the state estimation problem can be done by s different filters without any data exchange. Also, the initial information regarding the dynamics of the system and noise statistics is limited to a local level or that of the subsystem. The block diagonal elements of Kalman gain, the subsystem Kalman gain, could also be found by treating each subsystem individually. We recall that the Kalman filter of type (103)–(105) minimizes the mean-square estimation error,

$$\sigma \triangleq E\left[\left(a'x(t_f) - a'\hat{x}(t_f)\right)^2\right], \tag{107}$$

for all values of weighting vector a. Alternately σ, the mean-square estimation error, can be written in the matrix form

$$\sigma = E\left[a'\left(x(t_f) - \hat{x}(t_f)\right)'\left(x(t_f) - \hat{x}(t_f)\right)a\right] = a'Pa, \tag{108}$$

where P is the state estimation error covariance matrix.

Analogous with the control problem of the previous section, the state estimation can be written as a separate subsystem estimation problems minimizing the mean-square estimation error,

$$\sigma_i = a_i'P_ia_i, \tag{109}$$

subject to subsystem dynamics and observations. The value of the mean estimation error for the entire system is given by

$$\sigma = \sum_{I} \sigma_i. \tag{110}$$

The solution of the two different approaches are the same and can be used interchangeably.

B. NECESSARY CONDITIONS

As one may expect when the decentralized estimator (103) is used to estimate the state of the coupled system (93), the value of the mean estimation error σ^a would, in general, be different from σ^0 of the decoupled system. Again, as in the control problem, we bound σ^a from above by a multiple of σ^0.

Using the results of the duality theorem (Astom [47]), the decentralized estimator problem can be converted to a deterministic LQR problem. The results of Theorem 1 are also applicable to the deterministic case with minor modification on the performance index. The necessary changes for conversion of the estimation problem to convention optimal control are as follows:

$$A(t) \leftrightarrow A'(t_f - t), \tag{111}$$

$$C(t) \leftrightarrow B'(t_f - t), \tag{112}$$

$$R_v(t) \leftrightarrow Q_n(t_f - t + 1), \tag{113}$$

$$R_w(t) \leftrightarrow Q_u(t_f - t + 1). \tag{114}$$

With the above changes a new matrix H(t), corresponding to the F(t) matrix of Theorem 1, is defined:

$$H(t) \triangleq (A - KC)P(t - 1)(A - KC)' - P(t) + \mu\left[R_v + K(t)R_wK'(t)\right]. \tag{115}$$

Suboptimality of the decentralized estimator is assured when H(t) is negative semidefinite for all time intervals, as required by Theorem 1, and this can be formalized in the following theorem.

Theorem 7. The decentralized estimator

$$\hat{x}(t + 1) = A_D\hat{x}(t) + K(t)[y(t) - C\hat{x}(t)], \tag{116}$$

where K(t) is the block diagonal solution (104), is suboptimal for the coupled system

$$x(t + 1) = (A_D + A_C)x(t) + v(t), \tag{117}$$

$$y(t) = Cx(t) + w(t) \tag{118}$$

if the matrix H(t), defined as

$$H(t) \triangleq (A - KC)P(t - 1)(A - KC)' - P(t) + \mu\left[R_v + K(t)R_wK'(t)\right], \tag{119}$$

is negative semidefinite for any time interval (t_0, t_f) and the subsystem triples $\left(A_i', C_i', D_i'\right)$ are stabilizable and detectable, where D_i is defined as

$$D_iD_i' = R_{vi}. \tag{120}$$

Similar to the control problem σ^0, the mean estimation error of the decoupled system serves only as a reference point. The suboptimality index μ is a measure of goodness when the decentralized estimator is used to reconstruct the state of the coupled system. Also, as mentioned in the control problem, the set of coupling matrices A_C with finite degrees of suboptimality can be partitioned into three different subsets. The A_C^P class represents all matrices whose effect on the estimation problem is beneficial. The decentralized estimator when used in conjunction with the coupled system works better than when used with the decoupled system. A_C^N is the set of all matrices which result in an inferior performance when the decentralized estimator is used to construct the state of the system. When the coupling matrix A_C is specified the suboptimality index can be found using the following corollary.

Corollary 8. For the decentralized state estimation problem of Theorem 7, when the interconnection matrix A_C is specified, the state of the system can be estimated with a finite covariance matrix if

$$\mu^* = \min_t \eta(t) \triangleq \lambda_m[P(t)] - \lambda_M[(A - KC)'P(t - 1)(A - KC)] \tag{121}$$

is positive; furthermore, the suboptimality index is given by

$$\mu = \min_t[\eta(t)/\xi(t)], \tag{122}$$

where

$$\xi(t) \triangleq \lambda_M\Big[R_V + K(t)R_WK'(t)\Big]. \tag{123}$$

By restricting subsystems to use only their local measurements, the need for on-line data exchange between subsystems has been eliminated. Fewer communication links are to be established, resulting in reduced cost and increased reliability. Intuitively, the more subsystems are dependent on information being exchanged between them, the more the system as a whole is susceptible to errors and failures and hence is less reliable.

C. STEADY STATE DECENTRALIZED ESTIMATOR

General decentralized state reconstruction was considered in a previous part of this section. If the conditions of Theorem 7 or Corollary 8 are satisfied, the state of the system can be estimated with finite covariance using a decentralized filter for all time intervals. If we are only concerned with the steady state performance of the filter, alternative conditions can be derived. The duality theorem (Astrom [47]) can be used to extend the results derived previously for the steady state decentralized control problem to steady state decentralized estimation. The steady state Kalman filter gain is governed by the following equations:

$$\hat{x}(t+1) = A_D\hat{x}(t) + \bar{K}[y(t) - C\hat{x}(t)], \tag{124}$$

$$\bar{K} = A_D\bar{P}C'\left[C\bar{P}C' + R_W\right]^{-1}, \tag{125}$$

$$\bar{P} = \left[A_D - \bar{K}C\right]\bar{P}\left[A_D - \bar{K}C\right]' + R_V + \bar{K}R_W\bar{K}. \tag{126}$$

The steady state covariance matrix, when the above filter is used for the decoupled system, is given by $\bar{P}$ of Eq. (123). When the above filter is used to reconstruct the state of the coupled system, a covariance matrix different from $\bar{P}$ above is expected. However, if the matrix $\hat{P}$ corresponding to the infinite time control problem is skew symmetric, then the state of the system can be reconstructed with no deterioration. The following theorem summarizes the result.

Theorem 9. For the coupled system (117)–(118), the steady state of the system can be reconstructed from the decentralized

Kalman filter (124) with covariance matrix $\overline{P}$ of Eqs. (125)–(126) if the matrix $\hat{P}$ defined as

$$\hat{P} \triangleq A_C\overline{P}\left(1/2A_C + A_D - \overline{K}C\right)' \tag{127}$$

is skew symmetric and the matrix $A' - C'K'$ is stable.

V. SUBOPTIMALITY BOUNDS ON DECENTRALIZED CONTROL; INCOMPLETE AND NOISY MEASUREMENTS

A. PROBLEM DEFINITION

Thus far decentralized control for omplete state information and decentralized construction of the state of the system has been considered. Also, conditions for suboptimality of decentralized schemes have been considered. Now we focus our attention on the case where output of a decentralized filter is used in place of the state in controlling the system. Let us consider the interconnected system

$$x(t + 1) = A_Dx(t) + Bu(t) + A_Cx(t) + v(t), \tag{128}$$

$$y(t) = Cx(t) + w(t). \tag{129}$$

Matrices A_D, A_C, B, and C are the same as before, with v(t) and w(t) white sequences as defined in state estimation problems. The performance index to be minimized is the same as defined for the control problem with weighting matrices in diagonal form. When the coupling matrix $A_C = 0$, optimal control for the decoupled system

$$x(t + 1) = A_Dx(t) + Bu(t) + v(t), \tag{130}$$

$$y(t) = Cx(t) \tag{131}$$

is given by

$$u^0(t) = -L\hat{x}(t), \tag{132}$$

where $L(t)$ is the block diagonal matrix solution of Eqs. (17) and (18) and $x(t)$ is the output of the decentralized estimator of Eqs. (103)–(105). The linear control (132) minimizes the performance index (42), and the minimum value of the performance index is given by

$$J^0 = x'(t_0)S(t_0)x(t_0) + \text{tr}\ S(t_0)R_0 + \sum_T \text{tr}\ R_V S(t+1) + \sum_T \text{tr}\ P(t)L'(t)B'(t)S(t+1)A_D. \tag{133}$$

The decentralized estimator–controller (132), when used in conjunction with the coupled system (93), would, in general, result in a value of the performance index different from J^0. We propose to bound the value of the performance index from above by a multiple of J^0.

B. DERIVATION OF NECESSARY CONDITIONS

The dynamics of the system with the control law $u^0 = -L\hat{x}$ may be written as

$$x(t+1) = (A - BL)x(t) + BL\tilde{x}(t) + v(t), \tag{134}$$

where $\tilde{x}(t)$, the state estimation error, is governed by

$$\tilde{x}(t+1) = (A - KC)\tilde{x}(t) + A_C x(t) + v(t) - Kw(t). \tag{135}$$

Similar to the proof of Theorem 1, we find the term $\Delta(t)$ as defined previously:

$$\begin{aligned} x'(t+1)&S(t+1)x(t+1) \\ &= v'(t)S(t+1)v(t) + v'(t)S(t+1) \\ &\quad \times [(A - BL)x(t) + BL\tilde{x}(t)] \\ &\quad + [(A - BL)x(t) + BL\tilde{x}(t)]'S(t+1)v(t) \\ &\quad + x'(t)(A - BL)'S(t+1)BL\tilde{x}(t) + \tilde{x}'(t)L'B'S(t+1) \\ &\quad \times (A - BL)x(t) + \tilde{x}'(t)L\ B\ S(t+1)BL\tilde{x}(t), \end{aligned} \tag{136}$$

$$x'(t)S(t)x(t) = x'(t)\Big[(A_D - BL)'S(t+1)(A_D - BL)$$
$$+ L'Q_uL + Q_x\Big]x(t). \qquad (137)$$

Taking the expected value of the above terms, and since $v(t)$ is not correlated to $x(t)$ and $\tilde{x}(t)$, and taking the summation for $\Delta(x'Sx)$ from t_0 to t_{f-1} will result in

$$J^a = x'(0)S(t_0)x(0) + \text{tr}\, R_0S(t_0) + \sum_T \text{tr}\, R_VS(t+1)$$
$$+ E\sum_T x'(t)\Big[(A - BL)'S(t+1)(A - BL)$$
$$- (A_D - BL)'S(t+1)(A_D - BL)\Big]x(t)$$
$$+ E\sum_T x'(t)A_CS(t+1)BL\tilde{x}(t) + \tilde{x}'(t)L'B'S(t+1)A_Cx(t)$$
$$+ E\sum_T \tilde{x}'(t)L'B'S(t+1)A_D\tilde{x}(t). \qquad (138)$$

Therefore,

$$J^a = J^0 + E\Bigg\{\sum_T x'(t)\Big[(A - BL)'S(t+1)(A - BL)$$
$$- (A_D - BL)'S(t+1)(A_D - BL)\Big]x(t)$$
$$+ \sum_T x'(t)A_CS(t+1)BL\tilde{x}(t)$$
$$+ \tilde{x}'(t)L'B'S(t+1)A_Cx(t)\Bigg\}$$
$$+ \sum_T \text{tr}\, L'B'S(t+1)A_D(P^a(t) - P^0(t)). \qquad (139)$$

Subtracting $(1 - \mu)J^a$ from both sides results in

$$J^a - \mu J^0 = \sum_T\Big\{(A - BL)'S(t+1)(A - BL) - S$$
$$+ \mu\left(Q_x + L'Q_uL\right)x(t) + \tilde{x}(t)L'B'S(t+1)A_Cx(t)$$
$$+ (-1 + \mu)\tilde{x}'(t)L'Q_uLx(t)$$

$$+ x'(t)A_C'S(t+1)BL\tilde{x}(t) + (-1+\mu)x'(t)Q_u L\tilde{x}(t)$$

$$+ \tilde{x}'(t)L'B'S(t+1)A_D + (-1+\mu)L'Q_u L$$

$$- P^{-1/2}L'B'S(t+1)P^0 P^{-1/2}\tilde{x}(t)\Big\} \tag{140}$$

or

$$J^a - \mu J^0 = \sum_T \begin{bmatrix} x \\ \tilde{x} \end{bmatrix}' \times \begin{bmatrix} F_\mu(t) & A_C'S(t+1)BL + (1-\mu)L'Q_u L \\ L'B'S(t+1)A_C + (\mu-1)L'Q_u L & \tilde{H}_\mu(t) \end{bmatrix} \begin{bmatrix} x \\ \tilde{x} \end{bmatrix}. \tag{141}$$

If we define the F(t) matrix as

$$\hat{F}(t) \triangleq \begin{bmatrix} F_\mu(t) & A_C'S(t+1)BL + (\mu-1)L'Q_u L \\ L'B'S(t+1)A_C + (\mu-1)L'Q_u L & \tilde{H}_\mu(t) \end{bmatrix} \tag{142}$$

and

$$\tilde{H}_\mu(t) \triangleq L'B'S(t+1)A_D + (\mu-1)L'Q_u L - P^{-1/2}L'B'S(t+1)P^0 P^{-1/2}, \tag{143}$$

we can state the following theorem regarding the suboptimality of a decentralized estimator controller.

Theorem 10. The decentralized control of

$$u^0 = -L\hat{x}(t), \tag{144}$$

where L is the solution of Eqs. (17)–(18) and $\hat{x}(t)$ is the output of the decentralized estimator of

$$\hat{x}(t+1) = A_D\hat{x}(t) - BL\hat{x}(t) + K(t)[y(t) - C\hat{x}(t)], \tag{145}$$

$$\hat{x}(t_0) = x_0, \tag{146}$$

is suboptimal with degree μ for the coupled system (130)–(131) if the matrix $\hat{F}(t)$ as defined by Eqs. (142)–(143) is negative semidefinite for all time intervals and the triples (A_i, B_i, C_i) are complete.

This concludes the presentation of main results. The following section includes numerical examples to broaden comprehension of decentralized control as presented here and the applicability of the results. Theorems 1–10 provide a designer with alternative schemes for decentralized control utilizing a digital data processor as the control unit. By restricting the subsystems observed and by using only local measurements, the reliance of the system on a network of communication links is alleviated. Also, by reducing the size of the optimal control problems solved by each subsystem, the amount of data processed at each time frame was reduced considerably. This is of great importance if on-line control of a process is desired and the digital data processor is used for multiple purposes.

VI. EXAMPLES

The simple examples presented are intended for clarification of basic concepts and results as well as to suggest their applicability for analysis and design of large-scale systems. Some of the interesting and simple criteria obtained from these examples might be used to formulate an initial guess for the solution of more complex systems.

A. *NEUTRAL INTERCONNECTION*

Consider a simple case composed of two subsystems. Each subsystem is described by a scalar difference equation

$$x_i(t + 1) = ax_i(t) + bu_i(t), \quad i = 1, 2, \quad t \in T. \tag{147}$$

The performance index to be minimized is of quadratic form and is given by

$$J = \sum_{T} \left[x'(t) Q_x x(t) + u'(t) Q_u u(t) \right], \tag{148}$$

where Q_x and Q_u are diagonal matrices of dimension 2 × 2 and their diagonal elements are given by

$$Q_{xi} = q_x > 0, \quad i = 1, 2, \tag{149}$$

$$Q_{ui} = q_u > 0, \quad i = 1, 2. \tag{150}$$

The steady state feedback gain is given by

$$\bar{l} = \left(q_u + b^2 \bar{s}\right)^{-1} b \bar{s} a, \tag{151}$$

with $\bar{s}$ the positive solution of the following scalar ARE:

$$\bar{s} = (a - b\bar{l})^2 \bar{s} + l^2 q_u + q_x. \tag{152}$$

The resulting closed-loop system is asymptotically stable and is described by

$$x(t + 1) = \left(A_D - B\bar{L}\right) x(t), \tag{153}$$

$$A_D = \text{diag}[a, a], \tag{154}$$

$$B = \text{diag}[b, b], \tag{155}$$

$$\bar{L} = \text{diag}[\bar{l}, \bar{l}], \tag{156}$$

$$\bar{S} = \text{diag}[\bar{s}, \bar{s}]. \tag{157}$$

The interconnection matrix A_C is a 2 × 2 matrix whose elements are denoted by A_{ij}. We recall from previous sections, for a matrix to have no effect on steady state performance of the system, it is sufficient that the matrix $\hat{S}$, defined as follows, be skew symmetric:

$$\hat{S} \triangleq A_C' S (1/2 A_C + (A_D - BL)). \tag{158}$$

$A_D - BL$ is a 2 × 2 diagonal matrix whose diagonal elements are given by

$$\hat{a} = a - bl. \tag{159}$$

If the required matrix operations are done in expression (158) for $\hat{S}$, we obtain

$$2\hat{S} = \bar{s}\begin{bmatrix} a_{11}^2 + a_{21}^2 + 2a_{11}\hat{a} & a_{11}a_{12} + a_{22}a_{21} + 2a_{21}\hat{a} \\ a_{11}a_{12} + a_{22}a_{21} + 2a_{12}\hat{a} & a_{12}^2 + a_{22} + 2a_{22}\hat{a} \end{bmatrix}. \tag{160}$$

For the matrix $\hat{S}$ to be skew symmetric, it is necessary that the following conditions be met:

$$a_{11}^2 + a_{21}^2 + 2a_{11}\hat{a} = 0, \tag{161}$$

$$a_{11}a_{12} + a_{22}a_{21} + \hat{a}(a_{12} + a_{21}) = 0, \tag{162}$$

$$a_{12}^2 + a_{22}^2 + 2a_{22}\hat{a} = 0. \tag{163}$$

An additional condition required by Theorem 5 is that the closed-loop coupled system be stable. The stability criterion poses another quadratic constraint on the elements of matrix A_C. However, it will follow that the class of neutral interconnection is not void and has infinite elements.

A possible way to satisfy condition (162) is for the elements of A_C to satisfy the following conditions:

$$a_{22} = a_{11}, \tag{164}$$

$$a_{21} = -a_{12}. \tag{165}$$

The above expressions for a_{22} and a_{21}, when substituted in Eqs. (161) and (162), reduce both equations to one quadratic equation in terms of a_{11}, a_{12}, and $\hat{a}$:

$$\left(a_{11} + \hat{a}\right)^2 + a_{12}^2 = \hat{a}^2. \tag{166}$$

Equation (166) describes a circle with its center at $(-\hat{a}, 0)$ and radius $\hat{a}$. The stability condition for the closed-loop coupled system

$$x(t + 1) = \begin{bmatrix} a_{11} + \hat{a} & a_{12} \\ -a_{12} & a_{11} + \hat{a} \end{bmatrix} x(t) \tag{167}$$

is given by

$$\left(a_{11} + \hat{a}\right)^2 + a_{12}^2 < 1. \tag{168}$$

Inequality (168) defines the interior points of a unit circle with its center located at point $(-\hat{a}, 0)$ in the a_{11}, a_{12} plane. However, the circle defined by (166) lies entirely inside the unit circle of Eq. (168) due to the fact that the closed-loop subsystems with LQR design are asymptotically stable and therefore $\|\hat{a}\|$ is less than one. The ideas are graphically presented in Fig. 1.

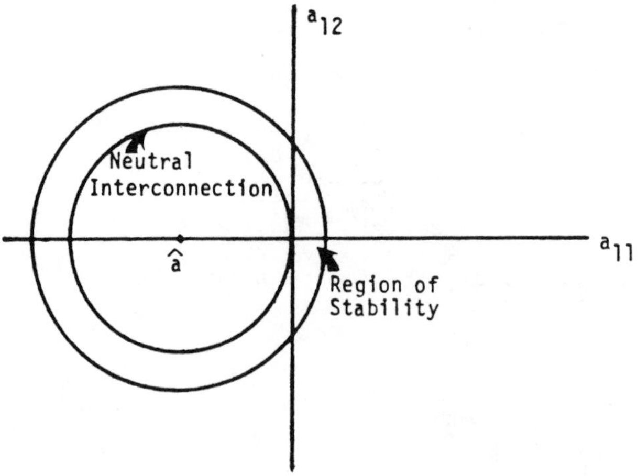

Fig. 1. Region of stability and neutral interconnection matrix.

B. *SUBOPTIMALITY INDEX*

The example to be considered for the suboptimality index is a 2 × 2 system composed of two scalar systems, each described by a scalar difference equation

$$x_i(t + 1) = x_i(t) + u_i(t), \quad t \in T, \quad i = 1, 2. \tag{169}$$

The performance index to be minimized is of quadratic form and is given by

$$Q_x = \mathrm{diag}[1, 1], \tag{170}$$

$$Q_u = \mathrm{diag}[1, 1], \tag{171}$$

$$J = \sum_T \left[x'(t)Q_x x(t) + u'(t)Q_u u(t)\right]. \tag{172}$$

The optimal feedback gain for the system

$$x(t + 1) = A_D x(t) + Bu(t), \tag{173}$$

$$A_D = \mathrm{diag}[1, 1], \tag{174}$$

$$B = \mathrm{diag}\ [1, 1] \tag{175}$$

is given by

$$u(t) = -L(t)x(t), \tag{176}$$

$$L(t) = \mathrm{diag}[l(t), l(t)]. \tag{177}$$

The sequence of scalar values $l(t)$, $t \in T$ is given by

$$l(t) = [1 + s(t + 1)]^{-1}s^2(t + 1), \tag{178}$$

$$s(t) = (1 - l(t))^2 s(t + 1) + 1 + l^2(t), \tag{179}$$

$$s(t_f) = 0. \tag{180}$$

Matrix S is also of diagonal form, with its elements given by Eqs. (178)–(180). For the system to be suboptimal with degree μ, matrix F_μ, as defined below, has to be negative semidefinite:

$$F_\mu(t) \triangleq (A - BL(t))'S(t + 1)(A - BL(t)) + \mu\left(Q_x + L'(t)Q_u L(t)\right). \tag{181}$$

Matrix A is defined as

$$A = A_C + A_D, \tag{182}$$

$$A_C = [a_{ij}]. \tag{183}$$

Motivated by the results from the previous example, let us consider only interconnection matrices of similar form, that is,

$$a_{22} = a_{11}, \tag{184}$$

$$a_{21} = -a_{12}. \tag{185}$$

With the above conditions on interconnection matrix A_C, we can proceed to evaluate terms in expression (181) for $F_\mu(t)$:

$$(A - BL(t))'S(t + 1)(A - BL(t))$$
$$= \begin{bmatrix} \left(a_{11} + \hat{a}(t)\right)^2 + a_{12}^2 & 0 \\ 0 & \left(a_{11} + \hat{a}(t)\right)^2 + a_{12}^2 \end{bmatrix} s(t+1) \tag{186}$$

where $\hat{a}(t)$ is defined as

$$\hat{a}(t) = a - bl(t), \tag{187}$$

$$= 1 - l(t). \tag{188}$$

In order for the suboptimality index to exist, it is necessary that the term $A_{C1}'S(t + 1)A_{cl} - S(t)$ be non-positive definite or

$$s(t + 1)\ \mathrm{diag}\left[\left(a_{11} + \hat{a}(t)\right)^2 + (a_{12})^2 - s(t)/s(t + 1),\right.$$
$$\left.\left(a_{11} + \hat{a}(t)\right)^2 + (a_{12})^2 - s(t)/s(t + 1)\right] \tag{189}$$

be negative semidefinite. For the diagonal matrix of expression (189) to be negative semidefinite, its diagonal elements must be nonpositive, that is,

$$\left(a_{11} + \hat{a}(t)\right)^2 + (a_{12})^2 \leq s(t)/s(t + 1), \quad t \in T. \tag{190}$$

The above set of inequalities corresponds to the interior points of a sequence of circles centered at $(\hat{a}(t), 0)$, with radius $(s(t)/s(t+1))^{1/2}$. The region interior to all circles, as given by Eq. (190), is the set of interconnection matrices with a finite degree of suboptimality. It should be emphasized that this is not the entire set but the cross section of such a set with hyperplanes (184)–(185) in the four-dimensional Euclidean space of the interconnection matrix A_C.

The sequences of values for $s(t)$ and $l(t)$ can be generated by solving the difference equations backward in time. Numerical values for $s(t)$ and $l(t)$ are summarized in Table I.

Table I is given in backward time and is terminated after five time instants since the values have reached their corresponding steady state values. The circle corresponding to the steady state case lies inside all other circles, and therefore its interior is the set of interconnection matrices A_C with finite suboptimality index μ.

The suboptimality index μ is given by Corollary 2 and

$$\mu^* = \min_t \left[\frac{s(t) - \left[(a_{11} + a(t))^2 + a_{12}^2\right] s(t+1)}{1 + l^2(t)} \right]. \tag{191}$$

Values for $s(t)$, $l(t)$, and $a(t)$ are given by Table I.

TABLE I. Numerical Values for s(t) and l(t)

Time	t_f	$t_f - 1$	$t_f - 2$	$t_f - 3$	$t_f - 4$	$t_f - 5$
$s(t)$	0.00	1.00	1.50	1.61	1.61	1.61
$\frac{s(t)}{s(t+1)}$	--	∞	1.50	1.06	1.00	1.00
$a(t)$	--	1.00	0.50	0.40	0.39	0.39
$l(t)$	--	0.00	0.50	0.60	0.61	0.61
$1 + l^2(t)$	--	1.00	1.25	1.36	1.37	1.37

An important and interesting result of expression (191) for μ is that the equivalent classes of interconnection matrices A_C are circles. This is due to the fact that the quadratic form $\left(a_{11} + \hat{a}(t)\right)^2 + a_{12}^2$ is invariant with respect to a_{11} and a_{12} so long as changes are limited to a circle centered at $(\hat{a}(t), 0)$.

The suboptimality index μ can be obtained for any pair (a_{11}, a_{12}) from expression (191). For pairs (0, 0) representing no interconnection and $(-2 \times 0.39, 0)$, the suboptimality index is 1. Therefore, for this example the class of neutral interconnection is the same as A_C^0 defined previously. The equivalent interconnection matrices resulting in the same degree of suboptimality are circles centered at (0.39, 0). Figure 2 graphically represents results obtained with respect to the suboptimality index.

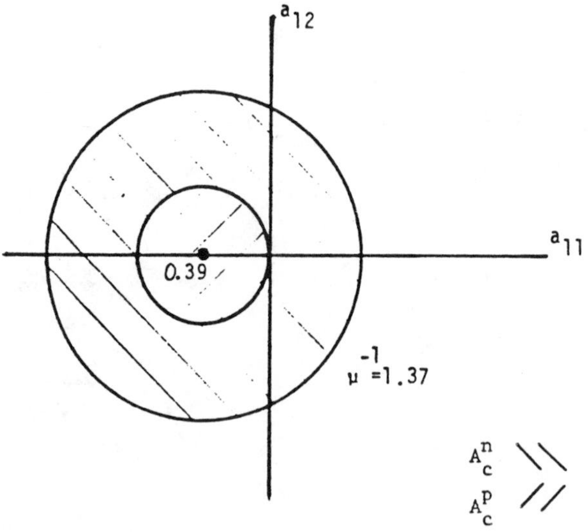

Fig. 2. Region of stability partitioned into classes of interconnection matrix.

VII. CONCLUSION

The on-line data exchange between different control stations of a large-scale system plays an important role in several aspects of an optimal design. For practical purposes a complicated network of communication links is not only costly to establish and maintain, it also results in vulnerability of the system due to the high possibility of errors in the links. For theoretical considerations the introduction of on-line data exchange generally implies extreme hardship in obtaining optimal solutions if they can be obtained.

The method presented here assumes that the system consists of smaller interacting subsystems, each controlled by a different controller. Ignoring the effect of interactions, each controller can find his optimal solution based only on the limited information and observations at that subsystem. The need for on-line and off-line information exchange between subsystems is therefore totally eliminated, avoiding the associated difficulties and achieving a more reliable system. Also, the number of operations required of digital computer for computation of optimal gains is proportional to the powers of the dimension of the system. Substantial savings on computer time results when the original large-scale system is treated as several lower order systems with their sum of dimensions equal to the order of the original problem. Also, considerable insight into the uncertainties associated with modeling large-scale systems is achieved.

REFERENCES

1. H. S. WITSENHAUSEN, "Separation of Estimation and Control for Discrete Time Systems," *Proc. IEEE 59* (1971).

2. W. M. WONHAM, "On the Separation Theorem of Stochastic Control," *SIAM J. Control 6*(2) (1968).

3. Y. BAR-SHALOM and E. TSE, "Concepts and Methods in Stochastic Control," *in* "Control and Dynamic Systems," Vol. 12 (C. T. Leondes, ed.), Academic Press, 1976.

4. Y. BAR-SHALOM and E. TSE, "Dual Effect, Certainty Equivalence and Separation in Stochastic Control," *IEEE Trans. Autom. Control AC-19*, No. 5, 494-500, October 1974.

5. N. R. SANDELL, P. VARAIYA, M. ATHANS, and M. G. SAFANOV, "Survey of Decentalized Control Methods for Large-Scale Systems," *IEEE Trans. Autom. Control AC-23*, No. 2, April 1978.

6. M. ATHANS, "Theory and Applications, Survey of Decentralized Control Methods," *Ann. Econ. Social Measurement 412*, 345-355 (1975).

7. M. D. MESAROIC, D. MACKO, and Y. TAKAHARA, "Theory of Hierarchical Multilevel Systems," Academic Press, New York, 1970.

8. D. A. WISMER, (ed.), "Optimization Methods for Large Scale Systems," McGraw-Hill, New York, 1971.

9. Y. C. HO and S. K. MITTER, (ed.), "Directions in Large Scale Systems," Plenum Press, New York, 1976.

10. M. G. SINGH, "Dynamical Hierarchical Control," North Holland, Amsterdam, 1977.

11. R. SACKS, (ed.), "Large-Scale Dynamical Systems," Point Lobos Press, North Hollywood, California, 1975.

12. M. JAMSHIDI, "Large Scale Systems, Modeling, Control and Applications," Elsevier-North Holland Publisher, New York, 1980.

13. D. D. SILJAK, "Large-Scale Dynamic Systems: Stability and Structure," North Holland, New York, 1978.

14. J. MARSCHAK, *Manage. Sci. 7*, 101 (1955).

15. I. B. RHODES and D. G. LYENBERGER, "Stochastic Differential Games with Constrained State Estimators," *IEEE Trans. Autom. Control AC-14*, 476-481, October 1969.

16. W. WILLIAM, "Formal Solutions for a Class of Stochastic Pursuit Evasion Games," *IEEE Trans. Autom. Control AC-14*, 504-509, October 1969.

17. H. S. WISTENHAUSEN, "A Counterexample in Stochastic Optimum Control," *SIAM J. Control 6*, No. 1 (1968).

18. T. YOSHIKAWA and H. KOBAYASHI, "Separation of Estimation and Control for Decentralized Stochastic Control Systems," *Proc., Int. Fed. Autom. Control Congr.* (1978).

19. Y. C. HO, "Team Decision Theory and Information Structures," *Proc. IEEE 68*, No. 6, June 1980.

20. Y. C. HO and K. C. CHU, "On the Equivalence of Information Structures in Static and Dynamic Team," *IEEE Trans. Autom. Control*, April 1973.

21. T. YOSHIKAWA, "Decomposition of Dynamic Team Decision Problems," *IEEE Trans. Autom. Control AC-23*, No. 4, August 1978.

22. Y. C. HO and K. C. CHU, "Team Decision Theory and Information Structures in Optimal Control Problems--Part I," *IEEE Trans. Autom. Control AC-217*, No. 1, February 1972.

23. K. C. CHUS, "Team Decision Theory and Information Structures in Optimal Control Problems--Part II," *IEEE Trans. Autom. Control AC-17*, No. 1, February 1972.

24. Y. C. HO and T. S. CHANG, "Another Look at the Nonclassical Information Structure Problem," *IEEE Trans. Autom. Control AC-25*, No. 3, June 1980.

25. Y. C. HO and G. HENNER, "Redundancy in Team Problems," *IEEE Trans. Autom. Control*, June 1975.

26. J. D. COLE and A. P. SAGE, "Multiperson Decision Analysis in Large-Scale Hierarchical Systems--Team Decision Theory," *Int. J. Control 22*, No. 1, 1-28 (1975).

27. Y. C. HO and K. C. CHU, "Information Structure in Dynamic Multi-Person Control Problems," *Automatica 10*, 341-351 (1974).

28. M. ATHANS, "The Matrix Minimum Principle," *Inf. Control 11*, 592-606.

29. K.-C. CHUS, "Comparison of Information Structures in Decentralized Dynamic Systems," *in* "Directions in Large Scale Systems," Plenum Press, New York, 1976.

30. D. P. LOOZE and N. R. SANDELL, JR., "Decentralization and Decomposition in Linear Stochastic Control," Proceedings of the Control and Decision Conference, 1980.

31. W. S. LEVINE and M. ATHANS, "On the Determination of the Optimal Constant Output Feedback Gains for Linear Multivariable Systems," *IEEE Trans. Autom. Control AC-15*, No. 1, February 1970.

32. C.-Y. CHONG, M. ATHANS, "On the Stochastic Control of Linear Systems with Different Information Sets," *IEEE Trans. Autom. Control AC-16*, No. 5, October 1978.

33. N. R. SANDELL, JR. and M. ATHANS, "Solution of Some Nonclassical LQG Stochastic Decision Problems," *IEEE Trans. Autom. Control AC-19*, No. 2, April 1974.

34. T. YOSHIKAWA, "Decentralized Control of Discrete-Time Stochastic Systems," *Proc. IFAC Symp. Sensitivity Adaptivity Optimality, 3rd*, 444-451 (1973).

35. V. L. PISACANE and V. D. VANDE LINDLE, "Stochastic Control of Linear Systems with Nonclassical Information and an Arbitrary Number of Controllers," Proceedings of the Control and Decision Conference, 1980.

36. M. K. SUNDARESHAN, "Generation of Multilevel Control and Estimation Schemes for Large Scale-Systems: A Perturbational Approach," *IEEE Trans. Syst. Man Cybern. SMC-7*, No. 3, March 1977.

37. M. K. SUNDARESHAN, "Decentralized Observation in Large Scale Systems," *IEEE Trans. Syst. Man Cybern. SMC-17*, No. 12, December 1977.

38. M. K. SUNDARESHAN, "Exponential Stabilization of Large Scale Systems: Decentralized and Multilevel Schemes," *IEEE Trans. Syst. Man Cybern.*, June 1977.

39. D. D. SILJAK and M. K. SUNDARESHAN, "A Multilevel Optimization of Large Scale Dynamic Systems," *IEEE Trans. Autom. Control*, February 1976.

40. D. D. SILJAK and M. B. VUKCEVIC, "Decentralization, Stabilization and Estimation of Large Scale Linear Systems," *IEEE Trans. Autom. Control*, June 1976.

41. M. DARWISH, H. M. SOLIMAN, and J. FANTIN, "Decentralized Stabilizations of Large Scale Dynamical Systems," *IEEE Trans. Syst. Man Cybern. SMC-9*, No. 11, November 1979.

42. J. J. RISSANEN, "Performance Deterioration of Optimum Systems," *IEEE Trans. Autom. Control AC-16*, 530-532, July 1966.

43. V. M. POPOV, "Criterion of Quality for Nonlinear Controlled Systems," *Proc. IFAC Congr. 1st*, Moscow, USSR, 173-176 (1960).

44. F. N. BAILEY and H. K. RAMAPRIYAN, "Bounds on Suboptimality in the Control of Linear Dynamic Systems," *IEEE Trans. Autom. Control*, October 1973.

45. A. J. LAUB and F. N. BAILY, "Suboptimality Bounds on Stability in the Control of Nonlinear Dynamic Systems," *IEEE Trans. Autom. Control*, June 1976.

46. R. KRTOLICA and D. D. SILJAK, "Suboptimality of Decentralized Stochastic Control and Estimation," *IEEE Trans. Autom. Control AC-25*, No. 1, February 1980.

47. K. A. ASTRÖM, "Introduction to Stochastic Control Theory," Academic Press, New York, 1976.

48. H. KWAKERNAAK and R. SIVAN, "Linear Optimal Control Systems," Wiley, New York, 1972.

Decentralized Control Using Observers

BAHRAM SHAHIAN

Department of Electrical Engineering
California State University, Long Beach
Long Beach, California

I. INTRODUCTION

The design of reduced-order Luenberger observers suitable for large-scale systems is considered first in this chapter. The system as a whole is modeled as an interconnection of lower order subsystems. Under local or subsystem observability conditions, observers are designed in such a way to assure that when interconnected, observation error converges asymptotically with the prescribed degree of convergence. In Section III, the observers are combined with locally optimal controllers and Liapunov-type conditions are obtained to yield exponential stability of the decentralized compensators for the coupled system.

Finally, in Section IV, the performance degradation due to decentralized design is obtained and cost increments are obtained to be used as guidelines for comparisons between different structures. It is noted that the cost increments due to incorrect observer initial conditions and effects of decentralization are separated to single out different effects. This chapter is based on Shahian [1], where generalization to heirarchical techniques and totally decentralized structures in which observer communication is severely limited are considered.

II. DECENTRALIZED OBSERVERS

A. *INTRODUCTION*

During the last two decades a great amount of effort has been devoted to analysis and design of observers following the pioneering work of Luenberger [2]. In this section the problem of design of reduced-order observers for large systems is presented. Since reduced-order observers have the benefit of size reduction, it seems natural that this advantage can be most efficiently and benefically used for large systems. The first work along these lines was presented by Siljak [3] and Sundareshan [4] for full-order observers, and their results are generalized here for the reduced-order case.

B. *SYSTEM MODEL AND OBSERVERS*

The system model is assumed to be an interconnection of δ lower order subsystems of the form

$$\dot{X}_i = A_i X_i + B_i U_i + \sum_{j=1}^{\delta} A_{ij} X_j, \tag{1}$$

$$Y_i = C_i X_i, \quad i = 1, \ldots, \delta, \tag{2}$$

or, in compact notation,

$$\dot{X} = (A + A_c)X + BU, \tag{3}$$

$$Y = CX, \tag{4}$$

where

$$X \in R^n,\ Y \in R^m,\ U \in R^r,\ X_i \in R^{n_i},\ Y_i \in R^{m_i},\ U_i \in R^{r_i}.$$

The matrices have appropriate dimensions. The A, B, and C matrices are diagonal matrices with elements A_i, B_i, and C_i, respectively. A_c is the coupling or interconnection matrix with elements A_{ij}. The system vector dimensions are also the sum of the subsystem dimensions, that is, $n = \Sigma_{i=1}^{\delta} n_i$, etc. It is proposed to design observers for the subsystems of order $n_i - m_i$ such that the "overall observer" has exponential stability properties for the whole system. To assure the stability of the error dynamics of the observers, it is necessary to allow certain limited exchange of information between subsystems. This means that the information structure of the system has to be specified. It is assumed that subsystems have access to or exchange their local estimates of states if they interact and also know the system coupling matrix, that is, the information structure is

$$I_i(t) = \left\{U_i,\ y_i,\ x_i,\ \hat{x}_j,\ A_i,\ B_i,\ C_i,\ A_{ij}\right\},$$
$$t \geq 0, \quad j \neq i \ni A_{ij} \neq 0.$$

The observer provides estimates of X_i based on measurements Y_i and accounts for system coupling based on $\hat{x}_j$. The following reduced-order system observers are proposed:

$$\hat{x}_i = M_i\hat{Z}_i + N_iY_i, \tag{5}$$

$$\dot{\hat{z}}_i = F_i \hat{z}_i + D_i Y_i + T_i B_i U_i + T_i \sum_{\substack{j=1 \\ j \neq i}}^{\delta} A_{ij} \hat{x}_j$$

$$+ L_i \left(\dot{Y}_i - E_i Y_i - G_i \hat{z}_i - C_i B_i U_i - C_i \sum_{\substack{j=1 \\ j \neq i}}^{\delta} A_{ij} \hat{x}_j \right). \quad (6)$$

The observer matrices are chosen as follows. The transformation matrix T_i is arbitrarily chosen such that

$$\begin{bmatrix} C_i \\ --- \\ T_i \end{bmatrix}^{-1} = [N_i \mid M_i]. \quad (7)$$

Then

$$F_i = T_i A_i M_i, \quad D_i = T_i A_i N_i, \quad (8)$$

$$G_i = C_i A_i M_i, \quad E_i = C_i A_i N_i. \quad (9)$$

The dimensions of T_i are $(n_i - m_i) \times n_i$, and this determines other parameter dimensions. The observer gain is given by

$$L_i = S_i G_i', \quad (10)$$

where S_i satisfies the following algebraic Ricatti equation:

$$S_i(F_i + \sigma_i I_i)' + (F_i + \sigma_i I_i)S_i - S_i G_i' G_i S_i + \overline{Q}_i = 0. \quad (11)$$

$\overline{Q}_i$ is an arbitrary positive semidefinite matrix and I_i is an $n_i - m_i$ identify matrix; σ_i determines the rate of convergence of the observer.

To avoid differentiation of the output, standard restructuring of the observer can be performed, and the modified structure presented below is obtained:

$$\hat{x}_i = M_i W_i + R_i Y_i, \quad (12)$$

$$\dot{W}_i = V_i A_i \hat{X}_i + V_i \left(B_i U_i + \sum_{\substack{j=1 \\ j \neq i}}^{\sigma} A_{ij} \hat{x}_j \right), \quad (13)$$

where

$$V_i = T_i - L_iC_i, \tag{14}$$

$$R_i = N_i + M_iL_i. \tag{15}$$

From standard observer theory the above structures are equivalent.

C. CONVERGENCE OF THE OBSERVER

Define the observer error as $\tilde{Z}_i = Z_i - \hat{Z}_i$. The estimation error is similarly defined as $\tilde{X}_i = X_i - \hat{X}_i$; then,

$$\begin{aligned}\tilde{X}_i &= X_i - \left(N_iY_i + M_i\hat{Z}_i\right) \\ &= X_i - N_iC_iX_i - M_i\hat{Z}_i \\ &= M_iT_i(N_iY_i + M_iZ_i).\end{aligned} \tag{16}$$

Hence $\tilde{X}_i = M_i\tilde{Z}_i$ and convergence of $\tilde{Z}_i$ implies that of $\tilde{X}_i$.

Using system and original observer equations, the error dynamics follow:

$$\begin{aligned}\dot{\tilde{Z}}_i &= (F_i - L_iG_i)\tilde{Z}_i + \sum_{\substack{j=1\\j\neq i}}^{\delta}(T_i - L_iC_i)A_{ij}\left(X_j - \hat{X}_j\right) \\ &= (F_i - L_iG_i)\tilde{Z}_i + \sum_{\substack{j=1\\j\neq i}}^{\delta}(T_i - L_iC_i)A_{ij}M_j\tilde{Z}_j \\ &= (F_i - L_iG_i)\tilde{Z}_i + \sum_{\substack{j=1\\j\neq i}}^{\delta}(T_iA_{ij}M_j - L_iC_iA_{ij}M_j)\tilde{Z}_j.\end{aligned} \tag{17}$$

Let F_c be a matrix with elements $F_{ij} = T_iA_{ij}M_j$, and let G_c be the matrix with elements $G_{ij} = C_iA_{ij}M_j$. Now, if F, L, G are diagonal matrices with elements F_i, L_i, G_i, respectively, we get error dynamics for the "system observer" with state $Z = \left[Z_1', \ldots, Z_\delta'\right]'$:

$$\dot{\tilde{Z}} = [(F + F_c) - L(G + G_c)]\tilde{Z}. \tag{18}$$

Let us choose $\mathscr{L}(\tilde{Z})$ as the Liapunov function for the error system:

$$\mathscr{L}(\tilde{Z}) = \tilde{Z}'S\tilde{Z}, \tag{19}$$

where S is a diagonal matrix with entries S_i that are solutions of Ricatti equations. Subsystem observability conditions, along with $\bar{Q}_i \geq 0$, imply that $S > 0$. Now,

$$\begin{aligned}\frac{d}{dt}\mathscr{L}(\tilde{Z}) &= \dot{\tilde{Z}}'S\tilde{Z} + \tilde{Z}'S\dot{\tilde{Z}} \\ &= \tilde{Z}'\Big[(F - LG)S + S(F - LG)' \\ &\qquad + (F_c - LG)S + S(F_c - LG_c)'\Big]\tilde{Z},\end{aligned} \tag{20}$$

and using the system Ricatti equation (11), we obtain

$$\begin{aligned}\frac{d}{dt}\mathscr{L}(\tilde{Z}) &= \tilde{Z}'\Big[(-2\sigma S - \bar{Q} - SG'GS) \\ &\qquad + (F_c - LG_c)S + S(F_c - LG_c)'\Big]\tilde{Z}.\end{aligned} \tag{21}$$

Now, let the coupling matrix A_c be such that

$$VA_cM = (T - LC)A_cM = F_c - LG_c = S(\Phi - \Psi), \tag{22}$$

where Ψ and Φ are arbitrary symmetric and skew-symmetric matrices, respectively, that is $\Psi' = \Psi$, $\Phi' = -\Phi$, with the above restriction on A_c:

$$\begin{aligned}(F_c - LG_c)S + S(F_c - LG_c)' &= S\Phi S - S\Psi S - S\Phi S - S\Psi S \\ &= -2S\Psi S.\end{aligned}$$

Defining Δ as

$$\Delta = \bar{Q} + SG'GS + 2S\Psi S \tag{23}$$

and assuming it to be positive semidefinite, we obtain

$$\frac{d}{dt}\mathscr{L}(\tilde{Z}) \leq -2\sigma\tilde{Z}S\tilde{Z} \quad \text{or} \quad \mathscr{L}(Z) \leq \mathscr{L}(Z(0))e^{-2\sigma t},$$

which implies

$$\|\tilde{z}(t)\|^2 \lambda_m(S) \leq \|z(0)\|^2 \lambda_M(S) e^{-2\sigma t} \quad \text{or}$$

$$\|\tilde{z}(t)\|^2 \leq \alpha \|\tilde{z}(0)\| e^{-\sigma t}, \tag{24}$$

where λ_m, λ_M are the smallest and largest eigenvalues of S:

$$\alpha = (\lambda_M(S)/\lambda_m(S))^{1/2}.$$

Therefore the observer converges exponentially. The rate of convergence is $\sigma = \min\{\sigma_i: i = 1, \ldots, \delta\}$. The above derivation proves the following theorem.

Theorem 1. Let $VA_cM = S(\Phi - \Psi)$, where Ψ and Φ are arbitrary symmetric and skew symmetric matrices, respectively, such that

$$\Delta = \bar{Q} + SG'GS + 2S\Psi S \geq 0. \tag{25}$$

Then the observer system (5)–(6) converges at least as fast as $\sigma = \min_i\{\sigma_i\}$, $i = 1, \ldots, \delta$.

Example 1. Consider the following fourth-order system:

$$\begin{bmatrix} \dot{X}_{11} \\ \dot{X}_{12} \\ \hline \dot{X}_{21} \\ \dot{X}_{22} \end{bmatrix} = \left[\begin{array}{cc|cc} 1 & 1 & 0 & 1 \\ 2 & 1 & 0 & 0 \\ \hline 0 & 0 & 1 & 2 \\ 1 & 0 & 1 & 1 \end{array}\right] \begin{bmatrix} X_{11} \\ X_{12} \\ \hline X_{21} \\ X_{22} \end{bmatrix} + \left[\begin{array}{cc} 1 & 0 \\ 0 & 0 \\ \hline 0 & 1 \\ 0 & 0 \end{array}\right] \begin{bmatrix} U_{11} \\ U_{12} \\ \hline U_{21} \\ U_{22} \end{bmatrix},$$

$$\begin{bmatrix} Y_1 \\ Y_2 \end{bmatrix} = \left[\begin{array}{cc|cc} 1 & 0 & 0 & 0 \\ \hline 0 & 0 & 0 & 1 \end{array}\right] \begin{bmatrix} X_{11} \\ X_{12} \\ \hline X_{21} \\ X_{22} \end{bmatrix}.$$

This system can be decomposed into two second-order systems:

$$\begin{aligned} \dot{X}_1 &= A_1X_1 + B_1U_1 + A_{12}X_2, \quad Y_1 = C_1X_1; \\ \dot{X}_2 &= A_2X_2 + B_2U_2 + A_{21}X_1, \quad Y_2 = C_2X_2. \end{aligned} \tag{26}$$

The subsystem matrices are

$$A_1 = \begin{bmatrix} 1 & 1 \\ 2 & 1 \end{bmatrix}, \quad B_1 = \begin{bmatrix} 1 & 0 \\ 0 & 0 \end{bmatrix}, \quad C_1 = [1 \quad 0],$$

$$A_2 = \begin{bmatrix} 1 & 2 \\ 1 & 1 \end{bmatrix}, \quad B_2 = \begin{bmatrix} 0 & 1 \\ 0 & 0 \end{bmatrix}, \quad C_2 = [0 \quad 1].$$

The coupling matrix is given by

$$A_c = \begin{bmatrix} 0 & 0 & 0 & 1 \\ 0 & 0 & 0 & 0 \\ 0 & 0 & 0 & 0 \\ 1 & 0 & 0 & 0 \end{bmatrix}.$$

Note that matrices $[C_1' \,:\, (C_1A_1)']'$ and $[C_2' \,:\, (C_2A_c)']'$ both have rank two and hence local observers can be built.

Choosing $T_1 = [0 \; 1]$, $T_2 = [1 \; 0]$, we obtain $F_1 = 1$, $F_2 = 1$, $G_1 = 1$, and $G_2 = 1$. Choosing also $\overline{Q}_1 = 5$ and $\sigma_1 = 1$, the Ricatti equation for this scalar observer is a quadratic algebraic equation:

$$S_1^2 - 4S_1 - 5 = 0 \Rightarrow S_1 = 5, \quad L_1 = 5, \quad V_1 = [-5 \quad 1],$$

$$R_1 = \begin{bmatrix} 1 \\ 5 \end{bmatrix}, \quad M_1 = \begin{bmatrix} 0 \\ 1 \end{bmatrix}.$$

Also, $\overline{Q}_2 = 7$ and

$$\sigma_2 = 2 \Rightarrow S_2 = 7, \quad L_2 = 7, \quad V_2 = [1 \quad -7],$$

$$R_2 = \begin{bmatrix} 7 \\ 1 \end{bmatrix}, \quad M_2 = \begin{bmatrix} 1 \\ 0 \end{bmatrix}.$$

The above completely specifies both observers. The convergence follows from application of Theorem 1:

$$\Delta = \begin{bmatrix} 5 & 0 \\ 0 & 7 \end{bmatrix} + \begin{bmatrix} 25 & 0 \\ 0 & 49 \end{bmatrix} + 2\begin{bmatrix} 25\Psi_{11} & 35\Psi_{12} \\ 35\Psi_{12} & 49\Psi_{22} \end{bmatrix}$$

$$= \begin{bmatrix} 30 + 50\Psi_{11} & 70\Psi_{12} \\ 70\Psi_{12} & 56 + 98\Psi_{22} \end{bmatrix} \geq 0$$

and

$$VA_cM = S(\Phi - \Psi) \Rightarrow \begin{bmatrix} 0 & 0 \\ 0 & 0 \end{bmatrix} = \begin{bmatrix} -5\Psi_{11} & 5\Psi_{12} - 5\Psi_{12} \\ -7\Psi_{12} - 7\Psi_{12} & -7\Psi_{22} \end{bmatrix}.$$

Therefore,

$$\Psi_{11} = \Psi_{22} = 0, \quad \Phi_{12} = \Psi_{12} = -\Psi_{12} \Rightarrow \Phi = \Psi = 0.$$

Note that with this choice, $\Delta = \text{diag}(30, 56)$, and hence is positive definite. The above design procedure has many degrees of freedom where, for a given rate of convergence σ, Q_1 and Q_2 are arbitrary but positive semidefinite. There is a degree of robustness involved in a way that Δ may be positive semidefinite even when system matrices change, and the observer performs well so long as the conditions of Theorem 1 are satisfied. The reduction of complexity and computational savings are apparent from this simple example in that for a fourth-order system, only scalar equations need be solved, which is the result of system decomposition and using reduced-order observers.

The designed observers are

$$\dot{W}_1 = -3\hat{X}_{11} - 4\hat{X}_{12} - 5U_1 - \left[5\hat{X}_{22}\right],$$

$$\dot{W}_2 = -6\hat{X}_{21} - 5\hat{X}_{22} - 7U_2 - \left[7\hat{X}_{11}\right].$$

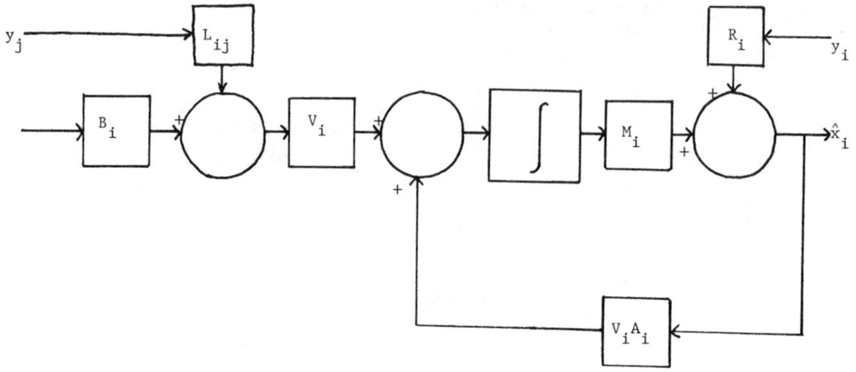

Fig. 1.

State estimates are given by

$$\begin{bmatrix} \hat{X}_{11} \\ \hat{X}_{12} \\ \hat{X}_{21} \\ \hat{X}_{22} \end{bmatrix} = \begin{bmatrix} 1 & 0 \\ 5 & 0 \\ 0 & 7 \\ 0 & 1 \end{bmatrix} \begin{bmatrix} Y_1 \\ Y_2 \end{bmatrix} + \begin{bmatrix} 0 & 0 \\ 5 & 0 \\ 0 & 1 \\ 0 & 0 \end{bmatrix} \begin{bmatrix} W_1 \\ W_2 \end{bmatrix}.$$

Figure 1 illustrates the observer and its simple structure.

III. DECENTRALIZED CONTROL WITH LOCAL OBSERVERS

The approach of the previous section will be followed here to obtain optimal local control laws under inaccessible measurements of the states. State estimates are obtained using local measurements, and the required exchange of information is limited to only state estimates $\hat{X}_j$ to the ith subsystem in case $A_{ij} \neq 0$; this allows guaranteed convergence of the scheme. Even though the control laws are only locally optimal and are suboptimal for the whole system, the conditions on A_c are given under which the system as a whole remains stable. As a design philosophy, one is trading optimality with assured stability, local autonomy, and overall system reliability under structural perturbations. This issue is clearly demonstrated by Siljak and Sundareshan [5]. The following observer—controller is proposed:

$$U_i = -K_i\hat{X}_i,$$

$$K_i = R_i^{-1}B_i'P_i, \tag{27}$$

$$(A_i + \mu_i I_{n_i})'P_i + P_i(A_i + \mu_i I_{n_i}) + Q_i - P_i B_i R_i^{-1} B_i' P_i = 0,$$

$$\hat{X}_i = M_i\hat{Z}_i + N_i Y_i,$$

$$\dot{\hat{Z}}_i = F_i\hat{Z}_i + D_i Y_i + T_i B_i U_i + L_i\left(\dot{Y}_i - E_i Y_i - G_i\hat{Z}_i - C_i B_i U_i\right)$$

$$+ V_i \sum_{\substack{j=1 \\ j\neq 1}}^{\delta} A_{ij}\hat{X}_j,$$

$$L_i = S_i G_i',$$

$$S_i(F_i + \sigma_i I_{n_i - m_i})' + (F_i + \sigma_i I_{n_i - m_i})S_i - S_i G_i' G_i S_i + \overline{Q}_i = 0.$$

Theorem 2. Assume that (A_i, B_i), (A_i, C_i) are controllable and observable pairs, respectively; $R_i > 0$, $Q_i \geq 0$, $\overline{Q}_i > 0$. Then $A_i - B_iK_i$ and $F_i - L_iG_i$ are stable matrices and the system objective functions J_i are minimized locally for $i = 1, \ldots, \delta$, where

$$J_i = \frac{1}{2}\int_0^\infty \left(X_i'Q_iX_i + U_i'R_iU_i\right)e^{2\mu_i t}\,dt \tag{28}$$

and $J = \Sigma_{i=1}^{\delta} J_i$. Also, if $\Omega > 0$, then $X(t)e^{\mu t} \to 0$ as $t \to \infty$, $\mu = \min_i\{\mu i\}$ $\sigma_i > \mu_i > 0$,

$$\Omega = \begin{pmatrix} \Delta_c & -K'RKM \\ -M'K'RK & \Delta_0 \end{pmatrix}, \tag{29}$$

$$\Delta_c = 2\mu P + Q + PBR^{-1}B'P - \left(PA_c + A_c'P\right),$$

$$\Delta_0 = 2\sigma S + \overline{Q} + SG'GS - \left[(VA_cM)S + S(VA_cM)'\right].$$

Proof. After the control U is applied, we obtain

$$\dot{X} = (A + A_c)X - BK\hat{X} = (A + A_c - BK)X + BKM\tilde{Z}. \tag{30}$$

Also, for $\tilde{Z}$ system we already know that

$$\dot{\tilde{Z}} = [(F + F_c) - L(G + G_c)]\tilde{Z}. \tag{31}$$

Hence we can instead consider the $(X, \tilde{Z})$ system, that is, the change coordinate system, where system and observer eigenvalues are now separated:

$$\begin{pmatrix} \dot{X} \\ \hline \dot{\tilde{Z}} \end{pmatrix} = \left(\begin{array}{c|c} A + A_c - BK & BKM \\ \hline 0 & (F + F_c) - L(G + G_c) \end{array}\right) \begin{pmatrix} X \\ \hline \tilde{Z} \end{pmatrix}. \tag{32}$$

choosing

$$\mathscr{L}[(X, \tilde{Z})] = \begin{bmatrix} X \\ \tilde{Z} \end{bmatrix}' \begin{bmatrix} P & 0 \\ 0 & S \end{bmatrix} \begin{bmatrix} X \\ \tilde{Z} \end{bmatrix}$$

as a Liapunov function, we obtain

$$\frac{d}{dt}\mathscr{L}[(X, \tilde{Z})] = \begin{bmatrix} X \\ \tilde{Z} \end{bmatrix}' \left\{ \begin{bmatrix} (A + A_c - BK)' & 0 \\ M'K'B' & (F + F_c)' - (G + G_c)'L' \end{bmatrix} \times \begin{bmatrix} P & 0 \\ 0 & S \end{bmatrix} + \begin{bmatrix} P & 0 \\ 0 & S \end{bmatrix} \times \begin{bmatrix} (A + A_c - BK) & BKM \\ 0 & (F + F_c) - L(G + G_c) \end{bmatrix} \right\} \times \begin{bmatrix} X \\ \tilde{Z} \end{bmatrix}. \tag{33}$$

Since a matrix and its transpose have the same spectrum, we can instead work with the $[(F + F_c) - L(G + G_c)]'$ matrix for the rest. Continuing, we obtain

$$\frac{d}{dt}\mathscr{L}[(X, \tilde{Z})] = \begin{bmatrix} X \\ \tilde{Z} \end{bmatrix}'$$

$$\times \begin{bmatrix} A'P + PA - K'B'P - PBK + PA_c + A_c'P & PBKM \\ M'K'B'P & [(F + F_c) - L(G + G_c)]S + S[(F + F_c) - L(G + G_c)]' \end{bmatrix}$$

$$\times \begin{bmatrix} X \\ \tilde{Z} \end{bmatrix}. \tag{34}$$

Using the control and observer Ricatti equations in the above matrices,

$$\frac{d}{dt}\mathscr{L}[(X, \tilde{Z})] = \begin{bmatrix} X \\ \tilde{Z} \end{bmatrix}'$$

$$\times \begin{bmatrix} -PBR^{-1}B'P - 2\mu P - Q + PA_c + A_c'P & K'RKM \\ M'K'B'P & -\bar{Q} - SG'GS - 2\sigma S + (F_c - LG_c)S + S(F_c - LG_c) \end{bmatrix}$$

$$\times \begin{bmatrix} X \\ \tilde{Z} \end{bmatrix}$$

$$= \begin{bmatrix} X \\ \tilde{Z} \end{bmatrix}' \begin{bmatrix} \Delta_c & -K'RKM \\ M'K'RK & \Delta_0 \end{bmatrix} \begin{bmatrix} X \\ \tilde{Z} \end{bmatrix} < 0 \quad \text{if} \quad \Omega > 0.$$

Therefore, if $\Omega > 0$, the system as a whole is exponentially stable (Anderson [6]). It converges as fast as the slowest subsystem with rate μ. Positive definiteness of the block matrix Ω, in terms of its component matrices Δ_c and Δ_0, is not known yet and is a fruitful area of investigation.

IV. PERFORMANCE DETERIORATION

It was stated earlier that one is trading optimality with other system properties such as reliability, subsystem autonomy, reduced computation, complexity reduction in communication links, and other side benefits of a decentralized structure. It is of practical importance from an engineering aspect to find out how much system performance deviates from an optimal solution which is centralized. Several measures of suboptimality can be used (Siljak [7]); here we suffice with only cost increments ΔJ, where ΔJ is the difference in cost between the centralized and decentralized cases. Note that several sources of errors are introduced and have to be treated separately. First, we recall from standard LQR theory that even in the optimal centralized case, introduction of observers causes some reduction in performance due to incorrect observer initial conditions. Second, the local subsystem controllers ignore the interconnection matrix in the Ricatti equations, hence controller gains are incorrect for the whole system. The third source of error is the dual problem, that is, the local observer gains are also incorrect for the system as a whole (Friedland [8]). These cases are treated separately to separate out the different effects. In the following derivations, it is assumed that conditions of Theorem 2 are satisfied such that an overall closed-loop stable system is obtained. Since suboptimality arises from using locally optimal gains, equations are repeated here for easy reference:

$$K = R^{-1}B'P, \qquad (35)$$

$$(A + \mu I)'P + P(A + \mu I) + Q - PBR^{-1}B'P = 0, \qquad (36)$$

$$L = SG', \tag{37}$$

$$S(F + \sigma I)' + (F + \sigma I)S + \overline{Q} - SG'GS = 0. \tag{38}$$

The corresponding optimal centralized control and observer gains are similarly obtained from

$$K_c = R^{-1}B'P_c, \tag{39}$$

$$(A + A_c + \mu I)'P_c + P_c(A + A_c + \mu I) + Q - P_cBR^{-1}B'P_c = 0, \tag{40}$$

$$L_c = S_c(G + G_c)', \tag{41}$$

$$S_c(F + F_c + \sigma I)' + (F + F_c + \sigma I)S_c + \overline{Q} - S_c(G + G_c)'(G + G_c)S = 0. \tag{42}$$

Note that K and L are block diagonal matrices but K_c and L_c are not. First, suppose that all states are accessible and observers are not needed and we apply the control input

$$U = -KX \tag{43}$$

to the system instead of the optimal control which has gain K_c; the closed-loop system is

$$\dot{X} = (A + A_c - BK)X. \tag{44}$$

Now, assuming that this control is stabilizing, the performance index is

$$J_1 = X'(0)P_1X(0), \tag{45}$$

where P_1 satisfies

$$(A + A_c + \mu I - BK)'P_1 + P_1(A + A_c + \mu I - BK) + (Q + K'RK) = 0. \tag{46}$$

Under centralized control with gain K_c, the cost would be

$$J_2 = X'(0)P_cX(0), \tag{47}$$

with P_c satisfying

$$(A + A_c + \mu I - BK_c)'P_c + P_c(A + A_c + \mu I - BK_c) + \left(Q + K_c'RK_c\right)$$
$$= 0, \tag{48}$$

which is, of course, a rearrangement of the control Ricatti equation for P_c. The dual of Eq. (46) for the state reconstruction problem is also

$$S_1[(F + F_c) - L(G + G_c)]' + [(F + F_c) - L(G + G_c)]S_1$$
$$+ (\bar{Q} + LL') = 0. \tag{49}$$

So far we have equations for costs incurred when decentralized gains are used in an otherwise interconnected system separately for control and estimation problems. Now, if a centrally designed observer is used in an optimal control system, it introduces additional cost due to incorrect observer initial conditions. It is straightforward to show that the new cost of the centralized observer – controller is given by

$$J_3 = X'(0)P_cX(0) + \tilde{Z}_0'M'\Gamma_c(22)M\tilde{Z}_0, \tag{50}$$

where $\tilde{Z}_0$ is the error in the observer initial conditions and $\Gamma_c(22)$ are the (22) elements of the following equation:

$$\bar{A}_c'\Gamma_c + \Gamma_c\bar{A}_c + \bar{Q}_c = 0, \tag{51}$$

where $\bar{A}_c$ is the closed-loop system matrix

$$\bar{A}_c = \begin{bmatrix} A + A_c - BK_c & BK_cM \\ 0 & (F + F_c) - L_c(G + G_c) \end{bmatrix}$$

and (52)

$$\bar{Q}_c = \begin{bmatrix} Q + K_c'RK_c & -K_c'RK_cM \\ -M'K_c'RK_c & M'K_c'RK_cM \end{bmatrix}.$$

It can be shown that $\Gamma_c(11) = P_c$, $\Gamma_c(12) = \Gamma_c(21) = 0$, and $\Gamma_c(22)$ satisfies

$$\Gamma_c(22)[(F + F_c) - L_c(G + G_c)] + [(F + F_c) - L_c(G + G_c)]'\Gamma_c(22) + M'K_c'RK_cM = 0. \tag{53}$$

Now let us use the decentralized gains K and L for the observer–controller system. Clearly we get the same closed-loop system matrix but with K and L instead:

$$\bar{A}'\Gamma + \Gamma\bar{A} + \bar{Q} = 0, \tag{54}$$

$$\bar{A} = \begin{bmatrix} A + A_c - BK & BKM \\ 0 & (F + F_c) - L(G + G_c) \end{bmatrix}, \qquad \bar{Q} = \begin{bmatrix} Q + K'RK & -K'RKM \\ -M'K'RK & M'K'RKM \end{bmatrix}. \tag{55}$$

Writing the above in component form and assuming stable $\bar{A}$, we obtain

$$\Gamma(11)(A + A_c - BK) + (A + A_c - BK)'\Gamma(11) + (Q + K'RK) = 0, \tag{56}$$

taking into account the exponential stability condition that is initially imposed. This modifies $(A + A_c - BK)$ to $(A + A_c + \mu I - BK)$, and by uniqueness of Eq. (54) for Γ, we conclude that $\Gamma(11) = P_1$. The uniqueness follows from stability of the closed-loop system matrix and noting that $\Gamma(11)$ and P_1 satisfy similar equations. Considering the (12) element of Γ,

$$\Gamma(12)[(F + F_c) - L(G + G_c)] + (A + A_c + \mu I - BK)'\Gamma(12) + [\Gamma(11) - P]BKM = 0. \tag{57}$$

Also, the (22) element is obtained from

$$\Gamma(22)[(F + F_c) - L(G + G_c)] + [(F + F_c) - L(G + G_c)]'\Gamma(22)$$
$$+ [PM + \Gamma(12)]'BR^{-1}B'[PM + \Gamma(12)]$$
$$- \Gamma(21)BR^{-1}B'\Gamma(12) = 0. \quad (58)$$

Therefore the final performance index when the decentralized observer–controller is used is given by

$$J = X'(0)P_1X(0) + 2\tilde{Z}'(0)M'\Gamma(12)X(0) + \tilde{Z}'(0)M'\Gamma(22)M\tilde{Z}(0). \quad (59)$$

Note that costs are now separated. If optimal centralized controller gains are used instead of K, L, we obtain $P = P_c = P_1$, which implies that $\Gamma(12) = \Gamma'(21) = 0$ and $\Gamma_c(22) = \Gamma(22)$ and $J = J_3$. If states are accessible or observer initial conditions are correct, that is, $\tilde{Z}(0) = 0$, we obtain $J = J_1$; if $K = K_c$, then $J = J_2$. Cost increments can also be obtained directly from the following derivations. Let

$$\Delta J \triangleq J_3 - J. \quad (60)$$

That is, we compare the centralized and decentralized observer–controller systems directly. Correspondingly, define

$$\Delta\Gamma \triangleq \Gamma_c - \Gamma, \quad \Delta K \triangleq K_c - K, \quad \Delta L \triangleq L_c - L. \quad (61)$$

Then ΔJ can be expressed in terms of elements of $\Delta\Gamma$:

$$\Delta\Gamma(11)(A + A_c + \mu I - BK) + (A + A_c + \mu I - BK)'\Delta\Gamma(11)$$
$$+ \Delta K'\left[RK_c - B'\Gamma_c(11)\right] + \left[RK_c - B'\Gamma_c(11)\right]'$$
$$- \Delta K - \Delta K'R\,\Delta K = 0. \quad (62)$$

Since $P_c = \Gamma_c(11)$ and $K_c = R^{-1}B'P_c$, we have that $\Delta P = \Delta\Gamma(11)$, where ΔP uniquely satisfies

$$\Delta P(A + A_c - \mu I - BK)$$
$$+ (A + A_c + \mu I - BK)\,\Delta P - \Delta K'R\,\Delta K = 0. \quad (63)$$

Note that $\Delta P \triangleq P_c - P_1$ and represents error in P_c when K is used instead of K_c:

$$\Delta\Gamma(12)[(F + F_c) - L(G + G_c)] + (A + A_c + \mu I - BK)' \Delta\Gamma(12) - (P_1 - P)BKM = 0, \tag{64}$$

$$\Delta\Gamma(22)[(F + F_c) - L(G + G_c)] + [(F + F_c) - L(G + G_c)]' \Delta\Gamma(22) + M'K_c'RK_cM - M'K'RKM - M'K'B'\Gamma(12) - \Gamma(21)BKM = 0. \tag{65}$$

Finally, the cost increment is

$$\Delta J = X'(0) \Delta\Gamma(11)X(0) + 2\tilde{Z}'(0)M\Gamma(12)X(0) + \tilde{Z}'(0)M' \Delta\Gamma(22)M\tilde{Z}(0). \tag{66}$$

Again note that when optimal gains are used, that is, $K_c = K$ and $L_c = L$, we have $P = P_1 \Rightarrow \Delta P = 0 \Rightarrow \Delta\Gamma(11) = 0$ and $\Delta\Gamma(12) = 0$. Also, $\Delta\Gamma(12) = 0 \Rightarrow \Delta\Gamma(22) = 0 \Rightarrow \Delta\Gamma = 0 \Rightarrow \Delta J = 0$ and $J = J_3$, which is the optimal performance.

V. CONCLUSIONS

The performance deterioration due to decentralized design can be used in actual design setting to determine the preferred structure. If observation and communication costs required for a centralized implementation including computer storage and computation cost are more than ΔJ, then a decentralized structure might be preferable if the system coupling matrix A_c satisfies conditions for stability under decentralized control. In general, comparisons between structures cannot be made more specific and will depend upon several specific costs, design specifications, and other criteria, but the above computations may serve as a basic guideline. This is the same for general LQR-based design, which is usually used as a guideline and measure with which alternative designs which have to meet other constraints are compared. The above design methods can be refined further by using other suboptimality measures.

REFERENCES

1. B. SHAHIAN, "Large Scale Systems: "Decentralized Control and Estimation Using Observers," Ph.D. in Engineering, University of California, Los Angeles (1981).

2. D. G. LUENBERGER, "Observing the State of a Linear System," *IEEE Trans. Military Electronics MIL-8*, 74-80, April 1964.

3. D. D. SILJAK, "Multilevel Stabilization of Large-Scale Systems," *Automatica 12*, 309-320 (1976).

4. M. K. SUNDARESHAN, "Decentralized Observation in Large-Scale Systems," *IEEE Trans. Syst. Man, Cybern. SMC-7*, 868-867, December 1977.

5. D. D. SILJAK and M. K. SUNDARESHAN, "Large-Scale Systems: Optimality vs. Reliability," *in* "Directions in Large-Scale Systems," (Y. C. Ho and S. K. Mitter, eds.), Plenum Press, New York, 1976.

6. B. D. O. ANDERSON and J. B. MOORE, "Linear Optimal Control," Prentice-Hall, Englewood Cliffs, New Jersey, 1971.

7. D. D. SILJAK and R. KROTOLICA, "Suboptimality of Decentralized Stochastic Control and Estimation," *IEEE Trans. Autom. Control AC-25*, No. 1, February 1980.

8. B. FRIEDLAND, "On the Effect of Incorrect Gain in Kalman Filter," *Corresp. Trans. Autom. Control*, October 1967.

System Zeros in the Decentralized Control of Large-Scale Systems

THOMAS A. KENNEDY

Design Analysis Department
Advanced Programs Division
Radar Systems Group
Hughes Aircraft Company
Los Angeles, California 90009

LIST OF ABBREVIATIONS

SZ	System zeros
DZ	Decoupling zeros
IDZ	Input decoupling zeros
ODZ	Output decoupling zeros
IODZ	Input – output decoupling zeros
TZ	Transmission zeros
IZ	Invariant zeros
SZ_i	ith channel system zeros
DZ_i	ith channel decoupling zeros
IDZ_i	ith channel input decoupling zeros
ODZ_i	ith channel output decoupling zeros
$IODZ_i$	ith channel input – output decoupling zeros
TZ_i	ith channel transmission zeros
IZ_i	ith channel invariant zeros
DSZ	Decentralized system zeros
DDZ	Decentralized decoupling zeros
DIDZ	Decentralized input decoupling zeros
DODZ	Decentralized output decoupling zeros
DIODZ	Decentralized input – output decoupling zeros
DTZ	Decentralized transmission zeros
DIZ	Decentralized invariant zeros
$IODZ_{ij}$	Input – output decoupling zeros of the triple (A, B_i, C_j)

LIST OF SYMBOLS

R	Real number field
C	Complex number field
C_o^-	Left-half-open complex plane

C^+	Right-half-closed complex plane
k'	The set of integers {1, ..., k}
Im	Image
β	Im B
Re	Real part
$\lVert\cdot\rVert$	Norm
$\langle\cdot, \cdot\rangle$	Inner product
$+$	Direct sum
$\cup$	Union
$\cap$	Intersection
$\subset$	Inclusion
$\langle\cdot\vert\cdot\rangle$	$\langle A\vert\beta\rangle$ is the controllable subspace of (A, B)
$\sigma(\cdot)$	$\sigma(A)$ is the spectrum of A
$W(\cdot)$	$W(A)$ is the numerical range of A
$*$	Indicates complex conjugate transpose (A^*)
T	Indicates transpose (A^T)
$\in$	$x \in R$, x is an element of R
$\forall$	For all
det	Determinant
diag	Diagonal
$\emptyset$	Empty set
inf	Greatest lower bound
$\perp$	Indicates orthogonal complement ($R^{\perp}$)

I. INTRODUCTION

Over the last decade, interest in the control and stabilization of large-scale systems has increased tremendously. The reason for this interest is that there are many complex physical systems in the world today and to realistically describe the behavior of these systems, one ends up with a high-dimensional model. Examples of large-scale systems that have been studied extensively include electric power systems [44,11], socioeconomic systems [59,4], chemical process control [19], information flow networks [51,1], traffic flow [26,27], and river pollution control [58,56]. In addition, with the advent of the Space Transportation System (Space Shuttle) and its ability to carry large structures into space, there has been a surge of research in the control and stabilization of large space structures [6,42].

Conventional modern control theory has been used extensively to design control laws for these large-scale systems. Some of the modern control theory techniques that were applied to these systems when the system states were available for feedback include linear–quadratic (LQ) optimal control [5] and pole placement [65]. Whenever it was impossible to instrument the system such that full state feedback was possible, Kalman filters [41,40] or Luenburger observers [38] were used to obtain estimates of the state variables. The main problem with all of these techniques is that they are based on a centralized control strategy. A centralized control strategy is a feedback control law for which every observed output affects every control input. This centralized control strategy results in a large number of interconnections or feedback loops. As the dimensionality of the system increases, so does the number of feedback loops. In many cases it is impossible to implement so many feedback loops. For example, electric power system generators are distributed over vast geographical regions. These generators are interconnected via hundreds of miles of high-voltage transmission lines. This physical separation makes it impractical and uneconomical to centrally monitor or control the interconnected power system.

As a result of the increased cost and complexity in applying centralized control laws to large-scale systems, and in view of the fact that the increased capability of microprocessors has significantly reduced the cost of distributed processing, a concept called decentralization has received a great deal of attention in control literature. Decentralized control systems have several local control stations or channels. At each station the controller observes only local system outputs and controls only local inputs. Thus the number of interconnections is greatly reduced.

Although the theory of centralized control has been well developed, direct application of its techniques in a decentralized strategy has had little success. The main reason for this difficulty is that the implementation of a decentralized control strategy results in varying degrees of information transfer between controllers. This reduction in communication of state variable information results in what is called a nonclassical information pattern [64].

II. ZEROS OF LINEAR MULTIVARIABLE SYSTEMS

A. *INTRODUCTION*

The zeros of a plant have played a crucial role in the classical design of single input – single output (SISO) feedback systems since the early 1950s. Rules were developed using graphical techniques, root loci, bode plots, Nichols charts, and Nyquist contours to obtain a desired response of the closed-loop SISO system [14]. Each of these methods requires a knowledge of the system zeros.

A plant was defined to be a minimum phase system if its zeros were in the left-half-closed complex plane. If the plant had zeros with positive real parts, the system was defined to be nonminimum phase [18]. Nonminimum phase SISO plants place a restriction on the allowable magnitude of feedback gain that can be tolerated and still maintain a closed-loop stable system. This is so since the open-loop root loci terminate at the system zeros and, as the feedback gain increases, the closed-loop system poles approach the system zeros along the loci.

Recent developments in multivariable systems theory [49,52,45] have brought a resurgence of interest in the zeros of multi input – multi output (MIMO) systems. Some of these developments were the results of studies in the area of noninteracting control, which result in decoupled systems [66]. In addition, work in disturbance rejection [63,46], parameter uncertainty [53], and cheap control [35,28,20,21] have indirectly enhanced the interest in multivariable zeros since these techniques result in high-gain feedback structures. It has been shown by Kouvaritakis and Shaked [33] that when high-gain output feedback is applied to a system, the zeros of the system "trap" some of the closed-loop characteristic frequencies as the gain approaches infinity, while the remaining poles tend to infinity. Many of the feedback design techniques for SISO systems, root locus, and Nyquist contours have been extended for MIMO systems [39]. As a result, various definitions of multivariable system zeros have been proposed [48–50,39].

Since this study investigates the use of high gain in a decentralized control law, a definition is proposed in Section II,B for the decentralized zeros of a system. The relationship of these zeros to the fixed modes of a decentralized system is also examined in this section.

B. DECENTRALIZED ZEROS

Although a considerable amount of research has been focused on on the centralized zeros of a system, little effort has been focused on the decentralized zeros of a system. The concept of decentralized zeros is crucial to this study since the decentralized control laws to be developed incorporate a decentralized high-gain feedback structure. As shown in [47], stabilizability of the system Σ under a high-gain decentralized control structure depends on the location of the decentralized transmission zeros and fixed modes of the system.

The model that will be used to define the decentralized zeros of a system Σ is a k-channel linear multivariable continuous time-invariant system defined by

$$\dot{x}(t) = Ax(t) + Bu(t) \tag{1a}$$

and

$$y(t) = Cx(t), \tag{1b}$$

where $x(t) \in R^n$, $u(t) \in R^m$, $A \in R^{n\times n}$, $B \in R^{n\times m}$, $y(t) \in R^q$, and $C \in R^{q\times n}$, with

$$B = [B_1, B_2, \ldots, B_k] \in R^{n\times m}, \tag{1c}$$

$$C = \left[C_1^T, C_2^T, \ldots, C_k^T\right]^T \in R^{q\times n}, \tag{1d}$$

$$u(t) = \left[u_1^T(t), u_2^T(t), \ldots, u_k^T(t)\right] \in R^m, \tag{1e}$$

$$y(t) = \left[y_1^T(t), y_2^T(t), \ldots, y_k^T(t)\right] \in R^q, \tag{1f}$$

where $B_i \in R^{n\times m_i}$, $C_i \in R^{q_i\times n}$, $m = \Sigma_{i=1}^k m_i$, and $q = \Sigma_{i=1}^k q_i$.

In this section and in the remainder of this study, a feedback control for the system Σ is defined to be decentralized if each local control u_i depends only on the local measurement y_i

for its implementation; that is,

$$u_i(t) = K_i y_i(t) \qquad (i = 1, \ldots, k), \tag{2}$$

where $K_i \in R^{m_i \times q_i}$. Thus the feedback gain for the closed-loop system is block diagonal:

$$K = \text{block diag}[K_1, K_2, \ldots, K_k] \in R^{m \times q}. \tag{3}$$

To maintain a similarity between centralized zeros and decentralized zeros, the structure of the definitions will be similar to those defined in [48–50]. The ith channel of the nondegenerate system Σ with k channels defined by Eq. (1) can be represented after Laplace transformation with zero initial conditions by the Rosenbrock polynomial matrix description [48] as follows:

$$P_i(s)\begin{bmatrix} x(s) \\ u_i(s) \end{bmatrix} = \begin{bmatrix} sI_n - A & -B_i \\ C_i & 0 \end{bmatrix}\begin{bmatrix} x(s) \\ u_i(s) \end{bmatrix} = \begin{bmatrix} 0 \\ y_i(s) \end{bmatrix}, \tag{4}$$

where $P_i(s)$ is the $(n + q_i) \times (n + m_i)$ ith channel polynomial system matrix. The oth channel is defined as the centralized system (i.e., $q_o = q$, $m_o = m$, $B_o = B$, $C_o = C$, K_o = centralized feedback gain matrix).

Definition 1. The complex scalar s is called an ith *channel system zero* (SZ_i) of the $(n + q_i) \times (n + m_i)$ polynomial matrix $P_i(s)$ if det $R_i(s) = 0$, where $R_i(s)$ is the monic greatest common divisor of all minors

$$P_i\begin{pmatrix} 1, 2, \ldots, n, n + i_1, n + i_2, \ldots, n + i_k \\ 1, 2, \ldots, n, n + j_1, n + j_2, \ldots, n + j_k \end{pmatrix} \tag{5}$$

and where k has a maximum value v such that $0 \leq v \leq \min(q_i, m_i)$ and such that at least one minor of that order is not identically zero.

Definition 2. The complex scalar s is called a *decentralized system zero* (DSZ) of the system Σ defined by Eqs. (1) if s is an element of the union of sets of ith channel system zeros for i = 1, ..., k:

$$\{DSZ\} = \left\{ s: s \in C,\ s \in \bigcup_{i=1}^{k} \{\text{ith channel system zeros}\} \right\}. \tag{6}$$

Definition 3.

(i) The complex scalar s is called an ith *channel input decoupling zero* (IDZ_i) of the system Σ defined by Eqs. (1) if

$$\operatorname{rank}[sI_n - A,\ B_i] < n. \tag{7}$$

(ii) An equivalent definition for an ith channel input decoupling zero (IDZ_i) is that, given $s \in C$, there exists a vector $v \in C^n$ such that the transpose of v, v^T, is a left-hand eigenvector of A, such that

$$v^T[sI_n - A,\ B_i] = 0. \tag{8}$$

The vector v is called an ith channel zero-input direction vector.

Definition 4. The complex scalar s is called a *decentralized input decoupling zero* (DIDZ) of the system Σ described by Eqs. (1) if s is an element of the union of sets of the ith channel input decoupling zeros for i = 1, ..., k:

$$\{DIDZ\} = \left\{ s: s \in C,\ s \in \bigcup_{i=1}^{k} \{\text{ith channel input decoupling zeros}\} \right\}. \tag{9}$$

Definition 5.

(i) The complex scalar s is called an ith *channel output decoupling zero* (ODZ_i) of the system Σ defined by Eqs. (1) if

$$\operatorname{rank}\begin{bmatrix} sI_n - A \\ C_i \end{bmatrix} < n. \tag{10}$$

(ii) An equivalent definition for an ith channel output decoupling zero (ODZ_i) is that, given $s \in C$, there exists a vector $\chi \in C^n$, where χ is an eigenvector of A such that

$$\begin{bmatrix} sI_n - A \\ C_i \end{bmatrix} \chi = 0. \tag{11}$$

The vector χ is called an ith channel zero-output direction vector.

Definition 6. The complex scalar s is called a *decentralized output decoupling zero* (DODZ) of the system Σ described by Eqs. (1) if s is an element of the union of sets of ith channel output decoupling zeros for i = 1, ..., k:

$$\{DODZ\} = \left\{ s: s \in C,\ s \in \bigcup_{i=1}^{k} \{\text{ith channel output decoupling zeros}\} \right\}. \tag{12}$$

Definition 7. The complex scalar s is called a *decentralized input–output decoupling zero* (DIODZ) of the system Σ described by Eqs. (1) if

$s \in \{DIDZ\} \cap \{DODZ\}$,

$$\{DIODZ\} = \{s: s \in C,\ s \in \{DIDZ\} \cap \{DODZ\}\}. \tag{13}$$

Definition 8. The complex scalar s is called an ith *channel transmission zero* (TZ_i) of the system Σ described by Eqs. (1) if s is a zero of the numerator polynomials of the Smith–McMillan [30] form of $G_i(s)$, where $G_i(s)$ is the ith channel transfer function matrix

$$G_i(s) = C_i\left(sI_n - A\right)^{-1}B_i. \tag{14}$$

A definition for the decentralized transmission zeros of the system Σ governed by Eqs. (1) and (2) can be determined by reformatting the closed-loop characteristic equation

$$\Phi(s) = \det[sI_n - A - gBKC], \tag{15}$$

where $u(t) = gKy(t)$, in terms of relatively right and left prime polynomial matrices for the cases $q_i \geq m_i$ and $m_i \geq q_i$ ($i = 1, \ldots, k$), respectively. It is assumed that the triple (A, B, C) is controllable, observable, and nondegenerate [11], but in general the triples (A, B_i, C_i) ($i = 1, \ldots, k$) may be uncontrollable and unobservable.

Case 1: $q_i \geq m_i$ ($i = 1, \ldots, k$)

The characteristic polynomial (15) can be expressed in terms of relatively right prime polynomial matrix factors (two polynomial matrices with the same number of columns that only have unimodular common right divisors) of the $q \times m$ system transfer function matrix

$$G(s) = C(sI_n - A)^{-1}B = V(s)T^{-1}(s); \tag{16}$$

$$q \geq m, \quad q = \sum_{i=1}^{k} q_i, \quad m = \sum_{i=1}^{k} m_i, \tag{17}$$

where V(s) is a $q \times m$ relatively right prime polymial matrix and T(s) is an $m \times m$ relatively right prime polynomial matrix. Since the zeros of the characteristic polynomial (15) are equivalent to the zeros of

$$\Phi(s) = \det\left[(sI_n - A) - gB(I_m)^{-1}KC\right] \det[I_m], \tag{18}$$

Shur's formula [22] can be used to obtain the equivalent determinant

$$\Phi(s) = \det[sI_n - A] \det\left[I_m - gKC(sI_n - A)^{-1}B\right], \tag{19}$$

which, by invoking Eq. (16), is equivalent to

$$\Phi(s) = \det[T_o(s)] \det\left[I_m - gKV(s)T^{-1}(s)\right], \tag{20}$$

where

$$\det[T_o(s)] = \det[sI_n - A]$$

is the open-loop characteristic polynomial. Since it was assumed that the triple (A, B, C) is controllable and observable, G(s) is irreducible [30], so

$$\det[T_o(s)] = \det[T(s)];$$

therefore

$$\Phi(s) = \det[T(s)] \det\left[I_m - gKV(s)T^{-1}(s)\right], \tag{21}$$

which, since T(s) is a square polynomial matrix, is equivalent to

$$\Phi(s) = \det[T(s) - gKV(s)]. \tag{22}$$

Now, applying the formula for the explicit form of the characteristic polynomial [22] to Eq. (21), it can be shown that

$$\Phi(s) = (-1)^m g^m \det[KV(s)] + \left\{s^n + \sum_{j=0}^{n-1} \alpha_j(g) s^j\right\}, \tag{23}$$

where $\deg \alpha_j(g) \leq \min(n - j, m - 1)$.

Case 2: $m_i \geq q_i$ *(i = 1, ..., k)*

For this case, the characteristic polynomial (15) can be expressed in terms of relatively left prime polynomial matrix factors (two polynomial matrices with the same number of rows that only have a unimodular common left divisor) of the $q \times m$ system transfer function matrix

$$G(s) = C(sI_n - A)^{-1}B = S^{-1}(s)U(s), \tag{24}$$

where $q = \Sigma_{i=1}^k q_i$, $m = \Sigma_{i=1}^k m_i$, S(s) is a $q \times q$ relatively left prime polynomial matrix, and U(s) is a $q \times m$ relatively left prime polynomial matrix. Recalling the closed-loop characteristic polynomial

$$\Phi(s) = \det[sI_n - A - gBKC] \tag{25}$$

and representing it in the equivalent form

$$\Phi(s) = \det\left[sI_n - A - gBK(I_q)^{-1}C\right] \det[I_q], \tag{26}$$

Shur's formula [22] can be used to obtain the equivalent determinant

$$\Phi(s) = \det[sI_n - A] \det\left[I_q - gC(sI_n - A)^{-1}BK\right]. \tag{27}$$

Now, by substituting Eq. (24) into Eq. (27), the following is obtained:

$$\Phi(s) = \det[S_o(s)] \det\left[I_q - gS^{-1}(s)U(s)K\right], \tag{28}$$

where $\det[S_o(s)] = \det[sI_n - A]$ is the open-loop characteristic polynomial. Given that the triple (A, B, C) is controllable and observable, G(s) is irreducible [30], so $\det[S_o(s)] = \det[S(s)]$, which results in the following:

$$\Phi(s) = \det[S(s)] \det\left[I_q - gS^{-1}(s)U(s)K\right]. \tag{29}$$

Since S(s) is a square polynomial matrix,

$$\Phi(s) = \det[S(s) - gU(s)K]. \tag{30}$$

Now, applying the formula for the explicit form of the characteristic polynomial [22] to Eq. (29), it can be shown that

$$\Phi(s) = (-1)^q g^q \det[U(s)K] + \left\{s^n + \sum_{j=0}^{n-1} B_j(s)s^j\right\}, \tag{31}$$

where $\deg \beta_j(g) < \min(n - j, q - 1)$. From Eqs. (23) and (31), it is obvious that as g approaches infinity, the finite closed-loop characteristic roots are zeros of the polynomials

$$\psi(s) = \det[KV(s)], \quad q \geq m \tag{32}$$

and

$$\chi(s) = \det[U(s)K], \quad m \geq q \tag{33}$$

provided that $\det[KV(s)] \neq 0$ and $\det[U(s)K] \neq 0$ for the cases $q \geq m$ and $m \geq q$, respectively.

Since the system Σ was assumed to be controllable and observable,

$$G(s) = C(sI_n - A)^{-1}B = V(s)T^{-1}(s), \quad q \geq m, \tag{34a}$$

$$G(s) = C(sI_n - A)^{-1}B = S^{-1}(s)U(s), \quad m \geq q \tag{34b}$$

is a minimal realization; therefore G(s) is irreducible, so the zeros of G(s) are equivalent to the zeros of the Smith forms of V(s) and U(s) for the cases $q \geq m$ and $m \geq q$, respectively [30].

For the case when the feedback matrix K belongs to the set K', where

$$K' = \{K: K \in R^{m\times q}, \text{ rank } K = \min(m, q)\}, \tag{35}$$

using the definition of centralized transmission zeros [49] and the definition of the Smith forms of V(s) and U(s), an alternate definition of the centralized transmission zeros is as follows.

(1) $q \geq m$:

$$\{TZ\} = \{s: s \in C, \text{ rank } V(s) < m\}. \tag{36}$$

(2) $m \geq q$:

$$\{TZ\} = \{s: s \in C, \text{ rank } U(s) < q\}. \tag{37}$$

When K' is restricted to be the set of decentralized feedback gains

$$K' = \left\{K: K = \text{block diag}[K_1, K_2, \ldots, K_k], K_i \in R^{m_i\times q_i}, \quad i = 1, \ldots, k\right\}, \tag{38}$$

V(s) and U(s) can be represented in the forms

$$V(s) = \begin{bmatrix} V_1(s) \\ V_2(s) \\ \vdots \\ V_k(s) \end{bmatrix}, \quad V_i(s) \in R^{q_i\times m} \quad (i = 1, \ldots, k) \tag{39}$$

and

$$U(s) = [U_1(s), U_2(s), \ldots, U_k(s)], \quad U_i(s) \in R^{q\times m_i} \quad (i = 1, \ldots, k). \tag{40}$$

Since the normal rank of $V_i(s) = m_i$ and the normal rank of $U_i(s) = q_i$, rank $V(s) < m$ when rank $V_i(s) < m_i$ and rank $U(s) < q$ when rank $U_i(s) < q_i$.

Defining the set

(1) $q_i \geq m_i$:

$$T_i = \{s\colon s \in C, \text{ rank } V_i(s) < m_i\} \qquad (i = 1, \ldots, k); \tag{41}$$

(2) $m_i \geq q_i$:

$$T_i = \{s\colon s \in C, \text{ rank } U_i(s) < q_i\} \qquad (i = 1, \ldots, k); \tag{42}$$

a definition for decentralized transmission zeros can be given as follows.

Definition 9. The complex scalar s is called *decentralized transmission zero* (DTZ) of the system Σ defined by Eqs. (1) if $s \in \{DTZ\}$, where

$$\{DTZ\} = \{TZ\} \cup T_1 \cup T_2 \cup \cdots \cup T_k. \tag{43}$$

Porter [47] first proposed a definition of decentralized transmission zeros similar to Definition 9 but with the restriction that $q_i \leq m_i$ for $i = 1, \ldots, k$.

Definition 10. The complex scalar s is called an ith *channel invariant zero* (IZ_i) of the system Σ described by Eqs. (1) if s is an element of the set of zeros of the polynomials $\{a_j(s)\colon j = 1, 2, \ldots, r_i\}$, where

$$r_i = \text{rank } P_i(s)$$

and

$$M_i(s) = \begin{bmatrix} \text{diag}[a_j(s)] & 0 \\ 0 & 0 \end{bmatrix}, \qquad j = 1, 2, \ldots, r_i \tag{44}$$

is the Smith form [22,24,30] of the ith channel polynomial matrix description $P_i(s)$.

Definition 11. The complex scalar s is called a *decentralized invariant zero* (DIZ) of the system Σ described by Eqs. (1) if s is an element of the union of sets of ith channel decentralized invariant zeros for i = 1, ..., k:

$$\{DIZ\} = \{s: s \in C, s \in \cup\{\text{ith channel invariant zeros}\}\}. \quad (45)$$

In summary, the following six sets of decentralized zeros have been defined for the system Σ governed by Eqs. (1):

(1) the set {DSZ} of decentralized system zeros,

(2) the set {DIDZ} of decentralized input decoupling zeros,

(3) the set {DODZ} of decentralized output decoupling zeros,

(4) the set {DIODZ} of decentralized input—output decoupling zeros,

(5) the set {DTZ} of decentralized transmission zeros, and

(6) the set {DIZ} of decentralized invariant zeros.

The next four theorems link the definitions of decentralized zeros to the concepts of controllability and observability.

Theorem 1. The set of decentralized input decoupling zeros is equivalent to the empty set

$$\{DIDZ\} = \emptyset$$

if and only if the system Σ is controllable from every ith channel, i = 1, ..., k.

Proof. Follows directly from the definition of centralized input decoupling zeros [48–50] and Definitions 3 and 4.

Theorem 2. The set of decentralized output decoupling zeros is equivalent to the empty set

$$\{DODZ\} = \emptyset$$

if and only if the system is observable from every ith channel, $i = 1, \ldots, k$.

Proof. Follows directly from the definition of centralized output decoupling zeros [48–50] and Definitions 5 and 6.

Theorem 3. If the system Σ described by Eqs. (1) is uncontrollable, then

$$\bigcap_{i=1}^{k} \{IDZ_i\} \neq \emptyset.$$

Proof. Given Σ is uncontrollable,

$$\operatorname{rank}[sI_n - A, B] < n \text{ for some } s \in C, \text{ say, } s_1$$

$$\Rightarrow \operatorname{rank}[s_1 I_n - A, B_i] < n \text{ for } s_1 \quad (i = 1, \ldots, k)$$

$$\Rightarrow s_1 \in \{IDZ_i\} \quad (i = 1, \ldots, k)$$

$$\Rightarrow s_1 \in \bigcap_{i=1}^{k} \{IDZ_i\}$$

$$\Rightarrow \bigcap_{i=1}^{k} \{IDZ_i\} \neq \emptyset. \quad \text{Q.E.D.}$$

Theorem 4. If the system Σ described by Eqs. (1) is unobservable, then

$$\bigcap_{i=1}^{k} \{ODZ_i\} \neq \emptyset.$$

Proof. Given Σ is unobservable,

$$\operatorname{rank}\begin{bmatrix} sI_n - A \\ C \end{bmatrix} < n \quad \text{for some} \quad s \in C, \text{ say, } s_1$$

$$\Rightarrow \operatorname{rank}\begin{bmatrix} s_1 I_n - A \\ C_i \end{bmatrix} < n \quad \text{for} \quad s_1 \quad (i = 1, \ldots, k)$$

$$\Rightarrow s_1 \in \{ODZ_i\} \quad (i = 1, \ldots, k)$$

$$\Rightarrow s_1 \in \bigcap_{i=1}^{k} \{ODZ_i\}$$

$$\Rightarrow \bigcap_{i=1}^{k} \{ODZ_i\} \neq \emptyset. \quad \text{Q.E.D.}$$

Note that, in general

$$\bigcap_{i=1}^{k} \{IDZ_i\} \neq \emptyset \not\Rightarrow \text{uncontrollability of } \Sigma,$$

$$\bigcap_{i=1}^{k} \{ODZ_i\} \neq \emptyset \not\Rightarrow \text{unobservability of } \Sigma.$$

The following example illustrates this fact.

Example 1. Consider the following three-channel system:

$$A = \begin{bmatrix} 1 & & & 0 \\ & 3 & & \\ 0 & & 3 & \\ & & & 2 \end{bmatrix}, \quad B = \begin{bmatrix} 0 & 0 & 1 \\ 1 & 0 & 0 \\ 0 & 1 & 0 \\ 1 & 0 & 0 \end{bmatrix} = [B_1, B_2, B_3],$$

$$C = \begin{bmatrix} 0 & 0 & 1 & 0 \\ 1 & 0 & 0 & 1 \\ 0 & 1 & 0 & 0 \end{bmatrix} = \begin{bmatrix} C_1 \\ C_2 \\ C_3 \end{bmatrix}.$$

The triple (A, B, C) is jointly controllable and observable. However,

$$\{IDZ_1\} = \{1, 3\}, \qquad \{ODZ_1\} = \{1, 3, 2\};$$

$$\{IDZ_2\} = \{1, 3, 2\}, \qquad \{ODZ_2\} = \{3, 3\};$$

$$\{IDZ_3\} = \{3, 3, 2\}, \qquad \{ODZ_3\} = \{1, 3, 2\}.$$

Thus

$$\bigcap_{i=1}^{3} \{IDZ_i\} = \{3\}, \qquad \bigcap_{i=1}^{3} \{ODZ_i\} = \{3\}.$$

As Example 1 shows, the fact that a system is jointly controllable and observable does not imply that

$$\bigcap_{i=1}^{k} \{IDZ_i\} = \emptyset, \qquad \bigcap_{i=1}^{k} \{ODZ_i\} = \emptyset.$$

This is so since the definitions of decentralized decoupling zeros do not allow for distinction between eigenvalues of the open-loop system that have the same value. The following two theorems apply for the restricted case when the system matrix A has distinct eigenvalues.

Theorem 5. Let the system Σ defined by Eqs. (1) have distinct eigenvalues. The system Σ is uncontrollable if and only if

$$\bigcap_{i=1}^{k} \{IDZ_i\} \neq \emptyset.$$

Proof. The "if" part: Given the system Σ has distinct eigenvalues and

$$\bigcap_{i=1}^{k} \{IDZ_i\} \neq \emptyset,$$

this implies there exists an $s \in \sigma(A)$ such that

$$v^T[sI_n - A, B_i] = 0 \qquad (i = 1, \ldots, k),$$

where v^T is a left eigenvector of the system matrix A. This implies that

$$v^T[sI_n - A, B_1, B_2, \ldots, B_k] = 0$$

$$\Rightarrow v^T[sI_n - A, B] = 0$$

which can be rewritten as

$$sv^T = v^TA, \quad v^TB = 0.$$

Therefore,

$$v^T AB - sv^T B = 0,$$

$$v^T A^2 B = sv^T AB = 0,$$

and

$$v^T A^{n-1} B = sv^T A^{n-2} B = 0,$$

so

$$v^T [B \cdot AB \cdots A^{n-1} \cdot B] = 0,$$

which means that the controllability matrix is singular. Thus the system is uncontrollable.

The "only if" part: follows directly from Theorem 3. Q.E.D.

Theorem 6. Let the system Σ defined by Eqs. (1) have distinct eigenvalues. The system Σ is observable if and only if

$$\bigcap_{i=1}^{k} \{ODZ_i\} \neq \emptyset.$$

Proof. The "if" part: Given the system Σ has distinct eigenvalues and

$$\bigcap_{i=1}^{k} \{ODZ_i\} \neq \emptyset,$$

this implies there exists an $s \in \sigma(A)$ such that

$$\begin{bmatrix} sI_n - A \\ C_i \end{bmatrix} \chi = 0 \quad (i = 1, \ldots, k),$$

where χ is an eigenvector of the system matrix A. This implies that

$$\begin{bmatrix} sI_n - A \\ C_1 \\ C_2 \\ \vdots \\ C_k \end{bmatrix} \chi = 0$$

$$\Rightarrow \begin{bmatrix} sI_n - A \\ C \end{bmatrix} \chi = 0,$$

or, equivalently,

$$s\chi = A\chi, \quad C\chi = 0.$$

Therefore,

$$\begin{aligned} sC\chi &= CA\chi = 0, \\ sCA\chi &= CA^2\chi = 0, \\ sCA^2\chi &= CA^2\chi = 0, \\ &\vdots \\ sCA^{n-2}\chi &= CA^{n-2}\chi = 0, \end{aligned}$$

so

$$\begin{bmatrix} C \\ CA \\ CA^2 \\ \vdots \\ CA^{n-1} \end{bmatrix} \chi = 0,$$

which implies that the observability matrix is singular. Thus the system is unobservable.

The "only if" part: follows directly from Theorem 4. Q.E.D.

The decentralized transmission zeros play a crucial role in determining if a system governed by Eqs. (1) can be stabilized via decentralized high-gain feedback. It is obvious from Eqs. (23)–(31) and Definition 9 that, as $g \to \infty$, the finite roots of the closed-loop characteristic polynomial are the decentralized transmission zeros for the case $K \in K'$, where

$$K' = \Big\{K: K = \text{block diag}[K_1, K_2, \ldots, K_k], \quad K_i \in R^{m_i \times q_i} \quad (i = 1, \ldots, k)\Big\}. \tag{46}$$

Note that the set of centralized transmission zeros is a subset of the set of decentralized transmission zeros. This is so since the transmission zeros of a system are invariant to static state and output feedback [48–50].

From the above discussion, the following lemma is apparent.

Lemma 1. The jointly controllable and observable system Σ governed by Eqs. (1) is stabilizable by decentralized high-gain output feedback as $g \to \infty$ if and only if

$$\{DTZ\} \subset C_o^-,$$

where $\{DTZ\}$ is the set of decentralized transmission zeros and C_o^- is the left-half-open complex plane.

Lemma 1 hints that the fixed modes of a system Σ subjected to decentralized high-gain output feedback are a subset of the set of decentralized transmission zeros, $\{DTZ\}$. The definition of the fixed modes found in Davison and Wang [13] will be repeated here so that it can be shown that when the system Σ is subjected to decentralized high-gain output feedback, the fixed modes of the system are a subset of the decentralized transmission zeros.

Definition 12. Given the triple (A, B, C) and the set of feedback gains

$$K' = \Big\{K\colon K = \text{block diag}[K_1, K_2, \ldots, K_k],\ K_i \in R^{m_i \times q_i},$$
$$K \in R^{m \times q}, \quad (i = 1, \ldots, k)\Big\}, \tag{47}$$

the set of fixed modes with respect to K' is defined as follows:

$$\Lambda(A, B, C, K) = \bigcap_{K \in K'} \{s\colon s \in C,\ \det[sI_n - A - BKC] = 0\}. \tag{48}$$

Observing that $\det[sI_n - A - BKC]$ is the closed-loop characteristic polynomial and g is a scalar, Theorem 7 follows immediately.

Theorem 7. The set of fixed modes $\Lambda(A, B, C, K)$ of the controllable, observable, and nondegenerate triple (A, B, C) under high-gain decentralized output feedback is given by

$$\Lambda(A, B, C, K) = \{s: s \in C, \det[sI_n - A] = 0\} \cap \{DTZ\}, \tag{49}$$

where {DTZ} is the set of decentralized transmission zeros.

Proof. From Eqs. (22) and (30), the characteristic polynomial equation

$$\Phi(s) = \det[sI_n - A - gBKC]$$

is equivalent to

$$\Phi(s) = \det[T(s) - gKV(s)] \quad \text{for} \quad q \geq m$$

and

$$\Phi(s) = \det[S(s) - gU(s)K] \quad \text{for} \quad m \geq q,$$

where

$$\det[T(s)] = \det[S(s)] = \det[sI_n - A].$$

Thus, under the limiting condition $g \to 0$, the set of fixed modes is a subset of the spectrum of A, $\sigma(A)$, where

$$\sigma(A) = \{s: s \in C, \det[sI_n - A] = 0\},$$

and from Eqs. (23) and (31),

$$\Phi(s) = (-1)^m g^m \det[KV(s)] + \left\{s^n + \sum_{j=0}^{n-1} \alpha_j(g) s^j\right\} \quad \text{for} \quad q \geq m,$$

where $\deg \alpha_j(g) \leq \min(n - j, m - 1)$ and

$$\Phi(s) = (-1)^q g^q \det[u(s)K] + \left\{s^n + \sum_{j=0}^{n-1} \beta_j(g) s^j\right\} \quad \text{for} \quad m \geq q,$$

where $\deg \beta_j(g) \leq \min(n - j, q - 1)$.

Under the limiting condition $g \to \infty$,

$$\Lambda(A, B, C, K) = \bigcap_{K \in K'} \{s: s \in C, \det[KV(s) = 0\}$$

$$= \bigcap_{K \in K'} \{s: s \in C, \text{rank } KV(s) < m\} \quad \text{for} \quad q \geq m$$

and

$$\Lambda(A, B, C, K) = \bigcap_{K \in K'} \{s: s \in C, \det[U(s)K] = 0\}$$

$$= \bigcap_{K \in K'} \{s: s \in C, \text{rank } U(s)K < q\} \quad \text{for} \quad m \geq q,$$

which, by Definitions 9 and 12, implies that

$$\Lambda(A, B, C, K) \subset \{DTZ\}.$$

Therefore, combining the two limiting conditions $g \to 0$ and $g \to \infty$,

$$\Lambda(A, B, C, K) = \{DTZ\} \cap \{s: s \in C, \det[sI_n - A] = 0\}$$

$$= \{DTZ\} \cap \sigma(A),$$

where $\sigma(A)$ is the spectrum of the matrix A. Q.E.D.

The next three corollaries follow directly from Theorem 7.

Corollary 1. If $\{DTZ\} = \emptyset$, then $\Lambda(A, B, C, K) = \emptyset$.

Corollary 2. If $\sigma(A) \cap \{DTZ\} = \emptyset$, then $\Lambda(A, B, C, K) = \emptyset$.

Corollary 3. If $\{DTZ\} \subset C_o^-$, then $\Lambda(A, B, C, K) \subset C_o^-$.

Porter [47] first defined Theorem 7 and Corollaries 1, 2, 3 for the case $m \geq q$. They have been extended here for the case $q \geq m$.

As shown by Lemma 1, the decentralized transmission zeros are crucial in determining the stability properties of the system Σ subject to decentralized high-gain output feedback. Theorem 7 and Corollaries 1, 2, 3 indicate that

$$\Lambda(A, B, C, K) \subset C_o^-$$

does not imply that the system Σ is stabilizable for a decentralized high-gain output feedback control law.

III. SINGLE-CHANNEL CONTROLLABILITY AND OBSERVABILITY

A. *INTRODUCTION*

In Section II, the concept of multivariable system zeros was extended to decentralized systems. In this section, the decentralized system zeros of a multivariable system will be shown to be crucial in determining conditions for local output feedbacks to exist such that the resulting closed-loop system is controllable and observable from a specified single channel.

The purpose of this section is to develop explicit conditions, in terms of the decentralized zeros of a multivariable system, such that a two-channel decentralized system can be made controllable and observable through a specified single channel. For the case when a system cannot be made controllable and observable through a specified single channel, conditions are developed in terms of the decentralized zeros to determine if the system can be made stabilizable and detectable through a specified single channel.

B. *BACKGROUND*

The effects of decentralized feedback on the closed-loop properties of k-channel, jointly controllable, and jointly observable linear systems was first addressed by Corfmat and Morse [9,10] and later by Fessas [16,17]. In [9], the concept of a complete system, a system which can be made controllable and observable through a single channel, was introduced for two-channel systems ($k = 2$). Later, in [10], the concept of a complete system was generalized to a k-channel system with $k \geq 2$. This generalization was based on the completeness of certain subsystems of Σ. These subsystems were termed complementary subsystems.

To describe these complementary subsystems of a linear time-invariant k-channel system Σ and the concept of completeness, consider the k-channel system governed by the following equations:

$$\dot{x}(t) = Ax(t) + \sum_{i=1}^{k} B_i u_i(t),$$
$$y_i(t) = C_i(t)x(t), \quad i \in k' \equiv \{1, \ldots, k\}, \tag{50}$$

where $u_i(t)$ and $y_i(t)$ are, respectively, the vectors of control input and measured output associated with channel i, and

$$x(t) \in R^n, \; y_i(t) \in R^{q_i}, \; u_i(t) \in R^{m_i}, \; A \in R^{n\times n}, \; B_i \in R^{n\times m_i},$$

and $C_i \in R^{q_i\times n}$. The total system's constant input and output matrices are

$$B = [B_1, B_2, \ldots, B_k], \quad B \in R^{n\times m}, \quad m = \sum_{i=1}^{k} m_i$$

and

$$C = \left[C_1^T, C_2^T, \ldots, C_k^T\right]^T, \quad C \in R^{q\times n}, \quad q = \sum_{i=1}^{k} q_i, \tag{51}$$

respectively. It is assumed that Σ is a jointly controllable and jointly observable system, that is,

$$\left\langle A \,\middle|\, \sum_{i=1}^{k} \beta_i \right\rangle = X = R^{n\times n},$$

$$\left\langle A^T \,\middle|\, \sum_{i=1}^{k} \mathrm{Im}\; C_i^T \right\rangle = X = R^{n\times n},$$

where $\beta_i = \mathrm{Im}\; B_i = \text{image } B_i$. Note that joint controllability and joint observability of Σ does not imply controllability and observability of the triple (A, B_i, C_i), $i \in k'$.

Definition 13. The system Σ is said to be single-channel controllable and observable if there exists local nondynamic controls of the form

$$u_i(t) = F_i y_i(t) + v_i(t), \tag{52}$$

where $F_i \in R^{m_i \times q_i}$, $v_i(t) \in R^{m_i}$, such that the resulting closed-loop system,

$$\dot{x}(t) = \left(A + \sum_{i=1}^{k} B_i F_i C_i\right) x(t) + \sum_{i=1}^{k} B_i v_i(t),$$

$$y_i(t) = C_i x(t), \quad i \in k', \tag{53}$$

is both controllable and observable through a single channel, say, j.

As mentioned earlier, Corfmat and Morse first introduced the concept of completeness for the case k = 2. In Corollary 4 of [9], Corfmat and Morse showed that their definition of completeness was equivalent to the following definition.

Definition 14 [9]. A triple (A, B, C) with $C(\lambda I_n - A)^{-1}B \neq 0$ (nondegenerate) is complete if

$$\text{rank } P(\lambda) = \text{rank}\begin{bmatrix} \lambda I_n - A & B \\ C & 0 \end{bmatrix} \geq n \quad \text{for all} \quad \lambda \in \sigma(A), \tag{54}$$

where $\sigma(A)$ is the spectrum of A.

From the definitions of invariant zeros and decoupling zeros in [48–50], the following lemmas are obvious.

Lemma 2. A triple (A, B, C) is complete if the pair (A, B) is controllable.

Proof. The pair (A, B) is controllable if and only if

$$\text{rank}[\lambda I_n - A, B] = n \quad \text{for all} \quad \lambda \in \sigma(A).$$

Thus (A, B) controllable implies

$$\text{rank } P(\lambda) \geq n \quad \text{for all} \quad \lambda \in \sigma(A).$$

So, by Definition 13, the triple (A, B, C) is complete. Q.E.D.

Lemma 3. A triple (A, B, C) is complete if the pair (A, C) is observable.

Proof. The pair (A, C) is observable if and only if

$$\text{rank}\begin{bmatrix} \lambda I_n - A \\ C \end{bmatrix} = n \quad \text{for all} \quad \lambda \in \sigma(A).$$

Thus (A, C) observable implies

$$\text{rank } P(\lambda) \geq n \quad \text{for all} \quad \lambda \in \sigma(A).$$

So by Definition 13 the triple (A, B, C) is complete. Q.E.D.

From the definition of invariant zeros [49], each $\lambda \in \sigma(A)$ that does not satisfy Eq. (54) is an invariant zero of the triple (A, B, C). Furthermore, using Lemmas 2 and 3 and the definitions of input and output decoupling zeros, it can be shown that any $\lambda \in \sigma(A)$ that does not satisfy Eq. (54) is an input–output decoupling zero.

Lemma 4. Given the triple (A, B, C) with $C(\lambda I_n - A)^{-1}B \neq 0$ if $\lambda \in \sigma(A)$ and

$$\text{rank}\begin{bmatrix} \lambda I_n - A & B \\ C & 0 \end{bmatrix} < n,$$

then $\lambda \in \{IDZ\} \cap \{ODZ\}$.

Proof. By contradiction. Assume

$$\lambda \notin \{IDZ\} \cap \{ODZ\}$$
$$\Rightarrow \lambda \notin \{IDZ\} \quad \text{or} \quad \lambda \notin \{ODZ\}.$$

By definition, if $\lambda \notin \{IDZ\}$, this implies that

$$\text{rank}[\lambda I_n - A, B] = n$$

$$\Rightarrow \text{rank } P(\lambda) = \text{rank}\begin{bmatrix} \lambda I_n - A & B \\ C & 0 \end{bmatrix} \geq n.$$

But by assumption, rank $P(\lambda) < n$, so $\lambda \notin \{IDZ\}$. By definition, if $\lambda \notin \{ODZ\}$, then

$$\operatorname{rank}\begin{bmatrix} \lambda I_n - A \\ C \end{bmatrix} = n$$

$$\Rightarrow \operatorname{rank} P(\lambda) = \operatorname{rank}\begin{bmatrix} \lambda I_n - A & B \\ C & 0 \end{bmatrix} \geq n.$$

But by assumption, rank $P(\lambda) < n$, so $\lambda \in \{ODZ\}$. Combining the above results,

$$\lambda \in \{ODZ\} \cap \{IDZ\} \quad \text{if} \quad \operatorname{rank} P(\lambda) \quad n. \qquad \text{Q.E.D.}$$

The following corollary of Corfmat and Morse [9] gives the necessary and sufficient conditions for decentralized control of a two-channel system, $k = 2$, governed by Eqs. (50) and (51) with the assumption that

$$\langle A | \beta_1 + \beta_2 \rangle = X = R^{n \times n},$$

which implies that the uncontrollable modes of channel i are the controllable modes of channel j ($i, j \in \{1, 2\}$, $i \neq j$), and the assumption

$$C(sI_n - A)^{-1}B \neq 0,$$

which implies that the triple (A, B, C) is nondegenerate.

Corollary 4 [9]. Given $\langle A \mid \beta_1 + \beta_2 \rangle = X$ and $C_i(sI_n - A)^{-1}B_j \neq 0$, there exists a map F_i such that

$$\langle A + B_i F_i C_i | \beta_j \rangle = X, \quad i \neq j, \quad i, j \in \{1, 2\}$$

if and only if the triple (A, B_j, C_i) is complete.

Proof. See [9].

In order to generalize the concept of completeness for a k-channel system with $k \geq 2$, Corfmat and Morse introduced the definition of a complementary subsystem. To describe these complementary subsystems for k-channel systems, consider the following notation: let v be a nonempty subset of k', $k' \equiv \{i: i = 1, \ldots, k\}$, with elements $i_1, i_2, \ldots, i_p$ ordered such that $i_1 < i_2 < \cdots < i_p$, and then define B_v and C_v to be

$$B_v = [B_{i_1} \quad B_{i_2} \quad \cdots \quad B_{i_p}],$$
$$C_v = \begin{bmatrix} C_{i_1}^T & C_{i_2}^T & \cdots & C_{i_p}^T \end{bmatrix}^T. \tag{55}$$

Thus (A, B_{v_1}, C_{v_2}) is a subsystem of Σ which models the relationship between channel inputs u_i, $i \in v_1$, and channel outputs y_j, $j \in v_2$. (A, B_{v_1}, C_{v_2}) is called a complementary subsystem of Σ if v_1 is a proper subset of k' and if $v_2 = k' - v_1$: a complementary subsystem $(A, B_v, C_{k'-v})$ is said to contain input channel j if $j \in v$.

Now, defining a k-channel system to be complete whenever all its comlementary subsystems are complete, the following theorem from Corfmat and Morse [10] can be stated.

Theorem 8 [10]. Let Σ be a jointly controllable and jointly observable k-channel system with $k \geq 2$, described by Eqs. (50) and (51), and let $j \in k'$ be fixed. There exists a nondynamic feedback matrix $F \in F'$, where

$$F' = \left\{F: F = \text{block diag}[F_1, F_2, \ldots, F_k],\ F_i \in R^{m_i \times q_i},\right.$$
$$\left.\sum_{i=1}^{k} m_i = m,\ \sum_{i=1}^{k} q_i = q,\ F \in R^{m \times q}\right\}$$

such that

$$\langle A + BFC | \beta_j \rangle = X$$

and

$$\left\langle (A + BFC)^T | \operatorname{Im}\left(C_j^T\right) \right\rangle = X$$

if and only if Σ is complete.

Proof. See Theorem 1 [10].

In [16] Fessas developed necessary and sufficient conditions for a two-channel system to be controllable and observable from a single channel based on certain properties of the system polynomial matrices. Later in [17] Fessas extended these results to k-channel systems using graph theoretic methods, such as strong connectedness. In [17] it was shown that Fessas's necessary and sufficient conditions for single-channel controllability and observability are algebraically equivalent to those of Corfmat and Morse as described above.

A subject that is tied closely to the concept of single-channel controllability and observability are the fixed modes in decentralized control. In Section II, the definition of the fixed modes of a decentralized system [13] was given. Recently, Anderson and Clements [2] presented algebraic characterizations for the existence of fixed modes of a linear closed-loop system with decentralized feedback control. It is interesting to note that this characterization of fixed modes of a decentralized system [2] uses the concept of complementary subsystems discussed previously with the minor change that some of the channels are assumed not to have feedback. Additionally, the rank condition on $P(\lambda)$ used to determine if a decentralized system is complete in Theorem 8 is used in Anderson and Clements' theorem. However, the condition $C_{v_1}(sI_n - A)^{-1}B_{v_2} \neq 0$ is not required. This means that although an information exchange is necessary between complementary subsystems for a decentralized system to be controllable and observable from a single channel, the lack of this condition does not necessarily mean that the system has fixed modes. The link between single-channel controllability and observability and the following theorem on fixed modes will be discussed further in the next section.

Theorem 9 [2]. Consider the system (50)–(51) with control law (52) for i = 1, ..., k - 1. A necessary and sufficient condition for

$$\left[\lambda I_n - A - \sum_{i=1}^{k-1} B_i F_i C_i\right]$$

to have rank < n - α for all F_i, some fixed complex λ, and non-negative α, $\alpha \geq 0$, is that for some partition of the set {1, ..., k - 1} into disjoint subsets $\{i_1, \ldots, i_r\}$ and $\{i_{r+1}, \ldots, i_{k-1}\}$, the following is satisfied:

$$\operatorname{rank}\begin{bmatrix} \lambda I_n - A & B_{i_1} & \cdots & B_{i_r} \\ C_{i_{r+1}} & 0 & \cdots & 0 \\ \vdots & & \ddots & \\ C_{i_{k-1}} & 0 & \cdots & 0 \end{bmatrix} < n - \alpha.$$

Proof. See [2].

Because α can be set to zero in Theorem 9 and from Lemma 4, the following corollary is obvious.

Corollary 5. Given the assumptions of Theorem 9, if for some fixed $\lambda \in C$

$$\left[\lambda I_n - A - \sum_{i=1}^{k-1} B_i F_i C_i\right]$$

has rank <n for all F_i, then

$\lambda \in \{IDZ\} \cap \{ODZ\}$

of some triple (A, B_{v_1}, C_{v_2}), where for some partition of the set {1, ..., k - 1} into disjoint subsets $v_1 = \{i_1, \ldots, i_r\}$

and $v_2 = \{i_{r+1}, \ldots, i_{k-1}\}$,

$$B_{v_1} = [B_{i_1} \cdots B_{i_r}], \quad C_{v_2} = \begin{bmatrix} C_{i_{r+1}} \\ \vdots \\ C_{i_{k-1}} \end{bmatrix}.$$

Proof. Follows directly from Theorem 9 and Lemma 4.

C. *PROBLEM STATEMENT AND PRELIMINARIES*

The problem of this section is, given the jointly controllable and jointly observable two-channel ($k = 2$) linear system Σ described by Eqs. (50) and (51), to find conditions, based on the decentralized decoupling zeros of Σ, for the existence of an output feedback matrix $F \in F'$:

$$F' = \left\{ F\colon F = \text{block diag}[F_1, F_2, \ldots, F_k], \right.$$
$$\left. F_i \in R^{m_i \times q_i},\ F \in R^{m \times q},\ \sum_{i=1}^{k} m_i = m,\ \sum_{i=1}^{k} q_i = q \right\} \quad (56)$$

such that

$$\langle A + BFC \mid \beta_i \rangle = X \quad (57)$$

and

$$\langle (A + BFC)^T \mid \operatorname{Im}(C_i^T) \rangle = X \quad (58)$$

for $i \in k' \equiv \{i\colon i = 1, \ldots, k\}$, where $\beta_i \equiv \text{image } B_i = \operatorname{Im} B_i$ and $X = R^{n \times n}$.

In other words, using the concept of decentralized decoupling zeros, find conditions for the existence of a decentralized nondynamic output feedback such that a two-channel system can be made controllable and observable from a single channel.

In general, it will be assumed that the triple (A, B_i, C_i), $i \in k'$, $k' = \{i: i = 1, \ldots, k\}$, is uncontrollable and unobservable. However, it will be assumed that

$$\operatorname{rank} C_i = q_i, \quad \operatorname{rank} B_i = m_i.$$

Since this chapter uses the concept of decentralized decoupling zeros to determine conditions for single-channel controllability and observability, the following definitions from Section II for the ith channel input and output decoupling zeros will be repeated here for convenience.

Definition 15. The zero $z \in C$ is called an ith channel input decoupling zero (IDZ_i) of the system Σ defined by Eqs. (50) and (51) if

$$\operatorname{rank}[zI_n - A, B_i] < n \quad \text{for} \quad z \in \sigma(A).$$

Definition 16. The zero $z \in C$ is called an ith channel output decoupling zero (ODZ_i) of the system Σ defined by Eqs. (50) and (51) if

$$\operatorname{rank}\begin{bmatrix} zI_n - A \\ C_i \end{bmatrix} < n \quad \text{for} \quad z \in \sigma(A).$$

From Definition 14 on completeness and Lemmas 2 and 3, which relate completeness to controllability and observability, the following is obvious.

Lemma 5. Given $C_j(zI_n - A)^{-1}B_i \neq 0$, the triple (A, B_i, C_j), $i, j \in k'$, is complete if either

$$\{IDZ_i\} = \emptyset, \quad i, j \in k',$$

or

$$\{ODZ_j\} = \emptyset, \quad i, j \in k'.$$

Proof. Given $C_j(zI_n - A)^{-1}B_i \neq 0$,

(i) $\{IDZ_i\} = \emptyset$

$$\Rightarrow \text{rank}[zI_n - A,\ B_i] = n \quad \text{for all} \quad z \in \sigma(A)$$

$$\Rightarrow \text{rank}\ P(z) = \text{rank}\begin{bmatrix} zI_n - A & B_i \\ C_j & 0 \end{bmatrix}$$

$$\geq n \quad \forall z \in \sigma(A)$$

$\Rightarrow$ (A, B_i, C_j) is complete.

(ii) $\{ODZ_j\} = \emptyset$

$$\Rightarrow \text{rank}\begin{bmatrix} zI_n - A \\ C_j \end{bmatrix} = n \quad \forall z \in \sigma(A)$$

$$\Rightarrow \text{rank}\ P(z) \geq n \quad \forall z \in \sigma(A)$$

$\Rightarrow$ (A, B_i, C_j) is complete. Q.E.D.

Thus, as will be shown throughout this chapter, decentralized decoupling zeros play a crucial role in determining system completeness. Note that in general

$$z \in \{IDZ_i\} \cap \{ODZ_j\}$$

does not imply that

$$\text{rank}\ P_{ij}(z) < n.$$

As discussed in Section II, the definitions of output decoupling and input decoupling zeros can be ambiguous when dealing with systems that possess nondistinct eigenvalues. The following example illustrates this point.

Example 2. Consider the two-channel system

$$A = \begin{bmatrix} -1.0 & 0 & 0 & 0 \\ -1.0 & -2.0 & 0 & 0 \\ 1.0 & 0 & -1.0 & 0 \\ 0 & 1.0 & -1.0 & -2.0 \end{bmatrix},$$

$$B_1 = \begin{bmatrix} 1 \\ 0 \\ 0 \\ 0 \end{bmatrix}, \quad B_2 = \begin{bmatrix} 0 \\ 0 \\ 1 \\ 0 \end{bmatrix},$$

$$C_1 = \begin{bmatrix} 1 & 0 & 0 & 0 \\ 0 & 1 & 0 & 0 \end{bmatrix}, \quad C_2 = \begin{bmatrix} 0 & 0 & 1 & 0 \\ 0 & 0 & 0 & 1 \end{bmatrix}.$$

We have

$$\{ODZ_1\} = \{-1.0, -2.0\},$$

$$\{IDZ_2\} = \{-1.0, -2.0\}.$$

Therefore,

$$\{-1.0, -2.0\} = \{IDZ_2\} \cap \{ODZ_1\}$$

However,

$$P_{21}(\lambda) = \begin{bmatrix} \lambda I_n - A & B_2 \\ C_1 & 0 \end{bmatrix} = 4 = n \quad \text{for} \quad \lambda = -1.0, -2.0$$

In order to circumvent this ambiguity, an extended definition for decoupling zeros will be developed in the following discussion.

Consider the controllability matrices of the triple (A, B_i, C_j) and its dual system $\left(A^T, C_j^T, B_i^T\right)$:

$$Q_i = \left[B_i, AB_i, \ldots, A^{n-1}B_i\right], \tag{59}$$

$$P_j = \left[C_j^T, A^TC_j^T, \ldots, A^{T(n-1)}C_j^T\right], \tag{60}$$

where n is the system state dimension. It can be shown via the Cayley–Hamilton theorem that $R(Q_i)$, the subspace of all controllable states of channel i, and $R(P_j)^{\perp}$, the subspace of all unobservable states of channel j, are invariant subspaces of A. Using the above invariance property of the controllable subspace and unobservable subspace, it has been shown [67] that a canonical transformation exists such that the state of the system described by the triple (A, B_i, C_j) can be decomposed into four distinct sectors. The first sector is completely controllable and completely observable; the second group of entries is controllable but not observable; the third group is observable but not controllable; and the last entries correspond to states neither controllable nor observable. Thus the state equations for the triple (A, B_i, C_j), $i, j = (1, 2)$, $i \neq j$,

$$\dot{x} = Ax + B_i u, \tag{61}$$

$$y_i = C_j x, \tag{62}$$

can be rewritten in the form

$$\dot{x}' = A'x' + B_i u, \tag{63}$$

$$y_i = C_j x', \quad i, j = (1, 2), \quad i \neq j, \tag{64}$$

where

$$A' = \begin{bmatrix} A_{co} & 0 & A_{13} & 0 \\ A_{21} & A_{c\bar{o}} & A_{23} & A_{24} \\ 0 & 0 & A_{\bar{c}o} & 0 \\ 0 & 0 & A_{43} & A_{\bar{c}\bar{o}} \end{bmatrix},$$

$$B_i' = \begin{bmatrix} B_{ico} \\ B_{ic\bar{o}} \\ 0 \\ 0 \end{bmatrix}, \tag{65}$$

$$C_j' = [C_{co} \quad 0 \quad C_{\bar{c}o} \quad 0],$$

and the state vector x' is partitioned as

$$x' = \begin{bmatrix} x_{co} \\ x_{c\bar{o}} \\ x_{\bar{c}o} \\ x_{\bar{c}\bar{o}} \end{bmatrix}. \tag{66}$$

The states represented by x_{co} are controllable and observable; the states of $x_{c\bar{o}}$ are controllable but not observable; the states of $x_{\bar{c}o}$ are uncontrollable but observable; and the states of $x_{\bar{c}\bar{o}}$ are uncontrollable and unobservable. From Eq. (65), it is obvious that

$$(A') = \sigma(A_{co}) \cup \sigma(A_{c\bar{o}}) \cup \sigma(A_{\bar{c}o}) \cup \sigma(A_{\bar{c}\bar{o}}). \tag{67}$$

Assuming this two-channel system is jointly controllable and observable,

$$\left\langle A \mid \beta_i + \beta_j \right\rangle = X = R^{n\times n},$$

$$\left\langle A^T \mid \mathrm{Im}\left(C_i^T\right) + \mathrm{Im}\left(C_j^T\right)\right\rangle = X = R^{n\times n}.$$

The transformation matrix T that transforms the triple (A, B_i, C_j) into the system described by Eq. (65) can be applied to B_j and C_i, yielding

$$B_j' = T^{-1}B_j = \begin{bmatrix} B_{jco} \\ B_{jc\bar{o}} \\ B_{j\bar{c}o} \\ B_{j\bar{c}\bar{o}} \end{bmatrix},$$

$$C_i' = C_iT = [C_{ico} \quad C_{ic\bar{o}} \quad C_{i\bar{c}o} \quad C_{i\bar{c}\bar{o}}]. \tag{68}$$

Now, applying channel j and channel i feedback of the form

$$u_k = F_k y_k, \quad k = i, j \tag{69}$$

to the system (63)–(65), the polynomial matrix description of the closed-loop system, assuming zero initial conditions, is

$$P_{ijCL}(s)\begin{bmatrix} x(s) \\ u(s) \end{bmatrix} = \begin{bmatrix} sI_n - A_{CL}' & -B_i' \\ C_j' & 0 \end{bmatrix}\begin{bmatrix} x(s) \\ u(s) \end{bmatrix} = \begin{bmatrix} 0 \\ y(s) \end{bmatrix}. \tag{70}$$

The closed-loop polynomial matrix description $P_{ijCL}(s)$ can be shown, using properties of partioned matrices [22], to be equivalent to

$$P_{ijCL}(s) = \begin{bmatrix} I_1 & 0 & 0 & 0 & -B_{jco}F_j \\ 0 & I_2 & 0 & 0 & -B_{jc\bar{o}}F_j \\ 0 & 0 & I_3 & 0 & -B_{j\bar{c}o}F_j \\ 0 & 0 & 0 & I_4 & -B_{j\bar{c}\bar{o}}F_j \\ 0 & 0 & 0 & 0 & I_5 \end{bmatrix}$$

$$\times \begin{bmatrix} s - A_{co} & 0 & -A_{13} & 0 & -B_{ico} \\ -A_{21} & s - A_{c\bar{o}} & -A_{23} & -A_{24} & -B_{ic\bar{o}} \\ 0 & 0 & s - A_{\bar{c}o} & 0 & 0 \\ 0 & 0 & -A_{43} & s - A_{\bar{c}\bar{o}} & 0 \\ C_{co} & 0 & C_{j\bar{c}o} & 0 & 0 \end{bmatrix}$$

$$\times \begin{bmatrix} I_1 & 0 & 0 & 0 & 0 \\ 0 & I_2 & 0 & 0 & 0 \\ 0 & 0 & I_3 & 0 & 0 \\ 0 & 0 & 0 & I_4 & 0 \\ F_iC_{ico} & F_iC_{ic\bar{o}} & F_iC_{i\bar{c}o} & F_iC_{i\bar{c}\bar{o}} & I_5 \end{bmatrix}, \qquad (71)$$

where I_i, $i = 1, \ldots, 5$, is an appropriately dimensioned identity matrix. It can be shown from Eq. (71) that

$$\text{rank } P_{ijCL}(s) = \text{rank } P_{ij}(s), \qquad (72)$$

which implies that the invariant factors of $P_{ijCL}(s)$ are equivalent to the invariant factors of $P_{ij}(s)$. Using the property of partitioned matrices [22] and row and column permutation, the following equivalence holds:

$$P_{ij}(s) \sim \begin{bmatrix} s - A_{co} & 0 & -B_{co} & 0 & 0 \\ -A_{21} & s - A_{c\bar{o}} & -B_{c\bar{o}} & 0 & 0 \\ 0 & 0 & 0 & s - A_{\bar{c}o} & 0 \\ C_{co} & 0 & 0 & C_{\bar{c}o} & 0 \\ 0 & 0 & 0 & 0 & s - A_{\bar{c}\bar{o}} \end{bmatrix} \qquad (73)$$

since the pair

$$\begin{bmatrix} A_{co} & 0 \\ A_{21} & A_{c\bar{o}} \end{bmatrix}, \begin{bmatrix} B_{co} \\ B_{c\bar{o}} \end{bmatrix}$$

is controllable:

$$\begin{bmatrix} s - A_{co} & 0 & -B_{co} \\ -A_{21} & s - A_{c\bar{o}} & -B_{c\bar{o}} \end{bmatrix} \sim \begin{bmatrix} I_1 & 0 & 0 \\ 0 & I_2 & 0 \end{bmatrix}.$$

Also, since $(A_{\bar{c}o}, C_{\bar{c}o})$ is observable,

$$\begin{bmatrix} s - A_{\bar{c}o} \\ C_{\bar{c}o} \end{bmatrix} \sim \begin{bmatrix} I_3 \\ 0 \end{bmatrix}.$$

Consequently,

$$P_{ij}(s) \sim \begin{bmatrix} I_1 & 0 & 0 & 0 & 0 \\ 0 & I_2 & 0 & 0 & 0 \\ 0 & 0 & 0 & I_3 & 0 \\ 0 & 0 & 0 & 0 & 0 \\ 0 & 0 & 0 & 0 & s - A_{\overline{co}} \end{bmatrix}. \tag{74}$$

Thus all $s \in C$ such that $s \in \sigma(A_{\overline{co}})$ are invariant factors of $P_{ij}(s)$ and s is an input – output decoupling zero of the triple (A, B_i, C_j). Since $s \in \sigma(A_{\overline{co}})$ implies $s \in \sigma(A)$, the following lemma is apparent.

Lemma 6. Given the decomposition of the triple (A, B_i, C_j), $i, j = 1, 2$, $i \neq j$, of Eq. (65) for the two-channel jointly controllable and jointly observable system (63)–(64), $s \in C$ is a fixed mode of the system if $s \in \sigma(A_{\overline{co}})$.

Proof. Given $s \in \sigma(A_{\overline{co}})$ implies by definition that $s \in \sigma(A)$. From Eq. (74) it is obvious that $s \in (A_{\overline{co}})$ is an input – output decoupling zero of the triple (A, B_i, C_j). Thus for all constant feedback matrices F_1, F_2,

$$s \in \sigma(A + B_1F_1C_1 + B_2F_2C_2),$$

and since $s \in \sigma(A)$, by definition s is a fixed mode of the two-channel system. Q.E.D.

The next definition uses the results discussed above and will be used in the following sections.

Definition 17. Given the decomposition of the triple (A, B_i, C_j) described by Eq. (65), if $s \in C$ such that $s \in \sigma(A_{\overline{co}})$, then s is called an ij input–output decoupling zero:

$s \in \{IODZ_{ij}\}$.

A review of Example 2 indicates that

$\{IDZ_2\} \cap \{IODZ_{21}\} = \emptyset$,

$\{ODZ_1\} \cap \{IODZ_{21}\} = \emptyset$.

Note that $\{IODZ_{ij}\} \neq \emptyset$ implies that

$$\langle A|\beta_i\rangle + \left\langle A^T|\mathrm{Im}\left(C_j^T\right)\right\rangle \subset R^{n\times n}.$$

In other words, it is impossible to form a basis for $R^{n\times n}$ from the columns of the controllability matrix of the ith channel and the rows of the observability matrix of the jth channel if $\{IODZ_{ij}\} \neq \emptyset$. This fact will be used in the following sections to aid in determining if for some system

$s \in \{IDZ_i\} \cap \{ODZ_j\}$

implies

$s \in \{IODZ_{ij}\}$.

In this study, the ij input–output decoupling zeros are found by determining the sets $\{IDZ_i\}$, $\{ODZ_j\}$; then the intersection of the sets is found:

$$\{\overline{IODZ}_{ij}\} = \{IDZ_i\} \cap \{ODZ_j\}. \quad (75)$$

Finally, the dimension of the subspace formed from the union of the controllable subspace of channel i and the observable subspace of channel j is calculated. If the dimension of this joint subspace is n, then

$$\{IODZ_{ij}\} = \emptyset. \quad (76)$$

If the dimension r of this joint subspace is less than n and the number of zeros of $\{\overline{IODZ}_{ij}\}$ is equal to n - r, then

$$\{IODZ_{ij}\} = \{\overline{IODZ}_{ij}\}. \quad (77)$$

When the dimension r of the joint subspace is less than n but the number of zeros of $\{IODZ_{ij}\}$ is greater than n - r, all that can be concluded (unless all zeros have the same value) is that

$$\{IODZ_{ij}\} \neq \emptyset. \quad (78)$$

An important property of system zeros is their invariance to static state and output feedback. Since this property will be used extensively in the proofs of theorems in this chapter, the following theorem on the invariance property of decentralized decoupling zeros is given.

Theorem 10. Let channel i of a k-channel system be described by the triple (A, B_i, C_i).

(1) The input decoupling zeros of the triple (A, B_i, C_i) are invariant under static state and output feedback of the form

$$u_i(s) = F_i x(s) + G_i y_i(s) + v_i(s),$$

where $v_i(s)$ is the new command vector.

(2) The output decoupling zeros of the triple (A, B_i, C_i) are invariant under static output feedback of the form

$$u_i(s) = G_i y_i(s) = G_i C_i x(s).$$

Proof.

(i) From Definition 3, $s \in C$ is an input decoupling zero of the triple $(A + B_iF_i + B_iG_iC_i, B_i, C_i)$ if

$$\operatorname{rank}[sI_n - A - B_iF_i - B_iG_iC_i, -B_i] < n,$$

which is equivalent to

$$\operatorname{rank}\left\{[sI_n - A, -B_i]\begin{bmatrix} I_n & 0 \\ F_i + G_iC_i & I_{m_j} \end{bmatrix}\right\} < n$$

$$\Rightarrow \operatorname{rank}[sI_n - A - B_iF_i - B_iG_iC_i, -B_i]$$

$$= \operatorname{rank}[sI_n - A, -B_i],$$

which implies that the input decoupling zeros of the ith channel are invariant under ith channel static state and output feedback.

(ii) From Definition 4, $s \in C$ is an output decoupling zero of the triple $(A + B_iG_iC_i, B_i, C_i)$ if

$$\operatorname{rank}\begin{bmatrix} sI_n - A - B_iG_iC_i \\ C_i \end{bmatrix} < n,$$

or, equivalently,

$$\operatorname{rank}\left\{\begin{bmatrix} I_n & -B_iG_i \\ 0 & I_{q_i} \end{bmatrix}\begin{bmatrix} sI_n - A \\ C_i \end{bmatrix}\right\} < n$$

$$\Rightarrow \operatorname{rank}\begin{bmatrix} sI_n - A - B_iG_iC_i \\ C_i \end{bmatrix} = \operatorname{rank}\begin{bmatrix} sI_n - A \\ C_i \end{bmatrix},$$

which implies that the output decoupling zeros of the ith channel are invariant under ith channel static output feedback.

D. SINGLE-CHANNEL CONTROLLABILITY (k = 2)

It is well known that the controllability of the pair (A, B_i) is invariant under local output feedback: $u_i = F_i y_i$, or, in other words,

$$\langle A|\beta_i\rangle = \langle A + B_i F_i C_i|\beta_i\rangle = R_i \subseteq X, \tag{79}$$

where R_i is the controllable subspace of the pair (A, B_i). Based on the above, the reduced problem considered in this section is under what conditions does there exist a local nondynamic output feedback $u_j = F_j y_j$ such that the resulting closed-loop system, with the system matrix

$$A_{CL} = A + B_j F_j C_j, \tag{80}$$

is controllable from channel i, that is,

$$\langle A_{CL}|\beta_i\rangle = X. \tag{81}$$

Since it is assumed that the system (50)–(51) is jointly controllable,

$$\langle A|\beta_i + \beta_j\rangle = X, \quad i, j = 1, 2, \quad i \neq j, \tag{82}$$

and that the pair (A, B_i) $(i = 1, 2)$ is uncontrollable, the controllable subspace of the pair (A, B_i), R_i, is a subspace of X,

$$\langle A|\beta_i\rangle = R_i \subset X, \tag{83}$$

while the controllable subspace of the pair (A, B_j), R_j, contains the complementary subspace of R_i. That is,

$$R_i + R_j = R_i \oplus R_i^\perp = X, \tag{84}$$

so

$$R_i^\perp \subseteq R_j. \tag{85}$$

The local output feedback $u_j = F_j y_j$ must change the structure of the system Σ so that the whole state space of the closed-loop system can be controlled by u_i.

From the preceding discussion, it is obvious that a necessary condition for channel i to be made controllable is that the uncontrollable subspace of channel i must be a subspace of the observable subspace of channel j. A less obvious condition is that the controllable subspace of channel i must not be a subspace of the unobservable subspace of channel j. To see this, consider the standard uncontrollable form of the triple (A, B_i, C_j):

$$\begin{bmatrix} \dot{x}_c \\ \dot{x}_{\bar{c}} \end{bmatrix} = \begin{bmatrix} A_c & A_{c\bar{c}} \\ 0 & A_{\bar{c}} \end{bmatrix} \begin{bmatrix} x_c \\ x_{\bar{c}} \end{bmatrix} + \begin{bmatrix} B_{ic} \\ 0 \end{bmatrix} u_i + \begin{bmatrix} B_{jc} \\ B_{j\bar{c}} \end{bmatrix} u_j,$$

$$y_j = [C_{jc} \quad C_{j\bar{c}}] \begin{bmatrix} x_c \\ x_{\bar{c}} \end{bmatrix}, \tag{86}$$

with channel j feedback of the form

$$u_j = F_j y_j. \tag{87}$$

If the pair (A_c, C_{jc}) is observable, the uncontrollable subspace of channel i can be observed from channel j. However, if the controllable subspace of channel i is a subspace of the unobservable subspace of channel j, then, by definition, assuming the system has been partitioned as in the system (86)–(87),

$$\begin{bmatrix} C \\ CA \\ \vdots \\ CA^{n-1} \end{bmatrix} \begin{bmatrix} X_c \\ 0 \end{bmatrix} = 0,$$

which implies that $C_{jc} = 0$. If $C_{jc} = 0$, then the pair (A_{CL}, B_i) with the system matrix

$$A_{CL} = \begin{bmatrix} A_c & A_{c\bar{c}} + B_{jc}F_jC_{j\bar{c}} \\ 0 & A_{\bar{c}} + B_{j\bar{c}}F_jC_{j\bar{c}} \end{bmatrix} \tag{88}$$

is uncontrollable.

The condition that the controllable subspace of channel i, R_i, must not be a subspace of the unobservable subspace of channel j, $O_j^{\perp}$, can be shown to be equivalent to the condition that the triple (A, B_i, C_j), i, j = 1, 2, i ≠ j, be nondegenerate, $C_j(sI_n - A)^{-1}B_i \neq 0$. The following lemma shows this.

Lemma 7. Given the jointly controllable and observable system (50)–(51) with k = 2, the triple (A, B_i, C_j), i, j = 1, 2, i ≠ j, is nondegenerate,

$$C_j(sI_n - A)^{-1}B_i \neq 0,$$

if and only if

$$R_i \not\subseteq O_j^{\perp}, \quad i, j = 1, 2, \quad i \neq j.$$

Proof. The "if" part:

Given:

$$\langle A | \beta_i + \beta_j \rangle = X, \ \langle A^T | \mathrm{Im}\ C_i^T + \mathrm{Im}\ C_j^T \rangle = X,$$

and since by assumption $R_i \neq X$ (i = 1, 2), this implies

$$\dim(R_i) = r < n, \quad r \neq 0.$$

Thus there exists an equivalence transformation $x = Px'$, where $P \in R^{n\times n}$ is a constant nonsingular matrix which transforms the system

$$\dot{x} = Ax + B_i u_i,$$

$$y_j = C_j x$$

into the standard uncontrollable form [30]

$$\begin{bmatrix} \dot{x}'_c \\ \dot{x}'_{\bar{c}} \end{bmatrix} = \begin{bmatrix} A_c & A_{c\bar{c}} \\ 0 & A_{\bar{c}} \end{bmatrix} \begin{bmatrix} x'_c \\ x'_{\bar{c}} \end{bmatrix} + \begin{bmatrix} B_{ic} \\ 0 \end{bmatrix} u_i,$$

$$y_j = [C_{jc} \quad C_{j\bar{c}}] \begin{bmatrix} x'_c \\ x'_{\bar{c}} \end{bmatrix}.$$

Now, $R_i \not\subseteq O_j^{\perp}$ implies that $C_{jc} \neq 0$. Thus, the transfer function matrix for the transformed system is

$$[C_{jc} \quad C_{j\bar{c}}]\begin{bmatrix} sI_n - A_c & -A_{c\bar{c}} \\ 0 & sI_n - A_{\bar{c}} \end{bmatrix}^{-1}\begin{bmatrix} B_{ci} \\ 0 \end{bmatrix}$$

$$= [C_{jc} \quad C_{j\bar{c}}]\begin{bmatrix} (sI_n - A_c)^{-1} & (sI_n - A_c)^{-1}A_{c\bar{c}}(sI_n - A_{\bar{c}})^{-1} \\ 0 & (sI_n - A_{\bar{c}})^{-1} \end{bmatrix}$$

$$\times \begin{bmatrix} B_{ci} \\ 0 \end{bmatrix}$$

$$- C_{jc}(sI_n - A_c)^{-1}B_{ic} \neq 0$$

$$\Rightarrow C_j(sI_n - A)^{-1}B_i \neq 0,$$

which implies that the triple (A, B_i, C_j) is nondegenerate. The "only if" part: Given the triple (A, B_i, C_j) is nondegenerate, then $C_j(sI_n - A)^{-1}B_i \neq 0$. Employing the inverse Laplace transform with $x(0) = 0$, the above implies

$$C_je^{At}B_i \neq 0 \Rightarrow e^{At}B_i \neq 0.$$

Expressing the matrix exponential in terms of its Taylor series expansion and postmultiplying by B_i yields

$$e^{At}B_i = B_i + AB_it + \frac{A^2B_it^2}{2!} + \cdots .$$

The subspace spanned by the column vectors of the infinite sequence of matrices B_i, AB_i, A^2B_i, ... is the controllable subspace of the pair (A, B_i), R_i. Thus

$$C_je^{At}B_i \neq 0,$$

which implies that there exists an $x(t) \in R_i$ such that $x(t) \notin N(C_j)$, but

$$X = N(C_j) + R\left(C_j^T\right) \Rightarrow x(t) \in R\left(C_j^T\right).$$

Therefore, since

$$\langle A^T | \operatorname{Im}(C_j^T) \rangle = O_j,$$

there exists $x(t) \in R_i \cap O_j$; therefore, $R_i \not\subseteq O_j^{\perp}$. Q.E.D. Note that from the definition of transmission zeros of a system, a degenerate triple (A, B, C) has an infinite number of transmission zeros.

Using the definition of the ij input–output decoupling zeros $\{IODZ_{ij}\}$ of Definition 17, the following theorem states the necessary and sufficient conditions for single-channel controllability with k = 2.

Theorem 11. Let Σ of Eqs. (50) and (51) be a two-channel system with $C_j(sI_n - A)^{-1}B_i \neq 0$, i, j = 1, 2, i ≠ j, and $\langle A|\beta_i + \beta_j\rangle = X$, $\langle A|\beta_i\rangle \subset X$. There exists a nondynamic output feedback matrix $F_j \in R^{m_j \times q_j}$ such that

$$\langle A + B_j F_j C_j | \beta_i \rangle = X \quad \text{if and only if} \quad \{IODZ_{ij}\} = \emptyset.$$

Proof. The "if" part:

Given: $\langle A|\beta_i + \beta_j\rangle = X$ implies $R_i + R_j = X$, where

$$\langle A|\beta_i\rangle = R_i, \quad \langle A|\beta_j\rangle = R_j.$$

Thus, since

$$R_i \oplus R_i^{\perp} = X, \quad R_j \oplus R_j^{\perp} = X$$

implies that

$$R_i^{\perp} \subseteq R_j, \quad R_j^{\perp} \subseteq R_i.$$

Now

$$\{IODZ_{ij}\} = \emptyset \quad \Rightarrow \quad R_i^{\perp} \cap O_j^{\perp} = \emptyset,$$

where

$$\langle A^T | \operatorname{Im}(C_j^T) \rangle = O_j \quad \Rightarrow \quad R_i + O_j = X.$$

Then,

$$O_j \oplus O_j^{\perp} = X \quad \Rightarrow \quad R_i^{\perp} \subseteq O_j.$$

Thus the uncontrollable modes of channel i are controllable and observable from channel j, and since $C_j(sI_n - A)^{-1}B_i \neq 0$ from Lemma 7, $R_i \not\subseteq O_j^{\perp}$. Considering the standard uncontrollable form [30] of the pair (A, B_i),

$$\begin{bmatrix} \dot{x}_c \\ \dot{x}_{\bar{c}} \end{bmatrix} = \begin{bmatrix} A_c & A_{c\bar{c}} \\ 0 & A_{\bar{c}} \end{bmatrix} \begin{bmatrix} x_c \\ x_{\bar{c}} \end{bmatrix} + \begin{bmatrix} B_{ic} \\ 0 \end{bmatrix} u_i + \begin{bmatrix} B_{jc} \\ B_{j\bar{c}} \end{bmatrix} u_j,$$

$$y_j = [C_{jc}.\ C_{j\bar{c}}] \begin{bmatrix} x_c \\ x_{\bar{c}} \end{bmatrix},$$

and a feedback control of the form

$$u_j = F_j C_{jc} x_c + F_j C_{j\bar{c}} x_{\bar{c}},$$

where, since

$$R_i^{\perp} \subseteq O_j; \quad R_i^{\perp} \subseteq R_j; \quad R_i \not\subseteq O_j^{\perp}$$

$$\Rightarrow C_{jc} \neq 0, \quad C_{j\bar{c}} \neq 0, \quad B_{j\bar{c}} \neq 0$$

and assuming the worst case $B_{jc} = 0$, the closed-loop system is

$$\begin{bmatrix} \dot{x}_c \\ \dot{x}_{\bar{c}} \end{bmatrix} = \begin{bmatrix} A_c & A_{c\bar{c}} \\ B_{j\bar{c}} F_j C_{jc} & A_{\bar{c}} + B_{j\bar{c}} F_j C_{j\bar{c}} \end{bmatrix} \begin{bmatrix} x_c \\ x_{\bar{c}} \end{bmatrix} + \begin{bmatrix} B_{ic} \\ 0 \end{bmatrix} u_i,$$

and F_j can thus be chosen such that the pair $(A + B_j F_j C_j, B_i)$ is controllable.

The "only if" part:

Given $\langle A | \beta_i \rangle = R_i \subset X$, $R_i \neq 0$, then $\dim\left(R_i^{\perp}\right) = p < n$. Then there exists p independent left eigenvectors/generalized eigenvectors, say, $v_k^T(z_k)$ $(k = 1, \ldots, p)$, such that

$$v_k^T(z_k)[z_k I_n - A, B_i] = 0 \quad (k = 1, \ldots, p),$$

where z_k are the eigenvalues associated with the uncontrollable modes of the pair (A, B_i). This implies that

$$v_k^T(z_k I_n - A) = 0, \quad v_k^T B_i = 0 \quad (k = 1, \ldots, p).$$

Now,

$$\langle A + B_j F_j C_j | \beta_i \rangle = X$$

$$\Rightarrow v_k^T(z_k)[z_k I_n - A - B_j F_j C_j, B_i] = \omega_k^T(z_k) \neq 0$$

$$\Rightarrow v_k^T(z_k) B_j F_j C_j = \omega_k^T(z_k) \neq 0.$$

Using the invariance property of the decoupling zeros, Theorem 10, implies that

$$z_k \notin \{IDZ_j\} \cap \{ODZ_j\}, \quad k = 1, \ldots, p$$

$$\Rightarrow z_k \notin \{ODZ_j\}, \quad k = 1, \ldots, p;$$

and thus using Definition 17, we have

$$z_k \notin \{IODZ_{ij}\}, \quad k = 1, 2, \ldots, p. \quad \text{Q.E.D.}$$

Assuming the triple (A, B_i, C_j) is nondegenerate, Theorem 11 gives the necessary and sufficient conditions for the single-channel controllability for a two-channel system. For the case when

$$\{IODZ_{ij}\} \neq \emptyset, \tag{89}$$

some or all of the uncontrollable modes of the pair (A, B_i) will be uncontrollable modes of the pair $(A + B_j F_j C_j, B_i)$. Thus the $z \in \sigma(A)$ that satisfy

$$z \in \{IODZ_{ij}\} \tag{90}$$

are invariant under output feedback of the form

$$u_j = B_j F_j C_j x \tag{91}$$

for all $F_j \in R^{m_j \times q_j}$. The following theorem states the conditions for a two-channel system to be stabilizable from a single channel when Eq. (89) is satisfied.

Theorem 12. Let Σ from Eqs. (50) and (51) be a two-channel system with $C_j(sI_n - A)^{-1}B_i \neq 0$ and $\langle A|\beta_i + \beta_j\rangle = X$, $\langle A|\beta_i\rangle \subset X$, $i, j = 1, 2$, $i \neq j$. There exists a nondynamic output feedback matrix F_j such that the pair $(A + B_jF_jC_j, B_i)$ is stabilizable if and only if for all

$$z \in \{IODZ_{ij}\},$$

z is in the left-half-complex plane, $z \in C_o^-$.

Proof. Theorem 11 provides the conditions for $z \notin \{IODZ_{ij}\}$, so only $z \in \{IODZ_{ij}\}$ need be considered.

The "if" part:

Given $z \in \{IODZ_{ij}\}$, this implies that

$$z \in \{IDZ_i\} \cap \{ODZ_j\}$$

by the invariance property of decoupling zeros (Theorem 10),

$$z \in \sigma(A + B_jF_jC_j)$$

and

$$\operatorname{rank}[zI_n - A - B_jF_jC_j, B_i] < n,$$

which implies that z is an input decoupling zero of the pair $(A + B_jF_jC_j, B_i)$. But $z \in C_o^-$, thus by the definition of stabilizability, the pair $(A + B_jF_jC_j, B_i)$ is stabilizable.

The "only if" part:

Given $z \in \{IODZ_{ij}\}$, this implies that

$$z \in \{IDZ_i\} \cap \{ODZ_j\};$$

thus z is invariant under static state and output feedback of the form

$$u_i = \tilde{F}_ix + F_iC_ix$$

and output feedback of the form

$$u_j = F_jC_jx.$$

Thus $z \in \sigma(A + B_jF_jC_j)$ and z is associated with an uncontrollable mode of the pair $(A + B_jF_jC_j, B_i)$. But, by assumption, $(A + B_jF_jC_j, B_i)$ is stabilizable, and thus $z \in C_o^-$. Q.E.D.

Theorems 11 and 12 show that knowledge of the decentralized decoupling zeros can aid in determining if a two-channel system can be made controllable or stabilizable from a single channel. The following example based on the river pollution problem [56] illustrates the usefulness of the decentralized decoupling zeros.

Example 3. Consider the dynamic model of the two-reach river pollution problem treated in [56]:

$$\begin{bmatrix} \dot{x}_1 \\ \dot{x}_2 \\ \dot{x}_3 \\ \dot{x}_4 \end{bmatrix} = \begin{bmatrix} -1.32 & 0 & 0 & 0 \\ -0.32 & -1.2 & 0 & 0 \\ 0.9 & 0 & -1.32 & 0 \\ 0 & 0.9 & -0.32 & -1.2 \end{bmatrix} \begin{bmatrix} x_1 \\ x_2 \\ x_3 \\ x_4 \end{bmatrix}$$

$$+ \begin{bmatrix} 0.1 \\ 0 \\ 0 \\ 0 \end{bmatrix} u_1 + \begin{bmatrix} 0 \\ 0 \\ 0.1 \\ 0 \end{bmatrix} u_2 + \begin{bmatrix} 5.35 \\ 1.9 \\ 4.19 \\ 1.9 \end{bmatrix},$$

$$y_1 = \begin{bmatrix} 10 & 0 & 0 & 0 \\ 0 & 10 & 0 & 0 \end{bmatrix} \begin{bmatrix} x_1 \\ x_2 \\ x_3 \\ x_4 \end{bmatrix},$$

$$y_2 = \begin{bmatrix} 0 & 0 & 10 & 0 \\ 0 & 0 & 0 & 10 \end{bmatrix} \begin{bmatrix} x_1 \\ x_2 \\ x_3 \\ x_4 \end{bmatrix}. \tag{92}$$

This system is jointly controllable and jointly observable. Also

$$C_2(sI_n - A)^{-1}B_1 = \begin{bmatrix} \dfrac{0.9}{(s + 1.32)^2} \\ \\ \dfrac{-0.576(s + 1.26)}{(s + 1.32)^2(s + 1.2)^2} \end{bmatrix} \neq 0$$

and

$$C_1(sI_n - A)^{-1}B_2 = 0.$$

Table I lists the poles and zeros for the joint system, channel 1 and channel 2. As Table I shows, this system has two non-distinct eigenvalues at s = -1.32, -1.2. Since $C_2(sI_n - A)^{-1}B_1 \neq 0$ and $\{IODZ_{12}\} = \emptyset$, using Theorem 11 it can be concluded that the system can be made controllable from channel 1. This is obvious since $\{IDZ_1\} = \emptyset$ implies channel 1 is already controllable.

TABLE I. Poles and Zeros of the River Pollution Control Problem

	Joint system	*Channel 1*	*Channel 2*
Poles	*-1.32, -1.2, -1.32, -1.2*	*-1.32, -1.2, -1.32, -1.2*	*-1.32, -1.2 -1.32, -1.2*
System zeros	*None*	*-1.32, -1.2*	*-1.32, -1.2*
Transmission zeros	*None*	*None*	*None*
Input decoupling zeros	*None*	*None*	*-1.32, -1.2*
Output decoupling zeros	*None*	*-1.32, -1.2*	*None*
Invariant zeros	*None*	*-1.32, -1.2*	*-1.32, -1.2*
No. of zeros at infinity	*Two*	*One*	*One*

Channel 2 has two input decoupling zeros at $s = -1.32, -1.2$, and channel 1 has two output decoupling zeros at $s = -1.32, -1.2$. Although $\{IDZ_2\} \cap \{ODZ_1\} \neq \emptyset$, the set $\{IODZ_{21}\} \neq \emptyset$ since the columns of the matrix $\begin{bmatrix} B_2 & AB_2 & C_1^T \end{bmatrix}$ span the system's four-dimensional state space, which implies that there does not exist a mode of the system which is both uncontrollable from channel 2 and unobservable from channel 1. But since $C_1(sI_n - A)^{-1}B_2 = 0$, there does not exist a feedback of the form $u_1 = F_1C_1x$ such that channel 2 can be made controllable.

Example 4. Consider the following linearized equations of motion ($\theta_i \simeq 0$, $i = 1, 2, 3$) for the system depicted in Fig. 1:

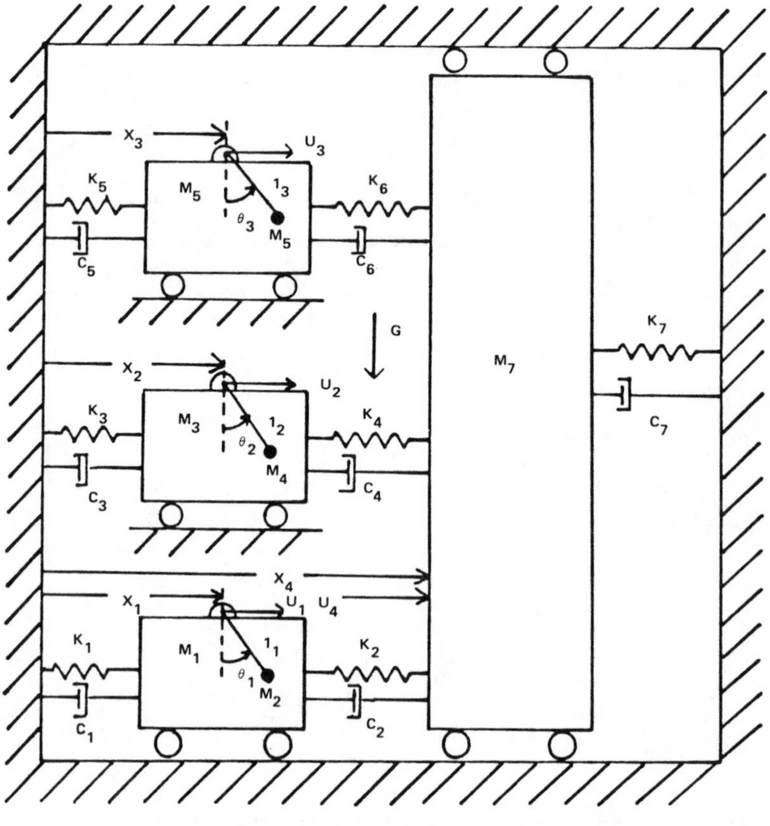

Fig. 1. System for Example 4.

$$\ddot{\theta}_1 = -\frac{(m_1 + m_2)g}{m_1 l_1}\theta_1 + \frac{k_1 + k_2}{m_1 l_1}x_1 + \frac{c_1 + c_2}{m_1 l_1}\dot{x}_1 - \frac{k_2}{m_1 l_1}x_4 - \frac{c_2}{m_1 l_1}\dot{x}_4 - \frac{u_1}{m_1 l_1}, \tag{93a}$$

$$\ddot{x}_1 = \frac{m_2 g}{m_1}\theta_1 - \frac{k_1 + k_2}{m_1}x_1 - \frac{c_1 + c_2}{m_1}\dot{x}_1 + \frac{k_2}{m_1}x_4 + \frac{c_2}{m_1}\dot{x}_4 + \frac{u_1}{m_1}, \tag{93b}$$

$$\ddot{\theta}_2 = -\frac{(m_3 + m_4)g}{m_3 l_2}\theta_2 + \frac{k_3 + k_4}{m_3 l_2}x_2 + \frac{c_3 + c_4}{m_3 l_2}\dot{x}_2 - \frac{k_4}{m_3 l_2}x_4 - \frac{c_4}{m_3 l_2}\dot{x}_4 - \frac{u_2}{m_3 l_2}, \tag{93c}$$

$$\ddot{x}_2 = \frac{m_4 g}{m_3}\theta_2 - \frac{k_3 + k_4}{m_3}x_2 - \frac{c_3 + c_4}{m_3}\dot{x}_2 + \frac{k_4}{m_3}x_4 + \frac{c_4}{m_3}\dot{x}_4 + \frac{u_2}{m_3}, \tag{93d}$$

$$\ddot{\theta}_3 = -\frac{(m_5 + m_6)g}{m_5 l_3}\theta_3 + \frac{k_5 + k_6}{m_5 l_3}x_3 + \frac{c_5 + c_6}{m_5 l_3}\dot{x}_3 - \frac{k_6}{m_5 l_3}x_4 - \frac{c_6}{m_5 l_3}\dot{x}_4 - \frac{u_2}{m_5 l_3}, \tag{93e}$$

$$\ddot{x}_3 = \frac{m_6 g}{m_5}\theta_3 - \frac{(k_5 + k_6)}{m_5}x_3 - \frac{(c_5 + c_6)}{m_5}\dot{x}_3 + \frac{k_6}{m_5}x_4 + \frac{c_6}{m_5}\dot{x}_4 + \frac{u_3}{m_5}, \tag{93f}$$

$$\ddot{x}_4 = -\frac{k_2 + k_4 + k_6 + k_7}{m_7}x_4 - \frac{c_2 + c_4 + c_6 + c_7}{m_7}\dot{x}_4 + \frac{k_2}{m_7}x_1 + \frac{k_4}{m_7}x_2 + \frac{k_6}{m_7}x_3 + \frac{c_2}{m_7}\dot{x}_1 + \frac{c_4}{m_7}\dot{x}_2 + \frac{c_6}{m_7}\dot{x}_3 + \frac{u_4}{m_7}. \tag{93g}$$

After substituting the parameter values for Table II into Eqs. (93a–g), a state space description for this system is

$$
\begin{bmatrix} \dot{\theta}_1 \\ \dot{x}_1 \\ \ddot{\theta}_1 \\ \ddot{x}_1 \\ \dot{\theta}_2 \\ \dot{x}_2 \\ \ddot{\theta}_2 \\ \ddot{x}_2 \\ \dot{\theta}_3 \\ \dot{x}_3 \\ \ddot{\theta}_3 \\ \ddot{x}_3 \\ \dot{x}_4 \\ \ddot{x}_4 \end{bmatrix}
=
\begin{bmatrix}
0 & 0 & 1.0 & 0 & 0 & 0 & 0 & 0 & 0 \\
0 & 0 & 0 & 1.0 & 0 & 0 & 0 & 0 & 0 \\
-35.2 & 5.0 & 0 & 0.2 & 0 & 0 & 0 & 0 & 0 \\
3.2 & -5.0 & 0 & -0.2 & 0 & 0 & 0 & 0 & 0 \\
0 & 0 & 0 & 0 & 0 & 0 & 1.0 & 0 & 0 \\
0 & 0 & 0 & 0 & 0 & 0 & 0 & 1.0 & 0 \\
0 & 0 & 0 & 0 & -35.2 & 5.0 & 0 & 0.2 & 0 \\
0 & 0 & 0 & 0 & 3.2 & -5.0 & 0 & -0.2 & 0 \\
0 & 0 & 0 & 0 & 0 & 0 & 0 & 0 & 0 \\
0 & 0 & 0 & 0 & 0 & 0 & 0 & 0 & 0 \\
0 & 0 & 0 & 0 & 0 & 0 & 0 & 0 & -35.2 \\
0 & 0 & 0 & 0 & 0 & 0 & 0 & 0 & 3.2 \\
0 & 0 & 0 & 0 & 0 & 0 & 0 & 0 & 0 \\
0 & 2.5 & 0 & 0.1 & 0 & 2.5 & 0 & 0.1 & 0
\end{bmatrix}
$$

TABLE II. Parameter Values for the Model of Example 4

Parameter	*Units*	*Value*
m_1, m_3, m_5, m_7	10^3 lb-sec^2/ft	1.0
m_2, m_4, m_6	10^3 lb-sec^2/ft	0.1
c_1, c_2, c_3, c_4	10^3 lb-sec/ft	0.1
c_5, c_6, c_7	10^3 lb-sec/ft	0.1
k_1, k_2, k_3	10^3 lb/ft	2.5
k_4, k_5, k_6	10^3 lb/ft	2.5
k_7	10^3 lb/ft	3.0
l_1, l_2, l_3	ft	1.0

$$\left.\begin{matrix} 0 & 0 & 0 & 0 & 0 \\ 0 & 0 & 0 & 0 & 0 \\ 0 & 0 & 0 & -2.5 & -0.1 \\ 0 & 0 & 0 & 2.5 & 0.1 \\ 0 & 0 & 0 & 0 & 0 \\ 0 & 0 & 0 & 0 & 0 \\ 0 & 0 & 0 & -2.5 & -0.1 \\ 0 & 0 & 0 & 2.5 & 0.1 \\ 0 & 1.0 & 0 & 0 & 0 \\ 0 & 0 & 1.0 & 0 & 0 \\ 5.0 & 0 & 0.2 & -2.5 & -0.1 \\ -5.0 & 0 & -0.2 & 2.5 & 0.1 \\ 0 & 0 & 0 & 0 & 1.0 \\ 2.5 & 0 & 0.1 & -10.5 & -0.4 \end{matrix}\right] \begin{bmatrix} \theta_1 \\ x_1 \\ \dot{\theta}_1 \\ \dot{x}_1 \\ \theta_2 \\ x_2 \\ \dot{\theta}_2 \\ \dot{x}_2 \\ \theta_3 \\ x_3 \\ \dot{\theta}_3 \\ \dot{x}_3 \\ x_4 \\ \dot{x}_4 \end{bmatrix} \qquad (94)$$

Channel 1 has u_1 as a control input and the following input and measurement matrices:

$$B_1 = \begin{bmatrix} 0 \\ 0 \\ -1.0 \\ 1.0 \\ 0 \\ 0 \\ 0 \\ 0 \\ 0 \\ 0 \\ 0 \\ 0 \\ 0 \\ 0 \end{bmatrix}, \qquad (95)$$

$$C_1 = \begin{bmatrix} 0 & 0 & 0 & 0 & 3 & 0 & 1 & 0 & 0 & 0 & 0 & 0 & 0 & 0 \\ 0 & 0 & 0 & 0 & 0 & 4 & 0 & 1 & 0 & 0 & 0 & 0 & 0 & 0 \end{bmatrix}.$$

Channel 2 has control inputs u_3 and u_4. Channel 2's input and measurement matrices are

$$B_2 = \begin{bmatrix} 0 & 0 \\ 0 & 0 \\ 0 & 0 \\ 0 & 0 \\ 0 & 0 \\ 0 & 0 \\ 0 & 0 \\ 0 & 0 \\ 0 & 0 \\ 0 & 0 \\ -1 & 0 \\ 1 & 0 \\ 0 & 0 \\ 0 & 1 \end{bmatrix}, \tag{96}$$

$$C_2 = \begin{bmatrix} 0 & 0 & 0 & 0 & 0 & 0 & 0 & 0 & 1.0 & 0 & 0 & 0 & 0 & 0 \\ 0 & 0 & 0 & 0 & 0 & 0 & 0 & 0 & 0 & 0 & 1.0 & 0 & 0 & 0 \\ 0 & 0 & 0 & 0 & 0 & 0 & 0 & 0 & 0 & 2.0 & 0 & 1.0 & 0 & 0 \end{bmatrix}.$$

The eigenvalues for this system are listed in Table III.

TABLE III. Eigenvalues of the System of Example 4

	Real part	Imaginary part
1:	-0.0166	5.982
2:	-0.0166	-5.982
3:	-0.2374	3.524
4:	-0.2374	-3.524
5:	-0.0460	1.554
6:	-0.0460	-1.554
7:	-0.0119	5.976
8:	-0.0119	-5.976
9:	-0.0881	2.115
10:	-0.0881	-2.115
11:	-0.0119	5.976
12:	-0.119	-5.976
13:	-0.0881	2.115
14:	-0.0881	-2.115

The system is jointly controllable and observable. However, the system is neither controllable nor observable from channel 1 or channel 2. The decoupling zeros for channel 1 and channel 2 are depicted in Table IV. Channel 1 and channel 2 are strongly connected; that is,

$$B_1(sI_n - A)^{-1}C_2 \neq 0,$$

$$B_2(sI_n - A)^{-1}C_1 \neq 0.$$

TABLE IV. Decoupling Zeros for the System of Example 4

Input	Output	Input — output
Joint system (A, B, C)		
None	None	None
Channel 1 (A, B_1, C_1)		
-0.0119 + i5.976	-0.0119 + i5.976	-0.0119 + i5.976
-0.0119 - i5.976	-0.0119 - i5.976	-0.0119 - i5.976
-0.0881 + i2.115	-0.0881 + i2.115	-0.0881 + i2.115
-0.0881 - i2.115	-0.0881 - i2.115	-0.0881 - i2.115
Channel 2 (A, B_2, C_2)		
-0.0119 + i5.976	-0.0119 + i5.976	-0.0119 + i5.976
-0.0119 - i5.976	-0.0119 - i5.976	-0.0119 - i5.976
-0.0881 + i2.115	-0.0881 + i2.115	-0.0881 + i2.115
-0.0881 - i2.115	-0.0881 - i2.115	-0.0881 - i2.115

Also, as shown in Table V,

$$\{IODZ_{12}\} = \emptyset \quad \text{and} \quad \{IODZ_{21}\} = \emptyset,$$

which implies by Theorem 11 that either channel can be made controllable. Applying channel 1 feedback of the form $u_1 = K_1C_1x$ with $K_1 = [-3\ -3]$ makes the pair $(A + B_1K_1C_1, B_2)$ controllable. Applying channel 2 feedback of the form

$$u_2 = K_2C_2x \quad \text{with} \quad K_2 = \begin{bmatrix} -1 & -2 & -1 \\ 5 & 5 & 2 \end{bmatrix}$$

results in the pair $(A + B_2K_2C_2, B_1)$ being controllable.

TABLE V. Decoupling Zeros for the System of Example 4

Input	Output	Input—output
(A, B_1, C_2)		
$-0.0119 + i5.976$	$-0.0119 + i5.976$	None
$-0.0119 - i5.976$	$-0.0119 - i5.976$	
$-0.0881 + i2.115$	$-0.0881 + i2.115$	
$-0.0881 - i2.115$	$-0.0881 - i2.115$	
(A, B_2, C_1)		
$-0.0119 + i5.976$	$-0.0119 + i5.976$	None
$-0.0119 - i5.976$	$-0.0119 - i5.976$	
$-0.0881 + i2.115$	$-0.0881 + i2.115$	
$-0.0881 - i2.115$	$-0.0881 - i2.115$	
$(A + B_1K_1C_1, B_2, C_2)$, $K_1 = [-3\ \ -3]$		
None	None	None
$(A + B_2K_2C_2, B_1, C_1)$, $K_2 = \begin{bmatrix} -1 & -2 & -1 \\ 5 & 5 & 2 \end{bmatrix}$		
None	None	None

E. SINGLE-CHANNEL OBSERVABILITY (k = 2)

Using the results of Section III,D on single-channel controllability and the concept of duality, it seems plausible that the decentralized decoupling zeros can also be used to determine if a two-channel system, described by Eqs. (50) and (51), can be made controllable and observable from a single channel. In this section conditions such that the jointly controllable and jointly observable system (50), (51) with two channels ($k = 2$) that are neither controllable nor observable,

$$\langle A|\beta_i\rangle = R_i \subset X,$$

$$\left\langle A^T|\mathrm{Im}\left(C_i^T\right)\right\rangle = O_i \subset X, \quad i = 1, 2, \tag{97}$$

can be made observable from a single channel are presented. These conditions use the concept of decentralized decoupling zeros to determine when there exists a local nondynamic channel j feedback of the form $u_j = F_jC_jx$ such that the resulting closed-loop system is completely observable from channel i:

$$\left\langle (A + B_jF_jC_j)^T|\mathrm{Im}\left(C_i^T\right)\right\rangle = X, \quad i, j = 1, 2, \quad i \neq j. \tag{98}$$

As in the single-channel controllability case, a necessary condition for channel i to be made observable under the conditions discussed above is that the triple (A, B_j, C_i) be nondegenerate, that is, $C_i(sI_n - A)^{-1}B_j = 0$. To see this, consider the standard unobservable form of the triple (A, B_j, C_i):

$$\begin{bmatrix} \dot{x}_o \\ \dot{x}_{\bar{o}} \end{bmatrix} = \begin{bmatrix} A_o & 0 \\ A_{o\bar{o}} & A_{\bar{o}} \end{bmatrix}\begin{bmatrix} x_o \\ x_{\bar{o}} \end{bmatrix} + \begin{bmatrix} B_{jo} \\ B_{j\bar{o}} \end{bmatrix}u_j,$$

$$y_i = [C_{io} \quad 0]\begin{bmatrix} x_o \\ x_{\bar{o}} \end{bmatrix}, \tag{99}$$

$$y_j = [C_{jo} \quad C_{j\bar{o}}]\begin{bmatrix} x_o \\ x_{\bar{o}} \end{bmatrix}.$$

From Lemma 7, $C_i(sI_n - A)^{-1}B_j = 0$ implies $R_j \subseteq O_i^{\perp}$ and thus $B_{jo} = 0$. Under this condition, applying channel j feedback of the form $u_j = F_j y_j$ yields the closed-loop matrix

$$A_{CL} = \begin{bmatrix} A_o & 0 \\ A_{o\bar{o}} + B_{j\bar{o}}F_jC_{co} & A_o + B_{j\bar{o}}F_jC_{c\bar{o}} \end{bmatrix}. \tag{100}$$

It is obvious that the pair (A_{CL}, C_i) is unobservable. In other words, the observable subspace

$$\left\langle (A + B_jF_jC_j)^T \middle| \operatorname{Im}\left(C_i^T\right)\right\rangle \tag{101}$$

is independent of F_j when

$$C_i(sI_n - A)^{-1}B_j = 0.$$

Now, using the above and the concept of ij input—output decoupling zeros, the following theorem presents necessary and sufficient conditions for single-channel observability.

Theorem 13. Let Σ from Eqs. (50) and (51) be a two-channel system with $C_i(sI_n - A)^{-1}B_j \neq 0$ $(i, j = 1, 2; i \neq j)$ and $\left\langle A^T \middle| \operatorname{Im}\left(C_i^T\right) + \operatorname{Im}\left(C_j^T\right)\right\rangle = X$, $\left\langle A^T \middle| \operatorname{Im}\left(C_i^T\right)\right\rangle \subset X$ $(i, j = 1, 2, i \neq j)$. There exists a nondynamic output feedback matrix $F_j \in R^{m_j \times q_j}$ such that

$$\left\langle (A + B_jF_jC_j)^T \middle| \operatorname{Im}\left(C_i^T\right)\right\rangle = X$$

if and only if

$$\{IODZ_{ji}\} = \emptyset.$$

Proof. The "if" part:

Given: $\left\langle A^T \middle| \operatorname{Im}\left(C_i^T\right) + \operatorname{Im}\left(C_j^T\right)\right\rangle = X$ implies

$$O_i + O_j = X,$$

where

$$\left\langle A^T \middle| \operatorname{Im}\left(C_i^T\right)\right\rangle = O_i \quad \text{and} \quad \left\langle A^T \middle| \operatorname{Im}\left(C_j^T\right)\right\rangle = O_j.$$

Thus,

$$O_i \oplus O_i^\perp = X, \quad O_j \oplus O_j^\perp = X;$$

$$\Rightarrow O_i^\perp \subseteq O_j; \quad O_j^\perp \subseteq O_i.$$

Now

$$\{IODZ_{ji}\} = \emptyset \quad \Rightarrow \quad R_j^\perp \cap O_i^\perp = \emptyset,$$

where

$$\langle A|\beta_j\rangle = R_j \quad \Rightarrow \quad R_j + O_i = X.$$

Then

$$O_i \oplus O_i^\perp = X \quad \Rightarrow \quad O_i^\perp \subseteq R_j.$$

Thus the unobservable modes of channel i are controllable and observable from channel j, and since $C_i(sI_n - A)^{-1}B_j \neq 0$ from Lemma 7, $R_j \not\subseteq O_j^\perp$. Consider the standard unobservable form of the pair (A, C_i),

$$\begin{bmatrix} \dot{x}_o \\ \dot{x}_{\bar{o}} \end{bmatrix} = \begin{bmatrix} A_o & 0 \\ A_{o\bar{o}} & A_{\bar{o}} \end{bmatrix}\begin{bmatrix} x_o \\ x_{\bar{o}} \end{bmatrix} + \begin{bmatrix} B_{jo} \\ B_{j\bar{o}} \end{bmatrix} u_j,$$

$$\begin{bmatrix} y_i \\ y_j \end{bmatrix} = \begin{bmatrix} C_{io} & 0 \\ C_{jo} & C_{j\bar{o}} \end{bmatrix}\begin{bmatrix} x_o \\ x_{\bar{o}} \end{bmatrix};$$

and a feedback control of the form

$$u_j = F_j C_{j\bar{o}} x_o$$

where it has been assumed that $C_{jo} = 0$. Since

$$O_i^\perp \subseteq R_j; \quad O_i^\perp \subseteq O_j; \quad R_j \not\subseteq O_i^\perp$$

$$\Rightarrow C_{j\bar{o}} \neq 0, \quad B_{jo} \neq 0, \quad B_{j\bar{o}} \neq 0,$$

the closed system is

$$\begin{bmatrix} \dot{x}_o \\ \dot{x}_o \end{bmatrix} = \begin{bmatrix} A_o & B_{jo}F_jC_{jo} \\ A_{o\bar{o}} & A_{\bar{o}} \end{bmatrix}\begin{bmatrix} x_o \\ x_{\bar{o}} \end{bmatrix},$$

$$y_i = [C_{io} \quad 0]\begin{bmatrix} x_o \\ x_{\bar{o}} \end{bmatrix},$$

where F_j can be chosen such that the pair $(A + B_jF_jC_j, C_i)$ is observable.

The "only if" part:

Given $\langle A^T | \mathrm{Im}(C_i^T) \rangle = O_i \subset X$, then $\dim(O_i^{\perp}) = p < n$ and there exists p independent right eigenvectors/generalized eigenvectors, say, $v_k(z_k)$ $(k = 1, \ldots, p)$, such that

$$\begin{bmatrix} C_i \\ z_kI_n - A \end{bmatrix} v_k(z_k) = 0 \qquad (k = 1, \ldots, p),$$

where the z_k are the eigenvalues associated with the unobservable modes of the pair (A, C_i), which implies that

$$C_iv_k(z_k) = 0, \qquad [z_kI_n - A]v_k(z_k) = 0 \qquad (k = 1, \ldots, p).$$

Now,

$$\langle (A + B_jF_jC_j)^T | \mathrm{Im}(C_i^T) \rangle = X$$

$$\Rightarrow \begin{bmatrix} C_i \\ z_kI_n - A - B_jF_jC_j \end{bmatrix} v_k(z_k) = w_k(z_k) \neq 0$$

$$\Rightarrow B_jF_jC_jv_k(z_k) \neq 0.$$

Using the invariance property of the decoupling zeros, Theorem 10 implies that $z_k \not\in \{IDZ_j\}$, $k = 1, \ldots, p$, and thus from Definition 17,

$$z_k \notin \{IODZ_{ji}\}, \quad k = 1, \ldots, p. \qquad \text{Q.E.D.}$$

For the case when

$$\{IODZ_{ji}\} \neq \emptyset, \tag{102}$$

it is of interest whether the pair (A, C_i) can be made detectable from a single channel when Eq. (102) is satisfied.

Theorem 14. Let Σ from Eqs. (50) and (51) be a two-channel system with $C_i(sI_n - A)^{-1}B_j \neq 0$ and

$$\left\langle A^T \middle| \operatorname{Im}\left(C_i^T\right) + \operatorname{Im}\left(C_j^T\right)\right\rangle = X, \qquad \left\langle A^T \middle| \operatorname{Im}\left(C_i^T\right)\right\rangle \subset X,$$

$$(i, j = 1, 2, i \neq j).$$

There exists a nondynamic output feedback matrix $F_j \in R^{m_j \times q_j}$ such that the pair $(A + B_jF_jC_j, C_i)$ can be made detectable if and only if for all $z \in \{IODZ_{ji}\}$, z is in the left half complex plane: $z \in C_o^-$.

Proof. Theorem 13 provides the conditions for $z \notin \{IODZ_{ji}\}$, so only $z \in \{IODZ_{ji}\}$ need be considered.

The "if" part:

Given

$$z \in \{IODZ_{ji}\} \subset C_o^- \quad \Rightarrow \quad z \in \{IDZ_j\} \cap \{ODZ_i\},$$

by the invariance property of decoupling zeros (Theorem 10)

$$z \in \sigma(A + B_jF_jC_j)$$

and

$$\operatorname{rank}\begin{bmatrix} C_i \\ zI_n - A - B_jF_jC_j \end{bmatrix} < n,$$

which implies that z is an output decoupling zero of the pair $(A + B_jF_jC_j, C_i)$. But $z \in C_o^-$, thus by definition of detectability [36], the pair $(A + B_jF_jC_j, C_i)$ is detectable.

The "only if" part:

Given

$$z \in \{IODZ_{ji}\} \quad \Rightarrow \quad z \in \{IDZ_j\} \cap \{ODZ_i\};$$

thus z is invariant under static state and output feedback of the form $u_j = \tilde{F}_jx + F_jC_jx$ and output feedback of the form $u_i = F_iC_ix$. Thus $z \in \sigma(A + B_jF_jC_j)$ and z is associated with an unobservable mode of the pair $(A + B_jF_jC_j, C_i)$. But by assumption $(A + B_jF_jC_j, C_i)$ is detectable, which implies that $z \in C_o^-$. Q.E.D.

The following examples illustrate the use of Theorems 13 and 14 in determining single-channel observability and detectability.

Example 5. Consider the river pollution control problem of Example 3. Since channel 2 has no output decoupling zeros, $\{ODZ_2\} = \emptyset$, the total system is observable from channel 2. Channel 1 has two output decoupling zeros at s = -1.32, -1.12, but since the matrix $\left[C_1^T\ B_2\ AB_2\right]$ has rank equal to n,

$$\left\langle A^T \middle| \operatorname{Im}\left(C_1^T\right)\right\rangle + \left\langle A \middle| \beta_2\right\rangle = X,$$

and therefore $\{IODZ_{21}\} \neq \emptyset$. However, $C_1(sI_n - A)^{-1}B_2 = 0$, and therefore channel 1 cannot be made observable by applying nondynamic output feedback to channel 2.

Example 6. Consider the system of Example 4. This system is strongly connected and the sets of ij input–output decoupling zeros of the triples (A, B_1, C_2), (A, B_2, C_1) are equal to the empty set.

The system is jointly observable but both channel 1 and channel 2 are unobservable. However, by Theorem 13 either channel can be made observable by applying nondynamic feedback to one of the channels. Applying channel 1 feedback of the form $u_1 = K_1C_1x$ with $K_1 = [-3, -3]$ results in the pair $(A + B_1KC_1, C_2)$ being observable, as shown in Table V. Applying channel 2 feedback of the form $u_2 = K_2C_2x$ with

$$K_2 = \begin{bmatrix} -1 & -2 & -1 \\ 5 & 5 & 2 \end{bmatrix}$$

results in the pair $(A + B_2K_2C_2, C_1)$ being observable.

F. SINGLE-CHANNEL CONTROLLABILITY AND OBSERVABILITY (k = 2)

By combining Theorem 11 with Theorem 13, a necessary and sufficient condition for single-channel controllability and observability for a two-channel system can be given. These conditions are stated in the following theorem.

Theorem 15. Given the jointly controllable and jointly observable two-channel system Σ from Eqs. (50) and (51) with

$$\langle A | \beta_i \rangle \subset X, \quad \langle A^T | \mathrm{Im}(C_i^T) \rangle \subset X, \quad i = 1, 2$$

and

$$C_i(sI_n - A)^{-1}B_j \neq 0, \quad i \neq j, \quad i, j = 1, 2,$$

there exists a nondynamic feedback matrix F_j such that the triple $(A + B_jF_jC_j, B_i, C_i)$ is completely controllable and observable if and only if

$$\{IODZ_{ij}\} = \emptyset, \quad i \neq j, \quad i, j = 1, 2.$$

Proof. Follows directly from Theorem 11 and Theorem 13.

Note that Theorem 15 requires a two-way communication link between the two systems:

$$C_i(sI_n - A)^{-1}B_j \neq 0, \quad i \neq j, \quad i, j = 1, 2.$$

Thus the two channels must be strongle connected.

Example 7. Consider the system of Example 4. As shown in Tables IV and V, the system is jointly controllable and observable; however, neither channel is controllable nor observable. Since the two channels are strongly connected, and

$$\{IODZ_{12}\} = \emptyset, \quad \{IODZ_{21}\} = \emptyset,$$

either channel can be made controllable or observable by applying nondynamic feedback to one of the channels. Applying channel 1 feedback of the form $u_1 = K_1C_1x$ with $K_1 = [-3\ -3]$

results in the triple $(A + B_1K_1C_1, B_2, C_2)$ being observable and controllable. Applying channel 2 feedback of the form $u_2 = K_2C_2x$ with

$$K_2 = \begin{bmatrix} -1 & -2 & -1 \\ 5 & 5 & 2 \end{bmatrix}$$

results in the triple $(A + B_2K_2C_2, B_1, C_1)$ being observable and controllable.

As Theorem 15 indicates, strong connectedness alone is not a sufficient condition for a jointly controllable and jointly observable system to be made single-channel controllable and observable. The following system model from [10] illustrates this.

Example 8. Consider the following two-channel system with

$$A = \begin{bmatrix} 0 & 1 & 0 & 0 \\ 0 & 1 & 0 & 0 \\ 0 & 0 & 1 & 0 \\ 0 & 0 & 0 & 1 \end{bmatrix}, \quad B_1 = \begin{bmatrix} 0 \\ 1 \\ 0 \\ 0 \end{bmatrix},$$

$$B_2 = \begin{bmatrix} 0 & 0 \\ 0 & 0 \\ 1 & 0 \\ 0 & 1 \end{bmatrix}, \quad C_1 = \begin{bmatrix} 1 & 0 & 0 & 0 \\ 0 & 1 & 0 & 0 \\ 0 & 0 & 0 & 1 \end{bmatrix},$$

$$C_2 = [0 \quad 1 \quad 1 \quad 0].$$

The spectrum of A is

$$\sigma(A) = \{0.0, 1.0, 1.0, 1.0\}.$$

This system is jointly controllable and observable. However, neither channel is controllable nor observable. The system is strongly connected;

$$C_1(sI_n - A)^{-1}B_2 \neq 0,$$

$$C_2(sI_n - A)^{-1}B_1 \neq 0.$$

The set of ij input–output decoupling zeros of the triple (A, B_2, C_1) is equal to the empty set $\{IODZ_{21}\} = \emptyset$. Thus, by

Theorems 11 and 13, channel 2 can be made controllable and channel 1 can be made observable by applying a nondynamic feedback of the form $u_1 = K_1C_1x$ and $u_2 = K_2C_2x$ to channel 1 and channel 2, respectively. However, the set of ij input–output decoupling zeros of the triple (A, B_1, C_2) is not empty: $\{IODZ_{12}\} = \{1.0\}$.

Hence by Theorems 11 and 13, channel 1 cannot be made controllable and channel 2 cannot be made completely controllable and observable from either channel. Furthermore, using Theorems 12 and 14, the system cannot be made stabilizable from channel 1 or detectable from channel 2, since for $s \in \{IODZ_{12}\} = \{1.0\}$, $s \in C^+$.

G. FIXED MODES

As pointed out in Section III,B, although an information exchange is necessary between complementary subsystems for decentralized controllability and observability, the lack of this condition does not necessarily mean that the system has fixed modes. Theorem 9 [2] clearly shows this.

Corollary 4 shows that if $\lambda \in C$ is a fixed mode of the triple (A, B, C), then it is an input–output decoupling zero of a complementary subsystem of the composite system. The concept of ij input–output decoupling zeros is stronger than the definition of input–output decoupling zeros given in this study. Thus, by extending the concept of ij input–output decoupling zeros to complementary subsystems, it seems feasible that the fixed modes of a system can be calculated using this concept. The following example has been used in many papers on fixed modes.

Example 9 [62,16,2]. Consider the jointly controllable and jointly observable three-channel system with plant matrix

$$A = \begin{bmatrix} 0 & 1 & 0 & 0 & 0 & 0 \\ 0 & 0 & 0 & 0 & 0 & 0 \\ 1 & 0 & 0 & 1 & 0 & 1 \\ 0 & 0 & 0 & 0 & 0 & 0 \\ 0 & 0 & 0 & 1 & 0 & 1 \\ 0 & 0 & 0 & 0 & 0 & 0 \end{bmatrix},$$

input matrices

$$B_1 = \begin{bmatrix} 0 \\ 1 \\ 0 \\ 0 \\ 0 \\ 0 \end{bmatrix}, \quad B_2 = \begin{bmatrix} 0 \\ 0 \\ 0 \\ 1 \\ 0 \\ 0 \end{bmatrix}, \quad B_3 = \begin{bmatrix} 0 \\ 0 \\ 0 \\ 0 \\ 0 \\ 1 \end{bmatrix},$$

and measurement matrices

$$C_1 = \begin{bmatrix} 1 & 0 & 0 & 0 & 0 & 0 \\ 0 & 1 & 0 & 0 & 0 & 0 \end{bmatrix},$$

$$C_2 = \begin{bmatrix} 0 & 0 & 1 & 0 & 0 & 0 \\ 0 & 0 & 0 & 1 & 0 & 0 \end{bmatrix},$$

$$C_3 = \begin{bmatrix} 0 & 0 & 0 & 0 & 1 & 0 \\ 0 & 0 & 0 & 0 & 0 & 1 \end{bmatrix}.$$

The eigenvalues of this system are (0, 0 , 0, 0, 0, 0). Taking the complementary subsystem (A, B_2, B_3, C_1), then

$$\{IDZ\} = \{0, 0, 0\}, \quad \{ODZ\} = \{0, 0, 0, 0\},$$

$$\{IDZ\} \cap \{ODZ\} = \{0, 0, 0\}.$$

The dimension of the union of the controllable subspace and observable subspace for this complementary subsystem is 5. Thus, the set $\{IODZ_{ij}\}$ has one member $(n - 5 = 1)$ with value $s = 0$. Accordingly, this system has a fixed mode at $s = 0$.

From this example, it is obvious that the concepts of ij input–output decoupling zeros and complementary subsystems can be used in conjunction to calculate fixed modes of a decentralized system.

H. SUMMARY AND CONCLUSION

In this section explicit conditions in terms of the decentralized zeros of a multivariable system were developed to determine when a two-channel decentralized system can be made controllable and observable through a specified single channel via nondynamic output feedback. The concept of ij input–output decoupling zeros was introduced and was used in the above explicit conditions. Two examples were used to illustrate this technique.

For the case when a system cannot be made controllable and observable through a specified single channel, conditions were developed using the concept of the ij input–output decoupling zeros to determine if the system could be made stabilizable and detectable through a specified single channel.

Finally, in Section III,G a method that calculates the fixed modes of a system based on the concept of ij input–output decoupling zeros was proposed. An example was given to illustrate this method.

In conclusion, it can be stated that the concept of ij input–output decoupling zeros is a powerful tool for evaluating the controllability and observability properties of decentralized systems.

IV. DECENTRALIZED STABILIZATION

A. INTRODUCTION

The high dimensionality and complexity of the interconnections in large-scale systems often presents computational and analytical difficulties in attempting to determine system stability. One method of dealing with this problem is to decompose the system into a number of subsystems, analyze each subsystem using classical stability theories and methods, and then combine these results with certain restrictions resulting from the structure of the system interconnections in order to determine the stability of the composite system. This approach has been termed the "composite system approach" [29].

Many of the methods of the composite system approach use Lyapunov functions to determine the composite system stability. Either vector Lyapunov functions [55] or a scalar Lyapunov function composed of a weighted sum of the Lyapunov functions of the individual subsystems [43] have been used.

In this section a new composite system approach that provides a sufficient condition for composite system stability is proposed. This method uses the properties of the numerical range [25] of an operator in finite dimension and the generalized Gerschgorin circle theorem for block matrices [15] in order to determine the stability of the composite system.

Two stabilization algorithms are introduced in this section. The first algorithm is a decentralized stabilization scheme that uses local subsystem feedback to stabilize the composite system. Satisfaction of this algorithm ensures that the composite system is connectively stable [55]. The second stabilization scheme uses a multilevel feedback consisting of local and global controls. The local controls are used to stabilize the subsystems, while the global controls are used to minimize the magnitude of the subsystem interconnections.

A necessary and sufficient condition for the existence of local output feedback control laws which stabilize a given system is that the fixed modes of the system must be stable. In the event that the system has unstable fixed modes, some transmission of output information among local stations is necessary to stabilize the system. In this section an algorithm that determines the necessary transmission of output information between stations to eliminate unstable fixed modes is proposed.

B. PROBLEM STATEMENT

Consider the continuous linear time-invariant system composed of k subsystems of the form

$$\dot{x}_i(t) = A_{ii}x_i(t) + \sum_{\substack{j=1 \\ j\neq i}}^{k} A_{ij}x_j(t) + B_iu_i(t) \quad (i = 1, \ldots, k), \tag{103}$$

where

$$x_i(t) \in C^{n_i}, \quad A_{ii} \in C^{n_i\times n_i}, \quad A_{ij} \in C^{n_i\times n_j},$$

$$B_i \in C^{n_i\times m_i}, \quad u_i(t) \in C^{m_i}, \quad \sum_{i=1}^{k} n_i = n, \quad \sum_{i=1}^{k} m_i = m.$$

Note that the scalar field H has been enriched from the previous sections. That is, H = C (the field of complex numbers). This enrichment is needed to use the concept of the numerical range of an operator. It is desired to determine the composite system stability based on the stability of the local subsystems and the strength of the interconnections. In the next subsection a sufficient condition for composite system stability is presented.

When the composite system is unstable, the decentralized stabilization problem is defined as follows: find k local feedback controls of the form

$$u_i(t) = -K_ix_i(t), \quad K_i \in C^{m_i\times n_i} \tag{104}$$

such that the composite system (103) in its closed-loop form is asymptotically stable. The multilevel stabilization problem is defined as follows: find k local and global feedback controls of the form

$$u_i(t) = u_i^l(t) + u_i^g(t), \tag{105}$$

where

$$u_i^l(t) = -K_i^l x_i(t), \quad K_i^l \in C^{m_i \times n_i} \tag{106}$$

and

$$u_i^g(t) = -\sum_{\substack{j=1 \\ j \neq i}}^{k} K_{ij}^g x_j(t), \quad K_{ij}^g \in C^{m_i \times n_j}, \tag{107}$$

such that the composite system is asymptotically stable. Since by assumption the composite system is continuous, linear, and time invariant, the asymptotical stability criteria can be satisfied by showing that the eigenvalues of the closed-loop system are elements of the open-left-half complex plane, C_o^-.

Stabilization schemes for both of these problems will be presented in this section. These schemes use the norm of the interconnection matrices. The norm

$$\|A_{ij}\|, \quad A_{ij} \in C^{n_i \times n_j}$$

is defined as usual as

$$\|A_{ij}\| = \sup_{x \neq 0} \|A_{ij}x\| / \|x\| = \sup_{\|x\|=1} \|A_{ij}x\|.$$

The following proposition will be needed in the development of the next section.

Proposition 1. If $A \in C^{n \times n}$ is invertible and $\|\cdot\|$ is a matrix norm on $C^{n \times n}$, then given $x \neq 0$, $\|Ax\| \geq \|x\| \, \|A^{-1}\|^{-1}$.

Proof. Given A is invertible, $A^{-1}A = I$, so $\|x\| = \|A^{-1}Ax\|$; by definition of $\|\cdot\|$,

$$\|x\| = \|A^{-1}Ax\| \leq \|A^{-1}\| \; \|Ax\|,$$

and thus

$$(\|A^{-1}\|)^{-1} \leq \|Ax\|/\|x\|, \quad x \neq 0,$$

and

$$(\|A^{-1}\|)^{-1} = \inf_{x \neq 0} \|Ax\|/\|x\|. \quad \text{Q.E.D.}$$

C. *COMPOSITE SYSTEM STABILITY*

As discussed in the introduction, most of the existing methods for determining the stability of large-scale systems decompose the system into smaller subsystems and then determine composite system stability based on the stability of the subsystems and the structure of the subsystem interconnections. The method to be presented in this section follows this decomposition methodology. This method provides an alternative to the so-called Lyapunov methods for large-scale systems since it does not require the formulation of Lyapunov functions.

The following definition of the numerical range of a finite dimensional operator $A \in C^{n\times n}$ will be needed in the development of the sufficient condition for composite system stability.

Definition 18 [25,23,37]. The numerical range or Hausdorff set of $A \in C^{n\times n}$ is the set W(A) of complex numbers of the form $\langle Ax, x\rangle$, $\|x\| = 1$, $x \in C^n$. That is,

$$W(A) = \{s \in C: s = \langle Ax, x\rangle \quad \text{for some} \quad x \in C^n, \; \|x\| = 1\}. \tag{108}$$

Note that in the finite-dimensional case, the numerical range of an operator (matrix) $A \in C^{n\times n}$ is a continuous image of a compact set and hence is compact (closed and bounded). Thus, the numerical range of a finite-dimensional operator (matrix) is equal to its closure. The numerical range of a finite-dimensional operator (matrix) is equal to its closure. The numerical range of a finite-dimensional complex matrix has many interesting properties. Some of the properties that will be used in this section are given in the following theorems.

Theorem 16 [37,25]. Let $A \in C^{n\times n}$; then the spectrum of A, $\sigma(A)$, is contained in the closure of W(A).

Theorem 17 [23]. The numerical range of any matrix $A \in C^{n\times n}$ is convex.

Theorem 18 [23]. The numerical range of every normal matrix $A \in C^{n\times n}$ $(AA^* = A^*A)$ is the convex hull of the spectrum of A, $\sigma(A)$.

The next corollary follows directly from Theorem 18.

Corollary 6. The numerical range of every diagonal matrix $A \in C^{n\times n}$ is the convex hull of its diagonal elements.

Proof. Given A is diagonal, this implies that the diagonal elements of A are the eigenvalues of A. Thus, from Theorem 18, W(A) is the convex hull of A's diagonal elements. Q.E.D.

As mentioned in the introduction to this section, the generalized Gerschgorin circle theorem for block matrices [15] is used in the development of the sufficient condition for composite system stability. This theorem is presented next.

Theorem 19 [15]. Let $A \in C^{n \times n}$ be any matrix partitioned in the following manner:

$$A = \begin{bmatrix} A_{11} & A_{12} & \cdots & A_{1k} \\ A_{21} & A_{22} & \cdots & A_{2k} \\ \vdots & \vdots & \ddots & \vdots \\ A_{k1} & A_{k2} & \cdots & A_{kk} \end{bmatrix}, \tag{109}$$

where the diagonal submatrices A_{ii} are square of order n_i $(i = 1, \ldots, k)$. With this partitioning, each eigenvalue of A satisfies

$$\left(\| (A_{ii} - zI_i)^{-1} \|\right)^{-1} < \sum_{\substack{j=1 \\ j \neq i}}^{k} \|A_{ij}\| \tag{110}$$

for at least one i $(i = 1, \ldots, k)$. Note that if the partitioning of Eq. (109) is such that all of the diagonal submatrices A_{ii} are 1×1 matrices and $\|\cdot\| = |\cdot|$, then Theorem 19 reduces to the well-known Gerschgorin circle theorem.

To obtain inclusion regions for the eigenvalues of $n \times n$ complex matrices, Feingold and Varga [15] defined sets called Gerschgorin sets.

Definition 19 [15]. For the partitioned $n \times n$ complex matrix A of Eq. (109), let the Gerschgorin set G_i be the set of all complex numbers z such that

$$\left(\| (A_{ii} - zI_i)^{-1} \|\right)^{-1} \leq \sum_{\substack{j=1 \\ j \neq i}}^{k} \|A_{ij}\| \quad (i = 1, \ldots, k).$$

The next lemma shows that the eigenvalues of each of the diagonal submatrices are members of the Gerschgorin sets.

Lemma 8. The Gerschgorin set G_i always contains the eigenvalues of A_{ii} independent of the magnitude of the right-hand side of Eq. (110) and independent of the vector norms used.

Proof. Using the equivalence from Proposition 1,

$$\left(\|(A_{ii} - zI_i)^{-1}\|\right)^{-1} = \inf_{x \neq 0}\left[\frac{\|(A_{ii} - zI_i)x\|}{\|x\|}\right],$$

it is obvious that for $z \in \sigma(A_{ii})$,

$$\left(\|(A_{ii} - zI_i)^{-1}\|\right)^{-1} = 0;$$

thus, since $\|\cdot\| \geq 0$, every $z \in \sigma(A_{ii})$ satisfies Eq. (110) irrespective of the vector norm used. Q.E.D.

Lemma 8 is important since certain norms may provide smaller inclusion sets (Gerschgorin sets) than others. This property will be used in the development of a sufficient condition for composite system stability.

For sets of complex numbers S, Z define

$$d(S, Z) = \inf\{|s - z|: s \in S, z \in Z\}.$$

The following lemma regarding the numerical range will be needed.

Lemma 9. Given $A \in C^{n\times n}$ and $z \notin W(A)$, then

$$0 < d(W(A), z) \leq \inf\{\|(A - zI)x\|, \|x\| = 1\}. \tag{111}$$

Proof. Since $z \notin W(A)$,

$$0 < d(W(A), z) = \inf\{|s - z|: s \in W(A)\}.$$

Using Definition 18,

$$d(W(A), z) = \inf\{|\langle Ax, x\rangle - z|, \|x\| = 1\}.$$

Now, since $\|x\| = 1$, $\|x\|^2 = \langle x, x\rangle = 1$, so

$$z = z\langle x, x\rangle = \langle zx, x\rangle.$$

Thus,

$$0 < d(W(A), z) = \inf\{|\langle(A - zI)x, x\rangle|, \|x\| = 1\}.$$

Applying the Cauchy – Schwarz inequality yields

$$0 < d(W(A), z) \leq \inf\{\|(A - zI)x\| \ \|x\|, \ \|x\| = 1\}$$

and, finally, since $\|x\| = 1$,

$$0 < d(W(A), z) \leq \inf\{\|(A - zI)x\|, \ \|x\| = 1\}. \qquad \text{Q.E.D.}$$

The next lemma gives a relationship between the numerical range of the submatrices of the partitioned matrix A [Eq. (109)] and the Gerschgorin sets G_i.

Lemma 10. Given the partitioned matrix $A \in C^{n\times n}$ [from Eq. (109)] and $z \in C$, with $z \notin W(A_{ii})$ and $z \in G_i$, then

$$d(W(A_{ii}), z) \leq \sum_{\substack{j=1 \\ j\neq i}}^{k} \|A_{ij}\| \quad (i = 1, \ldots, k). \tag{112}$$

Proof. From Definition 19, if $z \in G_i$, then

$$\left(\|(A_{ii} - zI_i)^{-1}\|\right)^{-1} \leq \sum_{\substack{j=1 \\ j\neq i}}^{k} \|A_{ij}\| \quad (i = 1, \ldots, k).$$

Now, employing the identity from Proposition 1,

$$\left(\|(A_{ii} - zI_i)^{-1}\|\right)^{-1} = \inf_{\|x\|=1} \|(A_{ii} - zI_i)x\|,$$

and the inequality (111),

$$d(W(A_{ii}), z) \leq \inf\{\|(A_{ii} - zI_i)x\|, \ \|x\| = 1\},$$

yields

$$d(W(A_{ii}), z) \leq \sum_{\substack{j=1 \\ j\neq i}}^{k} \|A_{ij}\| \quad (i = 1, \ldots, k). \qquad \text{Q.E.D.}$$

Lemma 10 provides a bound on the minimum distance from an element of the Gerschgorin set G_i to the numerical range of the matrix $A_{ii} \in C^{n\times n}$. From Theorem 19 and Definition 19, it is obvious that all of the eigenvalues of A lie in G, where G is defined as

$$G = \bigcup_{i=1}^{k} G_i. \tag{113}$$

The next theorem states a sufficient condition for matrix stability based on the inequality of Lemma 10.

Theorem 20. Let $A \in C^{n\times n}$ be partitioned as in Eq. (109) and $s \in C$; then A is a stable matrix ($\forall s \in \sigma(A)$, Re s < 0) if

$$\text{Re } s < -\sum_{\substack{j=1 \\ j\neq i}}^{k} \|A_{ij}\| \quad \forall s \in W(A_{ii}) \quad (i = 1, \ldots, k). \tag{114}$$

Proof. From Lemma 10, the minimum distance from any $z \in G_i$ to $W(A_{ii})$ satisfies

$$d(W(A_{ii}), z) \leq -\sum_{\substack{j=1 \\ j\neq i}}^{k} \|A_{ij}\|.$$

Let

$$\text{Re}(W(A_{ii})) < -\sum_{\substack{j=1 \\ j\neq i}}^{k} \|A_{ij}\| \quad (i = 1, \ldots, k).$$

Then for every $z \in G_i$ there exists an $s \in W(A_{ii})$ such that

$$\inf\{|s - z|\} \leq \sum_{\substack{j=1 \\ j\neq i}}^{k} \|A_{ij}\|$$

$$\Rightarrow \inf\{|\text{Re } s - \text{Re } z|\} \leq \sum_{\substack{j=1 \\ j\neq i}}^{k} \|A_{ij}\|,$$

but

$$\operatorname{Re} s < -\sum_{\substack{j=1 \\ j \neq i}}^{k} \|A_{ij}\| \qquad (i = 1, \ldots, k)$$

$$\Rightarrow \operatorname{Re} z < 0$$

$$\Rightarrow \text{for all } z \in G, \; G = \bigcup_{i=1}^{k} G_i.$$

From Theorem 19 and Definition 19, all of the eigenvalues of A are elements of G. Thus for all $z \in \sigma(A)$, Re $z < 0$. So by the definition of a stable matrix, Re $\sigma(A) < 0$, A is a stable matrix. Q.E.D.

Theorem 20 has a natural extension to decentralized systems since the composite system matrix of a decentralized system can be described by a partition similar to Eq. (109). A review of Eq. (103) clearly depicts this similarity. The next theorem basically restates Theorem 20 in terms of decentralized systems.

Theorem 21. Let the composite system matrix for the decentralized system governed by Eq. (103) be

$$A = \begin{bmatrix} A_{11} & A_{12} & \cdots & A_{1k} \\ A_{21} & A_{22} & \cdots & A_{2k} \\ \vdots & \vdots & \ddots & \vdots \\ A_{k1} & A_{k2} & \cdots & A_{kk} \end{bmatrix}. \tag{115}$$

A sufficient condition for the composite system to be asymptotically stable is that for all $s \in W(A_{ii})$ $(i = 1, \ldots, k)$,

$$\operatorname{Re} s < -\sum_{\substack{j=1 \\ j \neq i}}^{k} \|A_{ij}\|. \tag{116}$$

Proof. In the case of linear, time-invariant systems, the equilibrium point at the origin of $\dot{x}(t) = Ax(t)$ is asymptotically stable if and only if all the eigenvalues of A have negative real parts [60]. The rest of this proof follows directly from Theorem 20 and the above definition of asymptotic stability. Q.E.D.

It should be noted that Theorem 21 provides an alternative method for determining if the composite system is stable to the so-called "Lyapunov methos" of [54,43] for large-scale, continuous, time-invariant systems. Theorem 21 can also be used in studying the effects of structural perturbations of the interconnection matrices. For example, let

$$A'_{ij} = e_j A_{ij}, \quad e_j \in R. \tag{117}$$

Thus

$$\sum_{\substack{j=1 \\ j \neq i}}^{k} \|A'_{ij}\| = \sum_{\substack{j=1 \\ j \neq i}}^{k} e_j \|A_{ij}\|, \tag{118}$$

and now the effects of increasing or decreasing the strength of the interconnections on the stability of the composite system can be studied by increasing or decreasing e_j, $j = 1, 2, \ldots, k$, $j \neq i$.

To illustrate the use of the numerical range and the generalized Gerschgorin theorem in determining the stability of decentralized systems, an example will be given in which the subsystems have a dimension equal to two. The following theorem on the numerical range of a 2×2 complex matrix will be needed in the example.

Theorem 22 [25]. If A is a 2 × 2 matrix with distinct eigenvalues s_1 and s_2 and corresponding eigenvectors f and g, so normalized that $||f|| = ||g|| = 1$, then W(A) is a closed elliptical disk with foci at s_1 and s_2. If $r = |\langle f, g \rangle|$ and $q = \sqrt{1 - r^2}$, then the minor axis is $r|s_1 - s_2|/q$ and the major axis is $|s_1 - s_2|/q$. If A has only one eigenvalue s of multiplicity two, then W(A) is the circular disk with center s and radius $1/2||A - sI_2||$.

The system of the following example was used in [29] to illustrate a Lyapunov method. In this example, Theorem 21 will be used to determine the stability of the composite system, based on the numerical range of the subsystem plant matrices A_{ii}.

Example 10. Consider a fifth-order system decomposed into third- and second-order subsystems:

$$\dot{x}(t) = \begin{bmatrix} \dot{x}_1(t) \\ \dot{x}_2(t) \end{bmatrix} = \begin{bmatrix} -1.0 & 0.1 & 0.2 & 0.1 & 0.2 \\ 0.2 & -2.0 & 0.5 & 0.1 & 0.1 \\ 0.1 & -1.0 & -3.0 & 0.5 & 0.4 \\ 1.0 & 0 & 1.0 & -4.0 & 0.2 \\ 0.2 & 0.5 & 0 & 1.0 & -5.0 \end{bmatrix} \begin{bmatrix} x_1(t) \\ x_2(t) \end{bmatrix}.$$

It is desired to determine the asymptotic stability of the composite system. It is assumed that each subsystem only has knowledge of its own plant matrix and interconnection matrix.

For ease of illustration, the third-order subsystem will be decomposed into a second-order and a first-order subsystem. That is,

$$A'_{11} = \begin{bmatrix} -1.0 & 0.1 \\ 0.2 & -2.0 \end{bmatrix}, \quad A'_{12} = \begin{bmatrix} 0.2 \\ 0.5 \end{bmatrix}, \quad A'_{13} = \begin{bmatrix} 0.1 & 0.2 \\ 0.1 & 0.1 \end{bmatrix};$$

$$A'_{22} = -3.0, \quad A'_{21} = [0.1 \quad -1.0], \quad A'_{23} = [0.5 \quad 0.4].$$

Since A'_{11} is a two-dimensional matrix, its numerical range is an ellipse. This ellipse has foci at -2.0196 and -0.9804 (the eigenvalues of A'_{11}). Its major axis has length 1.0440 and its minor axis has length 0.0998. Thus, Re $W(A'_{11}) \leq -0.978$. Using the Euclidean norm $(\mathrm{tr}\, A^T A)^{1/2}$, the infinum distance of two of the eigenvalues of the composite system from $W(A'_{11})$ is less than or equal to

$$0.8547 = \|A'_{12}\| + \|A'_{13}\|.$$

Thus, these two eigenvalues have negative real parts. Since A'_{22} is one dimensional, the Gerschgorin circle theorem [15] can be applied directly. Thus, one of the eigenvalues of the composite system lies in a circle of radius 2.0 with the center at -3.0.

Subsystem two is a two-dimensional system, so its numerical range is an ellipse in the complex plane. This ellipse has foci at -3.8292 and -5.1708 (eigenvalues of A_{22}). Its major axis has length 1.5621 and its minor axis has length 0.8. Therefore,

$$\mathrm{Re}\, W(A_{22}) \leq -3.71895.$$

The infinum distance of the remaining two eigenvalues from this ellipse, using the Euclidean norm, is less than or equal to $1.5133 = \|A_{21}\|$, where

$$A_{21} = \begin{bmatrix} 1.0 & 0 & 1.0 \\ 0.2 & 0.5 & 0.0 \end{bmatrix}.$$

Therefore, the remaining two eigenvalues are in the left-half-open complex plane.

Since all of the Gerschgorin sets are subsets of the left-half-open complex plane, the composite system is asymptotically stable. This conclusion checks with a calculation of the composite system's eigenvalues, which are {-4.9436, -4.5216, -0.8991, -2.3178 ± i.5373}.

It is well known that the spectrum of a matrix $A \in C^{n\times n}$ is invariant under a linear nonsingular similarity transformation of the form

$$A' = T^{-1}AT, \quad T \in C^{n\times n},$$

where $T^{-1}T = I_n$. In other words, $\sigma(A') = \sigma(T^{-1}AT)$. However, the numerical range of a complex matrix is not necessarily invariant under the above transformation. The following example illustrates this fact.

Example 11. Consider the system of Fig. 2. The equations of motion for this system are

$$m_1\ddot{x}_1 = -(k_1 + k_2)x_1 + k_2x_2 - c_1\dot{x}_1 + u_1, \tag{119}$$

$$m_2\ddot{x}_2 = k_2x_1 - (k_2 + k_3)x_2 - c_2\dot{x}_2 + u_2. \tag{120}$$

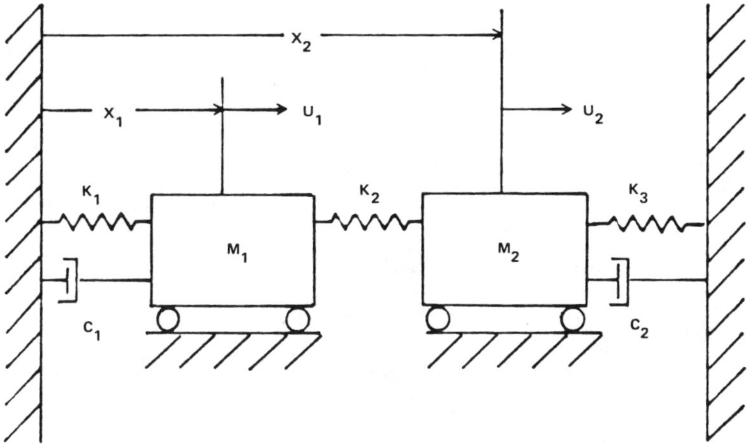

Fig. 2. System model for Example 11.

TABLE VI. Parameter Values for Example 11

Parameter	Units	Value
m_1, m_2	10^3 lb-sec^2/ft	1.0
c_1, c_2	10^3 lb-sec/ft	1.0
k_1, k_2	10^3 lb/ft	1.2
k_3	10^3 lb/ft	0.2

After substituting the values from Table VI into Eqs. (119) and (120), a state-space description for this system can be written as

$$\begin{bmatrix} \dot{x}_1 \\ \ddot{x}_1 \\ \dot{x}_2 \\ \ddot{x}_2 \end{bmatrix} = \begin{bmatrix} 0 & 1 & 0 & 0 \\ -1.2 & -1.0 & 0.2 & 0 \\ 0 & 0 & 0 & 1 \\ 0.2 & 0 & -1.2 & -1.0 \end{bmatrix} \begin{bmatrix} x_1 \\ \dot{x}_1 \\ x_2 \\ \dot{x}_2 \end{bmatrix} + \begin{bmatrix} 0 \\ 1 \\ 0 \\ 0 \end{bmatrix} u_1 + \begin{bmatrix} 0 \\ 0 \\ 0 \\ 1 \end{bmatrix} u_2. \quad (121)$$

This system can be decomposed into two subsystems of the form

$$\begin{bmatrix} \dot{x}_i \\ \ddot{x}_i \end{bmatrix} = \begin{bmatrix} 0 & 1 \\ -1.2 & -1.0 \end{bmatrix} \begin{bmatrix} x_i \\ \dot{x}_i \end{bmatrix} + \begin{bmatrix} 0 \\ 1 \end{bmatrix} u_i + \begin{bmatrix} 0 & 0 \\ 0.2 & 0 \end{bmatrix} \begin{bmatrix} x_j \\ \dot{x}_j \end{bmatrix}$$

$$i, j = 1, 2, \quad i \neq j.$$

Each subsystem has eigenvalues $s_{1,2} = -0.5 \pm i.975$, and thus both subsystems are asymptotically stable. The eigenvalues for the total system are $-0.5 \pm i1.072$ and $-0.5 \pm i.866$, and therefore the total system is asymptotically stable. The numerical range of the subsystem plant matrix

$$\begin{bmatrix} 0 & 1 \\ -1.2 & -1.0 \end{bmatrix}$$

can be shown using Theorem 22 to be an ellipse with foci at $-0.5 \pm i.975$. The major axis of this ellipse has length 2.2

and the minor axis has length 1.0198. Using the Euclidean norm for an operator, $||A|| = \sqrt{\text{tr } A^* A}$, the minimum distance of the eigenvalues of the total system from this ellipse (note that both subsystems are identical and thus have identical numerical ranges) is 0.2. Since the numerical range of both subsystems intersects the closed-right-half complex plane (C^+), Theorem 21 is inconclusive in determining if the total system is asymptotically stable although, as shown above, the system actually is asymptotically stable.

Now consider the linear nonsingular transformation matrix T composed of the eigenvectors of the plant matrix A_{ii}:

$$T = \begin{bmatrix} 1 & 1 \\ -0.5 + i.975 & -0.5 - i.975 \end{bmatrix}.$$

Applying the transformation

$$\begin{bmatrix} x_1' \\ \dot{x}_1' \\ x_2' \\ \dot{x}_2' \end{bmatrix} = \begin{bmatrix} T & 0 \\ & \\ & \\ 0 & T \end{bmatrix} \begin{bmatrix} x_1 \\ \dot{x}_1 \\ x_2 \\ \dot{x}_2 \end{bmatrix},$$

the subsystems now have the form

$$\begin{bmatrix} \dot{x}_i' \\ \ddot{x}_i' \end{bmatrix} = \begin{bmatrix} -0.5 + i.975 & 0 \\ 0 & -0.5 - i.975 \end{bmatrix} \begin{bmatrix} x_i' \\ \dot{x}_i' \end{bmatrix}$$

$$+ \begin{bmatrix} -i.1026 & -i.1026 \\ i.1026 & i.1026 \end{bmatrix} \begin{bmatrix} x_j' \\ x_j' \end{bmatrix}.$$

Using Theorem 22, it can be shown that the numerical ranges of the transformed subsystems are line segments from -0.5 + i.975 to -0.5 - i.975. Since $\text{Re}(W(A_{ii})) = -0.5$ and $||T^{-1}A_{ij}T|| = 0.145$ by Theorem 21, the composite system is asymptotically stable. This checks with the eigenvalues of the composite system, which are $\{-0.5 \pm i1.072, -0.5 \pm i.866\}$.

It can be concluded from Example 11 that the numerical range of a finite-dimensional complex matrix is not necessarily invariant under matrix similarity transformations. Thus it would be helpful if there existed a similarity transformation of a complex matrix A such that the numerical range of the transformed matrix was the minimum numerical range of all similarity transformations of A. For the 2×2 matrix case, Theorem 22 provides an efficient method for determining the numerical range of a matrix. However, when the subsystem dimension is greater than two, there is no set formula for calculating the numerical range of the subsystem plant matrix.

When the subsystem plant matrices have distinct eigenvalues, the problems discussed above can be resolved by using Corollary 6 after the subsystem plant matrices have been transformed to a diagonal form via a similarity transformation.

Note that even when the elements of a matrix A are real ($a_{ij} \in R$), A may have complex eigenvalues and therefore the matrices T, T^{-1} that transform A to a diagonal form and $T^{-1}AT$ will have complex entries in general. For small systems, as in Examples 10 and 11, this presents no problem. However, this fact does become computationally burdensome when dealing with large systems. It must be kept in mind that the reason for diagonalizing the subsystems is that by Theorem 18, the numerical range of a normal matrix is equivalent to the convex hull of its spectrum. Therefore, a similarity transformation that uses real matrices and transforms the system to a normal form would be desirable. Assuming that the eigenvalues of a matrix are distinct, the following theorem defines a real nonsingular transformation $T \in R^{n\times n}$ such that $T^{-1}AT$ is a normal matrix.

Theorem 23 [18]. Suppose a matrix $A \in C^{n\times n}$ has all real elements and has distinct eigenvalues

$$\lambda_i = \sigma_i + i\mu_i \quad (i = 1, 3, \ldots, m - 1),$$

$$\lambda_{i+1} = \sigma_i - i\mu_i = \lambda_i^*,$$

$$\lambda_i = \lambda_i \quad (i = m + 1, m + 2, \ldots, n)$$

and a set of eigenvectors

$$u_i = v_i + iw_i \quad (i = 1, 3, 5, \ldots, m - 1),$$

$$u_{i+1} = v_{i+1} - iw_i = u_i,$$

$$u_i = u_i \quad (i = m + 1, m + 2, \ldots, n).$$

Then the real-valued matrix

$$T = [v_1 \;\; w_1 \;\; v_3 \;\; w_3 \;\cdots\; v_{m-1} \;\; w_{m-1} \;\; u_{m+1} \;\; u_{m+2} \;\cdots\; u_n]$$

is nonsingular and may be used to put A in block diagonal form:

$$T^{-1}AT = \begin{bmatrix} \Lambda_1 & 0 & \cdots & 0 & 0 \\ 0 & \Lambda_3 & \cdots & 0 & 0 \\ \vdots & \vdots & \cdots & & 0 \\ 0 & 0 & \cdots & \Lambda_{m-1} & 0 \\ 0 & 0 & \cdots & 0 & \Lambda_{m+1} \end{bmatrix},$$

$$\Lambda_i = \begin{bmatrix} \sigma_i & \mu_i \\ -\mu_i & \sigma \end{bmatrix} \quad (i = 1, 3, 5, \ldots, m - 1),$$

and

$$\Lambda_{m+1} = \begin{bmatrix} \lambda_{m+1} & 0 & \cdots & 0 \\ 0 & \lambda_{m+2} & & \\ & 0 & & \\ \vdots & \vdots & & \vdots \\ 0 & 0 & \cdots & \lambda_n \end{bmatrix}.$$

The following corollary shows that the transformed matrix of Theorem 23 is a normal matrix.

Corollary 7. Given the assumptions of Theorem 23, the matrix $F = T^{-1}AT$ is a normal matrix.

Proof. By definition, a real matrix F is normal if $F^TF = FF^T$. Since by Theorem 23 F is real, it need only be shown that $F^TF = FF^T$. But F is in block diagonal form. Thus if each block is normal, then F is normal. Clearly, the blocks

$$\Lambda_{m+1} = \begin{bmatrix} \lambda_{m+1} & 0 & \cdots & 0 \\ 0 & \lambda_{m+2} & & \\ & 0 & & \\ \vdots & \vdots & & \vdots \\ 0 & 0 & \cdots & \lambda_n \end{bmatrix}$$

are diagonal and thus normal. For the blocks

$$\Lambda_i = \begin{bmatrix} \sigma_i & \mu_i \\ -\mu_i & \sigma_i \end{bmatrix}$$

it can be shown that

$$\Lambda_i^T\Lambda_i = \Lambda_i\Lambda_i^T.$$

Thus Λ_i is normal, all of the diagonal blocks of F are normal, and hence F is normal. Q.E.D.

Even in the case of systems with nondistinct eigenvalues, a similarity transformation T can be found such that $W(T^{-1}AT)$ is as close as desired to the convex hull of the spectrum of A, $\sigma(A)$. To see this, assume A has been transformed into the Jordan block of length r of the transformed matrix associated with $\lambda \in \sigma(A)$:

$$J = \begin{bmatrix} \lambda_1 & 1 & 0 & & \cdots & 0 \\ 0 & \lambda_2 & 1 & 0 & \cdots & 0 \\ \vdots & \vdots & & \ddots & & \vdots \\ & & & & \ddots & 1 \\ 0 & & & & \cdots & \lambda_r \end{bmatrix}.$$

Note that for $\alpha \in C$ this block can be transformed to

$$\begin{bmatrix} 1 & & & \\ & \alpha^{-1} & & \\ & & \ddots & \\ & & & \alpha^{-(r-1)} \end{bmatrix} \begin{bmatrix} \lambda_1 & 1 & 0 & \cdots & 0 \\ 0 & \lambda_2 & 1 & 0 \cdots & 0 \\ \vdots & \vdots & \ddots & \ddots & \vdots \\ & & & \ddots & 1 \\ 0 & & \cdots & & \lambda_r \end{bmatrix} \begin{bmatrix} 1 & & & \\ & \alpha & & \\ & & \ddots & \\ & & & \alpha^{(r-1)} \end{bmatrix}$$

$$= \begin{bmatrix} \lambda_1 & \alpha & 0 & \cdots & 0 \\ 0 & \lambda_2 & \alpha & 0 \cdots & 0 \\ & & \lambda_3 & \ddots & 0 \\ \vdots & & & \ddots & 0 \\ & & & & \alpha \\ 0 & 0 & 0 & \cdots & \lambda_r \end{bmatrix}.$$

Thus by taking α sufficiently small, the block becomes diagonal. After performing a similar transformation on every Jordan block of length greater than 1, the matrix can be transformed into a "nearly" diagonal form.

When the plant matrices of each subsystem have been transformed to a diagonal or nearly diagonal form, it is possible to approximate the location of the composite system eigenvalues to smaller regions of the complex plane than defined by the numerical range plus some delta. The following theorem of Feingold and Varga defines this method for partitioned matrices.

Theorem 24 [15]. Let the partitioned matrix A of Eq. (109) be such that its diagonal submatrices $A_{ii} \in C^{n_i \times n_i}$ are all normal. If the Euclidean vector norm is used in Eq. (110), then each Gerschgorin set G_i is the union of n_i circles with center λ_r, $\lambda_r \in \sigma(A_{ii})$, $i \leq r \leq n_i$, and radius less than or equal to

$$\sum_{\substack{j=1 \\ j \neq i}}^{k} \|A_{ij}\|.$$

Thus, once the subsystem plant matrices have been transformed to a normal form, checking if the composite system is asymptotically stable using Theorem 21 reduces to verifying that for all $\lambda \in \sigma(A_{ii})$ $i = 1, \ldots, k$,

$$\operatorname{Re} \lambda < -\sum_{\substack{j=1 \\ j \neq i}}^{k} \|A_{ij}\|, \quad i = 1, \ldots, k. \tag{122}$$

This fact is summarized in the following theorem.

Theorem 25. Let the plant matrix of each subsystem of the composite system (108) be in normal form; then, using the Euclidean norm, if for each $\lambda \in A_{ii}$, $i = 1, \ldots, k$,

$$\operatorname{Re} \lambda < -\sum_{\substack{j=1 \\ j \neq i}}^{k} \|A_{ij}\|, \quad i = 1, \ldots, k,$$

then the composite system will be asymptotically stable.

Proof. Given that the subsystem plant matrices are normal, by Theorem 24 the Gerschgorin sets G_i, $i = 1, \ldots, k$, consist of the union of n_i circles with centers at the eigenvalues of A_{ii} and with

$$\text{radii} \leq \sum_{\substack{j=1 \\ j \neq i}}^{k} \|A_{ij}\|.$$

Thus, since

$$\sigma(A) \subset \bigcup_{i=1}^{k} G_i$$

and since

$$\operatorname{Re} \lambda < -\sum_{\substack{j=1 \\ j \neq i}}^{k} \|A_{ij}\|, \quad \lambda \in A_{ii},$$

for each $s \in \sigma(A)$, Re $s < 0$, the total system is asymptotically stable. Q.E.D.

An important property of composite systems that satisfies the sufficient condition for asymptotic stability developed in this section is that they remain asymptotically stable when the interconnections between subsystems are broken. This is so since if an interconnection between subsystem i and subsystem j is broken, $A_{ij} = 0$ and thus $||A_{ij}|| = 0$ and the requirements of Theorems 21 and 25 are still maintained. Thus composite systems that meet this sufficient condition for asymptotic stability are very reliable with respect to structural perturbations of the interconnection matrices. Furthermore, it can be shown that these composite systems are "connectively stable systems" [54].

D. DECENTRALIZED STABILIZATION

In this section, based on the development of the sufficient condition for asymptotic stability of composite systems, two simple decentralized stabilization algorithms are proposed. Both algorithms assume the system has no unstable fixed modes.

The first algorithm assumes only local feedback is available for the linear time-invariant system represented by k channels of the form

$$\dot{x}_i(t) = A_{ii}x_i(t) + B_iu_i(t) + \sum_{\substack{j=1 \\ j\neq i}}^{k} A_{ij}x_j(t), \quad i = 1, \ldots, k, \tag{123}$$

where all vectors and matrices are of appropriate dimension as defined in Section IV,A and the pairs (A_{ii}, B_i) are controllable.

The local control $u_i(t)$ has the form

$$u_i(t) = u_i^d(t) + u_i^s(t),$$

where $u_i^d(t)$ is used to make the eigenvalues of the ith local subsystem distinct so that its plant matrix can be transformed into a normal form by a similarity transformation. If $\sigma(A_{ii})$ is distinct, then $u_i^d(t) = 0$. The control $u_i^s(t)$ is used to stabilize the local subsystem to a prespecified degree of stability. These control inputs have the form

$$u_i^d(t) = -K_i^d x(t), \quad K_i^d \in R^{m_i \times n_i}, \tag{124a}$$

$$u_i^s(t) = -K_i^s x(t), \quad K_i^s \in R^{m_i \times n_i}. \tag{124b}$$

The approach is to use a nonsingular similarity transformation of the form

$$T = \mathrm{diag}[T_1, \ldots, T_k], \tag{125}$$

where $T \in C^{n \times n}$, $T_i \in C^{n_i \times n_i}$ to transform each subsystem to a normal form. Once each susbsystem has been transformed into its normal form, the numerical range of each subsystem is equal to the convex hull of $\sigma\left(T_i^{-1} A_{ii} T_i\right)$ by Theorem 18. Thus, if

$$\mathrm{Re}\ \sigma(A_{ii}) = \mathrm{Re}\ \sigma\left(T_i^{-1} A_{ii} T_i\right) < -\sum_{\substack{j=1 \\ j \neq i}}^{k} \|T_i^{-1} A_{ij} T_j\| = -\alpha_i, \tag{126}$$

$i = 1, \ldots, k$, the composite system will be asymptotically stable by Theorem 25. Note that the spectrum of a matrix is invariant under a similarity transformation. The main objective of this algorithm is to determine a local feedback control law for each subsystem such that

$$\operatorname{Re} \sigma\left(A_{ii} - B_i K_i^d - B_i K_i^s\right) < -\sum_{\substack{j=1 \\ j \neq i}}^{k} \|L_i^{-1} A_{ij} L_j\| \tag{127}$$

for $i = 1, \ldots, k$, where L_i is a nonsingular similarity transformation matrix such that

$$L_i^{-1}\left(A_{ii} - B_i K_i^d - B_i K_i^s\right) L_i \tag{128}$$

is a normal matrix. Since by assumption the pair (A_{ii}, B_i) is controllable, the closed-loop spectrum for each subsystem can be freely assigned via a pole-placement algorithm [65,30,8] or an eigenvalue/eigenvector assignment algorithm [46].

Alternatively, each closed-loop subsystem using the performance index

$$J(\alpha_i) = \int_0^\infty e^{2\alpha_i t}\left[x_i^T(t) Q_i x_i(t) + u_i^T(t) R_i u_i(t)\right] dt, \tag{129}$$

where $Q_i \in R^{n_i \times n_i}$ and $R_i \in R^{m_i \times m_i}$ are positive semidefinite and positive definite matrices, respectively. The control which minimizes Eq. (129) is

$$u_i(t) = -R_i^{-1} B_i^T P_i x_i(t) = -K_i^s x_i(t), \tag{130}$$

where $P_i \in R^{n_i \times n_i}$ is the unique positive definite solution of the following algebraic matrix Ricatti equation:

$$\left(A_{ii} - B_i K_i^d + \alpha_i I_{n_i}\right)^T P_i + P_i\left(A_{ii} - B_i K_i^d + \alpha_i I_{n_i}\right)$$

$$- P_i B_i R_i^{-1} B_i^T P_i + Q_i = 0. \tag{131}$$

Assuming the pair $\left(A_{ii} - B_i K_i^d + \alpha_i I_{n_i}, B_i\right)$ is controllable and the pair $\left(A_{ii} - B_i K_i^d + \alpha_i I_{n_i}, Q_i^{1/2}\right)$ is observable, application of the control (130) to the ith subsystem yields

$$\operatorname{Re} \sigma\left(A_{ii} - B_i K_i^d - B_i K_i^s\right) < -\alpha_i. \tag{132}$$

This algorithm consists of two main steps. One is to ensure that

$$\mathrm{Re}\ \sigma\left(A_{ii} - B_iK_i^d - B_iK_i^s\right) < -\alpha_i \tag{133a}$$

and the other is to ensure

$$\|L_i^{-1}A_{ij}L_j\| \leq \|T_i^{-1}A_{ij}T_j\|. \tag{133b}$$

The following algorithm illustrates this stabilization scheme.

Algorithm 1.

(1) Check if the subsystem matrices A_{ii} have distinct eigenvalues. If not, use the control input $u_i^d(t)$ to assign distinct eigenvalues via any simple pole-placement scheme.

(2) Normalize the subsystem matrices using the transformation matrix T and determine the value of α_i from Eq. (126) for $i = 1, \ldots, k$.

(3) Use a simple pole-placement technique to assign the

$$\mathrm{Re}\ \sigma\left(A_{ii} - B_iK_i^d - B_iK_i^s\right) < -\alpha_i$$

for $i = 1, \ldots, k$ and such that the eigenvalues are distinct.

(4) Determine a new similarity transformation L_i that normalizes

$$A_{ii} - B_iK_i^d - B_iK_i^s, \quad i = 1, \ldots, k.$$

(5) If conditions (133a,b) are not satisfied, Step 3 can be repeated by choosing different eigenvalues or possibly a different L.

(6) Stop.

In order to compare this stabilization scheme against other decentralized stabilization schemes, two systems that had previously been used to demonstrate a decentralized stabilization scheme in the control literature were chosen to illustrate

Algorithm 1. The system of the first example is from [57]. The second example uses a system from [29]. Neither system has fixed modes.

Example 12. Consider the system

$$\dot{x}(t) = \begin{bmatrix} 0 & 1 & 1 \\ -2 & -3 & -0.5 \\ 1 & 2 & 3 \end{bmatrix} x(t) + \begin{bmatrix} 0 & 0 \\ 1 & 0 \\ 0 & 1 \end{bmatrix} u(t),$$

whose eigenvalues are {-0.690, -2.233, 2.922}. It is desired to stabilize this system via a decentralized local feedback by decomposing the problem into two subproblems, the first one with

$$\dot{x}_1(t) \begin{bmatrix} 0 & 1 \\ -2 & -3 \end{bmatrix} x_1(t) + \begin{bmatrix} 0 \\ 1 \end{bmatrix} u_1(t) + \begin{bmatrix} 1 \\ -0.5 \end{bmatrix} x_2(t)$$

and the second one with

$$\dot{x}_2(t) = [3]x_2(t) + u_2(t).$$

The first subsystem has eigenvalues {-1.0, -2.0} and the second system has an eigenvalue at {3.0}. Since these eigenvalues are distinct, $u_1^d = u_2^d = 0$. A set of transformation matrices T_1, T_1^{-1} that transforms the first subsystem to normal form is

$$T_1 = \begin{bmatrix} 0.778 & -1.555 \\ -0.778 & 3.111 \end{bmatrix},$$

$$T_1^{-1} = \begin{bmatrix} 2.571 & 1.285 \\ 0.643 & 0.643 \end{bmatrix}.$$

Since the second subsystem has a dimension of one, $T_2 = T_2^{-1} = 1$, the composite system stability bound using the euclidean norm for system one is

$$\alpha_1 = ||T_1^{-1}A_{12}T_2|| = 1.954$$

and for subsystem two is

$$\alpha_2 = ||T_2^{-1}A_{21}T_1|| = 4.7314.$$

Assigning the closed-loop eigenvalues $\{-2.0 \pm i2.5\}$ to subsystem 1 and $\{-5\}$ to subsystem 2 using the local controls

$$u_1^s(t) = -K_1 x_1(t), \quad u_2^s(t) = -K_2 x_1(t)$$

requires the feedback gains

$$K_1 = [8.25 \quad 1], \quad K_2 = [8].$$

The set of transformation matrices L_1, L_1^{-1} that transforms subsystem one's closed-loop plant matrix to diagonal form is

$$L_1 = \begin{bmatrix} 0.488 & -0.390 \\ 0 & 2.000 \end{bmatrix},$$

$$L_1^{-1} = \begin{bmatrix} 2.050 & 0.400 \\ 0 & 0.500 \end{bmatrix}.$$

Again, since subsystem two has dimension one, $L_2 = L_2^{-1} = 1$. The new composite system stability bound for subsystem one is

$$\alpha_1 = \|L_1^{-1} A_{12} L_2\| = 1.867$$

and for subsystem two is

$$\alpha_2 = \|L_2^{-1} A_{21} L_1\| = 3.643.$$

Thus for both subsystems $\operatorname{Re} \sigma(A_{ii} - B_i K_i) < -\alpha_i$, $i = 1, 2$, and

$$\|T_i^{-1} A_{ij} T_j\| \geq \|L_i^{-1} A_{ij} L_j\|, \quad i = 1, 2, \quad i \neq j,$$

and therefore by Theorem 25 the composite system is stable. This checks with a calculation of the closed-loop composite system eigenvalues, are $\{-1.592 \pm i3.033, -5.817\}$.

The system of the next example was used in [29] to illustrate a decentralized exponential stabilization scheme. The concept developed in this section will be used to stabilize this composite system via decentralized control.

Example 13. Consider the fourth-order system

$$\dot{x}(t) = \begin{bmatrix} 0 & 0 & 0 & -0.1 \\ 0.5 & -1.0 & 0.15 & 0 \\ -0.1 & 0 & 1.0 & -0.1 \\ 0 & 0.15 & 2.0 & -0.8 \end{bmatrix} x(t) + \begin{bmatrix} 1 & 0 \\ 0 & 0 \\ 0 & 1 \\ 0 & 0.2 \end{bmatrix} u(t),$$

with eigenvalues {-1.03, -0.05, -0.62, 0.89}. It is desired to stabilize this system via a decentralized control. It is assumed that this system is decomposed into two two-dimensional subsystems described by

$$\dot{x}_1(t) = \begin{bmatrix} 0 & 0 \\ 0.5 & -1.0 \end{bmatrix} x_1(t) + \begin{bmatrix} 1 \\ 0 \end{bmatrix} u_1(t) + \begin{bmatrix} 0 & -0.1 \\ 0.15 & 0 \end{bmatrix} x_2(t),$$

$$\dot{x}_2(t) = \begin{bmatrix} 1.0 & -0.1 \\ 2.0 & -0.8 \end{bmatrix} x_2(t) + \begin{bmatrix} 1 \\ 0.2 \end{bmatrix} u_2(t) + \begin{bmatrix} -0.1 & 0 \\ 0 & 0.15 \end{bmatrix} x_1(t),$$

with eigenvalues $\sigma(A_{11}) = \{0.0, -1.0\}$ and $\sigma(A_{22}) = \{0.88, -0.68\}$. The local controls $u_1(t)$ and $u_2(t)$ have the forms

$$u_1(t) = -K_1 x_1(t), \quad K_1 \in R^{1\times 2},$$

$$u_2(t) = -K_2 x_2(t), \quad K_2 \in R^{1\times 2}.$$

Note that because of the structure of the control input matrices B_1, B_2, there exists a local feedback for each subsystem that forces the closed-loop subsystem plant matrices $A_{ii} - B_i K_i$, $i = 1, 2$, to be in normal form. Thus, for this example, by restricting the allowable feedback gains to be such that the closed-loop subsystem plant matrices are in normal form, it is not necessary to calculate transformation matrices. Using this restriction on the feedback gains, the composite system stability bounds using the euclidean norm are

$$\alpha_1 = \|A_{12}\| = 0.1803, \quad \alpha_2 = \|A_{21}\| = 0.1803.$$

A feedback K_1 that normalizes subsystem one and satisfies $\mathrm{Re}\ \sigma(A_{11} - B_1K_1) < -\alpha_1$ is

$$K_1 = [1.0 \quad -0.5]$$

and yields

$$\sigma(A_{11} - B_1K_1) = \{-1.5, -0.5\}.$$

A feedback K_2 that normalizes subsystem two and satisfies $\mathrm{Re}\ \sigma(A_{22} - B_2K_2) < -\alpha_2$ is

$$K_2 = [10.0 \quad -0.1]$$

and yields

$$\sigma(A_{22} - B_2K_2) = \{-9.0 \quad -0.78\}.$$

Thus since both subsystems meet their composite system stability bounds, the closed-loop composite system is stable by Theorem 25. The closed-loop composite system plant matrix is

$$A_{CL} = \begin{bmatrix} -1.0 & 0.5 & 0 & -0.1 \\ 0.5 & -1.0 & 0.15 & 0 \\ -0.1 & 0 & -9.0 & 0 \\ 0 & 0.15 & 0 & -0.78 \end{bmatrix},$$

and it has eigenvalues

$$\sigma(A_{CL}) = \{-1.51, -0.53, -9.0, -0.74\}.$$

Thus the stabilization scheme checks out. Note that this stabilization scheme forces the system to be connectively stable [54], that is, if any of the interconnection matrices are set equal to zero, the composite closed-loop system will remain asymptotically stable.

The next decentralized stabilization scheme employs a multilevel control and thus is a type of hierarchical control. This multilevel control has the form

$$u_i(t) = u_i^l(t) + u_i^g(t), \tag{134}$$

with the ith local control, $u_i^l(t)$, and ith global control, $u_i^g(t)$, described by

$$u_i^l(t) = -K_i x_i(t), \tag{135}$$

$$u_i^g(t) = -\sum_{\substack{j=1 \\ j\neq i}}^{k} K_{ij} x_j(t), \tag{136}$$

where $K_i \in R^{m_i \times n_i}$, $K_{ij} \in R^{m_i \times n_j}$. Applying the controls (135) and (136) to Eq. (123) yields the closed-loop system

$$\dot{x}_i(t) = (A_{ii} - B_i K_i) x_i(t) + \sum_{\substack{j=1 \\ j\neq i}}^{k} (A_{ij} - B_i K_{ij}) x_j(t), \quad i = 1, \ldots, k. \tag{137}$$

From Eq. (137) it is obvious that the global controls have a direct effect on the interconnections between the subsystems. Thus it is possible to reduce the composite system stability bounds α_i on the subsystems by minimizing the following norm:

$$\|T_i^{-1}(A_{ij} - B_i K_{ij}) T_j\|, \quad i, j = 1, 2, \ldots, k, \quad i \neq j, \tag{138}$$

where T_i is a nonsingular transformation matrix that transforms the ith subsystem's plant matrix to a normal form. Minimizing Eq. (138) can be shown to be equivalent to minimizing

$$\|A_{ij} - B_i K_{ij}\|. \tag{139}$$

Assuming B_i has full rank, a feedback gain matrix K_{ij} that minimizes Eq. (139) is given by

$$\left(B_i^T B_i\right)^{-1} B_i^T A_{ij} = K_{ij}, \tag{140}$$

where $\left(B_i^T B_i\right)^{-1} B_i^T$ is the Moore–Penrose generalized inverse [7] of B_i. Also, it is possible to use the global controller to minimize adverse effects on the stability of the composite system due to structural perturbations of the interconnections.

The goal of this multilevel control scheme is to allow the local controllers more flexibility in assigning their respective closed-loop subsystem's eigenvalues. This is accomplished by reducing the composite system stability bounds on the subsystems, as discussed above. The following algorithm illustrates this stabilization scheme.

Algorithm 2.

(1) Assign the desired stable, distinct closed-loop poles of each subsystem using the local control u_i^l.

(2) Determine the transformation matrices T_i that transform each closed-loop subsystem's plant matrix to diagonal form. Calculate the composite system stability bound for each subsystem:

$$\sum_{\substack{j=1 \\ j\neq j}}^{k} \|T_i^{-1} A_{ij} T_j\| = \alpha_i.$$

(3) If the real part of the spectrum of some ith subsystem is greater than $-\alpha_i$, apply global feedback of the form

$$u_i^g(t) = -\sum_{\substack{j=1 \\ j\neq i}}^{k} \left(B_i^T B_i\right)^{-1} B_i^T A_{ij} x_j = -\sum_{\substack{j=1 \\ j\neq i}}^{k} K_{ij} x_j$$

and calculate

$$\sum_{\substack{j=1 \\ j\neq i}}^{k} \|T_i^{-1}(A_{ij} - B_i K_{ij}) T_j\| = \alpha_i'.$$

(4) If after applying global feedback all the closed-loop subsystems do not meet their revised composite system stability bounds $-\alpha_i'$, repeat steps 1 through 4, placing the poles of the subsystems that did not meet their composite system stability bound after global feedback further to the left in the complex plane.

(5) Stop.

The next example illustrates this algorithm. The system of this example was used in [29] to illustrate a different multi-level stabilization scheme.

Example 14. Consider the interconnected system

$$\dot{x}(t) = \begin{bmatrix} 0 & 1.0 & 0 & 1.0 & 1.0 \\ 0 & 0 & 1.0 & 0.1 & 1.0 \\ 4.0 & -1.0 & 2.0 & 0 & 0.5 \\ 0.4 & 0.2 & 0 & 0 & 1.0 \\ 0.5 & 0.2 & 1.0 & -1.0 & 2.0 \end{bmatrix} x(t) + \begin{bmatrix} 0 & 0 \\ 0 & 0 \\ 1 & 0 \\ 0 & 0 \\ 0 & 1 \end{bmatrix}.$$

The composite system has eigenvalues at (3.505, 0.469 ± j1.560, -0.221 ± j0.600), which indicates that the system is unstable. Assume that the composite system is decomposed into the following subsystems:

$$\dot{x}_1 = \begin{bmatrix} 0 & 1.0 & 0 \\ 0 & 0 & 1.0 \\ 4.0 & -1.0 & 2.0 \end{bmatrix} x_1 + \begin{bmatrix} 0 \\ 0 \\ 1 \end{bmatrix} u_1 + \begin{bmatrix} 1.0 & 1.0 \\ 0.1 & 1.0 \\ 0 & 0.5 \end{bmatrix} x_2,$$

$$\dot{x}_2 = \begin{bmatrix} 0 & 1 \\ -1 & 2 \end{bmatrix} x_2 + \begin{bmatrix} 0 \\ 1 \end{bmatrix} u_2 + \begin{bmatrix} 0.4 & 0.2 & 0 \\ 0.5 & 0.2 & 1.0 \end{bmatrix} x_1.$$

The eigenvalues of the subsystem plant matrices are

$$\sigma(A_{11}) = \{-0.157 \pm i1.3,\ 2.31\}, \qquad \sigma(A_{22}) = \{1,\ 1\}.$$

Clearly, subsystem 1 has distinct eigenvalues; however, subsystem 2 does not. Applying

$$u_2^l = -K_2^l x_2 \quad \text{with} \quad K_2^l = [4 \quad 6]$$

to subsystem 2 changes the eigenvalues of subsystem 2 to

$$\sigma\left(A_{22} - B_2K_2^l\right) = \{-2 \pm i\},$$

and subsystem 2 now has the form

$$\dot{x}_2 = \begin{bmatrix} 0 & 1 \\ -5 & -4 \end{bmatrix} x_2 + \begin{bmatrix} 0 \\ 1 \end{bmatrix} u_2 + \begin{bmatrix} 0.4 & 0.2 & 0 \\ 0.5 & 0.2 & 1.0 \end{bmatrix} x_1.$$

Applying the local feedback

$$u_1^l = -K_1x_1(t),$$

where

$$K_1^l = [294 \quad 128 \quad 22],$$

stabilizes subsystem 1 and assigns it the eigenvalues $\{-5.0 \pm i2.0, -10.0\}$. Subsystem 1 now has the form

$$\dot{x}_1(t) = \begin{bmatrix} 0 & 1 & 0 \\ 0 & 0 & 1 \\ -290 & -129 & -20 \end{bmatrix} x_1(t) + \begin{bmatrix} 0 \\ 0 \\ 1 \end{bmatrix} u_1^g(t) + \begin{bmatrix} 1.0 & 1.0 \\ 0.1 & 1.0 \\ 0 & 0.5 \end{bmatrix} x_2(t).$$

The transformation matrices that transform subsystems 1 and 2 to normal forms are

$$T_1 = \begin{bmatrix} -2.494 & 1.619 & 0.200 \\ 9.234 & -13.084 & -2.000 \\ -20.000 & 83.900 & 20.000 \end{bmatrix},$$

$$T_1^{-1} = \begin{bmatrix} -0.915 & -0.1521 & -0.006 \\ -1.411 & -0.447 & -0.031 \\ 5.000 & 1.724 & 0.1724 \end{bmatrix},$$

$$T_2 = \begin{bmatrix} 0.2 & -0.4 \\ 0 & 1.0 \end{bmatrix},$$

$$T_2^{-1} = \begin{bmatrix} 5.0 & 2.0 \\ 0 & 1.0 \end{bmatrix}.$$

The transformed system is represented by the following interconnected systems:

$$\dot{x}_1'(t) = \begin{bmatrix} -5.0 & 2.0 & 0 \\ -2.0 & -5.0 & 0 \\ 0 & 0 & -10.0 \end{bmatrix} x_1'(t) + \begin{bmatrix} -0.931 & -3.492 \\ -1.455 & -6.455 \\ 5.170 & 23.705 \end{bmatrix} x_2'$$

$$+ \begin{bmatrix} -0.006 \\ -0.031 \\ 0.1724 \end{bmatrix} u_1(t),$$

$$\dot{x}_2'(t) = \begin{bmatrix} -2.0 & 1.0 \\ -1.0 & -2.0 \end{bmatrix} x_2'(t) + \begin{bmatrix} -6.912 & 30.86 & 7.56 \\ -3.880 & 16.4 & 3.94 \end{bmatrix} x_1'(t)$$

$$+ \begin{bmatrix} 0.4 \\ 0.2 \end{bmatrix} u_2(t).$$

Since ($\|\cdot\|$ is the euclidean norm)

$$\|T_1^{-1}A_{12}T_2\| = 25.409 = \alpha_2 > -\text{Re}\ \sigma\left(A_{11} + B_1K_1^l\right)$$

and

$$\|T_2^{-1}A_{21}T_1\| = 36.851 = \alpha_2 > -\text{Re}\ \sigma\left(A_{22} - B_2K_2^l\right),$$

neither subsystem satisfies Theorem 25, and therefore no conclusion can be drawn about the stability of the composite system.

Now, utilizing step 3 of Algorithm 2, the interconnection gains were calculated to be

$$K_1^g = [30.671 \quad 140.263], \qquad K_2^g = [-17.704 \quad 78.138 \quad 19.06].$$

Employing these gains in the global feedback structure yields the new composite system stability bounds

$$\|T_1^{-1}(A_{12})T_2 - B_1'K_1^g\| = 3.565 = \alpha_1,$$

$$\|T_2^{-1}(A_{21})T_1 - B_2'K_2^g\| = 0.9723 = \alpha_2.$$

Clearly,

$$\text{Re}\ \sigma\left(A_{11} - B_1K_1^l\right) < -\alpha_1$$

and

$$\operatorname{Re} \sigma\left(A_{22} - B_2 K_2^{l}\right) < -\alpha_2,$$

and therefore the closed-loop composite system

$$\begin{bmatrix} \dot{x}_1 \\ \dot{x}_2 \end{bmatrix} = \begin{bmatrix} -5.0 & 2.0 & 0 & -0.745 & -2.642 \\ -2.0 & -5.0 & 0 & -0.515 & -2.158 \\ 0 & 0 & -10.0 & -0.118 & -0.476 \\ 0.170 & -0.3950 & -0.064 & -2.0 & -1.0 \\ -0.3390 & 0.7900 & 0.128 & 1.0 & -2.0 \end{bmatrix} \begin{bmatrix} x_1 \\ x_2 \end{bmatrix}$$

is stable by Theorem 25.

A check of the eigenvalues of the composite system, which are $\{-5.12 \pm i2.34, -1.88 \pm i1.01, -9.99\}$, verifies the above conclusion.

E. ELIMINATION OF FIXED MODES VIA LIMITED INFORMATION EXCHANGE

In this section a design technique is proposed that minimizes the information exchange between system channels that is necessary to eliminate unstable fixed modes (Definition 12). This technique is then combined with a scheme that minimizes transmission costs [61].

Consider the linear, time-invariant, jointly controllable and jointly observable multivariable system with k channels described by

$$\dot{x}(t) = Ax(t) + \sum_{i=1}^{k} B_i u_i(t), \tag{141a}$$

$$y_i(t) = C_i x(t), \quad i = 1, \ldots, k, \tag{141b}$$

where $x(t) \in R^n$, $u_i(t) \in R^{m_i}$, $y_i(t) \in R^{q_i}$, $A \in R^{n\times n}$, $B_i \in R^{n\times m_i}$, and $C_i \in R^{q_i \times n}$. It has been shown [13] that in order to stabilize this system via local output feedback with dynamic compensation, the system must have no fixed modes in the right-half-closed complex plane C^+. In the event the system does have unstable fixed modes, it is necessary to determine the minimum information exchange between channels that is needed to eliminate the unstable fixed modes.

By Theorem 9, if λ_o is a fixed mode of the system (141a,b), there exists some partition of the set $\{1, \ldots, k\}$ into disjoint subsets $v_1 = \{i_1, \ldots, i_r\}$ and $v_2 = \{i_{r+1}, \ldots, i_k\}$ such that the triple (A, B_{v_1}, C_{v_2}), where

$$B_{v_1} = [B_{i_1}, \ldots, B_{i_r}], \tag{142a}$$

$$C_{v_2} = \begin{bmatrix} C_{i_{r+1}} \\ \vdots \\ C_{i_k} \end{bmatrix}, \tag{142b}$$

satisfies

$$\operatorname{rank}\begin{bmatrix} \lambda_o I_n - A & B_{v_1} \\ C_{v_2} & 0 \end{bmatrix} < n. \tag{143}$$

The purpose of the limited information exchange between channels is to make the fixed mode observable to channels which can control the mode. Since by assumption the system is jointly observable,

$$\operatorname{rank}\begin{bmatrix} \lambda_o I_n - A & B_{v_1} \\ C_{v_2} & 0 \\ C_{v_1} & 0 \end{bmatrix} \geq n. \tag{144}$$

Thus, by making all information from channels belonging to the set v_1 available to the channels belonging to the set v_2, λ_o can be eliminated as a fixed mode. Note that it may not be necessary to transmit all information from the channels of v_1

to those of v_2. For example, there may exist a subset h_1 of v_1 such that

$$\text{rank}\begin{bmatrix} \lambda_o I_n - A & B_{v_1} \\ C_{v_2} & 0 \\ C_{h_1} & 0 \end{bmatrix} \geq n, \quad h_1 \subset v_1. \tag{145}$$

In this case only information from channels belonging to the set h_1 need to be transmitted to channels belonging to the set v_2.

Similarly, since the system is jointly controllable,

$$\text{rank}\begin{bmatrix} \lambda_o I_n - A & B_{v_1} & B_{v_2} \\ C_{v_2} & 0 & 0 \end{bmatrix} \geq n. \tag{146}$$

However, it is possible that there exists a subset h_2 of v_2 such that

$$\text{rank}\begin{bmatrix} \lambda_o I_n - A & B_{v_1} & B_{h_2} \\ C_{v_2} & 0 & 0 \end{bmatrix} \geq n, \quad h_2 \subset v_2. \tag{147}$$

If Eqs. (145) and (147) are satisfied, then information from channels belonging to the set h_1 need only be transmitted to the channels belonging to the set h_2.

When there exists more than one subset h_1 or h_2 such that Eq. (145) or (147) is satisfied, it is desirable to determine the information exchange with minimum transmission cost.

In [61], it was assumed that there was a certain amount of transmission cost, say, $\alpha_{ij} \geq 0$, of transmitting a scalar time function from station j to station i per unit time. To determine how many scalar time functions were being transmitted from station j to station i, the rank of the feedback matrix K_{ij} was calculated. Consider the following set of matrices:

$$K'(\rho_{ij}, i, j = 1, \ldots, k)$$

$$= \left\{ K \mid K = \text{block}\{K^{ij}\} \triangleq \begin{bmatrix} K^{11} & & \cdots & K^{1k} \\ \vdots & K^{22} & \cdots & \vdots \\ & & \ddots & \\ K^{k1} & & \cdots & K^{kk} \end{bmatrix}, \right.$$

$$\left. K^{ij} \in R^{m_i \times q_i}, \quad \text{rank } K^{ij} = \rho_{ij} \right\}. \tag{148}$$

The set of matrices K defined in Eq. (148) are used in the set of constant output feedback laws $u = Ky$. Each feedback law consists of a set of (sub)feedback laws $u_i = K^{ij} y_j$ which require the transmission of a time function with ρ_{ij} components from station j to station i. The total transmission cost resulting in using a $K \in K'$ as defined in [61] is

$$T_c(\rho_{ij}, i, j = 1, \ldots, k) = \sum_{j=1}^{k} \sum_{i=1}^{k} \rho_{ij} \alpha_{ij}. \tag{149}$$

The problem is to find a set of integers ρ_{ij}, $0 \leq \rho_{ij} \leq \min(m_i, q_i)$, in order to minimize Eq. (149) subject to the set of unstable fixed modes being eliminated. The process of minimizing Eq. (149) consists of determining all sets h_1 and h_2 such that Eqs. (145) and (147) are satisfied and then calculating the transmission cost associated with each combination.

The following algorithm presents an efficient method for stabilizing a large-scale decentralized system with unstable fixed modes with minimum transmission cost.

Algorithm 3.

(1) Determine the set of unstable fixed modes using the method in [13].

(2) Determine the complementary subsystems for each unstable fixed mode such that Eq. (143) is satisfied.

(3) Determine all the sets h_1 and h_2 such that Eqs. (145) and (147) are satisfied.

(4) Determine the sets h_1 and h_2 that minimize Eq. (149).

(5) Stop.

The following example [62] illustrates this algorithm.

Example 15. Consider the jointly controllable and jointly observable three-channel system of Example 9. This system has a fixed mode at the origin. The complementary subsystem (A, B_2, B_3, C_1) satisfies

$$\operatorname{rank}\begin{bmatrix} -A & B_2 & B_3 \\ C_1 & 0 & 0 \end{bmatrix} = 5 < n.$$

For $C_{h_1} = C_2$ or C_3,

$$\operatorname{rank}\begin{bmatrix} -A & B_2 & B_3 \\ C_1 & 0 & 0 \\ C_{h_1} & 0 & 0 \end{bmatrix} = 6.$$

Assume that the transmission cost is $\alpha_{11} = \alpha_{22} = \alpha_{33} = 0$, $\alpha_{12} = 2$, $\alpha_{13} = 1$. Since $\rho_{12} = \rho_{13} = 1$, transmitting information from channel 3 to channel 1 results in the least cost, $T_c = 1$. Thus the feedback matrix has the form

$$K = \begin{bmatrix} k_1^{11} & k_2^{11} & 0 & 0 & k_1^{13} & k_2^{13} \\ 0 & 0 & k_1^{22} & k_2^{22} & 0 & 0 \\ 0 & 0 & 0 & 0 & k_1^{33} & k_2^{33} \end{bmatrix}, \qquad k_1^{ij},\ k_2^{ij} \in R.$$

Applying the feedback control law u = Ky results in the closed-loop plant matrix

$$(A + BKC) = \begin{bmatrix} 0 & 1 & 0 & 0 & 0 & 0 \\ k_1^{11} & k_2^{11} & 0 & 0 & k_1^{13} & k_2^{13} \\ 1 & 0 & 0 & 1 & 0 & 1 \\ 0 & 0 & k_1^{22} & k_2^{22} & 0 & 0 \\ 0 & 0 & 0 & 1 & 0 & 0 \\ 0 & 0 & 0 & 0 & k_1^{33} & k_2^{33} \end{bmatrix}.$$

It is obvious that for a proper selection of K, $0 \notin \sigma(A - BKC)$. Thus the fixed mode at the origin has been eliminated. The next example is taken from [3], where the authors, Armentano and Singh, presented a fixed-mode elimination scheme using the Gerschgorin circle theorem for block matrices. The scheme in [3] is computationally burdensome compared to the scheme presented in this section.

Example 16. Consider the two-channel jointly controllable and jointly observable system

$$\begin{bmatrix} \dot{x}_1^1 \\ \dot{x}_2^1 \\ \dot{x}_1^2 \\ \dot{x}_2^2 \end{bmatrix} = \begin{bmatrix} 1 & 0 & 0 & 1 \\ 0 & 0 & 0 & 0 \\ 1 & 0 & 0 & 1 \\ 0 & 0 & 0 & 0 \end{bmatrix} \begin{bmatrix} x_1^1 \\ x_2^1 \\ x_1^2 \\ x_2^2 \end{bmatrix} + \begin{bmatrix} 0 \\ 1 \\ 0 \\ 0 \end{bmatrix} u_1 + \begin{bmatrix} 0 & 0 \\ 0 & 0 \\ 1 & 0 \\ 0 & 1 \end{bmatrix} u_2,$$

$$y_1 = \begin{bmatrix} 1 & 0 & 0 & 0 \\ 0 & 1 & 0 & 0 \end{bmatrix} x,$$

$$y_2 = [0 \quad 0 \quad 1 \quad 0]x.$$

This system has a decentalized fixed mode at the origin. The complementary subsystem (A, B_1, C_2) satisfies Eq. (143) since

$$\text{rank}\begin{bmatrix} -A & B_1 \\ C_2 & 0 \end{bmatrix} = 3 < n.$$

Therefore, to eliminate the fixed mode at the origin, information must be transmitted from channel 1 to channel 2. Thus, the feedback matrix has the form

$$K = \begin{bmatrix} k_1^{11} & k_2^{11} & 0 \\ k_1^{21} & k_2^{21} & k_1^{22} \\ k_3^{21} & k_4^{21} & k_2^{22} \end{bmatrix} = \begin{bmatrix} K^{11} & 0 \\ K^{21} & K^{22} \end{bmatrix}, \qquad k_r^{ij} \in R.$$

Applying the feedback control law $u = Ky$ results in the closed-loop plant matrix

$$A - BKC = \begin{bmatrix} 1 & 0 & 0 & 1 \\ k_1^{11} & k_2^{11} & 0 & 0 \\ 1 + k_1^{21} & k_2^{21} & k_1^{22} & 1 \\ k_3^{21} & k_4^{21} & k_2^{22} & 0 \end{bmatrix}.$$

It is obvious that for a proper selection of K, $0 \notin \sigma(A - BKC)$. Thus, the fixed mode at the origin has been eliminated.

F. SUMMARY AND CONCLUSION

In this section a sufficient condition for composite system stability based on the numerical range of the subsystem matrices and the structure of the system interconnections was proposed. This sufficient condition provides an alternative to the so-called Lyapunov methods [29] in determining if a composite system is asymtotically stable.

Two algorithms that provide feedback laws that stabilize an unstable composite system were proposed based on this sufficient condition for asymptotic stability. The first algorithm employs local feedback to stabilize the composite system. The second algorithm uses a multilevel approach. In this multilevel approach, a local feedback is used to stabilize the subsystems and a global control is used to minimize the effects of the system interconnections, thus resulting in an asymptotically stable composite closed-loop system.

In Section IV,E a method that eliminates the fixed modes of a system via limited information exchange was proposed. This method presents a way of choosing a new structure for the system feedback matrix such that the fixed modes are eliminated. This procedure was illustrated in two examples. It was shown that this method can be used to develop partially decentralized control systems.

V. CONCLUSIONS

As stated in the introduction of this article the purpose of this study was to investigate the use of system zeros in the decentralized control of large-scale systems. To meet this objective, Section II presented definitions and properties of decentralized system zeros. The decentralized transmission zeros of a system were shown to be crucial to the stability of the composite closed-loop system under high-gain decentralized feedback. Relations between a system's joint controllability and joint observability and its ith channel controllability and ith channel observability were developed using the concept of decentralized zeros.

Single-channel controllability and observability of two-channel systems were investigated in Section III. The concept of ij input–output decoupling zeros was introduced. Necessary and sufficient conditions in terms of the ij input–output decoupling zeros for a two-channel system to be made controllable and observable or stabilizable and detectable from a single-channel were presented. This result is significant since these conditions can be easily verified using the algorithms presented in Appendix A of [31]. Previous conditions [9,10,16,17], although mathematically equivalent to those mentioned above, lack a computationally attractive method of verification.

A sufficient condition for composite system stability based on the numerical range [25] of the subsystem plant matrices and the generalized Gerschgorin circle theorem for block matrices [15] was introduced in Section IV. It was shown that this sufficient condition provides an alternative procedure for determining the stability of the composite system to the so-called Lyapunov methods [29]. It was also shown that systems that satisfy this condition are connectively stable [55].

Two algorithms were proposed in Section IV to stabilize the composite system. The first method uses local feedback to ensure that the poles of the closed-loop subsystems meet their composite system stability bound requirements. The second method uses a multilevel feedback control to stabilize the composite system. This multilevel control consists of a local and a global control law. The local control stabilizes the subsystems, while the global control is used to minimize the subsystem interactions. Both of these methods were used to stabilize systems that had been used in the control literature to illustrate other decentralized stabilization schemes.

A method that eliminates the fixed modes of a system was also proposed in Section IV. This method was illustrated on two systems. It was shown that this method can be used to develop a partially decentralized control law when a system has unstable fixed modes.

REFERENCES

1. L. ALDERMESHIAN, "Model Reduction Techniques in the Stochastic Control of Data Communication Networks," M.S. Thesis, Massachusetts Institute of Technology, November 1975.

2. B. D. O. ANDERSON and D. J. CLEMENTS, "Algebraic Characterization of Fixed Modes in Decentralized Control," *Automatica 17*, No. 5, 703-712 (1981).

3. V. A. ARMENTANO and M. G. SINGH, "A Procedure to Eliminate Fixed Modes With Reduced Information Exchange," *IEEE Trans. Autom. Control AC-27*, No. 1, 258-260, February 1982.

4. M. ATHANS and D. KENDRICK, "Control Theory and Economics in a Survey, Forecast and Speculations," *IEEE Trans. Autom. Control AC-19*, No. 5, 518-523 (1974).

5. M. ATHANS and P. L. FALB, "Optimal Control," McGraw-Hill, New York, 1976.

6. M. J. BALAS, "Trends in Large Space Structure Control Theory: Fondest Hopes; Wildest Dreams," *IEEE Trans. Autom. Control AC-27*, No. 3, 522-535, June 1982.

7. S. CAMPBELL and C. MEYER, JR., "Generalized Inverses of Linear Transformations," Pitman Press, San Francisco, 1979.

8. C. T. CHEN, "Introduction to Linear System Theory," Holt, Rinehart and Winston, New York, 1970.

9. J. P. CORFMAT and A. S. MORSE, "Control of Linear Systems Through Specified Input Channels," *SIAM J. Control Optimization 14*, No. 1, 163-175 (1976).

10. J. P. CORFMAT and A. S. MORSE, "Decentralized Control of Linear Multivariable Systems," *Automatica 12*, 479-495 (1976).

11. E. J. DAVISON and N. K. TRIPATH, "The Optimal Decentralized Control of a Large Power System: Load and Frequency Control," *IEEE Trans. Autom. Control AC-23*, No. 2, 312-325, April 1978.

12. E. J. DAVISON, "The Decentralized Stabilization and Control of Unknown Nonlinear Time-Varying Systems," *Automatica 10*, No. 3, 309-316 (1974).

13. E. J. DAVISON and S. H. WANG, "On the Stabilization of Decentralized Control Systems," *IEEE Trans. Autom. Control AC-18*, 473-478, October 1973.

14. J. D'AZZO and C. H. HOUPIS, "Linear Control System Analysis and Design: Conventional and Modern," McGraw-Hill, New York, 1975.

15. D. G. FEINGOLD and R. S. VARGA, "Block Diagonally Dominant Matrices and Generalizations of the Gerschgorin Circle Theorem," *Pacific J. Math 12*, 1241-1250 (1962).

16. P. S. FESSAS, "Decentralized Control of Linear Dynamical Systems via Polynomial Matrix Methods Part I: Two Interconnected Scalar Systems," *Int. J. Control 30*, No. 9, 259-276 (1979).

17. P. S. FESSAS, "Decentralized Control of Linear Dynamical Systems via Polynomial Matrix Methods Part II: Interconnected Systems," *Int. J. Control 32*, No. 1, 127-147 (1980).

18. T. FORTMANN and K. HITZ, "An Introduction to Linear Control Systems," Marcel Dekker, New York, 1977.

19. A. S. FOSS, "Critique of Chemical Process Control Theory," *IEEE Trans. Autom. Control AC-18*, No. 6, 646-652 (1973).

20. B. A. FRANCIS and K. GLOVER, "Bounded Peaking in the Optimal Linear Regulator with Cheap Control," *IEEE Trans. Autom. Control AC-23*, No. 4, 608-617, August 1978.

21. B. A. FRANCIS, "The Optimal Linear-Quadratic Time Invariant Regulator with Cheap Control, " *IEEE Trans. Autom. Control AC-24*, No. 4, 616-621, August 1979.

22. F. R. GANTMACHER, "The Theory of Matrices," Vols. 1 and 2, Chelsea Publishing Company, New York, 1977.

23. I. GLAZMAN and J. LJUBIC, "Finite-Dimensional Linear Analysis: A Systematic Presentation in Problem Form," MIT Press, Cambridge, Massachusetts, 1974.

24. I. GOHBERG, P. LANCASTER, and L. RODMAN, "Matrix Polynomials Academic Press, New York, 1982.

25. P. R. HALMOS, "A Hilbert Space Problem Book," D. Van Nostrand Company, Princeton, New Jersey, 1967.

26. P. K. HOUPT, "Decentralized Stochastic Control of Finite State Systems with Application to Vehicular Traffic Flow," Ph.D. Thesis, Massachusetts Institute of Technology, 1974.

27. L. ISAKSEN and H. J. PAYNE, "Suboptimal Control of Linear Systems by Augmentation with Application to Freeway Traffic Regulation," *IEEE Trans. Autom. Control AC-18*, 1973.

28. A. JAMESON and R. E. O'MALLEY, JR., "Cheap Control of Time-Invariant Regulators," *Appl. Math. Optimization 1*, No. 4, 337-354 (1975).

29. M. JAMSHIDI, "Large-Scale Systems Modeling and Control," North Holland, New York, 1983.

30. T. KAILATH, "Linear Systems," Prentice-Hall, New Jersey, 1980.

31. T. A. KENNEDY, "High Gain and System Zeros in the Decentralized Control of Large Scale Systems," Ph.D. Thesis, UCLA, 1984.

32. B. KOUVARITAKIS and J. M. EDMUNDS, "Multivariable Root Loci: A Unified Approach to Finite and Infinite Zeros," *Int. J. Control 29*, No. 3, 393-428 (1979).

33. B. KOUVARITAKIS and U. SHAKED, "Asymptotic Behavior of Root Loci of Multivariable Systems," *Int. J. Control 23*, No. 3, 297-340 (1976).

34. H. KWAKERNAAK, "Asymptotic Root Loci of Multivariable Linear Optimal Regulators," *IEEE Trans. Autom. Control AC-21*, 378-382, June 1976.

35. H. KWAKERNAAK and R. SIVAN, "The Maximally Achievable Accuracy of Linear Optimal Regulators and Linear Optimal Filters," *IEEE Trans. Autom. Control AC-17*, No. 1, 79-86, February 1972.

36. H. KWAKERNAAK and R. SIVAN, "Linear Optimal Control Systems," Wiley, New York, 1972.

37. B. LIMAYE, "Functional Analysis," Wiley, New York, 1981.

38. D. LUENBERGER, "Observers for Multivariable Systems," *IEEE Trans. Autom. Control AC-11*, 190-197 (1966).

39. A. G. J. MacFARLANE and N. KARCANIAS, "Poles and Zeros of Linear Multivariable Systems: A Survey of the Algebraic, Geometric and Complex-Variable Theory," *Int. J. Control 24*, No. 1, 33-74 (1976).

40. P. S. MAYBECK, "Stochastic Models Estimation and Control," Vol. *1*, Academic Press, New York, 1979.

41. J. S. MEDITCH, "Stochastic Optimal Linear Estimation and Control," McGraw-Hill, New York, 1969.

42. L. MEIROVITCH and H. OZ, "An Assessment of Methods for the Control of Large Space Structures," *Joint Autom. Control Conf.*, Denver, Colorado, 1979.

43. A. MICHEL and R. MILLER, "Qualitative Analysis of Large Scale Dynamical Systems," Academic Press, New York, 1977.

44. M. A. PAI, "Power System Stability," North-Holland Publ., New York, 1981.

45. R. V. PATEL and N. MUNRO, "Multivariable Systems Theory and Design," Pergamon Press, New York, 1982.

46. B. PORTER and L. J. T. GRUJIC, "Continuous Time Tracking Systems Incorporating Lur'e Plants with Multiple Nonlinearities," *Int. J. Syst. Sci. 11*, No. 7, 827-840 (1980).

47. B. PORTER and A. BRADSHAW, "Decentralized Transmission Zeros," *Electron. Lett. 15*, 230-232 (1978).

48. H. H. ROSENBROCK, "State-Space and Multivariable Theory," Wiley, New York, 1970.

49. H. H. ROSENBROCK, "The Zeros of a System," *Int. J. Control 18*, No. 2, 297-299 (1973).

50. H. H. ROSENBROCK, "Correction to 'The Zeros of a System'," *Int. J. Control 20*, No. 3, 525-527 (1974).

51. A. SEGALL, "New Analytical Models for Dynamic Routing in Computer Networks," *Natl. Telecommunications Conf.*, New Orleans, December 1975.

52. U. SHAKED and B. KOUVARITAKIS, "The Zeros of Linear Optimal Control Systems and Their Role in High Feedback Gain Stability Design," *IEEE Trans. Autom. Control AC-22*, No. 4, 597-599, August 1977.

53. U. SHAKED, "Design of Multivariable Systems Having Zero Sensitive Poles," *IEEE Trans. Autom. Control AC-24*, No. 1, 117-119, February 1979.

54. D. D. SILJAK and M. B. VUKCEVIC, "Decentralization, Stabilization, and Estimation of Large Scale Linear Systems," *IEEE Trans. Autom. Control AC-21*, 363-366 (1976).

55. D. D. SILJAK, "Large-Scale Dynamic Systems: Stability and Structure," North-Holland, New York, 1978.

56. M. G. SINGH, "River Pollution Control," *Int. J. Syst. Sci. 6*, No. 1, 9-21 (1975).

57. M. G. SINGH, "Decentralized Control," North-Holland, New York, 1981.

58. H. TAMURA, "A Discrete Dynamic Model With Distributed Transport Delays and Its Hierarchical Optimization for Preserving Stream Quality," *IEEE Trans. Syst. Man Cybernetics SMC-4*, No. 5, 424-431, September 1974.

59. P. VARAIYA, "Trends in the Theory of Decision-Making in Large Systems," *Ann. Economic Social Measurement 1*, 493-500 (1972).

60. M. VIDYASAGAR, "Nonlinear Systems Analysis," Prentice-Hall, Englewood Cliff, New Jersey, 1978.

61. S. WANG and E. J. DAVISON, "Minimization of Transmission Cost in Decentralized Control Systems," *Int. J. Control 28*, No. 6, 889-896 (1978).

62. S. WANG, "An Example in Decentralized Control Systems," *IEEE Trans. Autom. Control AC-23*, No. 5, 938, October 1978.

63. J. L. WILLIAMS, "Disturbance Isolation in Linear Feedback Systems," *Int. J. Syst. Sci. 6*, No. 3, 233-238 (1975).

64. H. WITSENHAUSEN, "A Counter-Example in Stochastic Optimal Control," *SIAM J. Control 6*, No. 1, 131-147 (1968).

65. W. A. WOLOVICH, "Linear Multivariable Systems," Springer-Verlag, New York, 1974.

66. W. M. WONHAM, "Linear Multivariable Control: A Geometric Approach," Springer-Verlag, New York, 1979.

67. L. A. ZADEH and C. A. DESOER, "Linear Systems Theory: The State Space Approach," Robert E. Krieger Publ., Huntington, New York, 1979.

Direct Model Reference Adaptive Control for a Class of MIMO Systems

KENNETH M. SOBEL

Lockheed California Company
Burbank, California 91520

HOWARD KAUFMAN

Electrical, Computer, and Systems Engineering Department
Rensselaer Polytechnic Institute
Troy, New York 12181

I. INTRODUCTION

Model reference control is based upon matching the response of a system or "plant" to that of a reference model or "model." The plant design specifications are incorporated within the model such that a step input to the model would cause its outputs to respond with the specified rise time, overshoot, and settling time. The reference inputs are fed into the model, which responds in accordance with the design specifications which have been built into it. If the control system is properly designed, the inputs to the plant (which are generated from the model inputs, the model states, and the error between plant and model outputs) drive the outputs of the plant to equal the outputs of the model. A block diagram of a typical model reference control system is shown in Fig. 1.

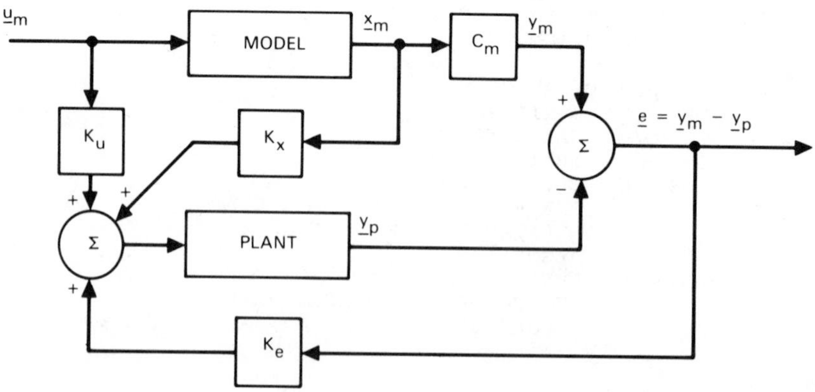

Fig. 1. Model reference control system.

When the designer has limited knowledge of the plant parameters, it may be desirable to utilize adaptive control, which adjusts the control law on-line to reduce the effects of the unknown parameters. This adaptive feature allows satisfactory performance with only limited knowledge of the plant parameters. Model reference adaptive control systems can be divided into the following two classes: (1) indirect adaptive controllers in which on-line estimates of the plant parameters are used for control law adjustment and (2) direct adaptive controllers in which no effort is made to identify the plant parameters, that is, the control law is directly adjusted to minimize the error between plant and model states. In this chapter, only direct model reference adaptive controllers will be considered.

A. BACKGROUND

The first direct model reference adaptive control system was designed by the performance index minimization method proposed by Whitaker [1] of the MIT Instrumentation Laboratory. This so-called "MIT design rule" was later improved upon by Donalson and Leondes [2], who used a more general performance index than that of Whitaker. However, neither method could ensure stability of the adaptive system.

Thus, subsequent studies were directed toward stable algorithms. The most common application of stability theory to direct model reference adaptive control has utilized Lyapunov's second method. Algorithms were developed by Butchart and Shakcloth [3], Parks [4], Phillipson [5,6], Monopoli [7], and Monopoli and Gilbart [8]. However, all these algorithms are restricted to single-input/single-output systems.

Early attempts at direct model reference control of multi-input/multi-output systems required the satisfaction of Erzberger's perfect model following conditions [9]. These conditions resulted from a general inability to satisfactorily alter all of the plant parameters. Papers describing these algorithms, with stability ensured by Lyapunov techniques, have been written by Grayson [10], Winsor and Roy [11], Porter and Tatnall [12], and Monopoli and Gilbart [13]. However, the perfect model following conditions require that there exist a certain structural relationship between the plant and the model. More specifically, the number of independent plant controllers must be sufficient to independently alter all the plant parameters which differ from the corresponding model parameters. These conditions are not always satisfied for model reference control systems. Furthermore, there is no general procedure for modifying a given model in order to satisfy the perfect model following conditions.

The hyperstability criterion of Popov [14] was first applied to direct model reference adaptive control system design by Landau [15]. This algorithm ensures stability for multi-input/multi-output continuous systems subject to the perfect model following conditions. These techniques were later applied by Bethoux [16] to single-input/single-output discrete systems which satisfy the perfect model following conditions.

Later, Monopoli [17], Narendra [18,19], and Morse [20] utilized an augmented error signal to provide stable algorithms for continuous single-input/single-output systems. This technique was subsequently applied to discrete single-input/single-output systems by Ionescu [21] and Narendra [22].

Results pertaining to direct model reference adaptive control for multi-input/multi-output systems which do not satsify the perfect model following conditions have been limited until recently. Monopoli [23] has proposed a scheme, based upon the augmented error signal concept, for plants which can be decomposed into multi-input/single-output subplants. Such an assumption can be restrictive in that it requires the designer to work with the individual elements of the plant transfer matrix rather than with the transfer matrix itself.

Mabius and Kaufman [24,25,26] have proposed a direct model reference adaptive controller for multi-input/multi-output plants which do not have to satisfy the perfect model following (PMF) conditions. This algorithm ensures asymptotic stability when PMF is satisfied. In addition, a bounded error is guaranteed when PMF does not hold, provided that certain inequality constraints independent of the model can be satisfied for all admissible plant parameter values. However, full state feedback is required.

More recently, Sobel [27], Sobel, Kaufman, and Mabius [28, 29], and Sobel and Kaufman [30,31] have proposed two new algorithms for direct model reference adaptive control of MIMO systems which do not satisfy the PMF conditions. Algorithm I guarantees asymptotic stability provided that certain inequality constraints independent of the model are satisfied for all admissible plant parameter values. Algorithm II guarantees that the error remains bounded under less restrictive inequality constraints than are required for Algorithm I.

Both algorithms require that only the plant outputs and model states be available for feedback.

B. OUTLINE

Section II presents some preliminary mathematical subjects and the formal statement of the model reference adaptive control problem. Section III presents the two adaptive control algorithms. The stability analysis is presented in Section IV, while most of the detailed mathematics appear in the appendixes. Section V describes various methods for satisfying the sufficient conditions for stability. The approaches taken include both time domain and frequency domain approaches. Finally, Section VI presents several examples to illustrate the applications of the adaptive control algorithms.

II. PROBLEM FORMULATION

A. PLANT AND MODEL DESCRIPTIONS

The continuous linear model reference control problem is solved for the linear process equations

$$\dot{x}_p(t) = A_p x_p(t) + B_p u_p(t), \tag{1}$$

$$y_p(t) = C_p x_p(t), \tag{2}$$

where $x_p(t)$ is the $n \times 1$ plant state vector, $u_p(t)$ is the $m \times 1$ control vector, $y_p(t)$ is the $q \times 1$ plant output vector, and A_p and B_p are matrices with the approapriate dimensions. The range of the plant parameters is assumed to be bounded. These bounds define the sets S^A and S^B as follows:

$$A_p \in S^A \quad \text{iff} \quad \underline{a}_{ij} \le a_{ij} \le \bar{a}_{ij}, \quad i = 1, \ldots, n, \; j = 1, \ldots, n;$$

$$B_p \in S^B \quad \text{iff} \quad \underline{b}_{ij} \le b_{ij} \le \bar{b}_{ij}, \quad i = 1, \ldots, n, \; j = 1, \ldots, m;$$

where a_{ij} is the i, jth element of A_p and b_{ij} is the i, jth element of B_p. It is also assumed that (i) all pairs A_p, B_p in S^A and S^B are controllable and output stabilizable, (ii) all pairs A_p, C_p are observable, and (iii) B_p has maximum rank. The objective is to find, without explicit knowledge of A_p and B_p, the control $u_p(t)$ such that the plant output vector $y_p(t)$ approximates "reasonably well" the output of the following model:

$$\dot{x}_m(t) = A_m x_m(t) + B_m u_m(t), \tag{3}$$

$$y_m(t) = C_m x_m(t), \tag{4}$$

where $x_m(t)$ is the $n_m \times 1$ model state vector, $u_m(t)$ is the $m \times 1$ model input or command, $y_m(t)$ is the $q \times 1$ model output vector, and A_m and B_m are matrices with the appropriate dimensions. The model is assumed to be bounded-input/bounded-state stable. Observe that the dimension of the model state may be less than the dimension of the plant state.

B. COMMAND GENERATOR TRACKER DESCRIPTION

To facilitate adaptive control algorithm development, it is useful to incorporate the command generator tracker concept[1] (CGT) developed by Broussard [32]. The CGT is a model reference control law for linear time-invariant systems with *known* coefficients. In this section, we shall review the basic elements of the command generator tracker.

When perfect output tracking occurs (i.e., when $y_p = y_m$ for $t \geq 0$), we define the corresponding state and control trajectories to be the ideal state and ideal control trajectories, respectively. These ideal trajectories will be denoted by

[1] *The idea of utilizing the CGT for adaptive control law development was originally proposed by Mabius [33].*

$x_p^*(t)$ and $u_p^*(t)$. By definition, the ideal plant is such that it satisfies the same dynamics as the real plant. In addition, the output of the ideal plant is defined to be identically equal to the model output. Mathematically, we have that

$$\dot{x}_p^* = A_p x_p^* + B_p u_p^* \quad \text{for all} \quad t \geq 0 \tag{5}$$

and

$$y_p^* = y_m \Rightarrow C_p x_p^* = C_m x_m. \tag{6}$$

Hence, when perfect tracking occurs the real plant trajectories become the ideal plant trajectories and the real plant output becomes the ideal plant output, which is defined to be the model output.

We shall assume that the ideal trajectories are linear functions of the model state and model input. Mathematically, we have that

$$\begin{bmatrix} x_p^*(t) \\ u_p^*(t) \end{bmatrix} = \begin{bmatrix} S_{11} & S_{12} \\ S_{21} & S_{22} \end{bmatrix} \begin{bmatrix} x_m(t) \\ u_m \end{bmatrix}. \tag{7}$$

In Eq. (7) we have restricted u_m to be a constant input; otherwise, derivatives of the model input may be required. Upon combining the ideal plant state equation (5) with the ideal plant output equation yields

$$\begin{bmatrix} \dot{x}_p^* \\ y_p^* \end{bmatrix} = \begin{bmatrix} A_p & B_p \\ C_p & 0 \end{bmatrix} \begin{bmatrix} x_p^* \\ u_p^* \end{bmatrix}, \tag{8a}$$

and upon substituting Eq. (7) into Eq. (8a), we obtain

$$\begin{bmatrix} \dot{x}_p^* \\ y_p^* \end{bmatrix} = \begin{bmatrix} A_p & B_p \\ C_p & 0 \end{bmatrix} \begin{bmatrix} S_{11} & S_{12} \\ S_{21} & S_{22} \end{bmatrix} \begin{bmatrix} x_m \\ u_m \end{bmatrix}. \tag{8b}$$

Now we differentiate the first equation in Eq. (7) to obtain

$$\dot{x}_p^* = S_{11}\dot{x}_m + S_{12}\dot{u}_m$$

and since u_m is a constant input, we have

$$\dot{x}_p^* = S_{11}\dot{x}_m. \tag{8c}$$

Now we substitute the equation for the model dynamics into Eq. (8c) to obtain

$$\dot{x}_p^* = S_{11}A_m x_m + S_{11}B_m u_m. \tag{8d}$$

We concatenate Eq. (8d) with Eq. (6) to obtain

$$\begin{bmatrix} \dot{x}_p^* \\ y_p^* \end{bmatrix} = \begin{bmatrix} S_{11}A_m & S_{11}B_m \\ C_m & 0 \end{bmatrix} \begin{bmatrix} x_m \\ u_m \end{bmatrix}. \tag{8e}$$

We equate the right-hand sides of Eqs. (8b) and (8e) to obtain

$$\begin{bmatrix} S_{11}A_m & S_{11}B_m \\ C_m & 0 \end{bmatrix} \begin{bmatrix} x_m \\ u_m \end{bmatrix} = \begin{bmatrix} A_p & B_p \\ C_p & 0 \end{bmatrix} \begin{bmatrix} S_{11} & S_{12} \\ S_{21} & S_{22} \end{bmatrix} \begin{bmatrix} x_m \\ u_m \end{bmatrix}, \tag{8f}$$

and noting that x_m and u_m are arbitrary, we obtain

$$\begin{bmatrix} S_{11}A_m & S_{11}B_m \\ C_m & 0 \end{bmatrix} = \begin{bmatrix} A_p & B_p \\ C_p & 0 \end{bmatrix} \begin{bmatrix} S_{11} & S_{12} \\ S_{21} & S_{22} \end{bmatrix}. \tag{8g}$$

If we define

$$\begin{bmatrix} \Omega_{11} & \Omega_{12} \\ \Omega_{21} & \Omega_{22} \end{bmatrix} = \begin{bmatrix} A_p & B_p \\ C_p & 0 \end{bmatrix}^{-1}, \tag{8h}$$

then the equations to be solved are

$$S_{11} = \Omega_{11}S_{11}A_m + \Omega_{12}C_m, \tag{8i}$$

$$S_{12} = \Omega_{11}S_{11}B_m, \tag{8j}$$

$$S_{21} = \Omega_{21}S_{11}A_m + \Omega_{22}C_m, \tag{8k}$$

$$S_{22} = \Omega_{21}S_{11}B_m. \tag{8l}$$

The existence of the inverse requires that the number of controls m equal the number of outputs q. If $m > q$ a psuedo-inverse may be required, while the case $m < q$ does not usually have a solution.

In summary, the existence of S_{ij} can be shown [32] provided that (i) u_m is a constant, (ii) the number of controls m is not less than the number of outputs q, and (iii) the product of the ith eigenvalue of Ω_{11} and the jth eigenvalue of A_m does not equal unity for all i, j.

When y_p differs from y_m at $t = 0$, we may achieve asymptotic tracking provided a stabilizing output feedback is included in the control law. To see this, we obtain the error equation as follows:

$$\dot{e} = \dot{x}_p^* - \dot{x}_p = A_p x_p^* + B_p u_p^* - A_p x_p - B_p u_p$$

$$= A_p e + B_p\left(u_p^* - u_p\right).$$

If the control law is

$$u_p = u_p^* + K(y_m - y_p) = u_p^* + KC_p e,$$

then the error equation becomes

$$e = (A_p - B_p K C_p) e$$

and the error will approach zero provided that K is a stabilizing output feedback gain.

The development of the adaptive algorithm will begin by defining a new error $e = x_p^*(t) - x_p(t)$, and we will seek a controller which guarantees that $e \to 0$ as $t \to \infty$. We observe that when $x_p(t) = x_p^*(t)$, we have $C_p x_p(t) = C_p x_p^*(t)$. By definition [see Eq. (6)] we know that $C_p x_p^*(t) = C_m x_m(t)$, and therefore we have $C_p x_p = C_m x_m$, which is the desired result.

The perfect model following conditions are a special case of the command generator tracker when the state vector is available and it is assumed that $x_p^*(t) = x_m(t)$. Since $x_p^*(t) = S_{11}x_m(t) + S_{12}u_m$, the PMF conditions imply that $S_{11} = I$ and $S_{12} = 0$. The ideal plant input is $u_p^*(t) = S_{21}x_m(t) + S_{22}u_m$, where S_{21} and S_{22} satisfy

$$A_m - A_p = B_pS_{21}, \tag{9a}$$

$$B_pS_{22} = B_m. \tag{9b}$$

These equations have a solution when the column vectors of the difference matrix $A_m - A_p$ and of the matrix B_m are linearly dependent on the column vectors of the matrix B_p.

If the matrices S_{21} and S_{22} which satisfy Eq. (9) exist, then a valid PMF controller becomes

$$u_p(t) = u_p^*(t) + K(x_m - x_p), \tag{10}$$

where K is a stabilizing feedback gain.

It should be noted that even though the CGT-based analysis is valid only when u_m is a step command, any command signal which can be described as the solution of a differential equation forced by a step input (or zero) can be used. This is true provided that the time-varying portion of the command signal is augmented to the model state vector and not to the model output vector.[2]

For example, suppose it is desired to follow a continuous model forced by the scalar command $r_m(t) = 1 + \sin t$. Then it should be noted that the following augmented system represents

[2] *Bar-Kana [34] has shown that the adaptive algorithm is stable even when the time-varying command is unknown.*

the original model forced by r_m:

$$\begin{bmatrix} \dot{x}_m(t) \\ \dot{z}_1(t) \\ \dot{z}_2(t) \end{bmatrix} = \begin{bmatrix} & A_m & & B_m & 0 \\ 0 & \cdots & 0 & 0 & 1 \\ 0 & \cdots & 0 & -1 & 0 \end{bmatrix} \begin{bmatrix} x_m(t) \\ z_1(t) \\ z_2(t) \end{bmatrix} + \begin{bmatrix} B_m \\ 0 \\ 0 \end{bmatrix} u_m,$$

$$z_1(0) = 0, \quad Z_2(0) = 1.$$

B_m would be the control distribution vector multiplying $z_1(t) + u_m$, u_m would be the unit step function, and $z_1(t)$, which equals $\sin t$, would be the output of the (z_1, z_2) system of differential equations.

C. SUMMARY

The perfect model following controller, represented by Eq. (10), may not be implementable because (i) the plant parameters are not known or (ii) the conditions for perfect model following do not hold.

Subsequent sections will describe two algorithms for model reference adaptive control which are applicable despite the following:

(1) the plant parameters are unknown but constrained to a set with known bounds;

(2) the perfect model following conditions are not satisfied;

(3) explicit parameter identification is prohibited.

III. CONTROL LAW DEVELOPMENT

A. *ALGORITHM I*

The CGT control for plants with known parameters was shown in the previous section to be

$$u_p(t) = S_{21}x_m(t) + S_{22}u_m + K(t)[y_m(t) - y_p(t)].$$

The adaptive control law is chosen to have a similar form to the CGT control law and is described by

$$u_p(t) = K_x(t)x_m(t) + K_u(t)u_m + K_e[y_m(t) - y_p(t)]. \tag{11a}$$

Substituting the definition from Eq. (6) that $y_m = y_p^*$ into Eq. (11a), we obtain

$$u_p(t) = K_x(t)x_m(t) + K_u(t)u_m + K_e(t)C_pe(t), \tag{11b}$$

where the gains $K_x(t)$, $K_u(t)$, and $K_e(t)$ are adaptive.

To simplify later computations, the adaptive gains are concatenated into the $m \times n_r$ matrix $K_r(t)$, which is defined as

$$K_r(t) = [K_e(t), K_x(t), K_u(t)]. \tag{12}$$

Correspondingly, the states are put into respective locations in the $n_r \times 1$ vector $r(t)$, which is defined as

$$r(t) = \begin{bmatrix} C_pe(t) \\ x_m(t) \\ u_m \end{bmatrix} = \begin{bmatrix} y_m(t) - y_p(t) \\ x_m(t) \\ u_m \end{bmatrix}; \tag{13}$$

then,

$$u_p(t) = K_r(t)r(t). \tag{14}$$

The gain is defined here as the sum of a proportional gain $K_p(t)$ and an integral gain $K_I(t)$, each of which is adapted as follows:[3]

[3] *Note that these equations are assuming that m, the number of controls, is equal to the number of outputs. If $m \geq q$, then either another output can be included or a control might be eliminated. Another approach might be to linearly combine two controls.*

$$K_r(t) = K_p(t) + K_I(t), \tag{15}$$

$$K_p(t) = v(t)r^T(t)\bar{T}, \tag{16}$$

$$\dot{K}_I(t) = v(t)r^T(t)T, \tag{17}$$

$$K_I(0) = K_{I0}, \tag{18}$$

$$v(t) = C_p e(t), \tag{19}$$

where T, $\bar{T}$ are $n_r \times n_r$ time-invariant weighting matrices, K_{I0} is the initial integral gain, and C_p is the time-invariant $m \times n$ plant output matrix. Selection of the weighting matrices T and $\bar{T}$ and the plant output matrix C_p is limited by the sufficient conditions for stability.

A stability result presented in Section IV shows that the closed-loop system which results from this algorithm gives rise to an asymptotically stable error provided that the matrices T and $\bar{T}$ are positive definite and positive semidefinite, respectively, and also provided that the stabilized plant input–output transfer matrix $C_p(sI - A_p + B_p\tilde{K}_eC_p)^{-1}B_p$ is strictly positive real for some feedback gain matrix $\tilde{K}_e$, which may be a function of A_p and B_p. Observe that the matrix $\tilde{K}_e$ is not required for implementation of the control algorithm.

Algorithm II relaxes the strict positive real condition on the plant and guarantees that the error will remain bounded.

B. *ALGORITHM II*

This section presents a modified version of Algorithm I which does not require that the stabilized plant satisfy the strict positive real property. Again K_p and K_I are adapted using Eqs. (16) and (17), but now v is redefined as follows:

$$v = QC_pe + G\left(u_p^* - u_p + \tilde{K}_eC_pe\right). \tag{20}$$

Then, with the error defined as $e(t) = x_p^*(t) - x_p(t)$, the error dynamics become

$$\begin{aligned}\dot{e}(t) &= \dot{x}_p^*(t) - \dot{x}_p(t)\\ &= A_p x_p^*(t) + B_p u_p^*(t) - A_p x_p(t) - B_p u_p(t)\\ &= A_p\left[x_p^*(t) - x_p(t)\right] + B_p\left[u_p^*(t) - u_p(t)\right]\\ &= \left(A_p - B_p \tilde{K}_e C_p\right)e(t) + B_p\left[u_p^*(t) - u_p(t) + \tilde{K}_e C_p e(t)\right]\\ &= \tilde{A}_p e(t) + B_p z(t), \end{aligned} \tag{21}$$

where $\tilde{A}_p = A_p - B_p \tilde{K}_e C_p$ and

$$z(t) = u_p^*(t) - u_p(t) + \tilde{K}_e C_p e(t).$$

Introducing the control algorithm into the error equation and recalling from Eq. (7) that $u_p^*(t) = S_{21}x_m(t) + S_{22}u_m$ gives

$$\begin{aligned}\dot{e}(t) = {} & \left(A_p - B_p \tilde{K}_e C_p\right)e(t)\\ & + B_p\Big[S_{21}x_m(t) + S_{22}u_m - K_I(t)r(t)\\ & \qquad - v(t)r^T(t)\bar{T}r(t) + \tilde{K}_e C_p e(t)\Big]. \end{aligned} \tag{22}$$

Asymptotic stability can be proven (see Section IV) provided that

$$J + C_p\left(sI - A_p + B_p\tilde{K}_e C_p\right)^{-1}B_p \tag{23}$$

is strictly positive real and $Q^{-1}G > J$ for some positive definite matrix Q.

Note that this is not as severe as the constraint given in Algorithm I, since it allows the addition of the matrix J to possibly compensate for any negativeness in $C_p\left(sI - A_p + B_p\tilde{K}_e C_p\right)^{-1}B_p$. However, implementation does require a priori knowledge of u_p^* and a priori knowledge of a fixed gain matrix $\tilde{K}_e$ that is stabilizing over all (A_p, B_p).

Since computation of the correct u_p^* requires values for A_p and B_p, it is proposed that a nominal value of u_p^* be used in Eq. (20). In fact, it is shown in Section IV that such use of a nominal value for u_p^* at worst results in stability with respect to a bounded error.

The requirement that a value for $\tilde{K}_e$ be available would clearly not be a problem if the plant to begin with were open-loop stable; in this case $\tilde{K}_e = 0$. Otherwise, some means of a priori designing a sufficiently robust feedback gain is necessary.

IV. STABILITY ANALYSIS

The two adaptive control algorithms presented in the previous section are now analyzed for stability. The equations which govern the closed-loop system are summarized in Table I.

TABLE I. Algorithm Summary

Algorithm I	*Algorithm II*
$r(t) = \begin{bmatrix} y_m(t) - y_p(t) \\ x_m(t) \\ u_m \end{bmatrix}$	
$K_r(t) = [K_e(t), K_x(t), K_u(t)]$	
$u_p(t) = K_r(t)r(t)$	
$K_r(t) = K_I(t) + K_p(t)$; $\dot{K}_I(t) = v(t)r^T(t)T$; $K_p(t) = v(t)r^T(t)\overline{T}$	
$v(t) = C_p e(t)$	$v(t) = QC_p e(t) + G\left[u_p^*(t) - u_p(t) + \tilde{K}_e C_p e(t)\right]$

First, asymptotic stability of the error for Algorithm I will be shown. Next, Algorithm II will be examined. Asymptotic stability of the error will be proven provided that $u_p^*(t)$ is known. However, since $u_p^*(t)$ cannot be known, because the plant is unknown, stability with respect to a bounded error will be proven provided that a nominal value for $u_p^*(t)$ exists.

In all cases, stability will be analyzed using a Lyapunov approach which involves (i) finding a Lyapunov candidate V, positive definite in the state variables, and (ii) evaluating the closed-loop stability by analyzing the sign of the derivative $\dot{V}$.

A. *ALGORITHM I*

The first step in the analysis is to form a quadratic function which is positive definite in the state variables of the adaptation system, $e(t)$ and $K_I(t)$. Before doing so, it is assumed that T^{-1} is a positive definite matrix, which is the first sufficient condition. Then, an appropriate choice of a positive definite function might be

$$V(e, K_I) = e^T(t)Pe(t) + \mathrm{Tr}\left[S(K_I - \tilde{K})T^{-1}(K_I - \tilde{K})^T S^T\right], \quad (24)$$

where P is an $n \times n$ positive definite symmetric matrix, $\tilde{K}$ is an $m \times n_r$ matrix (unspecified), and S is an $m \times m$ nonsingular matrix.

Since the matrix $\tilde{K}$ appears only in the function V and not in the control algorithm, it is referred to as a dummy gain matrix. It has the same dimensions as $K_r(t)$, which appears in V and can be partitioned as $\tilde{K} = \left[\tilde{K}_e, \tilde{K}_x, \tilde{K}_u\right]$ so that

$$\tilde{K}r = \tilde{K}_e C_p e + \tilde{K}_u u_m + \tilde{K}_x x_m, \quad (25)$$

where the three gains $\tilde{K}_x$, $\tilde{K}_u$, and $\tilde{K}_e$ are, like $\tilde{K}$, dummy gains.

The algebra involved in taking the time derivative of V appears in Appendix A. The elimination of cross product terms in the derivative establishes the second sufficient condition for stability, which is the following constraint on the output matrix C_p:

$$C_p = QB_p^T P \quad \forall A_p, B_p, \tag{26}$$

where $Q = (S^T S)^{-1}$. Next, with the choice $\tilde{K}_x = S_{21}$ and $\tilde{K}_u = S_{22}$, neither of which is required for implementation, the derivative of the function V becomes

$$\dot{V} = e^T(t)\left[P\left(A_p - B_p\tilde{K}_e C_p\right) + \left(A_p - B_p\tilde{K}_e C_p\right)^T P\right]e(t)$$
$$- 2e^T(t)PB_p(S^T S)^{-1}B_p^T Pe(t)r^T(t)\overline{T}r(t). \tag{27}$$

This derivative consists of two terms. It it is assumed that $\overline{T}$ is positive semidefinite (the third sufficient condition), then the second term is negative semidefinite in e(t). Requiring the quadratic term to be negative definite in e(t) establishes the fourth sufficient condition for stability. This condition is a constraint on P which can be stated as follows: the matrix P must be chosen such that there exists a $\tilde{K}_e$ such that

$$P\left(A_p - B_p\tilde{K}_e C_p\right) + \left(A_p - B_p\tilde{K}_e C_p\right)^T P \tag{28}$$

is negative definite for all A_p, B_p. Thus, two of the sufficient conditions for stability are constraints on the matrices C_p and P. With these sufficient conditions holding, the derivative of the function V is negative definite in the error e(t). Therefore, the plant output will asymptotically approach the model output. Furthermore, since the derivative of the function V is negative semidefinite in the augmented state $[e(t), K_I(t)]$, the adaptive gains will be bounded.

In order to determine the steady state behavior of the feedforward gains, it is useful to reconsider the error equation in the steady state.

With the error defined as $e(t) = x_p^*(t) - x_p(t)$, the error equation is

$$\begin{aligned}\dot{e}(t) &= A_p x_p^*(t) + B_p u_p^*(t) - A_p x_p(t) - B_p u_p(t) \\ &= A_p\left[x_p^*(t) - x_p(t)\right] + B_p\left[u_p^*(t) - u_p(t)\right] \\ &= A_p e(t) + B_p\left[u_p^*(t) - u_p(t)\right]. \qquad (29)\end{aligned}$$

After substituting the definitions for $u_p^*(t)$ from Eq. (7) and $u_p(t)$ from Eq. (11), we obtain

$$\begin{aligned}\dot{e}(t) = A_p e(t) + B_p [S_{21} x_m(t) + S_{22} u_m - K_x x_m(t) \\ - K_u u_m - K_e C_p e(t)]. \qquad (30)\end{aligned}$$

In steady state (i.e., $e = \dot{e} = 0$),

$$B_p\left[u_p^*(t) - u_p(t)\right] = B_p(S_{21} - K_x)x_m + B_p(S_{22} - K_u)u_m = 0.$$

Since B_p is assumed to have maximum rank, it follows that $u_p(t) \to u_p^*(t)$ as $t \to \infty$.

Finally, it should be noted that Eqs. (26) and (28) taken together are equivalent to requiring that the transfer matrix $Z(s) = C_p\left(sI - A_p + B_p\tilde{K}_e C_p\right)^{-1} B_p$ be strictly positive real for some feedback gain matrix $\tilde{K}_e$. Satisfaction of this constraint will be examined in Section V.

B. ALGORITHM II

This section presents a stability proof for the modified continuous algorithm which relaxes the constraint that the stabilized plant be strictly positive real. Asymptotic stability will only be ensured provided that the ideal plant control

$u_p^*(t)$ is known. Next, stability with respect to a bounded error will be guaranteed when only a nominal value for $u_p^*(t)$ is known.

1. Stability Analysis for Known Ideal Plant Trajectories

The first step in the analysis is to form a quadratic function which is positive definite in the state variables of the system, $e(t)$ and $K_I(t)$. Before doing so, it is assumed that T^{-1} is a positive definite matrix, which is the first sufficient condition. Then, a valid Lyapunov candidate is

$$V(e, K_I) = e^T(t)Pe(t) + \mathrm{Tr}\left[S\left(K_I - \tilde{K}\right)T^{-1}\left(K_I - \tilde{K}\right)^T S^T\right], \qquad (31)$$

where P is an $n \times n$ positive definite symmetric matrix, $\tilde{K}$ is an $m \times n_r$ matrix $\left(\tilde{K}_x, \tilde{K}_u \text{ unspecified}\right)$, and S is an $m \times m$ nonsingular matrix.

The matrix $\tilde{K}$ has the same dimensions as $K_r(t)$ and can be partitioned as $\tilde{K} = \left[\tilde{K}_e, \tilde{K}_x, \tilde{K}_u\right]$ so that

$$\tilde{K}r = \tilde{K}_e C_p e + \tilde{K}_u u_m + \tilde{K}_x x_m. \qquad (32)$$

The algorithm as given by Eqs. (16), (17), and (20) is repeated here for convenience:

$$K_p = vr^T\bar{T}, \qquad (33a)$$

$$\dot{K}_I = vr^T T, \qquad (33b)$$

$$v = QC_p e + G\left(u_p^* - u_p + \tilde{K}_e C_p e\right), \qquad (33c)$$

where $Q = (S^T S)^{-1}$.

The algebra involved in taking the derivative of V appears in Appendix B. As an aid to establishing conditions under which the derivative $\dot{V}$ is negative definite, the positive real lemma will be introduced as follows [36].

The transfer matrix $Z(s) = J + C(sI - A)^{-1}B$, with no poles for $\mathrm{Re}(s) > 0$ and only simple poles on the imaginary axis, is positive real if and only if there exists a real symmetric positive definite matrix P and real matrices L and W such that

$$PA + A^TP = -LL^T, \tag{34a}$$

$$PB = C^T - LW, \tag{34b}$$

$$W^TW = J + J^T. \tag{34c}$$

If in addition to Z(s) being positive real it is also true that Z(s) has no poles on the imaginary axis, then Z(s) is strictly positive real and

$$PA + A^TP = -LL^T < 0. \tag{35}$$

If it is assumed that the transfer matrix $Z(s) = J + C_p\left(sI - A_p + B_p\tilde{K}_eC_p\right)^{-1}B_p$ is strictly positive real for some matrices $\tilde{K}_e$ and J, then from Eq. (B18) $\dot{V}$ becomes

$$\dot{V} = -[L^Te + Wz]^T[L^Te + Wz] - 2v^TS^TSvr^T\bar{T}r - 2z^T(S^TSG - J)z. \tag{36}$$

Furthermore, $\dot{V}$ will be negative definite in e and z provided that

$$S^TSG > J \tag{37a}$$

and

$$\bar{T} \geq 0. \tag{37b}$$

From Eqs. (36) and (37) we observe that $V(e, K_I)$ cannot increase beyond its initial value $V(e(t_0), K_I(t_0))$. Thus from Eq. (24) it follows that the adaptive gain matrix $K_I(t)$ will be bounded.

It is interesting to note that if the stabilized plant transfer matrix $Z(s) = C_p\left(sI - A_p + B_p\tilde{K}_eC_p\right)^{-1}B_p$ is strictly positive real for some matrix $\tilde{K}_e$, then from Eq. (34) we may choose $G = J = W = 0$. With this choice of matrices Eq. (36)

reduces to

$$\dot{V} = e^T\left[P\left(A_p - B_p\tilde{K}_eC_p\right) + \left(A_p - B_p\tilde{K}_eC_p\right)^TP\right]e$$

$$- 2e^TPB_p(S^TS)^{-1}B_p^TPer^T\overline{T}r, \tag{38}$$

which is the derivative of the Lyapunov function obtained for Algorithm I. Indeed, when G = J = W = 0 is a valid choice, Algorithm II reduces to Algorithm I.

To summarize, the closed-loop system which results from the algorithm gives rise to an asymptotically stable error provided the following sufficient conditions are satisfied:

$$v(t) = (S^TS)^{-1}C_pe(t) + G\left[u_p^*(t) - u_p(t) + \tilde{K}_eC_pe(t)\right], \tag{39a}$$

$$Z(s) = J + C_p\left(sI - A_p + B_p\tilde{K}_eC_p\right)^{-1}B_p \tag{39b}$$

is strictly positive real for some matrices J and $\tilde{K}_e$,

$$S^TSG > J, \tag{40a}$$

$$\overline{T} \geq 0, \tag{40b}$$

$$T > 0. \tag{40c}$$

2. *Computation of the Plant Control Law*

In this section the problem involved in the implementation of the signal v(t) from Eq. (20) is considered. From Eq. (14) we have that

$$u_p(t) = K_r(t)r(t), \tag{41}$$

and upon substituting the expressions for $K_p(t)$ and r(t) from Eqs. (15) and (16) into Eq. (41), we obtain

$$u_p(t) = \left[v(t)r^T(t)\overline{T} + K_I(t)\right]r(t). \tag{42}$$

Recall from Eq. (20) that

$$v(t) = (S^TS)^{-1}C_pe(t) + G\left[u_p^*(t) - u_p(t) + \tilde{K}_eC_pe(t)\right]. \tag{43}$$

If we define $v_1(t)$ as

$$v_1(t) = (S^TS)^{-1} C_pe(t) + G\left[u_p^*(t) + \tilde{K}_eC_pe(t)\right], \tag{44}$$

then, combining Eqs. (43) and (44), we obtain that

$$v(t) = v_1(t) - Gu_p(t). \tag{45}$$

We see from Eq. (42) that $u_p(t)$ is a function of $v(t)$, while from Eq. (45) we note that $v(t)$ is a function of $u_p(t)$. Upon substituting Eq. (45) into Eq. (42), we obtain

$$u_p(t) = \left\{[v_1(t) - Gu_p(t)]r^T(t)\overline{T} + K_I(t)\right\} r(t), \tag{46}$$

and solving Eq. (46) for $u_p(t)$, we obtain

$$u_p(t) = [I + r^T(t)\overline{T}r(t)G]^{-1}\left[K_I(t) + v_1(t)r^T(t)\overline{T}\right]r(t). \tag{47}$$

It should be noted that a unique solution of Eq. (47) requires the nonsingularity of the matrix $[I + r^T(t)\overline{T}r(t)G]$ for all t.

3. *Selection of an Approximating Value for the Ideal Plant Trajectories*

Computation of the control law using Eq. (47) requires implementation of $u_p^*(t)$, as can be seen from Eq. (44). However, given a nominal set of plant matrices, it may be possible to find values of S_{11} and S_{12} such that the nominal $u_p^*(t)$ is not too far from the true value. Thus, $u_p^*(t)$ in Eq. (43) would be replaced by $u_{pnom}^*(t)$, which is a nominal value for the ideal plant control. This yields a modified $v(t)$ described by

$$v(t) = (S^TS)^{-1} C_pe(t) + G\left[u_{pnom}^*(t) - u_p(t) + \tilde{K}_eC_pe(t)\right], \tag{48}$$

and upon adding and subtracting $u_p^*(t)$ we obtain

$$v(t) = (S^TS)^{-1} C_p e(t) + G\left\{u_{pnom}^*(t) - u_p^*(t) + \tilde{K}_e C_p e(t) + \left[u_p^*(t) - u_p(t)\right]\right\}. \tag{49}$$

If we define

$$z(t) = u_p^*(t) - u_p(t) + \tilde{K}_e C_p e(t) \tag{50}$$

and define

$$\Delta u = u_{pnom}^* - u_p^*, \tag{51}$$

then upon substituting Eqs. (50) and (51) into Eq. (49) we obtain

$$v(t) = (S^TS)^{-1} C_p e(t) + G[\Delta u(t) + z(t)]. \tag{52}$$

Using the modified control law with the original Lyapunov candidate results in (see Appendix C)

$$\dot{V} = -[L^Te + Wz]^T [L^Te + Wz] - 2v^TS^TSvr^T\overline{T}r - 2z^T(G^TS^TS - J)z - 2\,\Delta u^T G^TS^TSz. \tag{53}$$

Observe that $\dot{V}$ is the same as that given by Eq. (36) except for one additional term which is linear in $z(t)$. Furthermore, Δu is bounded because x_m and u_m are bounded. Thus, from a result of LaSalle [37], we can state that $e(t)$ and $z(t)$ will be ultimately bounded. That is, there exists a $t_1 > 0$ with the property that $\|e(t)\| < b_1$ and $\|z(t)\| < b_2$ for all $t > t_1$.

The interpretation of this result is that outside some hypersurface where $e(t)$ and $z(t)$ are sufficiently large, the Lyapunov derivative will be negative. Thus, ultimately when the hypersurface is reached, a bound on the error is defined.

V. CONSTRAINT SATISFACTION

As a solution to the continuous adaptive control problem, which was introduced in Section II, two implementable algorithms have been presented. These algorithms may be characterized as follows.

(1) Algorithm I guarantees an asymptotically stable error provided that $T > 0$, $\bar{T} \geq 0$, and $Z(s) = C_p\left(sI - A_p + B_p\tilde{K}_eC_p\right)^{-1}B_p$ is strictly positive real for some $\tilde{K}_e(A_p, B_p)$; the matrix $\tilde{K}_e$ is not needed for implementation.

(2) Algorithm II guarantees a bounded error provided that $T > 0$, $\bar{T} \geq 0$, $S^TSG > J$, and $Z(s) = J + C_p\left(sI - A_p + B_p\tilde{K}_eC_p\right)^{-1}B_p$ is strictly positive real for some fixed and known matrices J and $\tilde{K}_e$.

In order to solve one of these adaptive control problems with time-invariant A_p and B_p, it is sufficient that the corresponding constraints be satisfied for all A_p and B_p in S^A and S^B, respectively. Thus, this section discusses techniques for satisfying the constraints for a bounded set of parameters.

A. CONSTRAINT SATISFACTION FOR ALGORITHM I

Both frequency and time domain approaches for validating that $Z(s) = C_p\left(sI - A + B_p\tilde{K}_eC_p\right)^{-1}B_p$ is strictly positive real will be discussed.

1. Frequency Domain Approach

By definition, $Z(s)$ is strictly positive real if and only if [35]

(1) all elements of $Z(s)$ are analytic in the closed-right-half plane $Re(s) \geq 0$ (i.e., they do not have poles in $Re(s) \geq 0$);

(2) the matrix $Z(j\omega) + Z^T(-j\omega)$ is positive definite Hermitian for all real ω.

Based upon the above definition, a modification of a procedure originally proposed by Mabius [26] is presented for validating that $Z(s)$ is strictly positive real for some matrix $\tilde{K}_e$.

Step 1. Choose the matrix product $\tilde{K}_e C_p$ such that the eigenvalues of $A_p - B_p \tilde{K}_e C_p$ have negative real parts.

Step 2. Define $Z(s) = C_p\left(sI - A_p + B_p \tilde{K}_e C_p\right)^{-1} B_p$ and define $F(\omega) = Z(j\omega) + Z^T(-j\omega)$.

Step 3. Validate that C_p is such that $F(\omega)$ is positive definite for all ω.

This last step is perhaps best carried out by checking that all m principal minors of $F(\omega)$ are positive. Each such minor can be expanded as a ratio of two polynomials in ω^2, each coefficient being a function of C_p, A_p, B_p, and $\tilde{K}_e$. In such an expansion the denominator can always be made positive and the numerator can then be written as

$$\sum_{i=0}^{N_m} f_i\left(C_p, A_p, B_p, \tilde{K}_e\right)\omega^{2i},$$

where N_m depends on the number of states and the order of the minor. In order to guarantee that $F(\omega)$ is positive for all ω, it is sufficient that each coefficient f_i in each minor be positive for all A_p, B_p in S^A, S^B. If not all the coefficients are positive, it is still possible that the principal minors are positive. To this effect, it may be desirable to test the positivity of the principal minors by using the Routh algorithms suggested by Siljak [38].

2. Time Domain Approach

A time domain approach for showing strict positive realness of the transfer matrix

$$Z(s) = J + H(sI - F)^{-1}G \tag{54}$$

is based upon the following results [36].

Temporary assumption: R is a nonsingular matrix.

A variational problem: given the system $\dot{x} = Fx + Gu$ with initial state vector $x(0) = x_0$, find u(t) so as to minimize

$$V(x_0, u, t_1) = \int_0^{t_1} (u^T Ru + 2x^T H^T u)\, dt, \tag{55}$$

where $R = J + J^T$.

Lemma [*Ref. 36, pp. 231–232*]. The performance index, given by Eq. (55), is bounded below for all x_0, u, t_1 independently of u and t_1 if and only if $Z(s) = J + H(sI - F)^{-1}G$ is positive real. Furthermore, reference to the above index shows that $V(x_0, u \equiv 0, t_1) = 0$ for all x_0 and t_1. Thus the optimal performance index is bounded above by zero for all x_0 and t_1.

The optimal performance index, $\min_u V(x_0, u, t_1) = V^O(x_0, t_1)$, is given by

$$V^O(x_0, t_1) = x_0^T \Pi(0, t_1) x_0,$$

where Π is a symmetric matrix defined as the solution of the Riccati equation

$$-\dot{\Pi} = \Pi(F - GR^{-1}H) + (F^T - H^T R^{-1} G^T)\Pi - \Pi G R^{-1} G^T \Pi - H^T R^{-1} H,$$

$$\Pi(t_1, t_1) = 0.$$

The associated optimal control is given by

$$u(t) = -R^{-1}[G^T \Pi(t, t_1) + H]x(t).$$

Furthermore, $\Pi(0, t_1)$ is negative semidefinite for all t_1 and it decreases monotonically with t_1.

Lemma [*Ref. 36, pp. 233–234*]. Suppose that Z(s) is positive real, so that the matrix $\Pi(t, t_1)$ exists for all $t \leq t_1$. Then

$$\lim_{t_1 \to \infty} \Pi(t, t_1) \leq \overline{\Pi}$$

exists and is independent of t; moreover, $\overline{\Pi}$ satisfies a limiting version of the Riccati differential equation, that is,

$$\overline{\Pi}(F - GR^{-1}H) + (F^T - H^TR^{-1}G^T)\overline{\Pi} - \overline{\Pi}GR^{-1}G^T\overline{\Pi} - H^TR^{-1}H = 0.$$

Furthermore, since $\Pi(t, t_1) = \Pi(0, t_1 - t)$, it follows that

$$\lim_{t_1 \to \infty} \Pi(t, t_1) = \lim_{t \to -\infty} \Pi(t, t_1),$$

and so in practice the formula $\overline{\Pi} = \lim_{t \to -\infty} \Pi(t, t_1)$ would be more appropriate for computation of $\overline{\Pi}$.

Lemma [*Ref. 36, pp. 235–236*]. If $\overline{\Pi}$ is defined as described in the preceding Lemma, then $\overline{\Pi}$ is negative definite.

Theorem [*Ref. 36, pp. 236–237*]. Let Z(s) be a positive real matrix of rational functions of s with $Z(\infty) < \infty$. Suppose that {F, G, H, J} is a minimal realization of Z(s) with $J + J^T = R$ nonsingular. Then there exists a negative definite matrix $\overline{\Pi}$ satisfying the equation

$$\overline{\Pi}(F - GR^{-1}H) + (F^T - H^TR^{-1}G^T)\overline{\Pi} - \overline{\Pi}GR^{-1}G^T\overline{\Pi} - H^TR^{-1}H = 0. \tag{56}$$

Furthermore,

$$\overline{\Pi} = \lim_{t_1 \to \infty} \Pi(t, t_1) = \lim_{t \to -\infty} \Pi(t, t_1),$$

where $\Pi(\cdot, t_1)$ is the solution of the Riccati equation

$$-\dot{\Pi} = \Pi(F - GR^{-1}H) + (F^T - H^TR^{-1}G^T)\Pi - \Pi GR^{-1}G^T\Pi - H^TR^{-1}H$$

with boundary condition $\Pi(t_1, t_1) = 0$. In addition, we may define

$$P = -\bar{\Pi}, \quad W_0 = R^{1/2}, \quad L = (\bar{\Pi}G + H^T)R^{-1/2},$$

and the matrices $\{P, L, W_0\}$ can be shown to satisfy the positive real lemma equations.

To summarize, we may state that the existence of a negative definite solution matrix $\bar{\Pi}$ to Eq. (56) is both a necessary and sufficient condition for Z(s), as given by Eq. (54), to be positive real.

However, since the above results require that $J + J^T$ be nonsingular, they are not applicable to transfer matrices for which $J = 0$. An alternate approach is based upon a test for the discrete positive realness of a transformed system [36]. To this effect define the following quantities:

$$A = (I + F)(I - F)^{-1}, \tag{57a}$$

$$B = \frac{1}{\sqrt{2}}(A + I)G, \tag{57b}$$

$$C^T = \frac{1}{\sqrt{2}}(A^T + I)H^T, \tag{57c}$$

$$J_D = J + C^T(A + I)^{-1}B, \tag{57d}$$

$$U = J_D + J_D^T. \tag{57e}$$

Then Z(s) as defined in Eq. (54) will be positive real (for any J including $J \equiv 0$) if and only if the following recursive difference equation has a negative definite steady state solution [36]:

$$\pi(n + 1) = A^T\pi(n)A - [A^T\pi(n)B + C][U + B^T\pi(n)B]^{-1} \times [B^T\pi(n)A + C^T], \tag{58}$$

$$\pi(0) = 0.$$

In order to interpret the significance of Eqs. (57), it is useful to replace s in Z(s) with the bilinear transformation

$$s = \frac{z - 1}{z + 1}. \tag{59}$$

This yields

$$S(z) = Z\left(\frac{z - 1}{z + 1}\right) = J + \left[\left(\frac{z - 1}{z + 1}\right)I - F\right]^{-1} G. \tag{60}$$

Furthermore, it can be shown that Z(s) is positive real if and only if S(z) is discrete positive real [39].

Alternatively, Eq. (60) may be rewritten as

$$S(z) = J_D + C(zI - A)^{-1}B, \tag{61}$$

with (A, B, C, J_D) given by Eq. (57). Thus the existence of a negative definite solution to the discrete Riccati equation (58) is equivalent to the establishment of the discrete positive realness of S(z) and the positive realness of Z(s).

To apply this test to continuous adaptive Algorithm I, (A, B, C, J_D) would be computed using the following relationships:

$$F = A_p - B_p\tilde{K}_e C_p, \tag{62a}$$

$$G = B_p, \tag{62b}$$

$$H = C_p, \tag{62c}$$

$$J = 0. \tag{62d}$$

All that remains is to show how Eq. (58) may be used to determine the strict positive realness of Z(s). The positive real lemma equations which were presented in Section IV are repeated below for convenience:

$$P\left(A_p - B_p\tilde{K}_e C_p\right) + \left(A_p - B_p\tilde{K}_e C_p\right)^T P = -LL^T, \tag{63a}$$

$$PB_p = C_p^T - LW, \tag{63b}$$

$$W^T W = J + J^T. \tag{63c}$$

If in addition to satisfying Eq. (63) the matrix $-LL^T$ is negative definite, then Z(s) is strictly positive real. This results in Eq. (63a) being replaced by

$$P\left(A_p - B_p\tilde{K}_eC_p\right) + \left(A_p - B_p\tilde{K}_eC_p\right)^TP = -LL^T < 0, \tag{64}$$

which is equivalent to the requirement that $A_p - B_p\tilde{K}_eC_p$ have no eigenvalues for $\mathrm{Re}(s) \geq 0$. Conversely, if Z(s) is strictly positive real, then the matrix $-LL^T$ is negative definite [35].

Finally, to utilize Eqs. (57) and (58) to determine the strict positive realness of Z(s) for satisfying the constraints for adaptive Algorithm I, we would use the relationships

$$F = A_p - B_p\tilde{K}_eC_p, \tag{65a}$$

$$G = B_p, \tag{65b}$$

$$H = C_p, \tag{65c}$$

$$J = 0, \tag{65d}$$

where the matrix F has no eigenvalues for $\mathrm{Re}(s) \geq 0$.

3. *Full State Availability*

In the event that the original system description does not yield a strictly positive real transfer matrix, then it becomes necessary to redesign the output configuration in order to utilize Algorithm I. This section discusses one possibility when all the states are measureable. An alternative approach is to utilize Algorithm II.

If measurements for all states are available, then it is possible to find an output matrix that will result in strict positive realness by solving the following linear quadratic regulator problem [40]:

$$\text{Minimize} \quad \int_0^\infty (x^TQx + u^TRu)\, dt \tag{66}$$

$$\text{Subject to} \quad \dot{x} = A_px + B_pu. \tag{67}$$

The well-known solution (when it exists) to this problem is

$$u = -Kx, \tag{68}$$

where

$$K = +R^{-1}B_p^T P, \tag{69}$$

$$\mathrm{Re}\ \lambda(A_p - B_p K) < 0, \tag{70}$$

and

$$A_p^T P + PA_p - PB_p R^{-1} B_p^T P + Q = 0. \tag{71}$$

Then selection of C_p as K and $\tilde{K}_e$ as the identity matrix will result in the strict positive realness of the matrix $C_p\left(sI - A_p + B_p\tilde{K}_e C_p\right)^{-1}B_p$.

Since such a design of C_p requires a priori knowledge of A_p and B_p, its use is contingent upon the availability of nominal A_p and B_p matrices belonging to S^A and S^B, respectively. The robustness of this output matrix in the sense of retaining positive realness for deviations in A_p and B_p must then be examined.

As an illustration of how this robustness can be determined, assume that Eq. (71) has been solved for nominal values A_p^0 and B_p^0, that is,

$$A_p^{0^T} P + PA_p^0 - PB_p^0 R^{-1} B_p^{0^T} P + Q = 0 \tag{72a}$$

and

$$\tilde{K}_e C_p = +R^{-1} B_p^{0^T} P. \tag{72b}$$

Assume further that

$$A_p = A_p^0 + \Delta A_p, \tag{73}$$

$$B_p = B_p^0 B, \tag{74}$$

where B is a positive definite symmetric matrix. Then constraint (63a) becomes

$$P\left(A_p^0 + \Delta A_p - B_p^0 B\tilde{K}_e C_p\right) + \left(A_p^0 + \Delta A_p - B_p^0 B\tilde{K}_e C_p\right)^T P < 0. \quad (75)$$

Using Eq. (72b), the above may be rewritten as

$$PA_p^0 + A_p^{0^T} P - PB_p^0 BR^{-1} B_p^{0^T} P - PB_p^0 R^{-1} BB_p^{0^T} P + P\,\Delta A_p + \Delta A_p^T P < 0. \quad (76)$$

Adding and subtracting $PB_p^0 R^{-1} B_p^{0^T} P$ to this equation and using Eq. (72a) gives

$$-Q + PB_p^0 R^{-1} B_p^{0^T} P - PB_p^0 BR^{-1} B_p^{0^T} P - PB_p^0 R^{-1} BB_p^{0^T} P$$
$$+ P\,\Delta A_p + \Delta A_p^T P < 0. \quad (77)$$

Thus Eq. (63a) will be satisfied if A_p and B_p [defined by Eqs. (73) and (74)] are such that

$$-Q + P\,\Delta A_p + \Delta A_p^T P + PB_p^0 R^{-1} B_p^{0^T} P - PB_p^0 [BR^{-1} + R^{-1}B] B_p^{0^T} P < 0. \quad (78)$$

With regard to Eq. (63b) with $W \equiv 0$, it should be noted that

$$C_p = R^{-1} B_p^{0^T} P$$

or

$$C_p = R^{-1}\left(B_p B^{-1}\right)^T P = R^{-1} B^{-1} B_p^T P. \quad (79)$$

Consequently, if it can be assumed that the variation B in B_p^0 is such that

$$BR = RB > 0, \quad (80)$$

then Eq. (79) can be rewritten as

$$C_p = B^{-1} R^{-1} B_p^T P, \quad (81)$$

which satisfies constraint (63b) with $W \equiv 0$. Under condition (80), Eq. (78) may be simplified to

$$-Q + P\,\Delta A_p + \Delta A_p^T P + PB_p^0 R^{-1} B_p^{0^T} P - 2PB_p^0[BR^{-1}]B_p^{0^T} P < 0. \quad (82)$$

Thus a gain matrix C_p determined by solving the LQR problem

$$\text{Minimize:} \quad J = \int_0^\infty (x^T Q x + u^T R u)\, dt$$

$$\text{Subject to:} \quad \dot{x} = A_p^0 x + B_p^0 u$$

will result in strict positive realness of the transfer matrix $C_p\left(sI - A_p + B_p\tilde{K}_e C_p\right)^{-1}B_p$ for all A_p and B_p given by Eqs. (73) and (74) provided that

$$BR = RB > 0, \quad (83)$$

$$-Q + P\,\Delta A_p + \Delta A_p^T P + PB_p^0 R^{-1} B_p^{0^T} P - 2PB_p^0[BR^{-1}]B_p^{0^T} P < 0. \quad (84)$$

B. *CONSTRAINT SATISFACTION FOR ALGORITHM II*

In order to satisfy the strictly positive real constraint for Algorithm II, with a time-invariant A_p and B_p, it is sufficient that this property be satisfied for all A_p and B_p in S^A and S^B, respectively. Thus given the sets S^A and S^B, an implementable procedure is needed in order to determine that

$$Z(s) = J + C_p\left(sI - A_p + B_p\tilde{K}_e C_p\right)^{-1}B_p \quad (85)$$

is strictly positive real. To this effect we shall discuss two procedures.

1. *Frequency Domain Approach*

As an extension to the frequency domain approach for satisfying the strictly positive real property for continuous Algorithm I, the following procedure is proposed for validating that the strictly positive real property is satisfied for some matrices J and $\tilde{K}_e$.

Step 1. Choose the matrix product $\tilde{K}_e C_p$ such that the eigenvalues of $A_p - B_p\tilde{K}_e C_p$ have negative real parts.

Step 2. Define $Z(s) = J + C_p\left(sI - A_p + B_p\tilde{K}_e C_p\right)^{-1}B_p$ and define $F(\omega) = Z(j\omega) + Z^T(-J\omega)$.

Step 3. Validate that C_p and J are such that $F(\omega)$ is positive definite for all ω.

2. *Time Domain Approach*

A time domain approach for determining a matrix J which results in the strict positive realness of the transfer matrix

$$Z(s) = J + C_p\left(sI - A_p + B_p\tilde{K}_e C_p\right)^{-1}B_p$$

is based upon results given by Eqs. (63), which are repeated here for convenience:

$$P\left(A_p - B_p\tilde{K}_e C_p\right) + \left(A_p - B_p\tilde{K}_e C_p\right)^T P = -LL^T < 0, \tag{86a}$$

$$PB_p = C_p^T - LW, \tag{86b}$$

$$W^T W = J + J^T. \tag{86c}$$

The procedure to choose the matrix J is given below.

Step 1. If A_p is a stable matrix, then choose $\tilde{K}_e = 0$. If A_p is not stable, then choose $\tilde{K}_e$ to output stabilize the plant.

Step 2. Choose L such that L^{-1} exists. Solve the Lyapunov equation (86a) for the positive definite symmetric matrix P.

Step 3. Solve Eq. (86b) for W yielding $W = L^{-1}\left(C_p^T - PB_p\right)$.

Step 4. Solve Eq. (86c) for the matrix J. Choosing J to be a symmetric matrix yields $J = \frac{1}{2}W^T W$.

Since such a design of J requires a priori knowledge of A_p and B_p, its use is contingent upon the availability of nominal A_p and B_p matrices belonging to S^A and S^B, respectively. The robustness of this matrix J in the sense of retaining the strict positive realness of Z(s) for deviations in A_p and B_p must then be examined.

As an illustration of how a matrix J [which results in Z(s) being strictly positive real for all A_p and B_p in S^A and S^B, respectively] can be determined, assume that there exist nominal values A_p^0 and B_p^0 for A_p and B_p. Assume further that

$$A_p = A_p^0 + \Delta A_p, \tag{87a}$$

$$B_p = B_p^0 B, \tag{87b}$$

where B is a positive definite symmetric matrix.

The procedure for choosing a matrix J which results in Z(s) being strictly positive real for all A_p and B_p described by Eq. (87) is given below.

Step 1. Obtain a fixed matrix $\tilde{K}_e$ which output stabilizes the plant for all A_p and B_p described by Eqs. (86) and (87).

Step 2. Choose a nonsingular matrix L. Solve Eq. (86a) for $P(\Delta A, B)$.

Step 3. Find $W(\Delta A, B) = L^{-1}\left[C_p^T - P(\Delta A, B)B_p^0 B\right]$.

Step 4. Find $J(\Delta A, B)$ using Eq. (86c). Choose G such that $S^T SG > \max_{\Delta A, B} J$.

It may be possible to obtain a different matrix $S^T SG$ which will result in improved performance by choosing $S^T SG > \min_L \max_{\Delta A, B} J$.

The procedure described by Eqs. (57) and (58) may be used to determine if a matrix J computed for A_{p1}, B_{p1} also results in Z(s) being strictly positive real for some other values A_{p2}, B_{p2}. This approach for demonstrating the strict positive realness of the transfer matrix

$$Z(s) = J + H(sI - F)^{-1}G \tag{88}$$

is identical to the procedure in Section V,A, with Eq. (65) replaced by

$$F = A_p - B_p \tilde{K}_e C_p, \tag{89a}$$

$$G = B_p, \tag{89b}$$

$$H = C_p, \tag{89c}$$

$$J = J, \tag{89d}$$

where the matrix F has no eigenvalues for $\mathrm{Re}(s) \geq 0$.

VI. EXAMPLES

This section presents several examples to illustrate the application of the adaptive control algorithms. The examples will include the lateral dynamics of the F-8 aircraft and the longitudinal dynamics of the L-1011 aircraft. The adaptive gains K_e, K_x, and K_u will be initialized at zero unless indicated otherwise in a particular example.

The plant, model, and adaptive algorithms will be simulated on a digital computer in order to determine the closed-loop system performance. Therefore, in the simulations of the continuous systems we approximate the integrations in a discrete representation with a step size of Δt. Thus, all the signals in the system are fixed for intervals of Δt, which is chosen for each example in a manner which trades off computation time and numerical accuracy. The control algorithm equation for integral gain update, given by Eq. (17), is integrated using

$$K_I(i\,\Delta t + \Delta t) = K_I(i\,\Delta t) + \Delta t\, v(i\,\Delta t) r^T(i\,\Delta t) T.$$

The model dynamics (3) are integrated using

$$x_m(i\,\Delta t + \Delta t) = e^{A_m \Delta t} x_m(i\,\Delta t) + \left(\int_0^{\Delta t} e^{A_m t}\, dt \right) B_m u_m(i\,\Delta t),$$

and the plant dynamics (1) are integrated using

$$x_p(i\ \Delta t + \Delta t) = e^{A_p \Delta t} x_p(i\ \Delta t) + \left(\int_0^{\Delta t} e^{A_p t}\, dt\right) B_p u_p(i\ \Delta t).$$

A. *LATERAL DYNAMICS OF THE F-8 AIRCRAFT*

The F-8 plant and model can be represented by four states and two inputs. The elements of the state vector are roll rate, yaw rate, sideslip angle, and bank angle. The elements of the input vector are aileron deflection and rudder deflection.

In addition to the fourth-order model, we will consider a second-order model involving only the bank angle and roll rate dynamics. The second-order plant and model matrices are extracted from the fourth-order F-8 aircraft dynamics by considering only those coefficients which are related to the bank angle, roll rate, and aileron deflection. This second-order problem is intended for illustrative purposes only and should not be construed to be a realistic aircraft control law design.

Example 1. Time-Varying Second-Order F-8 Aircraft

The states of the second-order system are bank angle and roll rate and the input is aileron deflection. The plant matrices are of the form

$$A_p = \begin{bmatrix} a_{11} & 0 \\ a_{21} & 0 \end{bmatrix}, \quad B_p = \begin{bmatrix} b_1 \\ 0 \end{bmatrix}, \tag{90}$$

where

$$-10.22 \le a_{11} \le -3.598, \quad 0.9947 \le a_{21} \le 0.9997, \tag{91a}$$

$$14.65 \le b_1 \le 77.86. \tag{91b}$$

To illustrate the control of a time-varying plant, the second-order plant will vary linearly between flight condition #1, described by

$$\begin{bmatrix} \dot{p} \\ \dot{\phi} \end{bmatrix}_p = \begin{bmatrix} -3.598 & 0 \\ 0.9947 & 0 \end{bmatrix} \begin{bmatrix} p \\ \phi \end{bmatrix}_p + \begin{bmatrix} 14.65 \\ 0 \end{bmatrix} \delta_{a_p}, \tag{92}$$

and flight condition #2, described by

$$\begin{bmatrix} \dot{p} \\ \phi \end{bmatrix}_p = \begin{bmatrix} -10.22 & 0 \\ 0.9997 & 0 \end{bmatrix} \begin{bmatrix} p \\ \phi \end{bmatrix}_p + \begin{bmatrix} 77.86 \\ 0 \end{bmatrix} \delta_{a_p}. \tag{93}$$

The reference model is described by

$$\begin{bmatrix} \dot{p} \\ \dot{\phi} \end{bmatrix}_m = \begin{bmatrix} -10 & 0 \\ 1 & 0 \end{bmatrix} \begin{bmatrix} p \\ \phi \end{bmatrix}_m + \begin{bmatrix} 20 \\ 0 \end{bmatrix} \delta_{a_m}, \tag{94}$$

where δ_{a_m} is a unit step input.

The selection of an allowable plant output matrix using the positive real procedure, described in Section V,A,1., will now be detailed. The characteristic equation of the plant is

$$\lambda^2 + \left(-a_{11} + b_1\tilde{k}_e c_1\right)\lambda + a_{21}b_1\tilde{k}_e c_2 = 0. \tag{95}$$

If the coefficients of this equation are always greater than zero, then the real part of the eigenvalues of $A_p - B_p\tilde{K}_e C_p$ will be negative as required in step one of the positive real procedure.

Thus, c_1, c_2, and $\tilde{k}_e$ must be chosen such that

$$-a_{11} + b_1\tilde{k}_e c_1 > 0, \tag{96}$$

$$a_{21}b_1\tilde{k}_e c_2 > 0. \tag{97}$$

Upon substituting Eq. (91) into Eqs. (96) and (97), we obtain

$$\tilde{k}_e c_1 > \frac{a_{11}}{b_1} > \frac{-3.598}{77.86} = -0.0462, \tag{98}$$

$$\tilde{k}_e c_2 > 0. \tag{99}$$

Next we proceed by using the definition of Z(s) from Section V,A,1 to obtain

$$Z(s) = \frac{b_1(c_1 s + a_{21}c_2)}{s^2 + \left(-a_{11} + b_1\tilde{k}_e c_1\right)s + a_{21}b_1\tilde{k}_e c_2} \tag{100}$$

and

$$Z(j\omega) = \frac{b_1[c_1 j\omega + a_{21}c_2]}{-\omega^2 + j\omega\left(-a_{11} + b_1\tilde{k}_e c_1\right) + a_{21}b_1\tilde{k}_e c_2}. \tag{101}$$

Thus, using $F(\omega) = Z(j\omega) + Z^T(-j\omega)$, we obtain

$$F(\omega) = \frac{\left(-a_{21}b_1c_2 - a_{11}b_1c_1 + b_1^2c_1^2\tilde{k}_e\right)\omega^2 + c_2^2b_1^2a_{21}^2\tilde{k}_e}{\left[a_{21}b_1\tilde{k}_e c_2 - \omega^2\right]^2 + \left[\left(-a_{11} + b_1\tilde{k}_e c_1\right)\omega\right]^2}. \tag{102}$$

If the coefficients of ω^2 and ω^0 in the numerator of Eq. (102) are positive for all A_p and B_p, then $F(\omega)$ is positive for all ω. Thus, using Eq. (91),

$$\tilde{k}_e > 0, \tag{103}$$

$$c_2 < 3.6c_1 + 14.65c_1^2\tilde{k}_e. \tag{104}$$

The selection of $C_p = [c_1 \; c_2]$ must be such that Eqs. (98), (99), (103), and (104) are satisfied. The selection $C_p = [1 \; 0.1]$ can be shown to satisfy these equations. A simulation is shown in Figs. 2a–d for a 10-sec flight interval where the plant parameters vary linearly from flight condition #1 to flight condition #2 over the first 5 sec and from flight condition #2 to flight condition #1 over the next 5 sec. C_m is chosen to be C_p, $T = \bar{T} = 0.1I$, and Algorithm I is implemented. The plant output and the two plant states tend to approach the corresponding model quantities.

A nonadaptive simulation is shown in Figs. 2e–h for a 10-sec flight interval where the plant parameters vary in the same manner as the adaptive simulation. The gain K_e is allowed to adapt

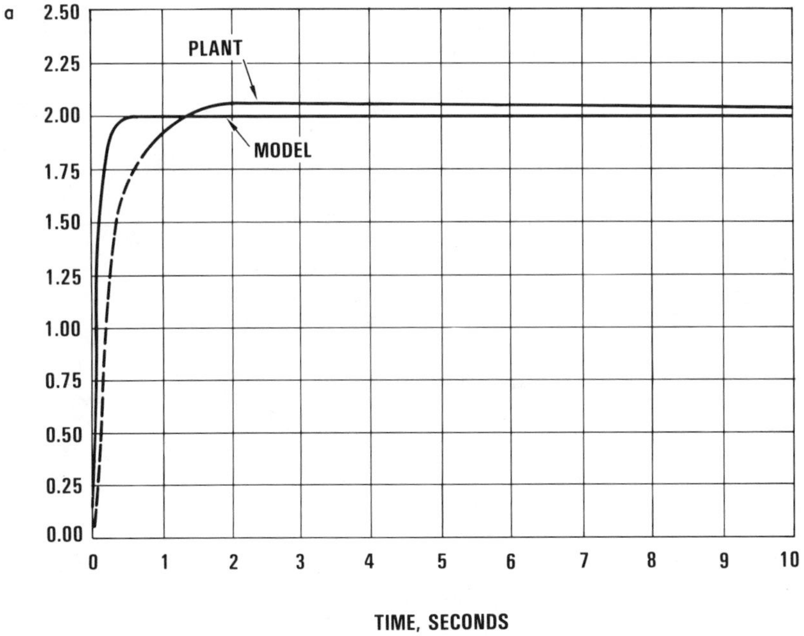

Fig. 2a. Plant and model roll rate using adaptive controller.

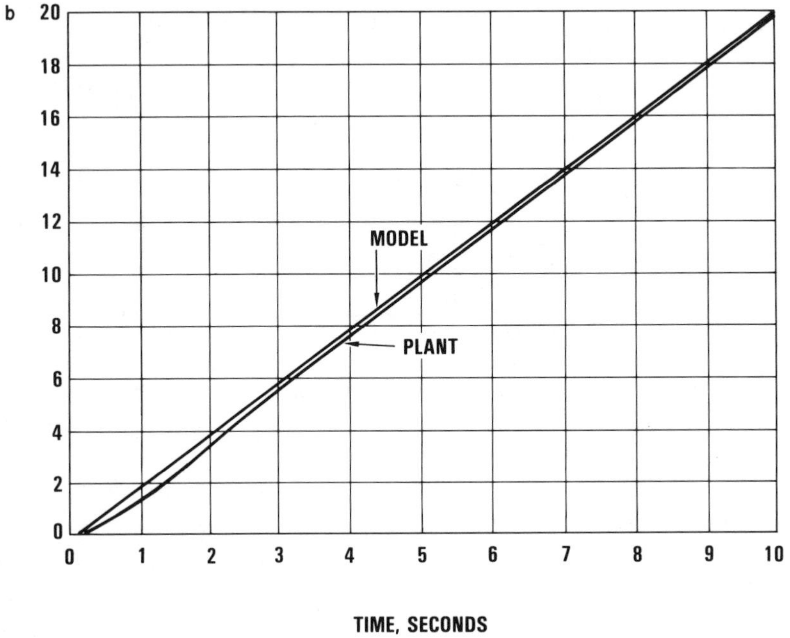

Fig. 2b. Plant and model bank angle using adaptive controller.

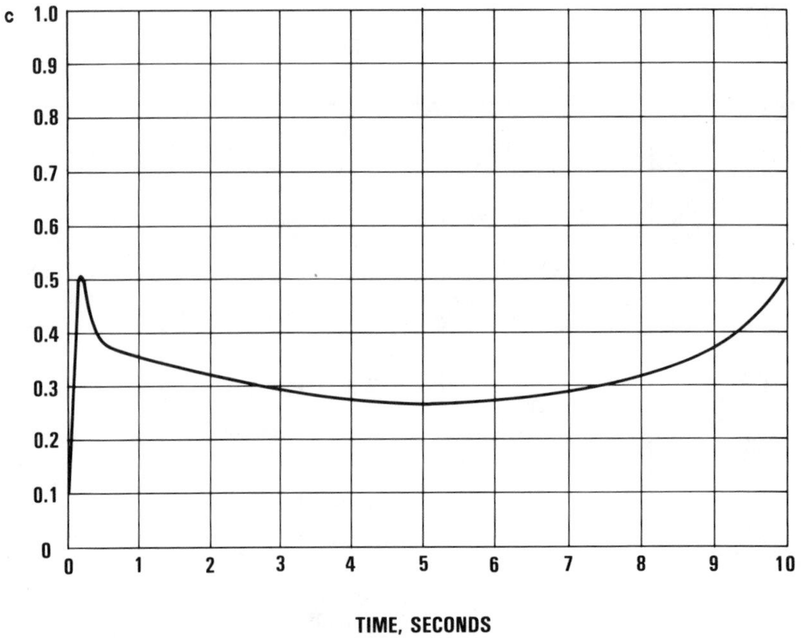

Fig. 2c. Plant aileron deflection using adaptive controller.

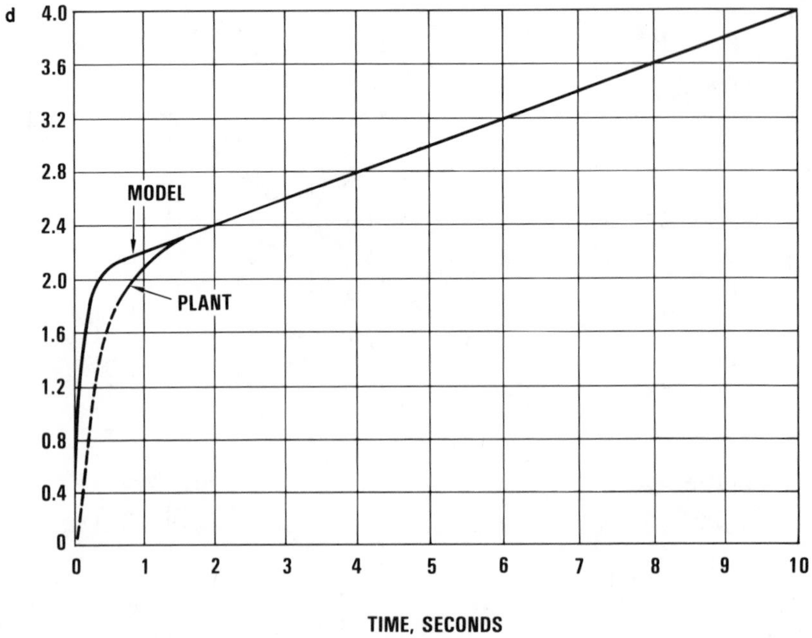

Fig. 2d. Plant and model output using adaptive controller.

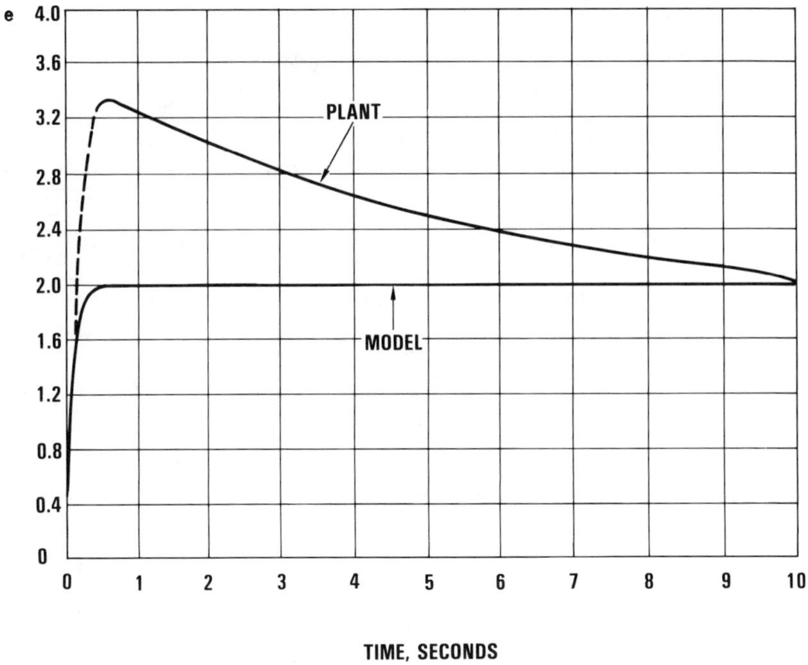

Fig. 2e. Plant and model roll rate using fixed gain controller.

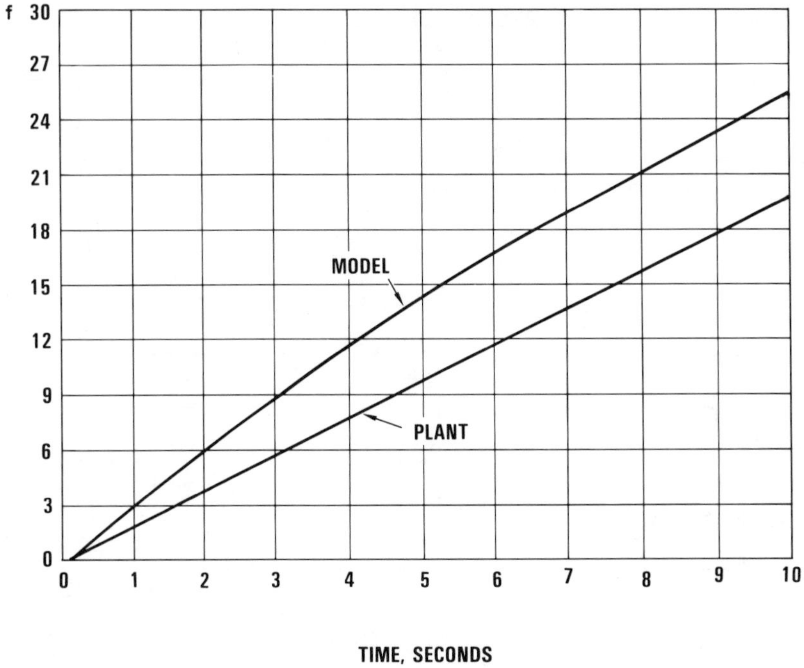

Fig. 2f. Plant and model bank angle using fixed gain controller.

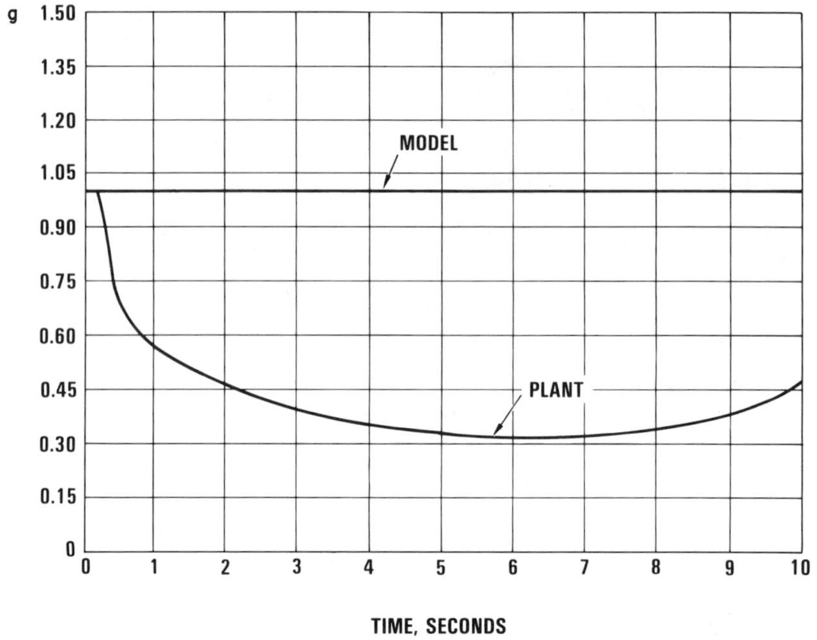

Fig. 2g. Plant and model aileron deflections using fixed gain controller.

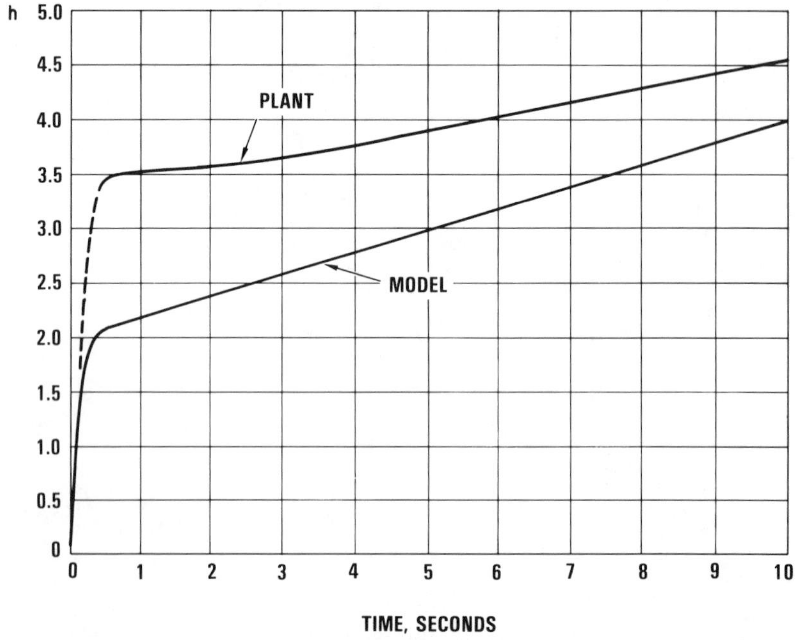

Fig. 2h. Plant and model outputs using fixed gain controller.

but $K_x = 0$ and $K_u = 1$. Thus, the plant input is equal to the model input plus the output feedback. The simulations demonstrate the advantages of using adaptive control.

Example 2. Fourth-Order Lateral F-8 Aircraft Dynamics with Limited Plant Parameter Knowledge

Consider the F-8 lateral dynamics described at flight condition #1 by

$$\begin{bmatrix} \dot{p} \\ \dot{r} \\ \dot{\beta} \\ \dot{\phi} \end{bmatrix}_p = \begin{bmatrix} -3.598 & 0.1968 & -35.18 & 0 \\ -0.0377 & -0.3576 & 5.884 & 0 \\ 0.0688 & -0.9957 & -0.2163 & 0.0733 \\ 0.9947 & 0.1027 & 0 & 0 \end{bmatrix} \begin{bmatrix} p \\ r \\ \beta \\ \phi \end{bmatrix}_p + \begin{bmatrix} 14.65 & 6.538 \\ 0.2179 & -3.087 \\ -0.0054 & 0.0516 \\ 0 & 0 \end{bmatrix} \begin{bmatrix} \delta_a \\ \delta_r \end{bmatrix}_p \tag{105}$$

and at flight condition #2 by

$$\begin{bmatrix} \dot{p} \\ \dot{r} \\ \dot{\beta} \\ \dot{\phi} \end{bmatrix}_p = \begin{bmatrix} -10.22 & -0.1416 & -147.8 & 0 \\ 0.0671 & -0.9610 & 29.43 & 0 \\ -0.0101 & -0.9958 & -0.5613 & 0.0309 \\ 0.9997 & 0.0245 & 0 & 0 \end{bmatrix} \begin{bmatrix} p \\ r \\ \beta \\ \phi \end{bmatrix}_p + \begin{bmatrix} 77.86 & 42.61 \\ 0.9165 & -14.40 \\ -0.0247 & 0.0864 \\ 0 & 0 \end{bmatrix} \begin{bmatrix} \delta_a \\ \delta_r \end{bmatrix}_p . \tag{106}$$

The model is described by

$$\begin{bmatrix} \dot{p} \\ \dot{r} \\ \dot{\beta} \\ \dot{\phi} \end{bmatrix}_m = \begin{bmatrix} -10 & 0 & -10 & 0 \\ 0 & -0.7 & 9 & 0 \\ 0 & -1 & -0.7 & 0 \\ 1 & 0 & 0 & 0 \end{bmatrix} \begin{bmatrix} p \\ r \\ \beta \\ \phi \end{bmatrix}_m + \begin{bmatrix} 20 & 2.8 \\ 0 & -3.13 \\ 0 & 0 \\ 0 & 0 \end{bmatrix} \begin{bmatrix} \delta_a \\ \delta_r \end{bmatrix}_m , \tag{107}$$

where p is the roll rate, r the yaw rate, β the sideslip angle, ϕ the bank angle, δ_a the aileron deflection, and δ_r the rudder deflection.

To attempt matching of the plant and model sideslip and bank angles over both flight conditions, we utilize the procedure which is described in Section V,A,3.

The optimal linear quadratic regulator gain for the plant at flight condition #1 with weighting matrices

$$Q = \mathrm{diag}(0.1,\ 0.1,\ 50,\ 1)$$

and

$$R = \begin{bmatrix} 1 & 0 \\ 0 & 0.001 \end{bmatrix}$$

can be shown to be

$$K = \begin{bmatrix} 0.2700 & 0.5305 & -1.966 & 0.9603 \\ 2.146 & -18.47 & 223.7 & 3.662 \end{bmatrix} \tag{108a}$$

with Riccati solution

$$P = \begin{bmatrix} 1.786E-02 & 3.499E-02 & -1.286E-01 & 6.351E-02 \\ 3.499E-02 & 7.557E-02 & -2.696E-01 & 1.260E-01 \\ -1.286E-01 & -2.696E-01 & 4.493E00 & -4.401E-01 \\ 6.351E-02 & 1.260E-01 & -4.401E-01 & 5.430E-01 \end{bmatrix}. \tag{108b}$$

The matrix Q was chosen to emphasize the fact that we wish to place the most penalty on the errors in sideslip angle and bank angle. The R matrix was chosen to allow large rudder commands, which may help to offset the small coupling between sideslip angle and rudder angle in Eqs. (105) and (106).

If we choose A_p and B_p for flight condition #1 as the nominal values of A_p and B_p $\left(A_{p1} = A_p^0 \text{ and } B_{p1} = B_p^0\right)$, then

$$\Delta A_p = A_{p2} - A_p^0 = \begin{bmatrix} -6.622 & -0.3384 & -112.62 & 0 \\ 0.1048 & -0.6034 & 23.546 & 0 \\ -0.0789 & -0.0001 & -0.345 & -0.0424 \\ 0.005 & -0.0782 & 0 & 0 \end{bmatrix}, \tag{109}$$

and a reasonable approximation for B as defined in Eq. (74) can be computed as

$$B \approx \begin{bmatrix} 5 & 0 \\ 0 & 5.5 \end{bmatrix}. \tag{110}$$

With these values for ΔA_p, A_p^0, B, and B_p^0, we shall attempt to verify that Eqs. (80) and (82) are satisfied. Since

$$BR = \begin{bmatrix} 5 & 0 \\ 0 & 5.5 \end{bmatrix}\begin{bmatrix} 1 & 0 \\ 0 & 0.001 \end{bmatrix} = \begin{bmatrix} 5 & 0 \\ 0 & 0.0055 \end{bmatrix} \tag{111a}$$

and

$$RB = \begin{bmatrix} 1 & 0 \\ 0 & 0.001 \end{bmatrix}\begin{bmatrix} 5 & 0 \\ 0 & 5.5 \end{bmatrix} = \begin{bmatrix} 5 & 0 \\ 0 & 0.0055 \end{bmatrix}, \tag{111b}$$

it is clear that BR = RB > 0 and Eq. (80) is satisfied. Furthermore, the matrix

$$-Q + P\,\Delta A_p + \Delta A_p^T P + PB_p^0 R^{-1} B_p^{0^T} P - 2PB_p^0 BR^{-1} B_p^{0^T} P$$

$$= \begin{bmatrix} -1.0092 & -1.1328 & -0.6263 & -2.7734 \\ -1.1312 & -6.615 & 48.713 & 4.0525 \\ -0.6251 & 48.713 & -570.23 & 4.842 \\ -2.7716 & -4.0565 & 4.828 & -9.3857 \end{bmatrix}. \tag{112}$$

The eigenvalues of Eq. (112) are

$$\lambda_1 = -0.574457E + 03, \qquad \lambda_2 = -0.117420E + 02,$$

$$\lambda_3 = -0.159935E + 00, \qquad \lambda_4 = -0.881069E + 00.$$

The matrix given by Eq. (112) is negative definite because all its eigenvalues are negative. Hence, Eq. (82) is satisifed and the matrix C_p as given by Eq. (108a) is a valid output matrix at both flight conditions.

Computer simulations over 5-sec intervals using Algorithm I with $C_p = C_m$, $T = 0.05I$, and $\overline{T} = 0.1I$ are shown in Figs. 3a–d and 4a–d for flight conditions #1 and #2, respectively. In both cases the output errors go to zero and β and ϕ of the plant agree closely with β and ϕ of the model.

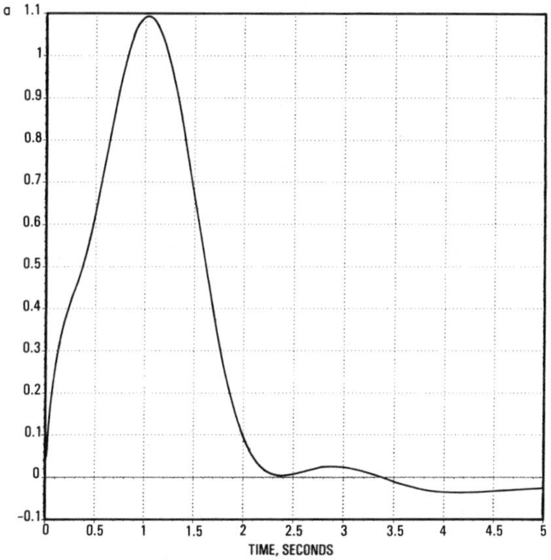

Fig. 3a. First component of output error vector at FC #1.

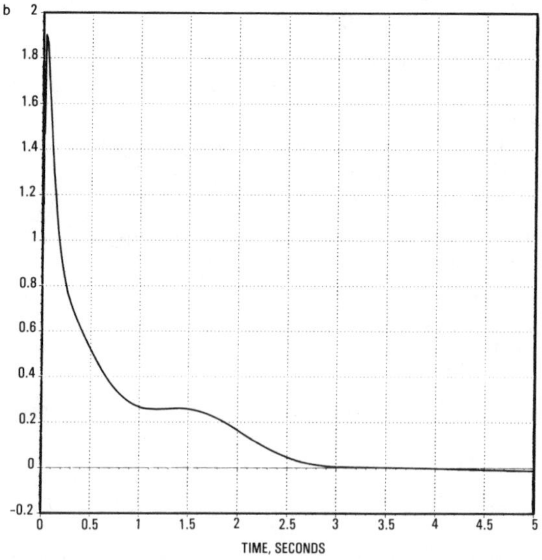

Fig. 3b. Second component of output error vector at FC #1.

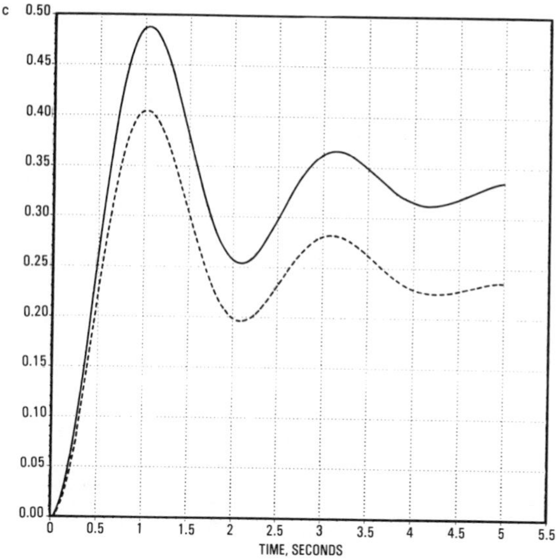

Fig. 3c. Plant and model sideslip angle at FC #1.

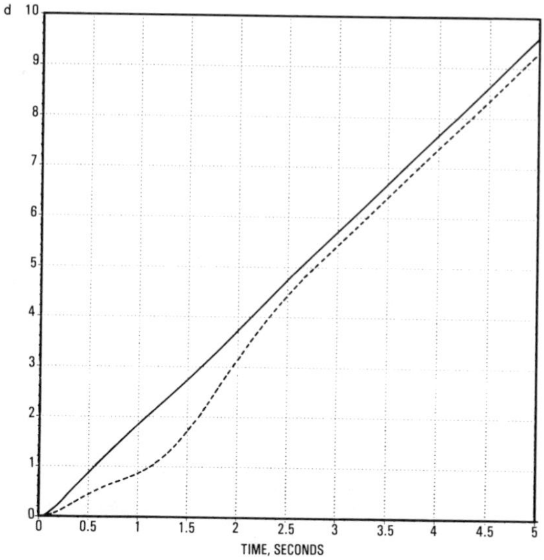

Fig. 3d. Plant and model bank angle at FC #1.

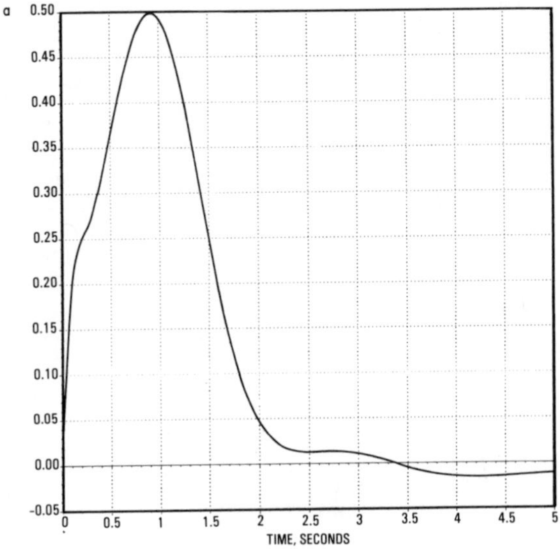

Fig. 4a. First component of output error vector at FC #2.

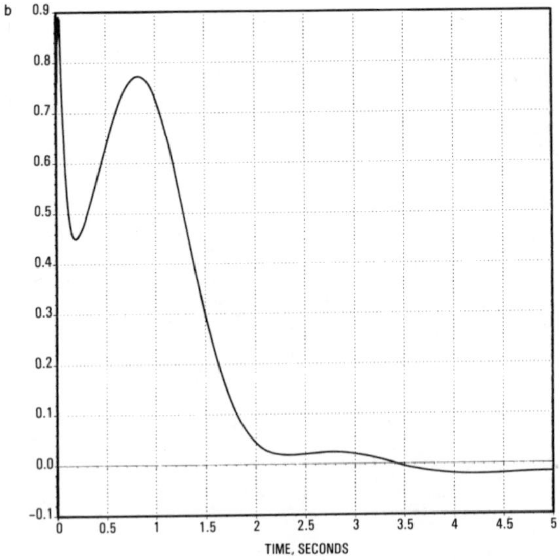

Fig. 4b. Second component of output error vector at FC #2.

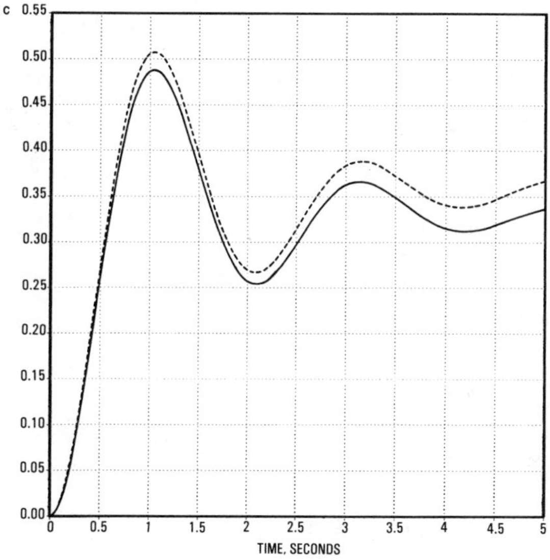

Fig. 4c. Plant and model sideslip angle at FC #2.

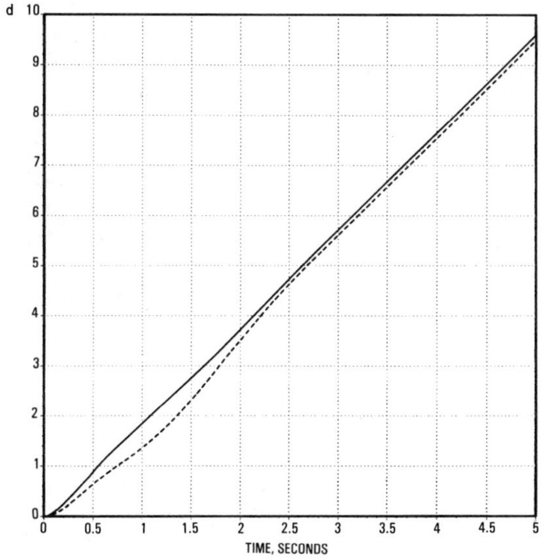

Fig. 4d. Plant and model bank angle at FC #2.

A nonadaptive simulation at flight condition #2 is shown in Figs. 5a–d. The gains are fixed at the values obtained at $t = 5$ sec when simulating the adaptive algorithm at flight condition #1. Comparison of the nonadaptive simulations with the corresponding adaptive simulations indicate that the adaptive algorithm yields significant improvements in error regulation and bank angle following.

B. LONGITUDINAL DYNAMICS OF THE L-1011 AIRCRAFT

Example 3.

The aircraft considered is an L-1011 transport with its center of gravity moved aft. The c.g. position is at 0.331 mean aerodynamic chord (MAC). The short period dynamics of this relaxed static stability vehicle (augmented with actuator dynamics and gyro and accelerometer low-pass filters) are described by

$$\frac{d}{dt}\begin{bmatrix} \alpha \\ q \\ q_f \\ n_{zf} \\ \delta_H \\ \dot{\delta}_H \end{bmatrix} = \begin{bmatrix} Z_\alpha & Z_q & 0 & 0 & Z_{\delta_H} & 0 \\ M_\alpha & M_q & 0 & 0 & M_{\delta_H} & 0 \\ 0 & 33.33 & -33.33 & 0 & 0 & 0 \\ 33.33c_1 & 33.33c_2 & 0 & -33.33 & 33.33c_3 & 0 \\ 0 & 0 & 0 & 0 & 0 & 1 \\ 0 & 0 & 0 & 0 & -125 & -26.25 \end{bmatrix}$$

$$\times \begin{bmatrix} \alpha \\ q \\ q_f \\ n_{zf} \\ \delta_H \\ \dot{\delta}_H \end{bmatrix} + \begin{bmatrix} 0 \\ 0 \\ 0 \\ 0 \\ 0 \\ 125 \end{bmatrix} \delta_{HC}, \tag{113}$$

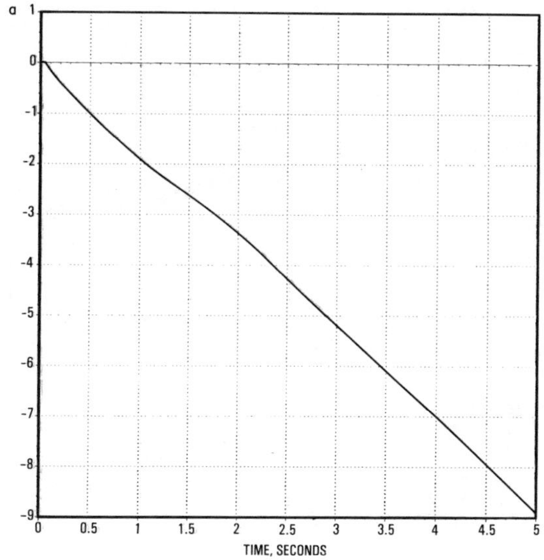

Fig. 5a. First component of output error vector with fixed gains.

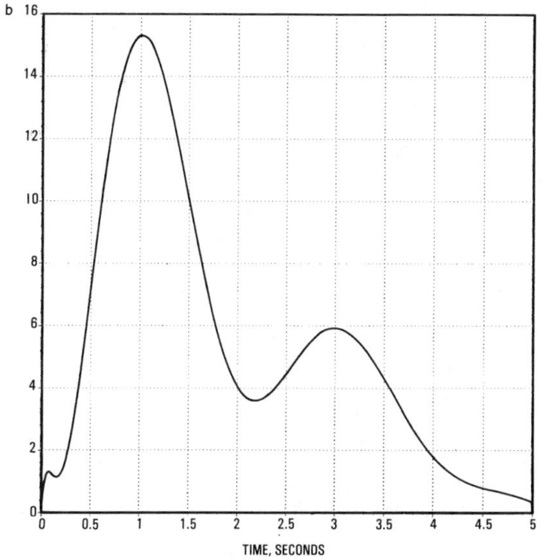

Fig. 5b. Second component of output error vector with fixed gains.

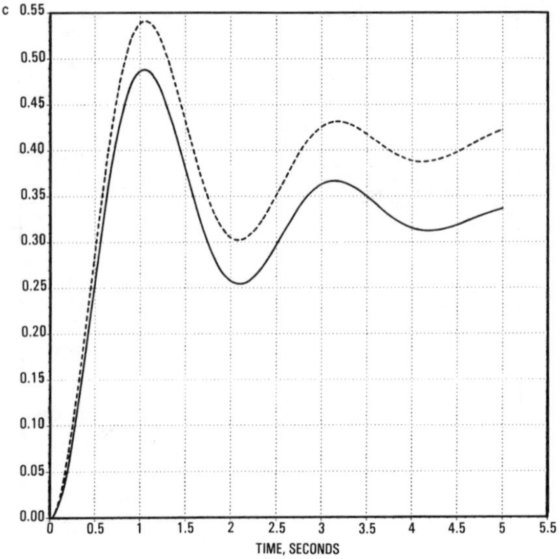

Fig. 5c. Plant and model sideslip angle with fixed gains.

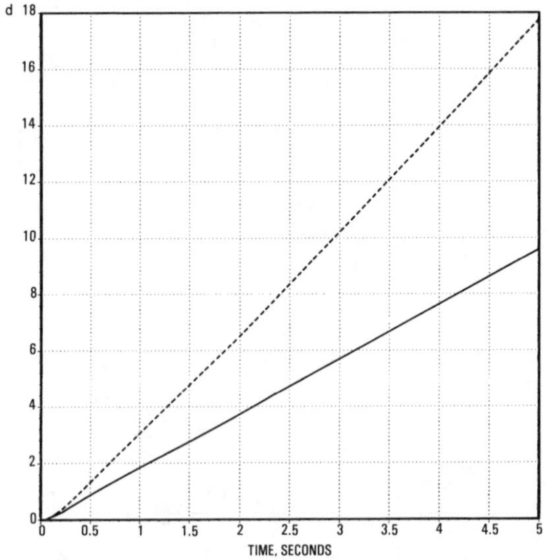

Fig. 5d. Plant and model bank angle with fixed gains.

$$\underline{y} = [n_{zf}, q_f]^T, \tag{114}$$

where

$$n_z = [c_1, c_2, c_3]\begin{bmatrix}\alpha \\ q \\ \delta_H\end{bmatrix}, \tag{115}$$

α is the angle of attack, q the pitch rate, q_f the low-pass filtered pitch rate, n_{zf} the low-pass filtered vertical acceleration, δ_H the horizontal stabilizer deflection, and δ_{HC} the horizontal stabilizer command.

The aircraft is assumed to vary linearly between four cruise flight conditions. These linearized operating points correspond to flight at 37,000 feet and Mach numbers 0.8, 0.83, 0.86, and 0.9, respectively. The aircraft stability and control derivatives for the four flight conditions are shown in Table II.

The sufficient conditions for stability described in Section V require that the number of inputs be at least equal to the number of outputs. Although this is not the case for this aircraft, the adaptive control algorithm will still be utilized. The performance of the algorithm will be demonstrated via computer simulation results. Thus, the algorithm will be shown to be applicable to flight vehicles even when the sufficient conditions for stability are difficult to satisfy.

TABLE II. Aircraft Stability and Control Derivatives

	Mach 0.8	*Mach 0.83*	*Mach 0.86*	*Mach 0.9*
Z_α	-0.537	-0.529	-0.573	-0.583
Z_q	0.984	0.984	0.984	0.983
M_α	-0.467	-0.285	-0.735	-0.166
M_q	-0.559	-0.598	-0.641	-0.694
Z_{δ_H}	-0.114	-0.118	-0.121	-0.125
M_{δ_H}	-4.32	-4.63	-4.94	-5.35

The reference model should be chosen so that it exhibits the desired response of the aircraft. Thus, a cruise model for the conventional aircraft with mid-position center of gravity is chosen as a starting point in the reference model development.

Next, a constant output feedback control law was designed for the preliminary model so that the closed-loop system has a damping factor $\zeta = 0.707$ and natural frequency $\omega_n = 1.6$. The feedback gain matrix is given by

$$F = [K_z, K_q] = [-0.0007, 0.149]. \tag{116}$$

Combining the preliminary model with Eq. (116) and allowing the pilot to command vertical acceleration yields

$$\frac{d}{dt}\begin{bmatrix} \alpha \\ q \\ q_f \\ n_{zf} \\ \delta_H \\ \dot{\delta}_H \end{bmatrix} = \begin{bmatrix} -0.573 & 0.984 & 0 & 0 & -0.125 & 0 \\ -1.27 & -0.616 & 0 & 0 & -4.88 & 0 \\ 0 & 33.33 & -33.33 & 0 & 0 & 0 \\ 450 & -7.33 & 0 & -33.33 & -59.7 & 0 \\ 0 & 0 & 0 & 0 & 0 & 1 \\ 0 & 0 & 125K_q & 125K_z & -125 & -26.25 \end{bmatrix} \times \begin{bmatrix} \alpha \\ q \\ q_f \\ n_{zf} \\ \delta_H \\ \dot{\delta}_H \end{bmatrix} + \begin{bmatrix} 0 \\ 0 \\ 0 \\ 0 \\ 0 \\ -125K_z \end{bmatrix} p_c, \tag{117}$$

$$\underline{y} = [n_{zf}, q_f]^T. \tag{118}$$

Unfortunately, due to lack of control over the closed-loop eigenvectors, the transfer function $n_{zf}(s)/p_c(s)$ has a zero near the origin, which results in an excessive maximum percentage overshoot. Therefore, a prefilter is utilized to process the pilot command. A diagram of the reference model is shown in Fig. 6.

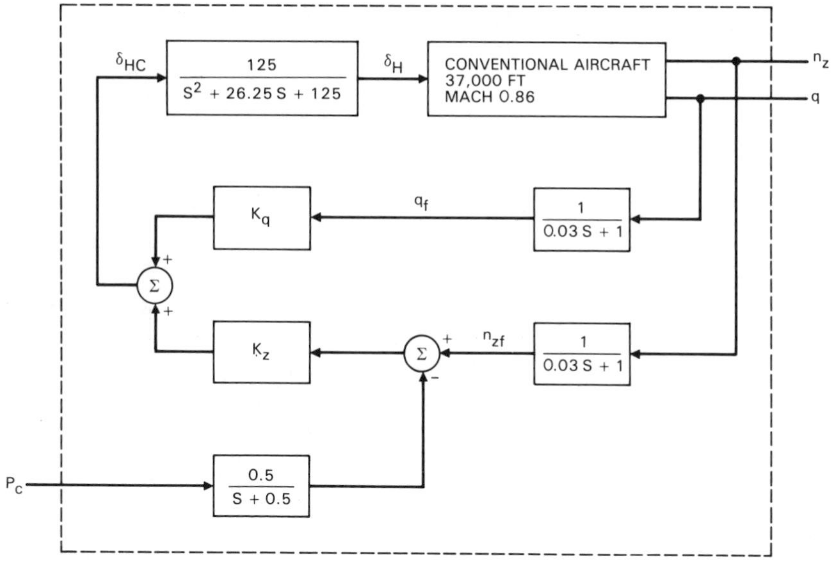

Fig. 6. L-1011 reference model.

The adaptive control system was simulated for the aircraft and reference model. The pilot vertical acceleration command is a square wave with an amplitude of 2.0g and a period of 40 sec.

The algorithm was tuned by trial and error, which resulted in the choice $\overline{T} = \text{diag}(10, 10^6, 10, 10, 10, 10, 10, 10, 10^{-2})$ and $T = \text{diag}(1, 10^5, 1, 1, 1, 1, 1, 1, 10^{-3})$. A simulation of the adaptive algorithm was performed with zero initial gains. Since the initial response was sluggish, the adaptive algorithm was initialized with the gains at their 90-sec values. The angle of attack, pitch rate, and vertical acceleration responses are shown in Figs. 7a,b,c, respectively.

Next, the simulation was repeated with constant gains. The gains were fixed at the same values which were used to initialize the adaptive algorithm. The alpha, pitch rate, and vertical acceleration responses are shown in Figs. 8a,b,c, respectively.

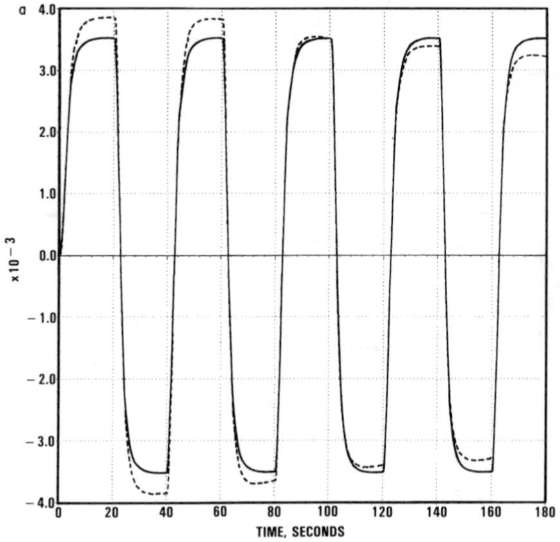

Fig. 7a. Adaptive gain angle of attack response.

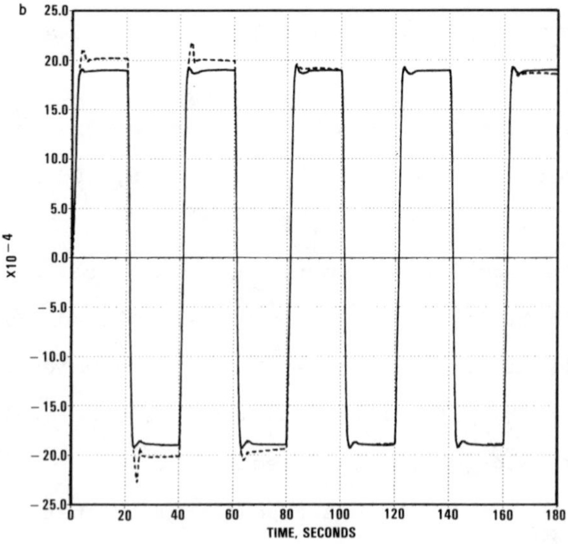

Fig. 7b. Adaptive gain pitch rate response.

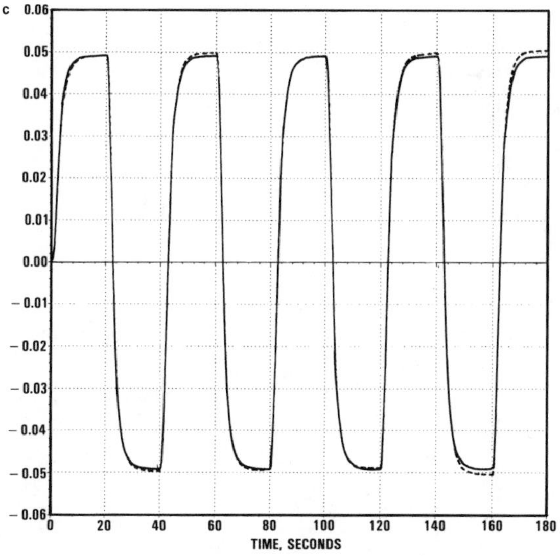

Fig. 7c. Adaptive gain normal acceleration response.

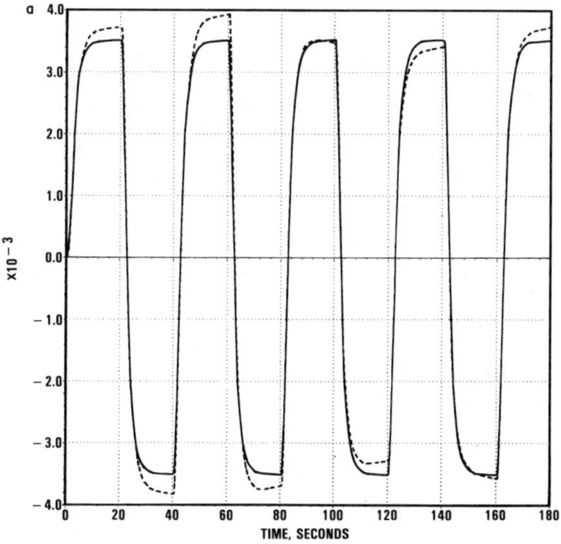

Fig. 8a. Fixed gain angle of attack response.

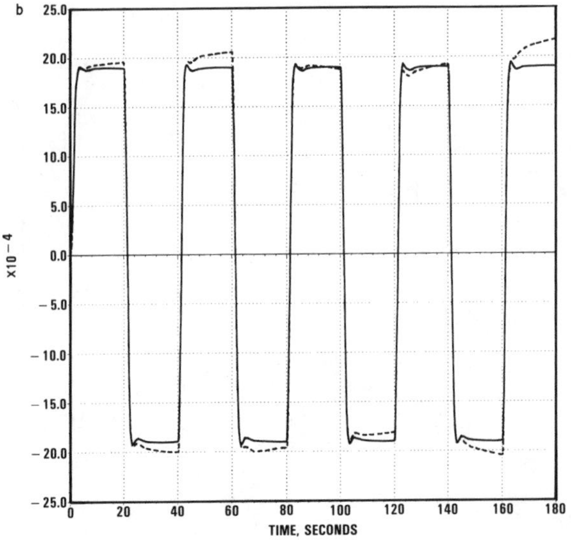

Fig. 8b. Fixed gain pitch rate response.

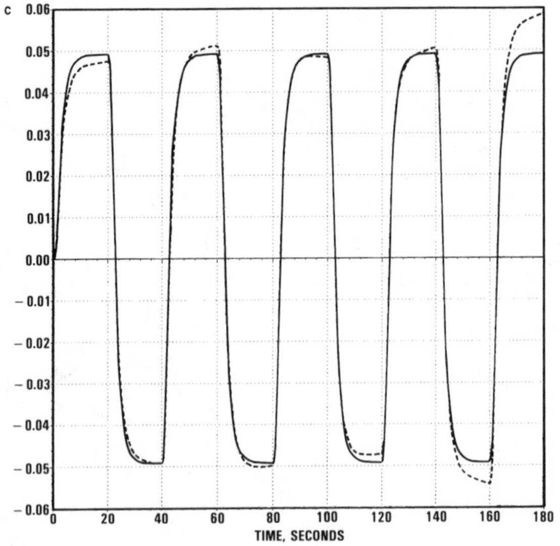

Fig. 8c. Fixed gain normal acceleration response.

A comparison between the adaptive and fixed gain algorithms indicates that the adaptive algorithm yields improved following in normal acceleration and pitch rate. Furthermore, note that model following in normal acceleration is particularly important because it is that quantity which is commanded by the pilot.

VII. CONCLUSIONS

This chapter has presented model reference adaptive control algorithms for multi-input/multi-output systems which do not necessarily satisfy the perfect model following conditions. Furthermore, none of the algorithms requires either an explicit on-line identifier or full state feedback. This research is significant because previous algorithms for model reference adaptive control of multi-input/multi-output systems required one or more of the above conditions.

Two adaptive algorithms for continuous systems have been presented. Asymptotic stability of the first continuous algorithm is ensured provided that the stabilized plant transfer matrix is strictly positive real. Stability, in terms of a bounded error, is ensured for the second algorithm provided that a certain auxiliary transfer matrix is strictly positive real. This is significant because in contrast with previous work, we can now ensure a bounded error even when the stabilized plant is not strictly positive real. Furthermore, a recent result of Bar-Kana [34] shows that Algorithm II can be modified to eliminate the need for an approximate $u_p^*(t)$.

The importance of the continuous positive real lemmas in the stability proofs of the adaptive algorithms is explained. Several methods are proposed for satisfying the sufficient conditions for stability over a set of admissible parameter values. The time domain methods are quite amenable to digital computer solution of the constraint satisfaction problem.

APPENDIX A. DERIVATION OF THE LYAPUNOV DERIVATIVE FOR CONTINUOUS ALGORITHM I

From Eq. (29), the error equation is

$$\dot{e}(t) = A_p e(t) + B_p\left[u_p^*(t) - u_p(t)\right].$$

After substituting the definitions for $u_p^*(t)$ from Eq. (7) and $u_p(t)$ from Eqs. (14), (15), and (16), the error equation becomes

$$\dot{e}(t) = \dot{x}_p^*(t) - \dot{x}_p(t)$$

$$= A_p e(t) + B_p\left[S_{21}x_m(t) + S_{22}u_m(t) - K_I(t)r(t) - C_p e(t)r^T(t)\overline{T}r(t)\right].$$

At this point the functional notation will be dropped for convenience. Thus the adaptive system is described by

$$\dot{e} = A_p e + B_p\left[S_{21}x_m + S_{22}u_m - K_I r - C_p e r^T\overline{T}r\right], \tag{A1}$$

$$\dot{K}_I = C_p e r^T T. \tag{A2}$$

The Lyapunov function is

$$V = e^T P e + \mathrm{Tr}\left[S\left(K_I - \tilde{K}\right)T^{-1}\left(K_I - \tilde{K}\right)^T S^T\right], \tag{A3}$$

and its time derivative is

$$\dot{V} = e^T P\dot{e} + \dot{e}^T P e + 2\ \mathrm{Tr}\left[S\left(K_I - \tilde{K}\right)T^{-1}\dot{K}_I^T S^T\right]. \tag{A4}$$

Substituting Eqs. (A1) and (A2) into Eq. (A4), we obtain

$$\dot{V} = e^T P\left[A_p e - B_p C_p e r^T\overline{T}r - B_p K_I r + B_p S_{21}x_m + B_p S_{22}u_m\right]$$
$$+ \left[A_p e - B_p C_p e r^T\overline{T}r - B_p K_I r + B_p S_{21}x_m + B_p S_{22}u_m\right]^T P e$$
$$+ 2e^T C_p^T S^T S\left(K_I - \tilde{K}\right)r,$$

$$\dot{V} = e^T\left(PA_p + A_p^TP\right)e - e^T\left(PB_pC_p + C_p^TB_p^TP\right)er^T\bar{T}r - 2e^TPB_pK_Ir$$

$$+ 2e^TPB_p(S_{21}x_m + S_{22}u_m) + 2e^TC_p^TS^TS\left(K_I - \tilde{K}\right)r,$$

$$\dot{V} = e^T\left(PA_p + A_p^TP\right)e - e^T\left(PB_pC_p + C_pB_p^TP\right)er^T\bar{T}r$$

$$+ 2e^T\left[C_p^TS^TS - PB_p\right]K_Ir - 2e^TC_p^TS^TS\tilde{K}r$$

$$+ 2e^TPB_p[S_{21}x_m + S_{22}u_m]. \tag{A5}$$

With the choice $C_p = (S^TS)^{-1}B_p^TP$, Eq. (A5) becomes

$$\dot{V} = e^T\left(PA_p + A_p^TP\right)e - 2e^TPB_p(S^TS)^{-1}B_p^TPer^T\bar{T}r - 2e^TC_p^TS^TS\tilde{K}r$$

$$+ 2e^TPB_p(S_{21}x_m + S_{22}u_m). \tag{A6}$$

Observe that $\tilde{K}r$ may be expanded as

$$\tilde{K}r = \tilde{K}_e(y_m - y_p) + \tilde{K}_xx_m + \tilde{K}_uu_m$$

$$= \tilde{K}_e\left(C_px_p^* - C_px_p\right) + \tilde{K}_xx_m + \tilde{K}_uu_m$$

$$= \tilde{K}_eC_pe + \tilde{K}_xx_m + \tilde{K}_uu_m. \tag{A7}$$

Substituting Eq. (A7) into Eq. (A6), we obtain

$$\dot{V} = e^T\left[P\left(A_p - B_p\tilde{K}_eC_p\right) + \left(A_p - B_p\tilde{K}_eC_p\right)^TP\right]e$$

$$- 2e^TPB_p(S^TS)^{-1}B_p^TPer^T\bar{T}r$$

$$+ 2e^TPB_p\left[\left(S_{21} - \tilde{K}_x\right)x_m + \left(S_{22} - \tilde{K}_u\right)u_m\right]. \tag{A8}$$

With the choice $\tilde{K}_x = S_{21}$ and $\tilde{K}_u = S_{22}$, Eq. (A8) reduces to

$$\dot{V} = e^T\left[P\left(A_p - B_p\tilde{K}_eC_p\right) + \left(A_p - B_p\tilde{K}_eC_p\right)^TP\right]e$$

$$- 2e^TPB_p(S^TS)^{-1}B_p^TPer^T\bar{T}r. \tag{A9}$$

APPENDIX B. DERIVATION OF THE LYAPUNOV DERIVATIVE FOR CONTINUOUS ALGORITHM II

From Eq. (21) the error equation is $\dot{e}(t) = \tilde{A}_p e(t) + B_p z(t)$, where $\tilde{A}_p = A_p - B_p \tilde{K}_e C_p$ and $z(t) = u_p^*(t) - u_p(t) + \tilde{K}_e C_p e(t)$. At this point the functional notation will be dropped for convenience. Thus the adaptive system is described by

$$\dot{e} = \tilde{A}_p e + B_p z, \tag{B1}$$

$$\dot{K}_I = v r^T T. \tag{B2}$$

The selected Lyapunov candidate is

$$V = e^T P e + \mathrm{Tr}\left[S\left(K_I - \tilde{K}\right)T^{-1}\left(K_I - \tilde{K}\right)^T S^T\right] \tag{B3}$$

with derivative

$$\dot{V} = e^T P \dot{e} + \dot{e}^T P e + 2\ \mathrm{Tr}\left[S\left(K_I - \tilde{K}\right)T^{-1}\dot{K}_I^T S^T\right]. \tag{B4}$$

Conditions will now be determined such that $\dot{V}$ is negative definite. The substitution of Eq. (B1) into the first two terms in Eq. (B4) yields

$$e^T P \dot{e} + \dot{e}^T P e = e^T\left(P\tilde{A}_p + \tilde{A}_p^T P\right)e + 2e^T P B_p z. \tag{B5}$$

The trace term becomes

$$2\left[\mathrm{Tr}\ S\left(K_I - \tilde{K}\right)T^{-1}\dot{K}_I^T S^T\right] = 2\ \mathrm{Tr}\left[S\left(K_I - \tilde{K}\right)T^{-1} T r v^T S^T\right]$$

$$= 2\ \mathrm{Tr}\left[S\left(K_I - \tilde{K}\right) r v^T S^T\right].$$

Using the inequality Tr[EF] = Tr[FE], we obtain

$$2\ \mathrm{Tr}\left[S\left(K_I - \tilde{K}\right)T^{-1}\dot{K}_I^T S^T\right] = 2\ \mathrm{Tr}\left[v^T S^T S\left(K_I - \tilde{K}\right) r\right]$$

$$= 2v^T S^T S\left(K_I - \tilde{K}\right) r. \tag{B6}$$

Next we substitute Eqs. (B5) and (B6) into Eq. (B4) to obtain

$$\dot{V} = e^T\left(P\tilde{A}_p + \tilde{A}_p^T P\right)e + 2e^T P B_p z + 2v^T S^T S\left(K_I - \tilde{K}\right) r. \tag{B7}$$

As an aid to establishing conditions under which the above expression for $\dot{V}$ is negative definite, the positive real lemma (which was introduced in Section IV) will again be stated as follows.

The transfer matrix $Z(s) = J + C_p\left(sI - A_p + B_p\tilde{K}_eC_p\right)^{-1}B_p$, with no poles for $\mathrm{Re}[s] > 0$ and only simple poles on the imaginary axis, is positive real if and only if there exists a real symmetric positive definite matrix P and real matrices L and W such that

$$PA + A^TP = -LL^T, \tag{B8a}$$

$$PB = C^T - LW, \tag{B8b}$$

$$W^TW = J + J^T. \tag{B8c}$$

If in addition to Z(s) being positive real it is also true that Z(s) has no poles on the imaginary axis, then Z(s) is strictly positive real and

$$PA + A^TP = -LL^T < 0. \tag{B9}$$

If it is assumed that the transfer matrix $Z(s) = J + C_p\left(sI - A_p + B_p\tilde{K}_eC_p\right)^{-1}B_p$ is strictly positive real for some matrices J and $\tilde{K}_e$, then substitution of Eq. (B8) into Eq. (B7) yields

$$\dot{V} = -e^TLL^Te + 2e^T\left[C_p^T - LW\right]z + 2v^TS^TS\left(K_I - \tilde{K}\right)r \tag{B10}$$

and using Eq. (B8c) yields

$$\dot{V} = -e^TLL^Te - 2e^TLWz - z^T[-J - J^T + W^TW]z$$
$$+ 2e^TC_p^Tz + 2v^TS^TS\left(K_I - \tilde{K}\right)r. \tag{B11}$$

Combining terms yields

$$\dot{V} = -[L^Te + Wz][L^Te + Wz]$$
$$+ 2z^TJz + 2e^TC_p^Tz + 2v^TS^TS\left(K_I - \tilde{K}\right)r. \tag{B12}$$

From Eqs. (7), (12)–(18), and (21) we obtain

$$z = S_{21}x_m + S_{22}u_m + \tilde{K}_e C_p e - \left[vr^T\overline{T} + K_I\right]r. \tag{B13}$$

The definition $\tilde{K} = \left[\tilde{K}_e, S_{21}, S_{22}\right]$, when substituted into Eq. (B13) along with Eq. (13), which is the definition of $r(t)$, yields

$$z = \tilde{K}r - \left[vr^T\overline{T} + K_I\right]r$$

or

$$z = \left[K_I - \tilde{K}\right]r - vr^T\overline{T}r, \tag{B14}$$

which can be solved for $\left[K_I - \tilde{K}\right]r$, yielding

$$\left[K_I - \tilde{K}\right]r = -z - vr^T\overline{T}r. \tag{B15}$$

Next we substitute Eq. (B15) into Eq. (B12) to obtain

$$\dot{V} = -[L^Te + Wz]^T[L^Te + Wz] + 2z^TJz + 2e^TC_p^Tz$$
$$- 2v^TS^TSz - 2v^TS^TSvr^T\overline{T}r. \tag{B16}$$

With the choice $v = Fe + Gz$, Eq. (B16) becomes

$$\dot{V} = -[L^Te + Wz]^T[L^Te + Wz] - 2v^TS^TSvr^T\overline{T}r$$
$$- 2z^T(S^TSG - J)z + 2e^T\left(C_p^T - F^TS^TS\right)z. \tag{B17}$$

Finally, with the choice $F = (S^TS)^{-1}C_p$, we obtain

$$\dot{V} = -[L^Te + Wz]^T[L^Te + Wz] - 2v^TS^TSvr^T\overline{T}r$$
$$- 2z^T(S^TSG - J)z. \tag{B18}$$

APPENDIX C. DERIVATION OF THE LYAPUNOV DERIVATIVE FOR CONTINUOUS ALGORITHM II WHEN UTILIZING A NOMINAL VALUE FOR THE IDEAL PLANT CONTROL $u_p^*(t)$

Choose the Lyapunov candidate

$$V = e^TPe + \mathrm{Tr}\left[S\left(K_I - \tilde{K}\right)T^{-1}\left(K_I - \tilde{K}\right)^TS^T\right]. \tag{C1}$$

If the transfer matrix $Z(s) = J + C_p\left(sI - A_p + B_p\tilde{K}_e C_p\right)^{-1}B_p$ is strictly positive real for some matrices J and $\tilde{K}_e$, then from Eq. (B16)

$$\dot{V} = -[L^Te + Wz]^T[L^Te + Wz] + 2z^TJz + 2e^TC_p^Tz$$
$$- 2v^TS^TSz - 2v^TS^TSvr^T\bar{T}r. \qquad (C2)$$

Substituting the expression for v(t) from Eq. (52) into the fourth term in Eq. (C2) yields

$$\dot{V} = -[L^Te + Wz]^T[L^Te + Wz] + 2z^TJz + 2e^TC_p^Tz$$
$$- 2\left\{(S^TS)^{-1}C_pe + G[\Delta u + z]\right\}^TS^TSz$$
$$- 2v^TS^TSvr^T\bar{T}r. \qquad (C3)$$

Upon expanding the fourth term we obtain

$$\dot{V} = -[L^Te + Wz]^T[L^Te + Wz] + 2z^TJz + 2e^TC_p^Tz - 2e^TC_p^Tz$$
$$- 2\,\Delta u^T\,G^TS^TSz - 2z^TG^TS^TSz - 2v^TS^TSvr^T\bar{T}r, \qquad (C4)$$

and upon combining terms we obtain

$$\dot{V} = -[L^Te + Wz]^T[L^Te + Wz] - 2v^TS^TSvr^T\bar{T}r$$
$$- 2z^T(S^TSG - J)z - 2\,\Delta u\,G^TS^TSz. \qquad (C5)$$

Note that we have used the fact that the transpose of a scalar is equal to that scalar.

REFERENCES

1. P. V. OSBORN, H. P. WHITAKER, and A. KEEZER, "New Developments in the Design of Adaptive Control Systems," *Inst. Aeronaut. Sci.*, Paper 61-39 (1961).

2. D. D. DONALSON and C. T. LEONDES, "A Model Referenced Parameter Tracking Technique for Adaptive Control Systems," *IEEE Trans. Appl. Ind.*, 241-262, September 1963.

3. R. L. BUTCHART and B. SHAKCLOTH, "Synthesis of Model Reference Adaptive Control Systems by Lyapunov's Second Method," *Proc. IFAC Symp. Theory Self-Adapt. Control Syst. 2nd, 1965*, 145-152 (1966).

4. P. C. PARKS, "Lyapunov Redesign of Model Reference Adaptive Control Systems," *IEEE Trans. Autom. Control AC-11*, 362-367, July 1966.

5. P. H. PHILLIPSON, "Design Methods for Model Reference Adaptive Systems," *Proc. Inst. Mech. Eng. 183*, 695-700, December 1968.

6. P. H. PHILLIPSON, "Concerning Lyapunov Redesign of Model Reference Adaptive Control Systems," *IEEE Trans. Autom. Control AC-12*, 625, October 1967.

7. R. V. MONOPOLI, "Lyapunov's Method for Adaptive Control Systems Design," *IEEE Trans. Autom. Control AC-12*, 334-335, August 1967.

8. R. V. MONOPOLI, J. W. GILBART, and W. D. THAYER, "Model Reference Adaptive Control Based on Lyapunov-Like Techniques," *Proc. IFAC Symp. Syst. Sensitivity Adaptivity*, F.24-F.31, August 1968.

9. H. ERZBERGER, "On the Use of Algebraic Methods in the Analysis and Design of Model Following Control Systems," *NASA Tech. Note D-4663*, 1963.

10. L. P. GRAYSON, "The Status of Synthesis Using Lyapunov's Method," *Automatica 3*, 91-121, December 1965.

11. C. A. WINSOR and R. J. ROY, "Design of Model Reference Adaptive Control Systems by Lyapunov's Second Method," *IEEE Trans. Autom. Control AC-13*, No. 2, 204, April 1968.

12. B. PORTER and M. L. TATNALL, "Stability Analysis of a Class of Multivariable Model Reference Adaptive Systems Having Time Varying Process Parameters," *Int. J. Control 11*, No. 2, 325-332 (1970).

13. J. W. GILBART and R. V. MONOPOLI, "A Modified Lyapunov Design for Model Reference Adaptive Control Systems," *Conf. Circuit Syst. Theory*, October 1969.

14. V. M. POPOV, "The Solution of a New Stability Problem for Controlled Systems," *Automation Remote Control 24*, 1-23 (1963).

15. I. D. LANDAU and B. COURTIOL, "Adaptive Model Following Systems for Flight Control and Simulation," *AIAA Aerosp. Sci. Meet. 10th No. 72-95*, January 1972.

16. B. BETHOUX and B. COURTIOL, "A Hyperstable Discrete Model Reference Adaptive Control System," *Proc. IFAC Symp. Sensitivity Adaptivity Optimality 3rd*, 287-289, June 1973.

17. R. V. MONOPOLI, "Model Reference Adaptive Control with an Augmented Error Signal," *IEEE Trans. Autom. Control AC-19*, No. 5, 474-483, October 1974.

18. K. S. NARENDRA and L. VALAVANI, "Stable Adaptive Controller Design-Direct Control," *IEEE Trans. Autom. Control AC-23*, pp. 570-583, August 1978.

19. K. S. NARENDRA, Y. H. LIN, and L. S. VALAVANI, "Stable Adaptive Controller Design — Part II: Proof of Stability," *IEEE Trans. Autom. Control AC-25*, No. 3, 440-448, June 1980.

20. A. S. MORSE, "Global Stability of Parameter Adaptive Control Systems," *IEEE Trans. Autom. Control AC-25*, No. 3, 433-439, June 1980.

21. T. IONESCU and R. MONOPOLI, "Discrete Model Reference Adaptive Control with an Augmented Error Signal," *Automatica 13*, 507-517 (1977).

22. K. S. NARENDRA and Y. H. LIN, "Stable Discrete Adaptive Control," *IEEE Trans. Autom. Control AC-25*, 456-461, June 1980.

23. R. V. MONOPOLI and C. C. HSING, "Parameter Adaptive Control of Multivariable Systems," *Int. J. Control 22*, No. 3, 313-327 (1975).

24. L. MABIUS and H. KAUFMAN, "An Implicit Adaptation Algorithm for a Linear Model Reference Control System," *Proc. 1975 IEEE Conf. Decision Control*, Houston, 864-865, December 1975.

25. L. MABIUS and H. Kaufman, "An Adaptive Flight Controller for the F-8 Without Explicit Parameter Identification," *Proc. 1976 IEEE Conf. Decision Control, Florida*, December 1976.

26. L. MABIUS, "An Implicitly Adaptive Model Reference Control Design for Linear Multi-Input Multi-Output Systems," Ph.D. Thesis, Rensselaer Polytechnic Institute, Troy, New York, June 1976.

27. K. M. SOBEL, "Model Reference Adaptive Control for Multi-Input Multi-Output Systems," Ph.D Thesis, Rensselaer Polytechnic Institute, Troy, New York, June 1980.

28. K. M. SOBEL, H. KAUFMAN, and L. MABIUS, "Model Reference Output Control Systems Without Parameter Identification," *Proc. 18th IEEE Conf. Decision Control, Fort Lauderdale*, 1979.

29. K. M. SOBEL, H. KAUFMAN, and L. MABIUS, "Implicit Adaptive Control for a Class of MIMO Systems," *IEEE Trans. Aerospace Electron. Syst. 18*, No. 5, September 1982.

30. K. M. SOBEL and H. KAUFMAN, "Design of Model Reference Adaptive Flight Controllers Without Parameter Identification," *in* "Methods and Applications in Adaptive Control," (H. Unbehauen, ed.), pp. 102-111, Springer-Verlag, Berlin, 1980.

31. K. M. SOBEL and H. KAUFMAN, "Design of Multivariable Adaptive Control Systems Without the Need for Parameter Identification," *Joint Autom. Control Conf., San Francisco*, August 1980.

32. J. R. BROUSSARD and M. J. O'BRIEN, "Feed-Forward Control to Track the Output of a Forced Model," *Proc. 17th IEEE Conf. Decision Control*, 1149-1155, January 1979.

33. L. MABIUS, "Development of Model Reference Adaptive Control Theory for Electric Power Plant Control Applications," The Analytic Sciences Corporation Report TR-1489-3, September 1982.

34. I. BAR-KANA, "Direct Multivariable Model Reference Adaptive Control with Applications to Large Structural Systems," Ph.D Thesis, Rensselaer Polytechnic Institute, Troy, New York, May 1983.

35. I. D. LANDAU, "Adaptive Control: The Model Reference Approach," Dekker, New York, 1979.

36. B. D. O. ANDERSON and S. VONGPANITLERD, "Network Analysis and Synthesis: A Modern Systems Theory Approach," Prentice-Hall, Englewood Cliffs, New Jersey, 1973.

37. J. LASALLE and S. LEFSCHETZ, "Stability by Lyapunov's Direct Method," Academic Press, New York, 1961.

38. D. SILJAK, "New Algebraic Criteria for Positive Realness," *Proc. Annu. Princeton Conf. Info. Sci. Syst. 4th*, 329-335, March 1970.

39. L. HITZ and B. D. O. ANDERSON, "Discrete Positive Real Functions and Their Application to System Stability," *Proc. IEE 116*, No. 1, 153-155, January 1969.

40. B. MOLINARI, "The Stable Regulator and Its Inverse," *IEEE Trans. Autom. Control AC-18*, No. 5, 454-459, October 1973.

Passive Adaptation in Control System Design

D. D. SWORDER

D. S. CHOU

Department of Applied Mechanics and Engineering Sciences
University of California, San Diego
La Jolla, California 92093

I. INTRODUCTION

Controllers and regulators are often designed on the basis of a simplified model of system behavior. Indeed, most of the analytical synthesis procedures assume that the system can be adequately described by a set of linear, ordinary differential equations. These equations are derived by first determining the nominal or desired operating condition of the system from

*This research was supported in part by the National Science Foundation under Grant. No. ECS-8003547.

the nonlinear equations which give a global characterization of the system. The nominal states and actuating signals derived from this analysis are typically time invariant. The linear model associated with a fixed operating point is the local relationship which exists between the perturbed state variables and the perturbed actuating signals. Because most systems are intrinsically nonlinear, the parameters of the linear model will vary from operating point to operating point.

As a simple example of this modeling process, consider the steam temperature regulator of a single panel of a solar-powered central receiver. On the California desert, there is an operational generating plant which uses insolation reflected from a field of 1818 heliostats to convert feedwater into superheated steam. The feedwater flow rate into each of the panels is regulated so as to maintain proper conditions of the exit steam.

At its simplest level, the design of a feedwater flow rate regulator seems to lend itself to conventional methods. From the known earth/sun/receiver geometry, a nominal value of panel insolation can be computed as a function of time and date. The insolation, the feedwater inlet conditions, and the desired outlet conditions can be used to calculate a suitable feedwater flow rate. Measured deviations from the desired outlet conditions can be fed back to modify appropriately the feedwater flow rate. While the nominal conditions are derived from the global (nonlinear) equations describing the system, the feedback compensation is based on a local (linear) perturbation model.

Design of a satisfactory regulator for this application is complicated by a number of external influences. For example, the diurnal variation in insolation causes the nominal operating point of the system to change over a wide range during the operating day. Because such changes are so slow, they can be accommodated by a regulator with time-variable gain. Changes in the number of operational heliostats can be dealt with in a similar fashion.

Other types of disturbances are not so easily dismissed. Variations in the reflectivity of the heliostats or the absorbency of the atmosphere will cause the insolation on the panel to differ from that which would be predicted on the basis of geometric considerations alone. Such disturbances act to produce biases in the equations describing the panel. Performance sensitivity to such influences can be substantially reduced by placing an integral factor in the regulator.

In the situations considered thus far, the customary controller synthesis methods are adequate. When the disturbances are both unpredictable and abrupt, however, the problem becomes more complicated. If, on a sunny summer day, a cloud passes between the sun and the heliostat field, the insolation will suddenly change and the nominal operating condition will change in concert. Because of the slow internal dynamics of the loop, disturbance rejection is most effectively accomplished with a mixed feedforward/feedback control policy. Sensors on the panel measure the current level of insolation, and from this, the nominal feedwater flow rate can easily be computed. The feedback portion of the controller acts to eliminate any residual errors. The local panel model is indexed by insolation, and the controller can use a set of regulator gains and time constants that are stored as a function of insolation to compensate for changes in panel dynamics.

The discussion of this example, although very superficial, illustrates several relevant issues related to the design of controllers that are insensitive to exogenous disturbances. When the disturbances are large enough that a simple, local model is an inadequate representation of the system, it may be advantageous to measure the disturbance and use a feedforward/feedback compensation as indicated above. An indexed set of feedback gains can often be found using existing algorithms [1].

Unfortunately, the cost and difficulty of installation often increases as the quality of the disturbance measurement increases. When the measurement of the disturbance is ambiguous, the controller is sure of neither the correct operating point nor the correct local dynamics. An adaptive controller may be required in this event because the dual functions of estimating the disturbance and maintaining the system near the correct operating point must be accomplished simultaneously.

As soon as the possibility of errors in the disturbance measurement is incorporated into the system model, the synthesis problem becomes exceedingly complex. At its most basic level, the regulator computes the conditional probability distribution function of the system operating point given all observations which relate to this operating point. This implies that the conditional distribution of the current value of the primary disturbance depends not only on its direct, albeit noisy, measurement, but also on noisy measurements of the input–output behavior of the system. Combining such disparate sources of data in a rational manner is difficult.

In most applications, these difficulties are avoided by the simple artifice of neglecting certain operational data and simplifying the remainder. For example, if the direct measurement of the disturbance is relatively accurate, the regulator might base its estimate on the direct measurement alone. The structure of the regulator would be simplified still more if the measurement noise were neglected, and the measured disturbance were used in a classical design algorithm in place of the actual disturbance. Some of the implications of this identification of these distinct quantities are discussed in [2].

A compelling reason for approximations such as those mentioned above is simplicity. In most applications, the regulator structure is severely restricted by the hardware and/or software available for its implementation. Even in systems with digital regulators, there is a strong bias in favor of simple controller algorithms. In most cases, small deviations from optimal performance are fully acceptable, if the controller can be made less complicated thereby.

In this article, an adaptive control problem of the type described above is investigated. It is assumed that the nominal operating point of the system depends on the abruptly changing external disturbance. The variation of this disturbance is assumed to be of sufficient importance to warrant its direct measurement by a sensor having small but nonnegligible errors. The controller is subdivided into a feedforward link and a feedback regulator. The output of the former may be incorrect because of uncertainties in estimating the disturbance. The latter must be designed to compensate for errors induced by the forward link while also providing satisfactory closed-loop stability margins. Further, the controller must be simple to implement.

The requirement of regulator simplicity is incompatible with optimal performance. Because simplicity takes precedence over optimality in the applications envisioned for this system, only "near optimal" performance will be sought. A low-order nonlinear model of a solar receiver panel is used to illustrate the proposed synthesis algorithm.

II. ADAPTIVE CONTROL OF A STOCHASTIC SYSTEM

A. PROBLEM FORMULATION

To make the ideas of the preceding section more tangible, consider a system described by the nonlinear, stochastic differential equation

$$d\xi_t = f(\xi_t, \nu_t, r_t)\, dt + g(r_t)\, dw_t, \quad t \geq 0, \tag{1}$$

$$\xi_0 = 0,$$

where ξ_t is the vector nonlinear system state, ν_t is the vector actuating signal, w_t is vector Brownian motion,

$$Ew_t = 0, \tag{2}$$

and

$$Ew_t w_s' = I \min(t, s).$$

The scalar random process $\{r_t\}$ represents the primary exogenous influence on the system. It will be assumed that $\{r_t\}$ is a finite-state Markov process, independent of w, with transition probability matrix Q, where $r_t \in S = \{1, \ldots, s\}$ and

$$\text{Prob}(r_{t+\Delta} = j \mid r_t = i) = \begin{cases} 1 + q_{ii}\,\Delta + o(\Delta), & i = j, \\ q_{ij}\,\Delta + o(\Delta), & i \neq j. \end{cases} \tag{3}$$

Equations (1)–(3) can be viewed in the context of the solar receiver model discussed earlier. Equation (1) models the panel dynamics with different components of ξ_t representing temperatures, pressures, and enthalpies at various points in the panel. The actuating signal ν_t is the feedwater flow rate. In this example, the dominant exogenous influence is the level of insolation is made finite, and transitions between levels are described by Eq. (3). The second term in Eq. (1) represents a collection of modeling approximations and disturbances which are essentially indistinguishable in the frequency band of interest. Such effects are conveniently combined into a "wide band" noise term. The noise intensity factor g may depend upon the operating point of the system but is assumed to be independent of the current values of state and control.

The dynamic equation of the system, Eq. (1), is indexed by r_t, and $\{r_t\}$ has enough structure to suggest the utility of feedforward compensation. If, for example, $\{r_t\}$ were measured without error, the actuating signal should be made to depend upon r_t, and partial compensation for changes in $\{r_t\}$ could be made thereby. Unfortunately, perfect measurement of r_t is seldom possible. Instead, an observation vector $\{\rho_t\}$ is typically available, from which information about $\{r_t\}$ must be deduced. On the basis of the observed values of $\{\rho_t\}$ and $\{\nu_t\}$, the controller must cause the system to perform in a satisfactory manner, and this may involve estimation of the current value of r_t.

To be more explicit, let (Ω, Ξ, P) be a probability space upon which the random processes $\{w_t, r_t, \rho_t; t \in [0, T]\}$ are defined. Let $\{\Xi_t\}$ be the sub σ-algebra generated by $\{\rho_t\}$. Let ϕ_t be a unit vector in R^s with a one in the kth component; if $r_t = k$,

$$\phi_t = (0, 0, 1, 0, \ldots, 0)'. \tag{4}$$

Define $\hat{\phi}_t$ by

$$\hat{\phi}_t = E\{\phi_t | \Xi_t\}. \tag{5}$$

Then $\hat{\phi}_t$ is the vector of conditional probabilities of r_t, and

$$\hat{\phi}_{t,i} = \text{Prob}(r_t = i \mid \Xi_t).$$

The $\{\Xi_t\}$-measurable random process $\{\hat{\phi}_t\}$ quantifies the information available to the regulator about the current value of r. If it were possible to deduce r_t from the past of $\{\rho_t\}$, then $\hat{\phi}_t$ would equal ϕ_t. Usually, the information available to the controller is not sufficient to unambiguously determine r_t. Indeed, even when r_t is "measured," $\hat{\phi}_t$ may not be degenerate.

Again, the solar panel provides a useful example. The insolation falls across the panel in a distributed manner, and r_t is a scalar-valued measure of "effective" insolation. There are several sensors on the panel which give an accurate, albeit local, measure of insolation, but because of the changing sun/earth/heliostat geometry, there is no practical way to determine the true value of the effective insolation from a finite number of sensor readings. Consequently, the "measured" insolation tends to differ from the actual insolation.

To use the usual analytical procedures of control system design, the equation of evolution of $\hat{\phi}$ must first be determined. This is often a very difficult task despite the fact that the state space of r is finite. If the system equation and the observation have the proper structure, it is possible to describe $\hat{\phi}$ in terms of another stochastic differential equation:

$$d\hat{\phi}_t = h\left(\rho_t, \nu_t, \hat{\phi}_t, t, r_t\right) dt + k\left(\rho_t, \nu_t, \hat{\phi}_t, t, r_t\right) d\eta_t, \tag{6}$$

where η_t is a Brownian motion process. Equation (6) gives the "learning" dynamics of the system.

The fundamental adaptive control problem is that of finding a control policy which is adapted to $\{\Xi_t\}$ and which causes the system described by Eqs. (1) and (6) to perform in a satisfactory manner. Suppose the vector ρ_t contains the nonlinear system state ξ_t. Then the relevant information contained in $\{\Xi_t\}$ is given by the vector processes $\{\hat{\phi}_t, \xi_t\}$. Suppose further that performance is measured by a criterion function of the form

$$J = E\left\{\int_0^T \left[c\left(\xi_s, \hat{\phi}_s, r_s\right) + d\left(\nu_s, \hat{\phi}_s, r_s\right)\right] ds\right\}. \tag{7}$$

The first term in Eq. (7) provides a (random) weighting on the state trajectory and the second term is a (random) weighting on the actuating signal. The desired control is one which minimizes J.

B. DYNAMIC PROGRAMMING AND BELLMAN'S EQUATIONS

To find the optimal control, the formalism of dynamic programming can conveniently be used. Because of the simple parameterization of $\{\Xi_t\}$, the minimum cost-to-go functional V can be expressed as

$$V\left(t, \xi_t, \hat{\phi}_t\right) = \min_{\nu} E\left\{\int_t^T \left[c\left(\xi_s, \hat{\phi}_s, r_s\right) + d\left(\nu_s, \hat{\phi}_s, r_s\right)\right] ds \,|\, \Xi_t\right\}. \tag{8}$$

A controller minimizing the right-hand side of Eq. (8) will be assumed to exist and it will be labeled $\left\{\nu_t^*\right\}$. Define[1]

$$V\left(t, \xi_t, \hat{\phi}_t, r_t\right) = E\left\{\int_t^T \left(c\left(\xi_s, \hat{\phi}_s, r_s\right) + d\left(\nu_s, \hat{\phi}_s, r_s\right)\right) ds \,|\, \Xi_t, r_t\right\}\Bigg|_{\nu=\nu^*}. \tag{9}$$

[1] *The cost-to-go function V will be used in a variety of contexts and with a variety of arguments. The symbol V will be used in all of these cases even though the functional dependence will, of course, be different. A subscripted variable may represent the value at a particular time (r_t) or the partial derivative of the variable (V_x). The meaning is clear from the context.*

Then

$$V\left(t, \xi_t, \hat{\phi}_t\right) = \sum_i V\left(t, \xi_t, \hat{\phi}_t, i\right)\hat{\phi}_{t,i}. \tag{10}$$

An algorithm for evaluating ν_t^* can be produced as long as all of the requisite functions are smooth. Expanding $V\left(t, \xi_t, \hat{\phi}_t, r_t\right)$,

$$V\left(t, \xi_t, \hat{\phi}_t, r_t\right) = \left[c\left(\xi_t, \hat{\phi}_t, r_t\right) + d\left(\nu_t^*, \hat{\phi}_t, r_t\right)\right] dt + E\left\{V\left(t + dt, \xi_{t+dt}, \hat{\phi}_{t+dt}, r_{t+dt}\right) \middle| \Xi_t, r_t\right\}. \tag{11}$$

The last term can be written as

$$\begin{aligned} &V\left(t + dt, \xi_{t+dt}, \hat{\phi}_{t+dt}, r_{t+dt}\right) \\ &\quad = V_t\left(t, \xi_t, \hat{\phi}_t, r_{t+dt}\right) dt + V_\xi \, d\xi_t + V_{\hat{\phi}} \, d\hat{\phi}_t \\ &\quad + \frac{1}{2}\left[\sum_{ij} V_{\xi_i \xi_j} d\left\langle \xi_i^c, \xi_j^c \right\rangle_t + \sum_{ij} V_{\hat{\phi}_i \hat{\phi}_j} d\left\langle \hat{\phi}_i^c, \hat{\phi}_j^c \right\rangle_t \right. \\ &\quad \left. + 2 \sum_{ij} V_{\hat{\phi}_i \xi_j} d\left\langle \hat{\phi}_i^c, \xi_j^c \right\rangle_t \right] \\ &\quad + V\left(t, \xi_t, \hat{\phi}_t, r_{t+dt}\right). \end{aligned} \tag{12}$$

Substituting Eq. (12) into Eq. (11)

$$\begin{aligned} &V\left(t, \xi_t, \hat{\phi}_t, i\right) \\ &\quad = \left[c\left(\xi_t, \hat{\phi}_t, i\right) + d\left(\nu_t^*, \hat{\phi}_t, i\right) + V_t + V_\xi f\left(\xi_t, \nu_t^*, i, t\right)\right. \\ &\quad \left. + V_{\hat{\phi}} h\left(\rho_t, \nu_t^*, \hat{\phi}_t, t, i\right)\right] dt \end{aligned}$$

$$+ \frac{1}{2}\left[\sum_{ij} V_{\xi_i \xi_j} d\left\langle \xi_i^c, \xi_j^c \right\rangle_t + V_{\hat{\phi}_i \hat{\phi}_j} d\left\langle \hat{\phi}_i^c, \hat{\phi}_j^c \right\rangle_t + 2V_{\hat{\phi}_i \xi_j} d\left\langle \hat{\phi}_i^c, \xi_j^c \right\rangle_t \right]$$

$$+ E\left[V\left(t, \xi_t, \hat{\phi}_t, r_{t+dt}\right) \middle| \Xi_t, r_t = i\right]. \tag{13}$$

In principle, Eqs. (1)–(13) can be combined to find the desired regulator.

Solving the indicated equations for $\{\nu_t^*\}$ is a formidable task. Equation (13) contains $\{\nu_t^*\}$ in terms involving both first and second partial derivatives of V. Even in the unlikely event that all of the equations could be solved, $\{\nu_t^*\}$ would have such a convoluted form that it would not be implemented in most applications. Equation (6) for $\{\hat{\phi}_t\}$ is the intermediary which expresses the dynamic constraints on identifying $\{r_t\}$. Since both $d\hat{\phi}_t$ and $d\xi_t$ depend upon ν_t, the regulator must cause $\{\xi_t\}$ to follow the desired path while simultaneously causing $\{\hat{\phi}_t\}$ to track $\{\phi_t\}$. Because these two demands will be contrary to some degree, the regulator design is called a dual control problem. There exist very few dual control solutions because of the inherent intractability of the synthesis equations.

In this article, attention will be focused on a subclass of the adaptive controllers described above. It will be assumed that

A1: h and k in Eq. (6) are independent of ν_t and ξ_t. (14)

Assumption A1 has some significant implications. Only two terms in Eq. (13) now involve ν_t. If f and d have the requisite properties, $\{\nu_t^*\}$ can be found as the unique solution to

$$\sum_i \hat{\phi}_{t,i}\Big[d_\nu\big(\nu_t, \hat{\phi}_t, i\big) + V_\xi\big(t, \xi_t, \hat{\phi}_t, i\big) f_\nu(\xi_t, \nu_t, i)\Big]\Big|_{\nu_t=\nu_t^*} = 0. \quad (15)$$

A complete solution to this restricted problem is not currently obtainable. Indeed, even if $\{r_t\}$ were a known, nonrandom constant, the explicit form of $\{\nu_t^*\}$ still seems inaccessible for the general equations of the system evolution and the general performance weightings given above.

Systems satisfying Assumption A1 can be thought of as being passively adaptive. The regulator "learns" the value of the randomly changing modal indicator, but the learning is passive in the sense that the actuating signal has no direct impact on the role at which r is identified. The regulator need only concern itself with the behavior of $\{\xi_t\}$, thus avoiding the dual aspect of the problem.

It will seldom be the case that Eq. (14) is satisfied exactly. Both ξ_t and ν_t are assumed to be contained in ρ_t. The indicator variable r_t indexes the current relationship between ξ_t and ν_t, and as a consequence, $d\hat{\phi}_t$ will depend to some extent upon (ξ_t, ν_t).

Still, in many situations this dependence will be weak. The regulator of a solar panel illustrates this. In principle, the current level of insolation manifests itself in the input/output relationship of the panel. Noise, modeling errors, etc. would make this such a low quality indicator of the operating condition as to render it essentially useless. The panel-mounted insolation sensors provide a much more accurate and expeditious measure of operating condition. While not noise free, these sensors provide such high-quality measurements that the $\{\xi_t, \nu_t\}$

measurement is of scant value for identifying r_t. In this case, Eq. (14) is an accurate approximation of the "learning" which actually takes place in the system. Moreover, the regulator of a solar panel does not have the sophisticated data manipulation capability required to make use of $\{\xi_t, \nu_t\}$ in estimating $\{r_t\}$ anyway. Hence, with the above caveat, Eq. (14) is quite frequently a reasonable approximation to the estimation dynamics of a regulator for a system subject to an exogenous influence that is important enough to warrant feedforward control.

III. NEAR OPTIMAL CONTROL OF A JUMP PARAMETER SYSTEM

A. NONLINEAR FILTER

The previous section described the basic features of passive adaptation. Without additional restrictions, the problem is not solvable. In this section, some further assumptions on the nature of the external disturbances will be made. While even in this case the complete solution of the synthesis equations is not possible, some interesting approximations to the optimal regulator can be deduced.

For reasons explored previously, partial adaptation to changing values of $\{r_t\}$ is accomplished by a direct, albeit noisy, measurement of r. Suppose the direct observation of $\{r_t\}$ is given by $\{y_t\}$, where

$$dy_t = b_t\ dt + \sigma\ dm_t \quad \text{if} \quad r_t = i. \tag{16}$$

If $r_t = 1$, for example, a signal b_1 is transmitted. The measurement is contaminated by wide band noise with intensity σ^2. The process $\{m_t\}$ will be assumed to be normalized Brownian motion, independent of $\{w_t\}$.

The observation equation (16) can be written more concisely. Let

$$B = (b_1, \ldots, b_s)',$$

$$\tilde{B} = \mathrm{diag}(b_1, \ldots, b_s), \tag{17}$$

$$B_t = B'\phi_t.$$

Then

$$dy_t = B_t dt + \sigma\, dm_t \tag{18}$$

and

$$\hat{B}_t = B'\hat{\phi}_t.$$

In terms of these quantities, the equation for $\{\hat{\phi}_t\}$ becomes (see, for example, Ref. [3], pp. 289)

$$d\hat{\phi}_t = Q'\hat{\phi}_t\, dt + \sigma^{-1}\left(\tilde{B} - \hat{B}_t I\right)\hat{\phi}_t\, d\mu_t, \tag{19}$$

where $\{\mu_t\}$ is the innovation process

$$d\mu_t = \sigma^{-1}\left(\left(\hat{\phi}_t - \hat{\phi}_t\right)'B\, dt + \sigma\, dm_t\right) = \sigma^{-1}\left(dy_t - d\hat{y}_t\right).$$

The innovation process is an $\{\Xi_t\}$-Brownian motion process. Equation (19) gives the equations of evolution of the identification portion of the regulator [compare with Eq. (6)]. In keeping with the earlier discussion, the high accuracy of the direct observation of r will be displayed in Eq. (18) by the assumption that σ is small.

B. *LINEARIZATION OF SYSTEM EQUATIONS*

With small noise in Eq. (18), the equation for $\{\xi_t\}$ can be approximated in a natural manner. The indicator variable r_t can take on only a finite number of different values. Corresponding to each of these values of r_t, it will be assumed there is a nominal system trajectory $\{x_n(i), \nu_n(i);\ i \in S\}$. The ith trajectory represents the desired operating condition when $r_t = i$. For convenience, it will be assumed that the set of trajectories are time invariant and satisfy

$$f(x_n(i),\ \nu_n(i),\ i) = 0, \quad i \in S, \tag{20}$$

although the more general time-variable case can be accommodated in a straightforward manner.

Because $\{r_t\}$ is piecewise constant and identifiable with high probability from the observation $\{y_t\}$, a useful approximation for the system dynamics is given by a linearization of Eq. (1) about the nominal trajectory associated with the ostensible operating point. Suppose that $\hat{\phi}_{t,l} \simeq 1$. Since $\hat{\phi}_t$ is the conditional probability vector, l is the most likely value of r_t given Ξ_t. In what follows l_t will denote the "most likely" value of the modal indicator at time t.

Because the regulator is inclined toward the operating condition l, it will attempt to maintain the system near $(x_n(l),\ u_n(l))$. The measured state error vector $\bar{x}_t$ is thus given by

$$\bar{x}_t = \xi_t - x_n(l), \tag{21}$$

which is the difference between the realized system trajectory and what the regulator assumes the desired trajectory to be. If $r_t = l$ and $\bar{x}_t$ were small, the dynamic equation for $\bar{x}_t$ would be the usual linearization of Eq. (1) about $(x_n(l),\ u_n(l))$. Suppose, however, that $r_t = r \neq l$, i.e., the modal indicator has recently changed, but the identification algorithm (19) has not yet deduced this from $\{y_t\}$. The linearization of Eq. (1) takes a different form in this case:

$$\begin{aligned} d\bar{x}_t &= [f(\xi_t,\ \nu_t,\ r) - f(x_n(l),\ u_n(l),\ r)]\ dt \\ &\quad + f(x_n(l),\ u_n(l),\ r)\ dt + g(r)\ dw_t \\ &\simeq \left[F_{lr}\bar{x}_t + G_{lr}u_t\right] dt + \Delta(l,\ r)\ dt + g(r)\ dw_t, \end{aligned} \tag{22}$$

where

$$F_{l,r} = f_\xi(\xi,\ u_n(l),\ r)|_{\xi=x_n(l)} \quad \text{with} \quad F_{ll} = F_l, \tag{23}$$

$$G_{l,r} = f_\nu(x_n(l),\ \nu,\ r)|_{\nu=u_n(l)} \quad \text{with} \quad G_{ll} = G_l, \tag{24}$$

$$\Delta(l,\ r) = f(x_n(l),\ u_n(l),\ r), \tag{25}$$

$$u_t = \nu_t - u_n(l). \tag{26}$$

Equation (22) has an interesting interpretation. If $l = r$, Eqs. (23)–(26) are the classical equations for the matrices which parameterize the linear dynamic model of the system. Further, from Eq. (25), $\Delta(l,\ l) = 0$. If $\hat{\phi}_t$ gives an incorrect indication of r_t, the regulator faces a more recalcitrant task. The dynamic matrices are now $(F_{l,r},\ G_{l,r})$, and there is a bias $\Delta(l,\ r)$ which the actuating signal must overcome to maintain close approach to what it perceives as the correct nominal path. The bias tends to drive $\bar{x}_t$ away from zero. Because the regulator is unaware of the source of the bias, ν_t will tend to counteract it and use an increased level of control energy.

Eqaution (22) gives the dynamic equation for the measured error variable $\bar{x}_t$ when l is continuous at time t. Suppose that $\{l_t\}$ makes a sudden change at time t, i.e., $l_t \neq l_{t^-}$. Then

$$\begin{aligned}\bar{x}_t &= \xi_t - x_n(l_t)\\ &= \xi_t - x_n(l_{t^-}) + x_n(l_{t^-}) - x_n(l_t)\\ &= \bar{x}_{t^-} + \delta(l_t,\ l_{t^-}).\end{aligned} \tag{27}$$

Although the nonlinear state is continuous for all t, the measured error of the regulator will have discontinuities whenever $\{l_t\}$ is discontinuous.

Equations (22) and (27) give the dynamic model of the linearized plant. When the identification procedure gives the correct operating mode, the correct linear model is used. Identification errors give rise to an atypical model, and there are discontinuities in the sensed error variables whenever there are discontinuities in $\{l_t\}$. Based upon the information available to it, $\{\Xi_t\}$, the regulator seeks to cause the system to behave in an appropriate manner. The true trajectory following error is given by $\xi_t - x_n(r_t)$, while the feedback gain is restrained by limiting the energy in u_t. The particular performance index to be used in this study is given by

$$J = E\left\{ \int_0^T \left(\|\xi_t - x_n(r_t)\|_M^2 + \|u_t\|_N^2 \right) dt \right\};$$

$$M \geq 0, \qquad N > 0. \tag{28}$$

Equation (28) is interesting because the forms of c and d are different. The state error weighting in Eq. (28) measures the actual deviation of the controlled system variables ξ_t from the true nominal $x_n(r_t)$:

$$c\left(\xi_s, \hat{\phi}_s, r_s\right) = \|\xi_s - x_n(r_s)\|_M^2.$$

On the other hand, the control deviation is referenced to the most likely value of the nominal actuating signal $u_n(l_t)$:

$$d\left(\nu_s, \hat{\phi}_s, r_s\right) = \|\nu_s - u_n(l_s)\|_N^2.$$

Since u_t is a deviation from the apparent nominal $u_n(l)$, $\{d_t\}$ is adapted to $\{\Xi_t\}$ while $\{c_t\}$ is not.

The performance index given by Eq. (28) shows the impact of the mixed feedforward/feedback control policy. The direct sensor noise in Eq. (18) is small, and this causes the regulator to be relatively confident that $l_t = r_t$. The feedforward component of $\{\nu_t\}$ reflects this and is simply the nominal actuating signal appropriate for l_t:

$$\nu_t = u_n(l_t) + u_t.$$

The feedback component of $\{\nu_t\}$ is also adapted to $\{\Xi_t\}$. It is contingent on the measured state error and the estimate of r_t; $\left\{\bar{x}_s, \hat{\phi}_s : s \in [0, t]\right\}$. It is the generalized energy in $\{u_t\}$ that is weighted in J. If the feedback link generating u_t were linear, $\{d_t\}$ could be viewed as a term whose effect is to limit the feedback gain.

With the performance index given in Eq. (28), the equation describing the feedback control, Eq. (15), is easily solved:

$$u_t = -\frac{1}{2} N^{-1} \sum_i V_\xi\left(t, \xi_t, \hat{\phi}_t, i\right)' f_\nu(\xi_t, \nu_t, i)\hat{\phi}_{t,i}. \tag{29}$$

The regulator design problem becomes that of solving for the factors $V_\xi(\ldots, i)$ in Eq. (29). Unfortunately, even this restricted problem is intractable.

The system changes operating modes at unpredictable time points. It will be assumed that these modal changes are infrequent enough that the sum of the times of the transients associated with changes in the exogenous variable is but a small fraction of the operating interval. That is, it will be assumed that the elements of Q [see Eq. (3)] are small by comparison to the important corner frequencies of the closed-loop system. Furthermore, the noise intensity in Eq. (18) will be assumed to be small enough that the time required for identifying a modal variation tends to be small compared to the intervals between occurrence of discontinuities in $\{r_t\}$.

In operation, the system will have long intervals of relatively normal operation in which $\hat{\phi}_t$ correctly identifies

$r_t (l_t = r_t)$ interspersed with brief transient periods associated with changes in r_t. An interval of ambiguity follows the modal changes during which $\hat{\phi}_t$ must identify the characteristic behavioral markers in its observation to find the current value of r_t. Even without a change in $\{r_t\}$, $\{\hat{\phi}_t\}$ may provide a false indication of change, but if σ is small such occurrences are infrequent.

Note that even when $l_t = r_t$, $\hat{\phi}_t$ is not degenerate. The regulator can never be certain that a jump in $\{r_t\}$ has not just occurred. The behavior of $\{\hat{\phi}_t\}$ after a jump is quite complicated [see Eq. (19)]. In response to a change in $\{r_t\}$, all of the components of $\{\hat{\phi}_t\}$ will move about until after an interval of variable length, the new value of r_t is identified, and $\{\hat{\phi}_t\}$ becomes concentrated near this value. Because of the complex dynamics of $\{\hat{\phi}_t\}$ in this transitional regime, and because of the relatively short amount of time spent there, the dynamics of l_t will be modeled with a simple discontinuous approximation. It will be assumed that there is a matrix $Q^o = [q^o_{ij}]$ such that

$$\text{Prob}(l_{t_0+t+\Delta} = j \mid l_{t_0+s} = i;\ s \in [0, t],\ r_{t_0} = j,\ r_{t_0^-} = i)$$

$$= \begin{cases} q^o_{ij}\ \Delta + o(\Delta), & j \neq i, \\ 1 + q^o_{ij}\ \Delta + o(\Delta), & j = i, \end{cases} \tag{30}$$

and $d\hat{\phi}_t = 0$ on the interval over which $l_t \neq r_t$.

Equation (30) simplifies the transition dynamics of $\{l_t\}$. If $\{r_t\}$ makes an $i \to j$ transition at time t_0, $\{l_t\}$ will make the same transition with a random delay. The elements of Q^o will be assumed to be large by comparison with elements of Q. This makes unlikely the event of multiple changes in $\{r_t\}$ without corresponding changes in $\{l_t\}$. Since $\{r_t\}$ is the basic

Markov process describing the modal state and $\{l_t\}$ is a process dependent on it, composite events can be easily introduced into the subsequent analysis. However, the separation in time scales of these events obviates the need to introduce them into the solution algorithm explicitly.

The basic dynamic model of the system is now essentially complete. The state error dynamics are given by Eq. (22) at continuity points of $\{l_t\}$ and by Eq. (27) where $\{l_t\}$ is discontinuous. The observation of $\{y_t\}$ leads to the modal estimation equation (19). The performance index is given by the quadratic functional (28). Because σ is assumed to be quite small, the behavior of $\{u_t\}$ [see Eq. (26)] in the neighborhood of $\sigma = 0$ is sought.

C. SMALL NOISE APPROXIMATION

Although the simplifications listed above do yield a less complex equation for the cost-to-go function V [see Eq. (13)], the design problem is still intractable for models with reasonable state dimension and a large number of allowable modes. To produce an easily computed approximation to $\left\{\nu_t^*\right\}$, the equation describing $\left\{\hat{\phi}_t\right\}$ must be studied in more detail. The modal observation equation is intended to model the direct measurement of $\{r_t\}$ with signal signature, b_r, and additive high-frequency noise. Equation (18) is written as an Ito stochastic differential equation and $\{m_t\}$ is a Brownian motion process. Because σ is a constant Eq. (18) could as easily be interpreted as a white-noise differential equation [4] with the integral of the second term thought of as a white-noise integral.

Based upon $\{y_t\}$, the Ito equation for $\hat{\phi}_t$ is given in Eq. (19). Observe that the multiplier of the martingale $\{\mu_t\}$ is the $\{\Xi_t\}$ predictable process $\sigma^{-1}\left(\tilde{B} - \hat{B}_t I\right)\hat{\phi}_t$. For ease in calculations involving $\left\{\hat{\phi}_t\right\}$, it is expedient to rewrite Eq. (19) in the Stratonovich form. Such a transformation yields a dynamic equation which satisfies the formal rules of calculus, specifically the chain rule of differentiation [4].

From Eq. (19),

$$d\hat{\phi}_t = \left[Q'\hat{\phi}_t + \sigma^{-2}\left(\tilde{B} - \hat{B}_t I\right)\hat{\phi}_t\left(\phi_t - \hat{\phi}_t\right)'B\right] dt$$
$$+ \sigma^{-1}\left(\tilde{B} - \hat{B}_t I\right)\hat{\phi}_t \, dm_t. \tag{31}$$

The Stratonovich form of Eq. (31) can be produced by subtracting a correction term from the right-hand side; (Ref. [4], Eq. (5.34)). Denote

$$\beta = \sigma^{-1}\left(\tilde{B} - \hat{\phi}_t' BI\right)\hat{\phi}_t = (\beta_i).$$

The correction term for the Stratonovich integral is

$$-\frac{1}{2}\sum_k \frac{\partial \beta_l}{\partial \hat{\phi}_k}\beta_k = -\frac{\sigma^{-2}}{2}\left[-B_t^2 + \hat{B}_t^2 + \left(b_i - \hat{B}_t\right)^2\right]\hat{\phi}_{t,i} \tag{32}$$

with

$$\hat{B}_t^2 = \sum_i b_i^2 \hat{\phi}_{t,i}. \tag{33}$$

Substituting Eq. (32) into Eq. (31)

$$d\hat{\phi}_t = Q'\hat{\phi}_t \, dt + \sigma^{-2}\left[\left(\tilde{B} - \hat{B}_t I\right)\phi_t' B - \frac{1}{2}\left(\widetilde{B^2} - \hat{B}_t^2 I\right)\right]\hat{\phi}_t \, dt$$
$$+ \sigma^{-1}\left(\tilde{B} - \hat{B}_t I\right)\hat{\phi}_t \, dm_t^s, \tag{34}$$

where

$$\widetilde{B^2} = \text{diag } b_1^2, \ldots, b_s^2 \tag{35}$$

and the last term of Eq. (34) is to be interpreted as a Stratonovich stochastic integral.

The effect of identification errors becomes clearer if attention is focused on the difference between $\{\phi_t\}$ and $\{\hat{\phi}_t\}$. Define

$$\tilde{\phi}_t = \hat{\phi}_t - \phi_t. \tag{36}$$

Suppose t is a continuity point of l_t and r_t and that $l_t = r_t = r$. This represents typical operation of the system. All of the components of $\tilde{\phi}_t$ except rth are nonnegative and

$$\tilde{\phi}_{t,r} = -\sum_{j \neq r} \tilde{\phi}_{t,j}. \tag{37}$$

It is the vector $\tilde{\phi}_t$ which gives a quantitative indication of the uncertainty with which the regulator views its knowledge of r_t. Because $\tilde{\phi}_{t,r}$ is redundant, a reduced dimension vector $\tilde{\phi}_t^*$ can be used in place of $\tilde{\phi}_t$, i.e., the pair $(\tilde{\phi}_t^*, l_t)$ contains the same information conveyed by $\hat{\phi}_t$, and it is convenient to express V in terms of this pair.

At continuity points of r_t, $d\phi_t = 0$. Except for intervals shortly after the transition in $\{r_t\}$, $||\tilde{\phi}_t||$ will be small. Neglecting higher order terms in $\tilde{\phi}_t$, it follows from Eq. (34) that if $i \neq r$,

$$d\tilde{\phi}_{t,i} = \left[q_{ri} - \left(Q'\tilde{\phi}_t\right)_i - \frac{\sigma^{-2}}{2}(b_r - b_i)^2\tilde{\phi}_i\right] dt$$
$$+ \sigma^{-1}(b_r - b_i)\tilde{\phi}_i \; dm_t^s. \tag{38}$$

If the elements of Q are of comparable size, $Q'\tilde{\phi}$ can be neglected as compared with q_{ri}.

The implications of Eq. (38) become apparent when its qualitative behavior is analyzed. The equation for $\{\tilde{\phi}_{t,i}\}$ can be formally viewed as

$$\tilde{\phi}_{t,i} = \alpha_i + \beta_i n_t,$$

where n_t is a wide band (near white noise) process. Under quasi-steady state conditions $\tilde{\phi}_{t,i}$ tends to vary about an offset given by the solution to $\alpha_i = 0$. The term $\beta_i n_t$ is a forcing term which gives rise to an irregular variation about this bias. From Eq. (8), if $\alpha_i = 0$, then

$$\tilde{\phi}_{t,i} \simeq \frac{2\sigma^2 q_{li}}{(b_r - b_i)^2}, \qquad r \neq i, \qquad l = r. \tag{39}$$

The offset is proportional to the product of the intensity of the observation noise and the transition probability from l to i.

If σ^2 is small, the multiplier of dt in Eq. (38) is small. Near the value of $\tilde{\phi}_t$ given by Eq. (39), the noise intensity is given by

$$\|\sigma^{-1}(b_r - b_i)\tilde{\phi}_i\|^2 = O(\sigma^2). \tag{40}$$

Thus, it is clear that the amplitude of the wide band noise term in Eq. (38) tends to be small when σ is small. Note that m_t^s is not a martingale. Nevertheless, the contribution of this factor in the equation for $\tilde{\phi}_t$ is negligible when $\{y_t\}$ provides a high-quality measurement of $\{r_t\}$.

With the above rationale, it is now possible to produce a near optimal regulator for an adaptive system. It is advantageous to reparameterize the cost-to-go function. Noting that $\xi_t = \overline{x}_t + x_n(l_t)$, V can be written as $V\left(t, \overline{x}_t, \tilde{\phi}_t, l_t, r_t\right)$. There are two possible cases to consider.

Case 1: $r_t = l_t$.

$$V(t, \bar{x}_t, \tilde{\phi}_t, l_t, l_t)$$
$$= E\Big\{\big(\bar{x}_t' M \bar{x}_t + u_t' N u_t + V_t\big)\, dt + \frac{1}{2}\sum_{ij} V_{\bar{x}_i \bar{x}_j}\, d\langle \bar{x}_i^c, \bar{x}_j^c \rangle_t$$
$$+ V_{\bar{x}}\, d\bar{x}_t + V_{\tilde{\phi}}\, d\tilde{\phi}_t$$
$$+ V\big(t, \bar{x}_t, \tilde{\phi}_t, l_t, r_{t+dt}\big) \mid \Xi_t, r_t \Big\}\Big|_{\nu_t = \nu_t}. \tag{41}$$

Case 2: $r_t \neq l_t$.

$$V\big(t, \bar{x}_t, \tilde{\phi}_t, l_t, r_t\big)$$
$$= E\Big\{\big(\|\bar{x}_t + \delta(l_{t+dt}, l_t)\|^2 M + u_t' N u_t + V_t\big)\, dt$$
$$+ \frac{1}{2}\sum_{ij} V_{\bar{x}_i \bar{x}_j}\, d\; \bar{x}_i^c, \bar{x}_j^c\; {}_t + V_{\bar{x}}\, d\bar{x}_t$$
$$+ V\big(t, \bar{x}_t + \delta(l_{t+dt}, l_t), l_{t+dt}, r_t\big) \mid \Xi_t, r_t \Big\}\Big|_{\nu = \nu_t}. \tag{42}$$

$$V(T, \cdot, \cdot, \cdot, \cdot) = 0. \tag{43}$$

Solving Eqs. (41)–(42) in conjunction with Eq. (43) in a neighborhood of $\sigma = 0$ yields an explicit equation for the near optimal regulator. The calculations are direct but tedious, and they have been placed in the appendix. Observe that the choice of the Stratonovich model for $\{\tilde{\phi}_t\}$ avoids the second-order terms in Eqs. (41)–(43) associated with $d\tilde{\phi}_t$.

The equation for the feedback portion of the regulator is given by

$$u_t = -N^{-1}\Big[G_l'\big(P_o^{ll}\bar{x} + p_o^{ll}\big) + \sum_k G_{lk}'\big(P_o^{lk}\bar{x} + p_o^{lk}\big)\tilde{\phi}_k\Big], \tag{44}$$

where

$$\dot{P}_o^{ll} = F'P_o^{ll} - P_o^{ll}F_l + P_o^{ll}G_lN^{-1}G_l'P_o^{ll} - M - \sum_k q_{lk}P_o^{lk}; \tag{45}$$

$$\dot{P}_o^{lk} = P_o^{lk}\left(F_{lk} - G_{lk}N^{-1}G_l'P_o^{ll}\right) - M - P_o^{ll}G_lN^{-1}G'P_o^{ll}$$
$$- \left(F_{lk} - G_{lk}N^{-1}G_l'P_o^{ll}\right)'P_o^{lk} - q_{lk}^o\left(P_o^{kk} - P_o^{lk}\right); \tag{46}$$

$$P_o^{ll}(T) = P_o^{lk}(T) = 0, \quad l, k = 1, \ldots, s, \quad l \neq k;$$

$$\dot{p}_o^{ll} = \left(P_o^{ll}G_lN^{-1}G_l' - F_l'\right)p_o^{ll} - \sum_k q_{lk}p_o^{lk}; \tag{47}$$

$$\dot{p}_o^{lk} = \left(P_o^{ll}G_lN^{-1}G_{lk}' - F_{lk}'\right)p_o^{lk} - M\,\delta(k, l) - P_o^{ll}G_lN^{-1}G_l'p_o^{ll}$$
$$+ P_o^{lk}G_{lk}N^{-1}G_l'p_o^{ll} - P_o^{lk}\,\Delta(l, k)$$
$$- q_{lk}^o\left[P_o^{kk}\,\delta(k, l) + \left(p_o^{kk} - p_o^{lk}\right)\right]; \tag{48}$$

$$p_o^{ll}(T) = p_o^{lk}(T) = 0, \quad l, k = 1, \ldots, s, \quad l \neq k.$$

The full feedforward/feedback control becomes

$$\nu_t^* = u_n(l_t) - N^{-1}\left[G_l'\left(P_o^{ll}\bar{x}_t + p_o^{ll}\right) + \sum_k G_{lk}'\left(P_o^{lk}\bar{x}_t + p_o^{lk}\right)\tilde{\phi}_k\right]. \tag{49}$$

Equations (44)–(49) provide an approximation to the equations of the optimal adaptive regulator for systems with accurate measurement of the external disturbance. The individual terms in Eq. (49) give the feedforward/feedback structure of ν_t^* explicitly. The feedforward component is the "most likely" nominal. The feedback component is a linear function of the "measured" state error plus a bias. The full controller is simple to mechanize based upon the observable signals.

The performance of the system is given by V. It is shown in the appendix that to the first order in $||\tilde{\phi}||$,

$$V(t, \bar{x}, \tilde{\phi}, l) = \bar{x}'\left(P_o^{ll} + \sum_k P_o^{lk}\tilde{\phi}_k\right)\bar{x} + 2\bar{x}'\left(p_o^{ll} + \sum_k p_o^{lk}\tilde{\phi}_k\right)$$

$$+ q_o^{ll} + \sum_k q_o^{lk}\tilde{\phi}_k, \tag{50}$$

where the equations for $\left\{q_o^{lk}\right\}$ are given in Eqs. (A19) and (A27). The equations which characterize the regulator and the performance index are rather convoluted, and for this reason they do not lend themselves to an easy interpretation. They are suitable to direct computational solution. Equations (45) and (46) are matrix ordinary differential equations with the indicated terminal condition. After integrating Eqs. (45)–(46), the coefficients for Eqs. (47)–(48) become known, and the ordinary differential equations for p_o^{lk} can be integrated. Equations (A19), (A26), and (50) complete the description of V.

Some qualitative insight into the behavior of the adaptive regulator is possible if the limiting form of the design equations is inspected. Consider for purposes of illustration the primary gain factor in Eq. (44), P_o^{ll}. It has been shown in [1] that if there are no errors in measuring $r_t (\sigma \equiv 0)$,

$$u_t = -N^{-1}G_r'(P^r\bar{x} + p^r), \tag{51}$$

where

$$\dot{P}^r = -F_r'P^r - P^rF_r + P^rG_rN^{-1}G_r'P^r - M - \sum_k q_{rk}P^k, \tag{52}$$

$$P^r(T) = 0, \quad r \in S.$$

Observe that even when $||\tilde{\phi}|| = 0$, Eq. (44) does not reduce to Eq. (51) because the equation for P^r is not the same as the equation for P_o^{rr}. They differ in the last term with P^r using a weighted sum of $\{P^k\}$ and P_o^{rr} using a weighted sum of $\left\{P_o^{rk}\right\}$. The matrix P_o^{rk}, $k \neq l$, tends to be larger than P_o^{rr} because the former is associated with the cost-to-go when the regulator is making an erroneous inference about the true value of r, while the latter is evaluated under the conditions that the inference is correct. As a result of this, and the nonnegativity of the q_{ij} for $i \neq j$, P_o^{rr} tends to be larger than P^r of Eq. (52). The adaptive regulator is, thus, a "higher" gain system.

Note that as $\sigma \to 0$, $q_{ij}^o \to \infty$ for all permissible $i \to j$ transitions; for example, as the measurement noise strength decreases, the transient interval of identification decreases. In this event Eq. (46) indicates that

$$\lim_{\sigma^2 \to 0} P_o^{rk} = P_o^{rr}. \tag{53}$$

In the limit, therefore, Eqs. (45)–(46) are equivalent to the single equation (52).

Of course, $||\tilde{\phi}|| \neq 0$ during normal operation. If σ^2 is small, one may still replace P_o^{lk} in Eq. (49) by P^l with small error. This makes the evaluation of $\{u_t\}$ even easier because the coupling between Eq. (45) and Eq. (46) is neglected. Such a regulator will tend to have degraded performance when compared with that given in Eq. (49). Similar approximations can be used in Eqs. (47)–(48) when expedient.

IV. AN EXAMPLE

To illustrate the details of the synthesis procedure of the previous sections, consider a control problem motivated by the solar-powered central receiver described earlier. A functional block diagram of the system is shown in Fig. 1. The insolation

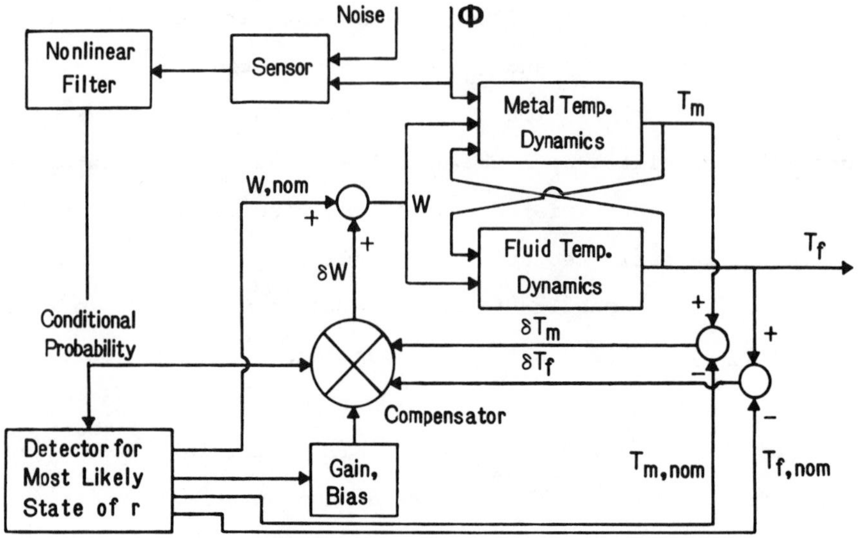

Fig. 1. Block diagram of the adaptive control system.

heats the metal panel structure, causing its temperature (T_m, °F) to change. A variation in metal temperature leads to a change in the fluid (steam–water) flowing through small pipes within the panel. For the purposes of this analysis, the distributed fluid temperature will be aggregated into a single "effective" temperature (T_f, °F). It will be assumed that the temperatures (T_m, T_f) can be measured directly (T_m) or inferred from direct measurements (T_f).

A simplified set of equations describing the panel condition is given by

$$\dot{T}_m = K_1\left[\Phi - 50W^{0.8}(T_m - T_f)\right], \tag{54}$$

$$\dot{T}_f = K_2\left[50W^{0.8}(T_m - T_f) - 6480W - 6144T_f + 5.076 \times 10^6\right], \tag{55}$$

where K_1 and K_2 are thermodynamic or heat transfer coefficients of the metal and fluid. The control variable W is the feedwater flow rate in lbs/min.

The incident insolation is given by Φ in Eq. (54). For simplicity it will be supposed that Φ takes on only two possible values, representing a dense cloud or alternatively unobscured sun:

$$\Phi = \begin{cases} \Phi_1, & 6 \times 10^4 \text{ BTU/min}, \quad r = 1; \\ \Phi_2, & 24 \times 10^4 \text{ BTU/min}, \quad r = 2. \end{cases} \tag{56}$$

The fluid temperature T_f is an average. Ideally, the exit temperature would be invariant (960°F) to changes in insolation. With unobscured sun ($r = 2$), the nominal feedwater flow rate is increased over that suitable for cloudy conditions and the inlet temperature is lowered. It will be supposed that

$$T_{f,\text{nom}} = \begin{cases} 780°\text{F}, & r = 1; \\ 765°\text{F}, & r = 2. \end{cases} \tag{57}$$

Substituting Eqs. (56) and (57) into Eqs. (54)–(55) with $K_1 = 10^{-3}$ and $K_2 = 2.5 \times 10^{-4}$ yields the static metal temperature and feedwater flow rate:

$$T_{m,\text{nom}} = \begin{cases} 830.1°\text{F}, & r = 1; \\ 890.6°\text{F}, & r = 2; \end{cases} \tag{58}$$

$$W_{\text{nom}} = \begin{cases} 53 \text{ lb/min}, & r = 1; \\ 95 \text{ lb/min}, & r = 2. \end{cases} \tag{59}$$

While Eqs. (57)–(59) give the desired operating conditions for the system under each of the level of insolation, transients produced by variations in Φ will preclude truly static operation. It will be supposed that r and hence Φ is a Markov process with transition matrix Q [see Eq. (3)]:

$$Q = \begin{bmatrix} -0.43 & 0.43 \\ 0.23 & -0.23 \end{bmatrix}. \tag{60}$$

The Q matrix given by Eq. (60) yields a random process Φ which matches the mean residence times of an observed sample at insolation on a partly cloudy day at the Barstow CA site of a solar-thermal central receiver.

Insolation sensors on the panel can be used to make a probabilistic inference of the level of insolation. Unfortunately the noise in the received signal precludes making an unambiguous determination of $\{\Phi_t\}$. Suppose that the insolation measurement model is given by [see Eq. (19)]

$$dy_t = (r_t - 1)\, dt + 0.1\, dm_t. \tag{61}$$

If $r_t = 1$, the observation is noise alone. If it is sunny ($r_t = 2$), the low-level noise rides on a bias.

As shown in Fig. 1, the observation $\{y_t\}$ is translated into a vector of conditional probabilities $\left\{\tilde{\phi}_t\right\}$ which is then used to determine both the nominal temperatures and flow rates as well as the feedback gains. Simulation of the block which generates the conditional probability suggests that a suitable model for $Q°$ would be

$$Q° = \begin{bmatrix} -6 & 6 \\ 6 & -6 \end{bmatrix} \tag{62}$$

Although crude, Eq. (62) indicates that the mean time to identify a transition in insolation is an order of magnitude less than mean residence time in either insolation mode.

To complete the problem description, suppose that the weighting matrices in the performance index are

$$N = 1, \qquad M = \begin{bmatrix} 0 & 0 \\ 0 & 12 \end{bmatrix}. \tag{63}$$

The performance index associates a state penalty with errors in fluid temperature alone. The matrix N acts to control the gain of the state-variable feedback.

The design algorithm given in this paper can be carried out in a direct manner by first linearizing Eqs. (54)–(55). The jump conditions given by Eqs. (57)–(59) can be used in Eq. (44) to produce the regulator block shown in Fig. 1. The calculation is direct. From Eq. (49) it is evident that u_t takes the form

$$u_t = -\Gamma_i(x + \alpha_i) \quad \text{if} \quad l_t = i, \tag{64}$$

where Γ_i is a gain dependent upon $\hat{\phi}_t$ and α_i is a variable offset. The bias α_i represents a "preferred" operating state in the sense that if $x = -\alpha_i$, then $u_t = 0$.

Using Eqs. (44)–(46) to calculate the gain Γ_i produces no surprises. For future reference, however, it is interesting to display the bias explicitly:

$$\alpha_i \simeq \begin{cases} \begin{bmatrix} 0.089 + 2.61\hat{\phi}_2 \\ 1.89 + 44.85\hat{\phi}_2 \end{bmatrix} & \text{if} \quad l_t = 1; \quad (65) \\ \begin{bmatrix} -0.20 - 2.7\hat{\phi}_1 \\ -4.2 - -48.8\hat{\phi}_1 \end{bmatrix} & \text{if} \quad l_t = 2. \quad (66) \end{cases}$$

To gain insight into the efficacy of the proposed regulator, it is interesting to compare its performance with that attained using a reasonable alternative. One might view the regulator synthesis problem in the following way. Since the insolation sensors are quite accurate, it is possible to identify l_t with the true operating point with little error. Hence, an algorithm based upon a noise-free measurement of r_t could be used if l_t were substituted for r_t. Note that this controller, call it ν^a, uses the same estimate of Φ_t as does ν^*. The algorithm of [1] can be used to produce this "noise-free" control:

$$\nu_t^a = u_n(l_t) - \Gamma_i^a\left(x + \alpha_i^a\right) \quad \text{if} \quad l_t = i. \tag{67}$$

This controller uses the same feedforward control that is proposed in Eq. (49) for ν_t^*. Only the gain Γ_i^a and α_i^a differ from their counterparts in Eq. (49). Direct calculation leads to the conclusion that $\Gamma_i^a \simeq \Gamma_i$. Surprisingly, however, the biases differ significantly:

$$\alpha_i^a = \begin{cases} \begin{bmatrix} 7.6 \\ 0.086 \end{bmatrix} & \text{if } \quad l_t = 1; \qquad (68) \\ \begin{bmatrix} -6.94 \\ -0.43 \end{bmatrix} & \text{if } \quad l_t = 2. \qquad (69) \end{cases}$$

Comparing Eqs. (65)–(66) with Eqs. (68)–(69), it is clear that $\alpha_i^a \neq \alpha_i|_{\hat{\phi}=0}$. While the fact that the two biases differ even

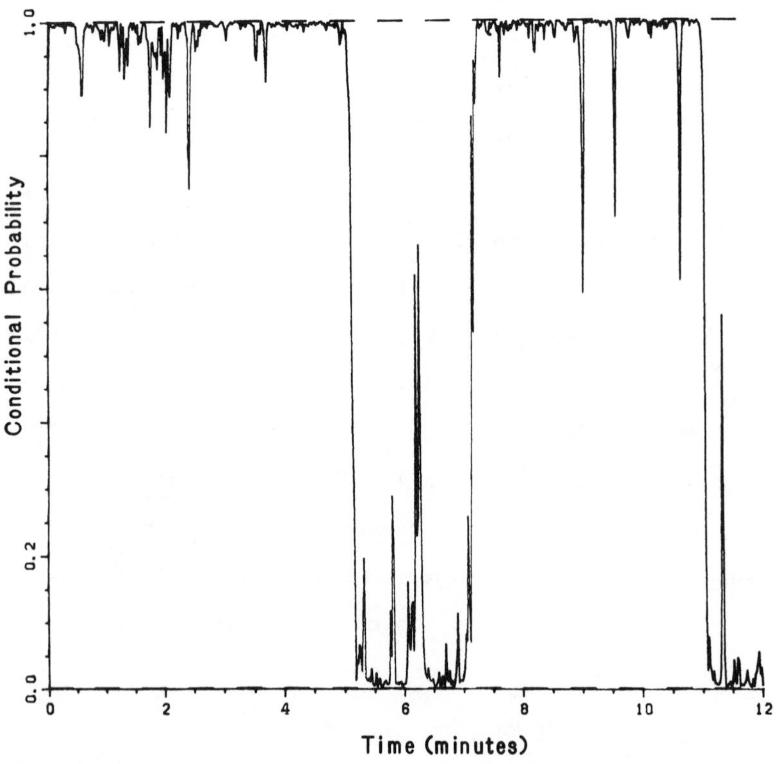

Fig. 2. A sample function of $\hat{\phi}_{t,1}$ with jumps in $\{r_t\}$ at t = 5, 7, and 11.

in the absence of estimation error $\tilde{\phi}$ should have been expected, the size of the difference is unexpectedly large. A simulation study provides an empirical rationale for the anomalous bias in ν^*. A sample function of $\{r_t\}$ with $r_0 = 1$ and discontinuities at t = 5, 7, and 11 min was used as a test function. Figure 2 shows the output of the modal identifier. The plotted function is $\left\{\hat{\phi}_{t,1}\right\}$. A threshold for detecting changes in r_t was set at $\tilde{\phi} = 0.8$, that is,

$$l_t \neq l_{t^-} \quad \text{if} \quad \hat{\phi}_{l_{t^-}} < 0.2.$$

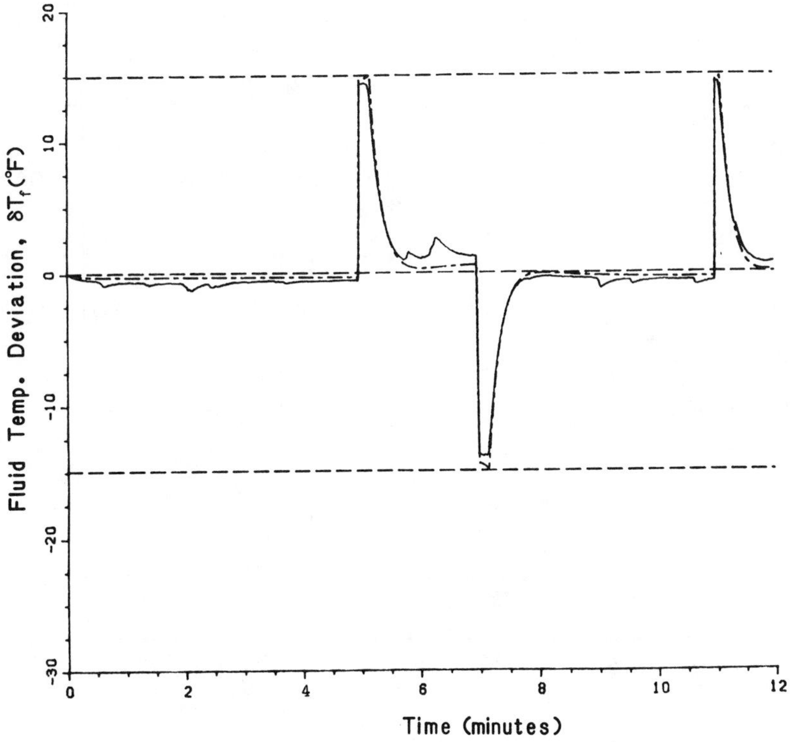

Fig. 3. Control of T_f using ν^* and using ν^a.

Both ν^* and ν^a use the same probabilistic information and hence have the same feedforward control. As mentioned earlier, they differ primarily in their respective bias terms. Figure 3 shows the sample function deviation in fluid temperature from nominal for the two regulators as an overlay. Figures 4 and 5 show the associated feedwater flow rate sample paths.

Because ν^a is oblivious to variations in $\{\hat{\phi}_t\}$ below the decision threshold, the fluid temperature and flow rate paths associated with ν^a are smoother than those observed when ν^* is

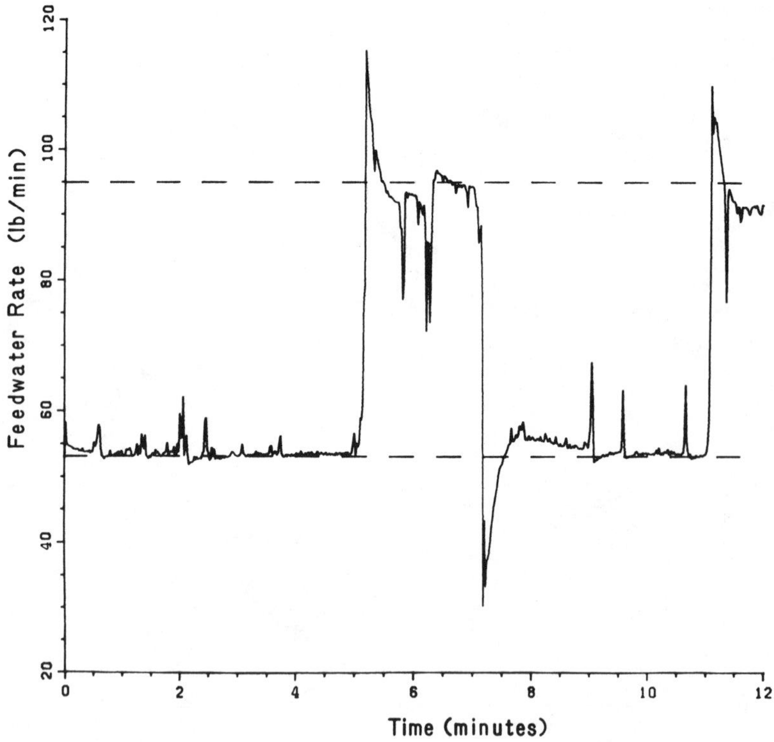

Fig. 4. Feedwater flow rate using ν^*.

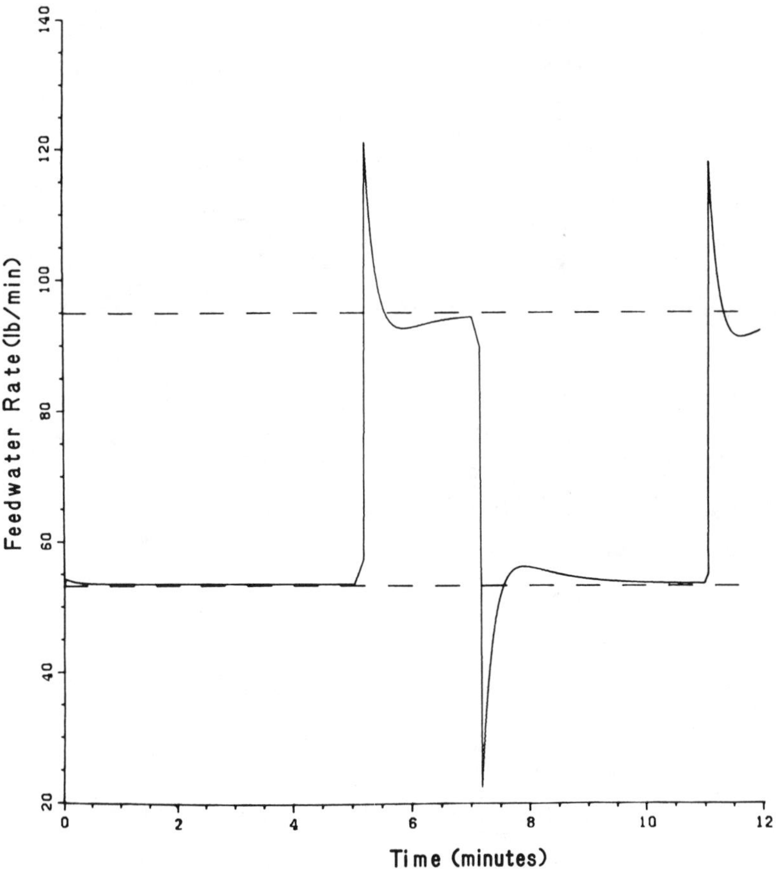

Fig. 5. Feedwater flow rate using ν^a.

used. The indicated volatility of the ν^* paths would be lessened in an actual system by the (unmodeled) dynamics of the feedwater control valve.

To understand the way in which the variable offset in ν^* effects performance, consider the system response to the transition in $\{r_t\}$ at t = 5 sec. The static metal temperature bias of ν^* is 2°F [see Eq. (65)], while that of ν^a is 0.1°F. Further, the bias in ν^* is quite sensitive to $\hat{\phi}_2$. Hence, ν^* is faster to respond to a transition in r_t than ν^a is. This is evidenced in the transient behavior of the loop beginning at

$t = 5$. The maximum error in T_f is 2% less when ν^* is used than it is when ν^a is the controller. This performance improvement is achieved despite the fact that the peak in the feedwater flow rate is 10% greater when ν^a is the controller.

In this example, the performance improvement associated with ν^* occurs in intervals with close time proximity to the discontinuities in $\{r_t\}$. This is not surprising since the quadratic performance index emphasizes large path following errors. The closed-loop response of ν^* during quiescent intervals is not as good as ν^a because of the volatility introduced by the variability in $\hat{\phi}_t$. To the extent that the transient behavior is the primary determinant of system performance, the passive adaptive regulator is superior to its simplistic counterpart.

V. CONCLUSION

This paper has proposed an approach to adaptive control which will be useful in those applications which permit an accurate determination of structured external disturbances. The controller has both feedforward and feedback links. The former tries to compensate for the "most likely" value of the disturbance, while the latter uses a more detailed statistical description of the disturbance to compensate for any residual errors. The final implementation is little more complicated than that of an ingenuous regulator which makes use of a coarse measure of the uncertainty surrounding the measurement of $\{r_t\}$.

VI. APPENDIX

An outline of the calculations leading to Eq. (49) are given in this appendix. Consider first Case 1, $r_t = l_t = l$. First observe that

$$u_t = -\frac{1}{2} N^{-1}\left[G_l' V_{\bar{x}}'(t, \bar{x}, \tilde{\phi}, l, l) + \sum_k G_{lk}' V_{\bar{x}}'(t, \bar{x}, \tilde{\phi}, l, k)\tilde{\phi}_k\right]. \tag{A1}$$

Under the assumption that $\tilde{\phi}$ is of order σ^2,

$$u_t = -\frac{1}{2} N^{-1} G_l' V_{\bar{x}}'(t, \bar{x}, \tilde{\phi}, l, l) + O(\sigma^2). \tag{A2}$$

The control dependent terms in Eq. (41) can be written

$$u_t' N u_t + V_{\bar{x}}' G_l u_t = -\frac{1}{4} V_{\bar{x}} G_l N^{-1} G_l' V_{\bar{x}}' + O(\sigma^4). \tag{A3}$$

Equation (41) can be written as

$$0 = \left(\bar{x}' M \bar{x} - \frac{1}{4} V_{\bar{x}} G_l N^{-1} G_l' V_{\bar{x}}' + V_t + V_{\bar{x}} F_l \bar{x}\right) dt + \frac{1}{2} \sum_{ij} V_{\bar{x}_i \bar{x}_j} d\left\langle x_i^c, x_j^c\right\rangle_t + E\left\{V_{\tilde{\phi}}' \, d\tilde{\phi}_t \mid r_t = l_t = l\right\} + dt \sum_j q_{lj} V(t, \bar{x}, \tilde{\phi}, l, j) + O(\sigma^4). \tag{A4}$$

To obtain an approximation to the solution to Eq. (A1), it will be assumed that V has a particular form:

$$V(t, \bar{x}, \tilde{\phi}, l, r) = \bar{x}' P^{lr} \bar{x} + 2\bar{x}' p^{lr} + q^{lr}, \tag{A5}$$

where P, p, and q all depend upon $\tilde{\phi}$, P can be written as

$$P^{lr} = P_o^{lr} + \sum_k P_k^{lr} \tilde{\phi}_k + \sum_{jk} P_{jk}^{lr} \tilde{\phi}_j \tilde{\phi}_k + o(\|\tilde{\phi}\|^2), \tag{A6}$$

with P_o, $\left\{P_k^{lr}\right\}$, and $\left\{P_{jk}^{lr}\right\}$ all symmetric matrices of comparable size with $P_{jk} = P_{kj}$. To avoid redundancy, it will be assumed that $P_l^{lr} = P_{lj}^{lr} = 0$. The functions p^{lr} and q^{lr} will be assumed to have analogous expansions.

From Eq. (A6), if higher order terms are neglected,

$$\frac{\partial P^{ll}}{\partial \tilde{\phi}_k} = P_k^{ll} + 2 \sum_j P_{jk}^{ll} \tilde{\phi}_j. \tag{A7}$$

Combining Eq. (A7) with Eq. (38),

$$\left[\frac{\partial}{\partial \phi}(\overline{x}' P^{ll} \overline{x})\right]' d\tilde{\phi}$$

$$= \overline{x}' \sum_k \left[P_k^{ll} + 2 \sum_j P_{jk}^{ll} \tilde{\phi}_j\right]$$

$$\times \left[\left(q_{lk} - \frac{(b_l - b_k)^2}{2\sigma^2} \tilde{\phi}_k\right) dt + \left(\frac{(b_l - b_k)\tilde{\phi}_k}{\sigma} dm_t^s\right)\right] \overline{x}. \tag{A8}$$

The forcing term m_t^s is not a martingale, but as noted earlier, its multiplier is of order σ. Hence, for sufficiently small σ,

$$E\left\{P_k^{ll} \frac{b_l - b_k}{\sigma} \tilde{\phi}_k \, dm_t^s \middle| \Xi_t, r_t = l_t = l\right\} \simeq 0. \tag{A9}$$

With Eqs. (A6) and (A9), the quadratic terms in $\overline{x}$ in Eq. (A4) can be written as

$$0 = M - \left\|P_o^{ll} + \sum_k P_k^{ll} \tilde{\phi}_k + \sum_{jk} P_{jk}^{ll} \tilde{\phi}_j \tilde{\phi}_k\right\|^2_{G_l N^{-1} G_l}$$

$$+ \left(\dot{P}_o^{ll} + \sum_k \dot{P}_k^{ll} \tilde{\phi}_k + \sum_{jk} \dot{P}_{jk}^{ll} \tilde{\phi}_j \tilde{\phi}_k\right)$$

$$+ \left(P_o^{ll} + \sum_k P_k^{ll} \tilde{\phi}_k + \sum_{jk} P_{jk}^{ll} \tilde{\phi}_j \tilde{\phi}_k\right) F_l$$

$$+ F_l' \left(P_o^{ll} + \sum_k P_k^{ll} \tilde{\phi}_k + \sum_{jk} P_{jk}^{ll} \tilde{\phi}_j \tilde{\phi}_k\right)$$

$$+ \sum_k \left[P_k^{ll} + 2 \sum_j P_{kj}^{ll} \tilde{\phi}_j\right] \left[q_{lk} - \frac{(b_l - b_k)^2}{2\sigma^2} \tilde{\phi}_k\right]$$

$$+ \sum_s q_{ls} \left[P_o^{ls} + \sum_k P_k^{ls} \tilde{\phi}_k + \sum_{jk} P_{jk}^{ls} \tilde{\phi}_j \tilde{\phi}_k\right]. \tag{A10}$$

The implications of Eq. (A10) become clearer when like powers of $\tilde{\phi}$ are equated. For example

$$0 = M - P_o^{ll} G_l N^{-1} G_l' P_o^{ll} + \dot{P}_o^{ll} + P_o^{ll} F_l + F_l' P_o^{ll} + \sum_k P_k^{ll} q_{lk} + \sum_s q_{ls} P_o^{ls}, \tag{A11}$$

$$0 = P_k^{ll}\left(-G_l N^{-1} G_l' P_o^{ll} + F_l - \frac{(b_l - b_k)^2}{4\sigma^2} I\right) + \left(-G_l N^{-1} G_l' P_o^{ll} + F_l - \frac{(b_l - b_k)^2}{4\sigma^2} I\right)' P_k^{ll} + \dot{P}_k^{ll} + 2\sum_j P_{jk}^{ll} q_{lj} + \sum_s q_{ls} P_k^{ls},$$

$$k = 1, \ldots, s, \qquad k \neq l. \tag{A12}$$

The dominant terms in Eq. (A12) can be written

$$-\dot{P}_k^{ll} = -\frac{(b_l - b_k)^2}{2\sigma^2} P_k^{ll} + 2\sum_j P_{jk}^{ll} q_{lj} + \sum_j q_{lj} P_k^{lj}, \qquad P_k^{ll}(T) = 0. \tag{A13}$$

The stationary solutions of Eq. (A13) are of order $\sigma^2 \|Q\|$, where $\|Q\| = \max_{i,j} |q_{ij}|$.

The forcing term for P_o^{ll} is $M - \Sigma_k P_k^{ll} q_{lj}$. Because of the small size of the P_k^{ll},

$$M - \sum_k P_n^{ll} q_{lk} = M + O(\sigma^2 \|Q\|^2 \simeq M. \tag{A14}$$

Both $\|Q\|$ and σ^2 are small. There is little error, therefore, in neglecting the high-order forms. Disregarding the contribution due to P_k^{ll} amounts to a slight modification of the state weighting index in V. Since M has a large subjective component anyway, the small deviation terms in Eq. (A14) are inconsequential. Neglecting the higher order terms,

$$\dot{P}_o^{ll} = -F_l' P_o^{ll} - P_o^{ll} F_l + P_o^{ll} G_l N^{-1} G_l' P_o^{ll} - M - \sum_j q_{lj} P_o^{lj},$$

$$P_o^{ll}(T) = 0, \quad l = 1, \ldots, s; \tag{A15}$$

$$P_k^{ll} = O(\sigma^2 \|Q\|), \quad k = 1, \ldots, s, \quad k \neq l. \tag{A16}$$

An identical argument leads to analogous equations for p^{ll} and q^{ll}:

$$\dot{p}_o^{ll} = \left(P_o^{ll} G_l N^{-1} G_l' - F_l'\right) p_o^{ll} - \sum_k q_{lk} p_o^{lk},$$

$$p_o^{ll}(T) = 0, \quad l = 1, \ldots, s; \tag{A17}$$

$$p_k^{ll} = O(\sigma^2 \|Q\|), \quad k = 1, \ldots, s, \quad k \neq l; \tag{A18}$$

$$\dot{q}_o^{ll} = p_o'^{ll} G_l N^{-1} G_l' p_o^{ll} - dt^{-1} \sum_{ij} \left(P_o^{ll}\right)_{ij} d\langle x_i^c, x_j^c \rangle_t$$

$$- \sum_k q_{lk} q_o^{lk},$$

$$q_o^{ll}(T) = 0, \quad l = 1, \ldots, s; \tag{A19}$$

$$q_k^{ll} = O(\sigma^2 \|Q\|), \quad k = 1, \ldots, s, \quad k \neq l. \tag{A20}$$

Equations (A15)–(A20) provide the dominant coefficients for V when $l_t = r_t = l$. To complete the solution, the coefficients for V for $l_t = l \neq r_t = r$ must be deduced. Equation (42) is now the relevant equation. Substitution of Eqs. (A5) and (A6) into Eq. (A2) yields

$$u_t = -N^{-1} G_l' \left(P_o^{ll} \bar{x} + p_o^{ll}\right) + O(\sigma^2). \tag{A21}$$

Hence

$$u'Nu + V'G_l u = \left[\left(P_o^{ll}\bar{x} + p_o^{ll}\right)'G_l - 2\left(P_o^{lr}\bar{x} + p_o^{lr}\right)'G_{lr}\right]N^{-1}G_l' \times \left(P_o^{ll}\bar{x} + p_o^{ll}\right) + O(\sigma^2). \tag{A22}$$

Substituting Eqs. (A5) and (A22) into Eq. (42) yields

$$\begin{aligned} 0 = {} & \|\bar{x} + \delta(r, l)\|_M^2 \\ & + \left[\left(P_o^{ll}\bar{x} + p_o^{ll}\right)'G_l - 2\left(P_o^{lr}\bar{x} + p_o^{lr}\right)'G_{lr}\right]N^{-1}G_l'\left(P_o^{ll}\bar{x} + p_o^{ll}\right) \\ & + \bar{x}'\dot{P}_o^{lr}\bar{x} + 2\bar{x}'\dot{p}_o^{lr} + \dot{q}_o^{lr} + dt^{-1}\sum_{ij}\left(P_o^{lr}\right)_{ij} d\left\langle \bar{x}_i^c, \bar{x}_j^c\right\rangle_t \\ & + 2\left(P_o^{lr}\bar{x} + p_o^{lr}\right)'\left(F_{lr}\bar{x} + \Delta(l, r)\right) \\ & + q_{lr}^o\Big[\|\bar{x} + \delta(r, l)\|_{P_o^{rr}}^2 - \|\bar{x}\|_{P_o^{lr}}^2 + 2p_o^{rr'}(\bar{x} + \delta(r, l)) \\ & - 2p_o^{lr'}\bar{x} + \left(q_o^{rr} - q_o^{lr}\right)\Big], \end{aligned} \tag{A23}$$

where $O(\sigma^2)$ terms and $O(\|Q\|)$ terms have been neglected.

Equation (A23) can be solved directly to yield

$$\begin{aligned} \dot{P}_o^{lr} = {} & -P_o^{lr}\left(F_{lr} - G_{lr}N^{-1}G_l'P_o^{ll}\right) - \left(F_{lr} - G_{lr}N^{-1}G_l P_o^{ll}\right)'P_o^{lr} \\ & - M - P_o^{ll}G_l N^{-1}G_l'P_o^{ll} - q_{lr}^o\left(P_o^{rr} - P_o^{lr}\right), \end{aligned}$$

$$P_o^{lr}(T) = 0, \quad l, r = 1, \ldots, s, \quad l \neq r; \tag{A24}$$

$$\begin{aligned} \dot{p}_o^{lr} = {} & \left(P_o^{ll}G_l N^{-1}G_{lr}' - F_{lr}'\right)p_o^{lr} - M\,\delta(r, l) - P_o^{ll}G_l N^{-1}G_l'p_o^{ll} \\ & + P_o^{lr}G_{lr}N^{-1}G_l'p_o^{ll} - P_o^{lr}\,\Delta(l, r) - q_{lr}^o \\ & \times \left[P_o^{rr}\,\delta(r, l) + p_o^{rr} - p_o^{lr}\right], \end{aligned}$$

$$p_o^{lr}(T) = 0, \quad l, r = 1, \ldots, s, \quad l \neq r; \tag{A25}$$

$$\dot{q}_o^{lr} = -\delta(r, l)'M\,\delta(r, l) - \left(p_o^{ll'} G_l - 2p_o^{lr'} G_{lr}\right)N^{-1}G_l' p_o^{ll}$$

$$- dt^{-1} \sum_{ij} \left(P_o^{lr}\right)_{ij} d\left\langle \bar{x}_i^c, \bar{x}_j^c \right\rangle_t - 2p_o^{lr'} \Delta(l, r)$$

$$- q_{lr}^o \Big[\delta(r, l)' P_o^{rr} \delta(r, l) + 2\,\delta(r, l)' p_o^{rr}$$

$$+ \left(q_o^{rr} - q_o^{lr}\right)\Big],$$

$$q_o^{lr}(T) = 0, \quad l, r = 1, \ldots, s. \tag{A26}$$

In terms of the above functions it is possible to evaluate the performance of the system. The cost-to-go becomes

$$V(t, \bar{x}, \tilde{\phi}, l) = E\left\{V(t, \bar{x}, \tilde{\phi}, l, r) \,|\, \Xi_t\right\}$$

$$= V(t, \bar{x}, \tilde{\phi}, l, l) + \sum_k V(t, \bar{x}, \tilde{\phi}, l, k)\tilde{\phi}_k.$$

From Eq. (A5),

$$V(t, x, \tilde{\phi}, l) = \bar{x}'\left(P_o^{ll} + \sum_k P_o^{lk}\tilde{\phi}_k\right)\bar{x}$$

$$+ 2\bar{x}'\left(p_o^{ll} + \sum_k p_o^{lk}\tilde{\phi}_k\right) + q_o^{ll} + \sum_k q_o^{lk}\tilde{\phi}_k.$$

REFERENCES

1. D. D. SWORDER and R. O. ROGERS, "An LQ-Solution to a Control Problem Associated with a Solar Thermal Receiver," *IEEE Trans. Autom. Control AC-28* No. 10, 971-978 (1983).

2. D. D. SWORDER, "Control of Systems Subject to Small Measurement Disturbances," *Trans. ASME J. Dyn. Syst. Meas. Control 106*(2), 182-189 (1984).

3. R. J. ELLIOTT, "Stochastic Calculus and Applications," Springer-Verlag, New York, 1982.

4. E. WONG, "Stochastic Processes in Information and Dynamical Systems," McGraw-Hill, New York, 1971.

INDEX